The Health of the Presidents

The Health of the Presidents

The 41 United States Presidents Through 1993 from a Physician's Point of View

by JOHN R. BUMGARNER, M.D.

with a foreword by WALTER L. FLOYD, M.D.

McFarland & Company, Inc., Publishers
Jefferson, North Carolina, and London

British Library Cataloguing-in-Publication data are available

Library of Congress Cataloguing-in-Publication Data

Bumgarner, John R. (John Reed)
   The health of the presidents : the 41 United States Presidents through
1993 from a physician's point of view / by John R. Bumgarner.
      p.   cm.
   Includes bibliographical references and index.
   ISBN 0-89950-956-8 (lib. bdg. : 50# alk. paper) ∞
   1. Presidents—United States—Health.   I. Title.
E176.1.B9314   1994
973'.099—dc20   93-42000
                                           CIP

Manufactured in the United States of America

McFarland & Company, Inc., Publishers
  Box 611, Jefferson, North Carolina 28640

To my wife Evelyn
whose patience and encouragement
enabled me to persevere long enough
to complete the writing of this book.

Acknowledgments

Drs. George and Judy Cheatham of the English Department, Greensboro College, who helped me to keep my syntax orderly; Ms. Karen Webb, transcriptionist, who typed, retyped, and retyped the manuscript; Ms. Shirley Windham, librarian, Greensboro Public Libraries, who helped me to gather relevant material from near and far; my wife, Evelyn, for her endless patience while I struggled to complete this manuscript; and to my brother, Bill, and his wife, Miriam, for their advice and assistance in indexing this manuscript.

Contents

Foreword

In the early 1960s when I was a young cardiologist at Duke University Medical Center, I first met Dr. John R. Bumgarner who, at the time, was in the private practice of internal medicine in Greensboro, N.C. During his years in practice Dr. Bumgarner had taken a particular interest in cardiovascular disease and a major portion of his practice was devoted to patients with heart and blood vessel disease.

The decade of the 1960s was characterized by an extraordinarily rapid advance in our ability to diagnose and treat patients with heart disease. Prior to that time, we were powerless to effectively treat the majority of disease conditions we encountered, but during that decade a variety of surgical procedures including coronary bypass surgery were developed, effective means of reviving individuals from the death of a heart attack were devised, and heart pacemakers were introduced. These are only a few of the innovations made during that decade and primarily were related to the rapidly advancing technology of medicine. Such extraordinary advances made it almost impossible for a physician in practice outside of teaching institutions to remain current in his knowledge and provide the optimum care for his patients.

Dr. Bumgarner, an astute physician who has always had an unusual compassion and concern for his patients, recognized this problem and, as a result, sought a more effective way of advancing his knowledge than the usual attendance at medical meetings and reading the medical literature. Rather, he arranged to come to Duke for one day of each week to become a part of the clinical programs of our cardiology division. In this way, he became a member of the clinical activities of the division and not just an observer. His willingness to do this was at considerable expenditure of time and money. He continued this practice for several years and, as a result of this and other efforts, he became certified in the subspecialty of cardiovascular disease by the American Board of Internal Medicine in 1967. He has an inquisitive, innovative mind which, in addition to his remarkable personality, has made him a joy to work with.

These characteristics of Dr. Bumgarner have not been lost to society by his retirement from the practice of medicine in 1985. His work on the health of U.S. presidents has occupied most of the entire decade and the research required has reflected the remarkable ingenuity and perseverance which he demonstrated for so many years as a physician.

The individual chapters devoted to each president are entertaining and historically interesting but, at the same time, raise many questions as to the adverse impact which a president's ill health may have had on our society and the world. For instance, Franklin Roosevelt was obviously very ill at the time of the Yalta Conference and, most certainly, his stamina and decisionmaking capacity were impaired. How much did this influence the turn of events at Yalta, ultimately contributing to the cold war and decades-long loss of freedom for Eastern Europe? How would the world have been different if he had enjoyed even the less than perfect health of previous years? Such questions are conjecture but ones that will intrigue historians for years to come.

As physicians, Dr. Bumgarner and I are sworn to uphold the confidentiality of our patients. I have always abhorred the frenzy of the press in picking apart the private lives of presidents and other prominent elected officials, particularly when it entails the intimacy of their medical problems. However, it is evident from Dr. Bumgarner's book that in years past the opposite extreme has existed, in that poor presidential health which may have influenced elections has been withheld from the public. We require rigid health standards for entry into the military and advancement to ranks of major responsibility by military leaders but we do not require any standard for our commander in chief, whose wide-ranging decisions involve much more than military matters. Should our society consider some type of publicized medical evaluation for some of our public officials, particularly presidents and presidential candidates? How strong should the restrictions on health be? Should we ignore the contributions of so many of our statesmen who have given their greatest contributions in less than perfect health?

Dr. Bumgarner's book—like all good research, whether historical or scientific—raises more questions than provides answers. It should serve as a source of reference for inquiring minds as well as enjoyment for the leisure reader.

Walter L. Floyd, M.D.
Professor of Medicine
Duke University Medical Center
Durham, North Carolina

Preface

During the years that I was engaged in the active practice of medicine, I had little time to do one of the things I liked best — read. Therefore, I limited my reading to biography. Then later I further narrowed my attention to the lives of America's foremost statesmen, and I found myself growing greatly interested in the health problems of the presidents. It was somehow surprising to discover that the presidents were subject to the same ills as other mortals. I learned that some of these leaders who, very ill, were surrounded by sycophants and others bound by a code of silence; for example, Franklin D. Roosevelt, Woodrow Wilson, and John Fitzgerald Kennedy very skillfully and deliberately kept the truth from the electorate. I became further interested in the inception and enactment of the Twenty-fifth Amendment, which is presumed to provide for the removal of an impaired president — but which is not a perfect instrument.

The subject of this book, the illnesses of presidents, is a fascinating one and my interest led me following retirement to gather material and begin writing the manuscript, a process that would take five years. My chief sources were biographies, medical journals, newspapers, private communications, and periodicals. I wish to thank the many reference librarians who were most helpful in my search for the latest and most accurate material on some of the presidents.

John R. Bumgarner, M.D.

1

George Washington

George Washington, the first president of the United States, was born at Wakefield on Pope's Creek Farm in Westmoreland County, Virginia, February 22, 1732.[1]

Most of us think of Washington as a powerful, austere, commanding individual who moved in great strides across the American continent, never subject to the ills that beset mere mortals; however, he had his share and more of such problems.

In discussing the illnesses of George Washington, we must admit a great deal of ignorance about his childhood health problems—if he had any. Childhood illnesses in Washington's time were not a matter of public record and were, in fact, taken as a matter of course. After his adolescence, however, there is a more complete record of his health problems available from the letters and diaries of Washington and knowledge obtained from doctors, family, and acquaintances. When Washington was licensed as a surveyor at the age of 17, he was exposed to malaria-carrying mosquitoes when camping out, and suffered from his first of many attacks of malaria, called "ague" at that time.[2] Many areas of Virginia were then covered by swampland and the attendant swarms of malaria-carrying mosquitoes. In Washington's era, especially in his childhood and youth, the etiology of malaria was a complete mystery, and it is almost certain that in Washington's early years there was no treatment available for the disease. Peruvian bark, or Jesuit's bark—which was later extracted to obtain the quinine alkaloid—was available to both the Continental and British armies as early as the Revolutionary War, although late in the war the supply became exhausted. It was not until 1820 that quinine was isolated, making the treatment of malaria easier, and not until 1880 that C. L. A. Laveran, a medical officer in the French Army, discovered the parasite of malaria.[3]

At the age of 19 (1751) Washington went with Lawrence, his half brother, to Barbados, hoping that the climate would be a curative for Lawrence's pulmonary tuberculosis. The climate was not helpful, however, and Lawrence later died. At about the time of this trip Washington had a severe case of smallpox, which left him greatly scarred. In addition, due to nursing Lawrence, Washington had such a prolonged and intimate exposure to tuberculosis that he later developed tuberculous pleurisy, which, after he returned to Mount Vernon, came almost on the heels of the smallpox. The recovery was slow, and he was in poor health for two years.

By late 1752, however, Washington had recovered enough to enter the military service, becoming a major in the Virginia militia. In the following year he went on a military expedition against the French at Fort Duquesne. Washington had barely returned from this mission when he developed a severe attack of malaria, which required considerable time for recovery.

In May 1755 Washington left Fort Cumberland with General Edmond Braddock. The army had to cover 100 rugged miles to reach Fort Duquesne, where they hoped to defeat the French. At the very onset of this adventure Washington was suffering from a severe case of dysentery. His distress became so great that he had to tie pillows on his horse's back in order to be able to ride. One wonders if perhaps Washington had hemorrhoids which were greatly aggravated by the dysentery. Such a problem could have explained the need of pillows to soften the horseback ride. His problem finally became so severe that he had to remain behind while the army advanced. Suffering from a headache, fever, and a bloody flux, he was so sick that he became unable to ride on his horse. His discomfort was augmented by the fact that the ride was over a crude, bumpy road.[4]

A physician tried without success to treat Washington. General Braddock ordered Washington to remain in bed, and he also ordered the physician to give Washington a treatment of powder concocted by Dr. Robert James. The powders were a generally used treatment at that time for fevers of all kinds and the powder prescribed was definitely not a specific. Washington, however, believed in it because his fever and other complaints were much relieved after four days. On July 4 he was almost fully recovered and followed the main body of the army in a wagon. Still weak, he joined one contingent on July 8.[5] On July 9 Braddock's forces were attacked with disastrous results. Although so weak that he could barely mount his horse, Washington nevertheless fought with a great courage as an aide to Braddock.

Following the battle Washington, still weak, started home, reaching Mount Vernon on July 25. He remained so weak and worn that he found some difficulty in riding around his plantation.[6] Even so, he continued to serve as commander of the Virginia militia and continued to struggle with the British officers to obtain the proper treatment and preferment for himself and his fellow colonial officers. This endeavor helped to undermine his health. Over a prolonged period of time Washington was afflicted with recurrent and increasingly severe attacks of fever and dysentery, and toward the end of 1755 Dr. James Craik persuaded him to retire to Mount Vernon.[7]

In the autumn of 1757 Washington became very ill with a recurrence of severe dysentery. In addition, he suffered from severe pleuritic chest pain and fever. It must be assumed that his long exposure to his brother Lawrence had left him with tuberculosis infection. Washington was deathly ill during this period. Dr. Craik didn't know what to do, so he bled him. Washington became so weak that he had difficulty walking and was transported to Mount Vernon by carriage.

Washington at the time was in love with the wife of his dearest friend, Lord Fairfax, and sent a plea to Sally Fairfax to visit him at Mount Vernon. During this illness Wasington was, as he was at other times during an illness, deeply depressed. Part of his dejection was due to the fact that Sally Fairfax visited him less frequently than he wished. Washington tried to travel to Williamsburg where he felt he might possibly get better medical attention, but was so weak he had to turn back.[8]

In the spring of 1758 Washington had recovered sufficiently from his various illnesses — including his love for Sally Fairfax — to give suit to a widow and heiress, Mrs. David Park Custis.[9] In late 1758, due to his poor health and frustration at his failure to become a regular in the British Army, Washington gave up his commission and retired from the service. His marriage to Mrs. Custis took place soon after, on January 16, 1759.

What is perhaps Washington's most famous health problem was already evident by this time: his teeth were in poor shape. Washington went to see the Rev. Charles Green of Alexandria, who treated the physical as well as the spiritual. However, the cleric could offer no remedy for Washington's dental problems. The best deduction one can make is that he had peridontal disease or pyorrhea. The only treatment offered in Washington's time for dental problems was extraction. The Rev. Green did advise Washington to cure his dysentery by avoiding flesh, and eating only "jellies and such kinds of food."[10]

Washington was acutely and dangerously ill again in 1761, with his old ailments dysentery and malaria. So ill that he almost despaired, he went to the famous spa at Berkeley Springs. The ride to the springs was taken in extreme summer heat, and when he arrived he was greatly fatigued. While at the spa his fever abated, but his pains grew worse until he was unable to sleep. However, on his return home in the fall he said,

"Thank God I have now got the better of my disorder, and shall soon be restored to perfect health again."[11] Apparently, his wishes were to a degree rewarded. He had had his last major attacks of malaria and dysentery, but less severe attacks would continue. As late as 1786 Washington was still suffering from malaria. His private physician, Dr. James Craik, then for the first time treated Washington with Peruvian or Jesuit's bark, and with excellent results. The extract of this bark is quinine, but quinine the active principle was not isolated until 1820. As early as 1776 the extract of Peruvian bark had been used on the colonial troops. It is strange that Washington never derived the benefit of its effect on his malaria until 1784.[12]

When Washington did become ill he was always haunted by premonitions of death. His father and brother Lawrence had both died at a premature age. In all aspects of his life, he was, as Jefferson wrote, "inclined to gloomy apprehensions." Washington was less likely to be depressed when he was very busy with his plantation activities.[13]

Some mention should be made of Washington's mother. Mary Ball Washington is described as a domineering woman given to neither acquiescence nor compromise.[14] When Washington was commander in chief, for example, and even when he was president, she objected to his occupation, complaining violently that he was ungratefully neglecting his duties to her.[15] This attempted dominance on the part of his mother may have influenced some of Washington's later behavior. Among our presidents Washington was not alone in this regard. FDR also had a domineering, managing mother. Alexander Hamilton made a great deal of comment about Washington's stressful relationship with his mother. Hamilton was said to have referred to a well-known portrait which depicted Washington looking at his mother: "That look of pain on George's face describes his relationship to her precisely." After the war his mother's demands for money became so strong that Washington suggested she sell her house and go to live with one of the children. He quickly added that this was not an invitation to Mount Vernon.[16]

Washington's Revolutionary War years, of course, involved a number of health issues. Perhaps the most interesting occurred in 1779. When the troops under Washington were encamped in Morristown, a smallpox epidemic in the army caused several deaths. Approximately one-third of this entire force suffered from the disease. The disease was spreading rapidly when Washington resorted to inoculation of his whole army, the first mass inoculation in America. The experiment was an amazing success.[17] In addition, in the spring of 1779, while Washington and his army were still encamped at Morristown, he had a severe attack of quinsy (tonsillar abscess). He was so weak and feverish that he feared for his own survival. He instructed General Nathaniel Green to take over if he failed to survive.[18]

Once Washington was even able to use his own physical frailty to avert a possible mutiny among his troops. In the spring of 1783, while the troops were in camp and not yet demobilized, there was a great deal of discontent. The officers and men had not for some time been paid for their valiant services. A laggard and ungrateful Congress had failed to provide money to pay the armed services. There was actually some threat of rebellion. Washington greatly desired to retreat to Mount Vernon, but the crisis persuaded him to stay with his troops. Washington had been informed by Hamilton that when peace came the army threatened to resort to arms to get justice. On March 13, 1783, Washington met with a group of the mutinous officers who came to present their case to him. As Washington faced the men, he gave a speech which seemed to fail in changing their mood. He then remembered that he had with him a letter from a congressman which contained good news for the army. However, when he drew the letter from his pocket, he paused and seemed paralyzed. He only stared at the letter. He then removed something from his pocket—something only those nearest to him had seen before—his eyeglasses. "Gentlemen," he said, "you will permit me to put on my glasses, for I have not only grown gray but almost blind in the service of my country."[19] This final gesture and statement did what his speech had failed to do. The hardened veterans wept. Washington had eased a great crisis and saved his country from domestic turmoil.

In the early months of 1784, the long war behind him, Washington's thoughts turned toward simply becoming a farmer at Mount Vernon. He was worn both physically and mentally, his health indifferent, and he continued to have a great deal of trouble with his teeth.[20] At middle life Washington had lost all of his teeth, and some genius made him a remarkable set of dentures. This marvelous contraption was furnished with a steel spring hung at the back. We do not know if the purpose of the spring was to aid in opening or in closing, or whether Washington had an opening or a closing snap. This piece of machinery protruded so far in front that it displaced his lips forward. This distortion was obvious in some of the portraits made at this time. When Washington sat first for a portrait by Stuart, he had a new set of teeth formed from seahorse ivory to imitate both teeth and gums. These teeth filled his mouth and distorted his lips. They were so uncomfortable and clumsy that they even interfered with his speech. Judge Bushrod Washington, nephew of George Washington, is quoted as having said that these teeth gave his mouth the appearance of "being rinsed with water."[21]

The Peale portrait of 1776 shows General Washington in uniform with a large scar along the left cheek. This was related by the artist to be due to an incision for an abscessed tooth. His dental problems were to be virtually endless. He wore several kinds of dentures—hippopotamus ivory, human teeth, and the teeth of pigs, cows, and elks. One set of his false teeth, set in lead and held by steel springs, weighed three pounds.[22]

During his first term as president Washington developed two serious illnesses—in 1789 a tumor on the thigh and in 1790 pneumonia. The tumor on the thigh was what the doctors called a malignant carbuncle, probably due to staphylococcus infection. He was quite ill for several weeks. He was treated by Dr. Samuel Bard who attended the president day and night. Dr. Bard finally drained the carbuncle by incision, and the president's health began to improve almost immediately. He was finally able, after a week, to go for a ride in his coach, lying down on a specially prepared bed. Also in 1789, early in his first term, Washington went on a trip to New England where he was exposed for a lengthy period to rainy, stormy weather, following which he developed a severe cold and conjunctivitis.[23] In May 1790 Washington was very ill with pneumonia, so ill that his life was felt to be threatened. His recovery was slow. In 1791 Washington developed another carbuncle, not as severe as the first, but severe enough to confine him to bed for quite a while.[24]

More generally, during his later years Washington's hearing was markedly impaired. This has been attributed to his numerous upper respiratory infections and his prolonged use of quinine. His deafness made it difficult for him to carry on a conversation and caused him to seem more aloof than he really was.

At least one notable accident occurred in June 1794. Washington was on his way to Mount Vernon for a vacation when his horse stumbled over a rough spot. In his words, "My horse blundered and continued blundering until by violent exertion on my part to save him and myself from falling on the rocks, I got such a wrench of my back" that he found it impossible to ride, and difficult to sit up straight; he was for a while unable to attend to plantation affairs.[25]

In the spring of 1797, at the age of 65, Washington declined a third term as president and returned to Mount Vernon for what would be a brief retirement. In 1798 he had a recurrence of his malaria, which responded poorly to the bark.[26] Then on Thursday, December 12, 1799, the end began. Washington rode over his estate for nearly five hours in the cold, rain, and sleet. That evening as he read by the fireside his secretary, Tobias Lear, noticed that he was hoarse and suggested that he take something for his cold, but Washington said he preferred "to let it go as it came."

At 3:00 A.M. Washington awoke with his throat so swollen that he had difficulty in breathing and speaking. Martha was not permitted to call in anyone until daybreak. Dr. Craik was called, but before he arrived Washington was bled by the overseer. A total of three other physicians arrived besides Dr. Craik. Their consensus was that Washington suffered from quinsy. Quinsy, a term that belongs to medical history, is defined as an inflammation of the tonsils with fever, swelling, pain, and local accumulation of pus. Since the attending physicians didn't know what to do, Washington was bled by cupping at least three more times. Then Spanish fly was applied to his throat (Spanish fly from the blister beetle was used as a vesicant or a blistering agent applied over the afflicted area as a counterirritant). And to add insult to injury, he was purged. The technique of cupping as a method of bleeding a patient was in common use during Washington's lifetime. The first step was the use of a lancet to make small cuts in the skin to produce bleeding (scarification). The cupping glass was heated and then placed over the lacerated area. As the cup cooled a partial vacuum was formed which drew blood into the cup. Sometimes a cupping glass was applied without scarification for the relief of congestion.

One of the doctors, a young surgeon, gave the only sensible and rational advice, which was rejected out of hand by the other three doctors. He suggested that he be allowed to do a tracheotomy. The doctor who suggested the tracheotomy was Dr. Elisha Dick, a young surgeon with excellent training. If Dr. Dick had been permitted to proceed with his surgery, there is a good chance that Washington's life might have been prolonged. Washington finally requested that he be allowed to die in peace; at 10:00 P.M., December 14, 1799, the president expired.

There can never be an exact diagnosis of Washington's terminal illness. We can only examine the clinical picture as it is presented to us from many sources. We know that in his final illness there was an acute onset followed by pain in his throat, difficulty in swallowing, and difficult respiration. The type of onset and the cluster of symptoms indicate an acute infection in Washington's throat which caused obstruction to breathing and swallowing. Unfortunately, no doctor at Washington's bedside peeped down his throat and gave us a word picture of the pathology which lay there. Also in that era there were no bacteriologists around to tell us what type of organism was responsible for the infection. However, after nearly 200 years, we can come to a conclusion which may have some logic. For many decades it has been assumed that Washington had died of diphtheria, then called croup. But as time has passed and we have learned more about the clinical course of individual infectious diseases, it would appear that Washington's clinical picture best fits acute streptococcal infection of the throat, involving the larynx and vocal cords. This type of infection involving the structures of the throat can cause marked swelling and subsequent obstruction to breathing and swallowing.

References

1. David C. Whitney, *The American Presidents*, p. 1.
2. Rudolph Marx, *The Health of the Presidents*, p. 19.
3. Edgar Erskine Hume, *Victories of Army Medicine*, p. 160.
4. James Thomas Flexner, *Washington: The Indispensible Man*, p. 22.
5. John R. Alden, *George Washington: A Biography*, p. 46.
6. Ibid., pp. 49–51.
7. Washington Irving, *George Washington: A Biography* (Garden City, N.Y.: Doubleday, 1976), p. 6.
8. Flexner, *Washington*, pp. 30–31.
9. Alden, *George Washington*, p. 72.
10. Ibid., p. 71.
11. Alden, *George Washington*, p. 91.
12. Hume, *Victories of Army Medicine*, p. 60.
13. Flexner, *Washington*, p. 45.
14. Ibid., p. 3.
15. Ibid., p. 3.
16. Ibid., p. 222.
17. Burke Davis, *George Washington and the American Revolution*, p. 197.
18. Ibid., p. 197.
19. Flexner, *Washington*, pp. 177–78.
20. Marcus Cunliffe, *George Washington, Man and Monument*, p. 129.
21. Daniel Boorstin, "The Mythologizing of George Washington," in *George Washington: A Profile*, p. 283.
22. Davis, *George Washington and the American Revolution*, p. 84.
23. Marx, *The Health of the Presidents*, p. 23.
24. Homer F. Cunningham, *The Presidents' Last Years*, p. 4.
25. Flexner, *Washington*, p. 316.
26. Ibid., pp. 177–78.

2

John Adams

John Adams, the first of the Adams dynasty and the second president of the United States, was born on October 30, 1735, in Braintree (now Quincy), Massachusetts.

There is very little to be found regarding any illness affecting John Adams as a baby or as a youth. It is noted that he was agile and muscular and that he prided himself in his prowess as a wrestler.[1] Adams was very conscious of his small size though, and perhaps as a consequence through his short temper, sharp tongue, and belligerence he made enemies all of his life.

Adams was described in his teens as his father saw him: "He was almost a man grown. He wasn't tall, not above five feet tall, but his shoulders were heavy. He was well knit, muscular, and quick and sure in his movements. His color was unusually high; just now his face was red from exertion, his blue eyes blazed."[2]

Adams was always an avid reader. At the age of 20 he read a text by the great Dutch physician Boerhaave and for a while thought of becoming a physician. He later decided that he was better suited to the law.[3]

Adams was admitted to Harvard at the age of 15. The food at that institution was described as being very poor. His breakfast, for example, consisted of beer and bread. In addition, the students' living quarters were very poorly heated in the winter, which may have contributed to Adams's respiratory problem. When he went home for the winter vacation of six weeks, he had a very severe cold. His mother looked at him in alarm: "He was positively puny, and where were his fine red cheeks?" At the end of February, when the time had come for him to return to Harvard, there was an outbreak of smallpox in Boston. His mother was alarmed. She had experienced the awful smallpox epidemic of 1721. Adams had not been inoculated against the disease. Inoculation would require a four-week absence from classes, and Adams was so anxious to return that he decided to take the risk and forego the inoculation.[4]

In 1756, while still studying law at Worcester, Massachusetts, Adams was having recurring attacks of depression. During his stay at Worcester he began the first of his lifelong string of illnesses. On one occasion he rode to Shrewsbury to attend the wedding of a friend and developed a cold which left him "weak and aching." His physician, Dr. Willard, attributed his illness to Adam's long and close hours of study which had "corrupted the whole mass of [his] blood and juices." The doctor prescribed then what was the trend in medicine—a milk diet. Adams was enjoined to leave off "all meats, spices, and spirits; and to subsist on bread, milk, vegetables and water." Adams improved, but he was burdened with a severe heartburn, relieved only with large portions of tea.[5]

In the winter of 1764, while Adams was practicing law in Boston, there was an epidemic of smallpox in Boston and Braintree. Adams at that time was courting Abigail Smith, his future wife. The epidemic caused a separation of several months between Adams and his sweetheart. Adams's mother, insisted that this time he be vaccinated. He finally went with a group of friends to be treated by a Dr. Perkins. He and his friends were housed five to a room, dieted, and denied bread, milk, and pudding. After they were inoculated they suffered aches and fever, with the pustules and scabs associated with smallpox vaccination.[6]

It is somewhat interesting to note that the smallpox vaccine was introduced in the United States by a noted physician, Dr. Benjamin Waterhouse (1754–1846), who was a contemporary of Thomas Jefferson and John Adams. Waterhouse was greatly inspired by work in England in developing the smallpox vaccine. In July 1800 Waterhouse secured some of the generous vaccine from England and bravely vaccinated his own children and several servants. The vaccine proved to be successful in immunizing against smallpox. None of Waterhouse's patients who were vaccinated developed the disease.[7]

In the winter of 1766–67, while Adams was still practicing law in Braintree, he and Abigail were discussing the pros and cons of moving from Braintree to Boston. Abigail's wish was to wait until the new baby was born in July 1767. John, however, felt that his frail constitution would never stand the town life of Boston, and he also felt that his health was beginning to fail him. He was prone to colds, and excitement would make him wheeze. The cough and wheezing interfered with his sleep. The cough, wheeze, and the duration of his illnesses would cause one to think of an allergy. Abigail must have understood that intrinsically his constitution was relatively sound. "Your health will bear town life very well," Abigail told him a little dryly. "If I tell you that you have the constitution of an ox, it will offend you."[8]

In April 1768, John, Abigail, and family moved to Boston. After he had arrived and established a thriving law practice, Abigail noted that, instead of injuring his health, the climate of Boston had apparently done wonders for him. "He really had never seemed better, his appetite was prodigious, his cheeks were round and rosy, he seemed altogether chunkier and stronger than ever."[9]

As a lawyer Adams's most significant case was the defense of a British officer, Captain Preston, and eight British soldiers who fired on a mob in the Boston Massacre on March 5, 1770. This defense of Preston and the eight soldiers was a move which made Adams unpopular with the people of Boston. After his successful defense Adams was elected as a delegate to the General Court from the town of Boston. After his election he dwelt on the sacrifices that his new position would cause him to undergo. He was in a large law practice at that time; his health was judged to be feeble; and he was still on his diet of milk and toast.[10]

He later reminisced concerning his acceptance of the job as delegate to the General Court: "My health was feeble. I was throwing away as bright prospects as any man had ever had before him."[11] Indeed, a few months after his election, he developed a pain in his breast which was said to have threatened his life. The pain was referred to as occurring when he was a delegate to the General Court in Boston. There is no description of the type of pain, the duration of the pain, or what brought on the pain. We are left with the knowledge that he had chest pain, but with no idea of its cause. In the spring of 1771 Adams moved back to Boston. He was very despondent and he fell into a period of depression caused by his concern over his health.[12] The season of occurrence, the duration, and the symptoms themselves of his illness would make it unlikely that Adams suffered from a common cold. The occasional reference to red and inflamed eyes would incline one to suspect again that he suffered from allergies. In August 1771 his eyes would tire quickly and were often red and inflamed. He grew increasingly nearsighted.[13]

Adams was described as having the swift mood changes of his mother. He and his mother had quick tempers and the same shifts from high spirits to the deepest despondency.[14] There were times when Adams was very meek and other times when he was extremely rash in behavior. His mood swings were from cautious to explosive. These features of his temperament led some to think that he was manic depressive. Benjamin Franklin wrote to the secretary of foreign affairs in Congress that Adams "is always an honest man, often a wise man, but sometimes in some things absolutely out of his sense." Jefferson concurred in this assessment.[15]

There are those who feel that Adams was basically a relatively sound man physically. There is evidence that his genes were good. His family history was relatively free of serious health problems. There is not a great deal written about Adams' exercise habits. However, in a letter from Adams to Abigail on May 12, 1774, he wrote: "I rise at 5:00 A.M., walk three miles, keep the air all day, and walk again in the afternoon. These walks have done me more good than anything."[16]

In a letter to Abigail April 26, 1777, Adams wrote: "Indeed I feel not a little out of humor from this indisposition of body. You know I cannot pass a spring or a fall without an ill turn and I have one of these for four or five weeks—a cold as usual. Warm weather and a little exercise with a little medicine, I suppose, will cure me as usual."[17] And again in May 1777 Adams wrote to Abigail: "I am suffering every day from the want of my farm to ramble over. I have been now for ten weeks in a drooping disagreeable way, and am constantly with a cold. If the warm weather, which is now coming on, should not cure me of my cold and make me better I must come home. I expect that I shall be chained to this cold until my constitution both mind and body shall be destroyed and rendered wholly useless to myself and to my family for the remainder of my days."[18] These last two letters were written while attending the Continental Congress as a delegate from Massachusetts.

In May 1777 Adams was apparently suffering from the maritime crunch which deprived him of his favorite alcoholic beverages. He wrote to Abigail on May 22, 1777: "I would give three guineas for a barrel of your cyder. Not one drop of it to be had here for gold, and wine is not to be had under sixty-eight dollars per gallon, and that very bad. I would give a guinea for a barrel of your beer. A small beer here is wretchedly bad. In short, I am getting nothing that I can drink, and I believe that I shall be sick from this cause alone. Rum is forty shillings a gallon, and bad water will never do in this hot climate in summer where acid liquors are necessary against infection."[19] This letter was written during his last year as a member of the Continental Congress.

From 1780 to 1781 Adams, while on his diplomatic mission to Europe, spent most of his time in the Netherlands. In Amsterdam on October 9, 1781, he wrote to Abigail, relating to her the details of his recent illness. He described it as "a nervous fever of a dangerous kind, bordering on putrid. It seized upon my head in such a manner that for four or five days I was lost. My friends were so good to me as to send me an excellent physician and surgeon, whose skill and faithful efforts, with the blessing of heaven have saved my life. I am, however, still weak; and whether I shall be able to recover my health among the pestilential vapors from these stagnant waters?"[20] There is no question that Adams was very ill. He was in a coma for five days, and Thaxter, his private secretary, despaired of his life. No specific causal agent has been named, but the term "Dutch complaint" was attached to his illness.[21] Even after the crest of the fever had passed, he was too weak to carry on any state business. He became ill again in August 1781, and it was the middle of October before he could resume the work as agent to the Dutch Netherlands.[22]

After Adams left the Netherlands he continued his European mission in France. During this time he was impatiently waiting on an appointment to the court of St. James. It was soon after he left Holland that he developed numerous boils. Apparently, Adams had developed the boils before he left Amsterdam, because they were referred to in a letter from John Thaxter to John Adams, dated April 20, 1782, from Amsterdam. John Thaxter referred to a boil as a tumor.[23]

In 1783, just following the signing of the Treaty of Paris, Adams again became ill. He had just been appointed to the court of St. James. This breakdown likely occurred due to the strain involved in the negotiations of the treaty. He had been working extremely long hours in very stuffy quarters and had also abandoned his regular program of rest and exercise. He was advised by a French physician to move to the suburbs and take long walks every day.

For many years Adams had a tremor which became much worse as he grew older. In May 1789, while Adams was vice president, he went with a member of the Senate to Washington to address the Senate. His hand shook so badly that he had to try to steady it by holding it against his hat which he held in the other hand, but he could read only with difficulty. He did finally gain more control and was able to finish.[24]

In 1798, during the second year of his presidency after a prolonged struggle with Hamilton over the peace mission, Adams became exhausted, and it took him several months to recover enough strength to resume the struggle. In October 1799 he finally ordered the peace mission to sail. He had prior to that time been away from his office trying to recover his strength and health.

Apparently, there was a period of several years, beginning during his presidency and lasting until the final few years of his life, when his health was relatively good. On January 21, 1812, Jefferson wrote to Adams, "I have heard with pleasure that you are retaining good health and a greater power of exercise and walking than I do."[25] Adams replied almost immediately on February 3, 1812, "I have never yet seen the day I could say that I have had no pleasure, or that I have had more pain than pleasure, but I have a complaint that only the ground can cure."[26]

As late as the age of 78 Adams continued to do a great deal of horseback riding for long distances. Into his mid–80s he took long rides over the hilly terrain of Quincy. In his later years he was unable to write, and in his last years his eyesight failed so fast that he had to be read to. Otherwise the last years of John Adams were spent with relatively good health. He must have been basically sound, since he survived to the ripe old age of 92. He complained of rheumatism, sciatica, and bad eyesight; however, none of his complaints and illnesses would be calculated to shorten one's life. He had a severe tremor of his hands which he called "quiverations" and which interfered with his handwriting. In the fall of 1820 Adams went to Boston to the Massachusetts Constitutional Convention. The trip and the convention were very tiring for a man of his age, and the sessions were long and arduous. The pressures of the convention proved to be too much for him. In the spring of 1821 he developed a fever which kept him in bed for two months. The cause of the fever is unknown.[27]

Adams was invited to Boston to attend the celebration of the fiftieth anniversary of the Declaration of Independence, but he was too weak to go. During the celebration Adams was near death. With his family around him, on the morning of July 4 he became comatose. About noon he regained consciousness briefly and then slipped back into an unconscious state. At 6:00 P.M. on July 4, 1826, he expired. Thomas Jefferson expired on that same day.

To try to establish exactly the cause of death of a man who died at 92 is difficult. The ex-president had for several months been unable to go for his customary walks. He was compelled to spend the long days sitting in an easy chair propped up with cushions. His mind remained clear, but he breathed with difficulty. It is probable, although we should like more evidence, that John Adams died of congestive heart failure.

References

1. Page Smith, *John Adams*, 1:9.
2. Catherine Drinker Bowen, *John Adams and the American Revolution*, p. 50.
3. Rudolph Marx, *The Health of the Presidents*, p. 30.
4. Bowen, *John Adams and the American Revolution*, p. 75.
5. Smith, *John Adams*, 1:35.
6. Bowen, *John Adams and the American Revolution*, p. 243.
7. Edgar Erskine Hume, *Victories of Army Medicine*, p. 119.
8. Bowen, *John Adams and the American Revolution*, p. 298.
9. Ibid., p. 305.
10. Smith, *John Adams*, 1:126.
11. John T. Morse, *John Adams*, 8:841.
12. Ibid., p. 41.
13. Smith, *John Adams*, 1:316.

14. Bowen, *John Adams and the American Revolution*, p. 227.

15. Jack Shepherd. *The Adams Chronicles: Four Generations of Greatness*, p. 7.

16. Charles Francis Adams, *Familiar Letters of John Adams and His Wife Abigail Adams*, 1:1.

17. L. H. Butterfield, editor in chief. *Adams Family Correspondence, The Adams Papers*, p. 225.

18. Ibid., pp. 238–39.

19. Ibid., p. 246.

20. Ibid., 4:224.

21. Smith, *John Adams*, 1:515–81.

22. Ibid., 2:502.

23. Butterfield, *Adams Family Correspondence*, 2:312.

24. Smith, *John Adams*, 2:758.

25. Paul Wilstach, editor, *The Correspondence of John Adams and Thomas Jefferson*, p. 35.

26. Ibid., p. 37.

27. Smith, *John Adams*, 2:1130.

3

Thomas Jefferson

Thomas Jefferson was born at his father's farm, Shadwell, in Albemarle County, Virginia, on April 13, 1743. Jefferson seems to have had no significant illness as an infant and child.

To try to write about the various illnesses of the adult Jefferson, however, is very difficult. Jefferson was a very complicated individual with rather advanced ideas about exercise and doctors, and some of his health problems were not organic. His headaches, for example, which at times severely incapacitated him, were apparently precipitated by stress.

From at least the age of 19 onward, Jefferson was subject at times of stress and grief to severe disabling headaches. When in 1762 he met Rebecca Burwell, age 16, she was his first recorded love. He apparently admired her from afar, fearing that pursuit of this young lady would go unrequited. When he finally summoned the courage to dance with Rebecca in the Apollo Room of the Raleigh Tavern in Williamsburg, he found himself almost at a total loss for words. He was so distressed by his lack of aptitude as a lover that on March 20, 1764, in a letter to a friend telling of the finality of his loss, he admitted having been racked with violent headaches for two days.[1]

Jefferson was thereafter, during periods of severe stress and grief, afflicted by headaches that could at times be severe, prolonged, and incapacitating. During these periods of stress and headache (to make him more miserable), he was afflicted with some sort of inflammation of his eyes. He said, "The whites of my eyes have become red."[2] These headaches struck Jefferson several times during his life, usually at intervals of seven to eight years. It is usually possible to correlate the headaches with deep personal loss, complicated by indecision and deeply buried rage.[3]

Soon after his mother's death, for example, on March 31, 1776, Jefferson himself became ill. It is known that the illness was a severe headache that lasted for six weeks.

Again in 1785, soon after Jefferson arrived in Paris to begin his mission as minister to France, he was suffering from migraine headaches (or tension), depending on one's evaluation from such a distance. This episode lasted for about six weeks. He was unhappy and homesick in Paris.[4]

In 1790 the headaches recurred. In April of that year he received word that his friend, Maria Cosway, had been very ill but was now recovered. This news and the burden of his duties as secretary of state overwhelmed him.

While undergoing these multiple stresses he developed another series of severe headaches. These were described as coming on each day at sunrise and staying with him till sunset. He continued his arduous labors in spite of the headaches. This particular attack lasted six weeks.[5]

Still again, in 1807, during the second term of Jefferson's presidency, Jefferson's headaches returned with great severity and lasted for a long time. The Embargo Act had been passed by both houses, and the difficulties arising from this act caused much havoc to the fortunes of the country. Several members of his cabinet left him, and Jefferson was troubled by the thought that he was causing great troubles for the economy of his country and destroying his party.[6]

Jefferson was an ardent and lifelong advocate of exercise and physical fitness. In a letter to his favorite nephew, Peter Carr, he related what his views were on exercise. First, however, in that letter he delivered a Polonius-like sermon to his nephew about all the virtues, and wrote, "The deficit of these virtues can never be made up by all other acquirements of body and mind." Then after the catalogue of virtues which must be observed by Peter Carr, he extolled the virtues of exercise. His letter was dated from Paris, August 19, 1785:

> To Peter Carr. Consider what hours you have free from school and the exercises of the school. Give about two or three hours every day to exercise, for health must not be sacrificed to learning. A strong body makes the mind strong. As to the species of exercise I advise the gun. While this gives a moderate exercise to the body, it gives boldness, enterprise, and independence. Games played with the ball and others of that nature are too violent for the body, and stamp no character on the mind. Let the gun, therefore, be the constant companion of your walks. Never think of taking a book with you. The object of walking is to relax the mind. You should, therefore, not permit yourself even to think while you walk; but divert yourself by the objects surrounding you. Walking is the best possible exercise. Habituate yourself to walk very far. The Europeans value themselves on having subdued the horse to the use of man, but I doubt whether we have not lost more than we have gained by the use of the animal. By the use of the animal one has occasioned the degeneracy of the human body. The Indian goes on foot nearly as

far on a long journey as our enfeebled white does on his horse; and he will tire the best horses. There is no habit you will value so much as that of walking for long distance without fatigue. I would advise you to take your exercise in the afternoon, not because it is the best time for exercise, for certainly it is not, but because it is the best time to spare from your studies, and habit will soon reconcile it to the health and render it nearly as useful as if you gave it to the more precious hours of the day. A little walk of half an hour in the morning when you first rise is advisable also. It shakes off sleep, and produces other good effects on the animal economy. Rise at a fixed and early hour, and go to bed at a fixed and early hour. Sitting up late at night is injurious to the health and not useful to the mind.[7]

Jefferson gave his opinion in this letter on those who rode horseback and thus did little walking. We wonder what his comments would have been about our excessive use of the automobile and the avoidance of walking. One is interested in getting Jefferson's ideas on preserving one's health. So far as I have been able to determine, no other president or world leader has outlined such explicit and detailed ideas on the mode of living that might preserve one's health. His advice was sane and far ahead of what one might expect in his time.

His family apparently was productive of a great deal of stressful situations. His headaches, their manner of production, their severity, and their length remind one of those suffered by Woodrow Wilson several scores of years after Jefferson.

One may understand Jefferson better by reading about his attitude toward doctors. Jefferson had a much better understanding about what doctors at that time had to offer their patients than did Washington and other of his comtemporaries. Indeed, there was no American president who understood better than he the deficiencies of medicine as practiced in their respective times. He, for a great number of years, had distrusted doctors and abhorred their use of bleeding and purging. Jefferson was fond of telling the story that "whenever he saw three physicians together he looked up to discover whether there was not a turkey buzzard in the neighborhood."[8] Such an attitude toward doctors did show some insight into the shortcomings of their profession in his day. George Washington, Andrew Jackson, and James Madison apparently accepted without question what the medical profession had to offer, including excessive bleeding.

Jefferson outlined this feeling about the deficiency of medicine in a letter to Dr. Casper Wistar. The letter is dated June 21, 1807, from Washington.

The disorders of the animal body, and the symptoms indicating them are as various as the elements of which the body is composed. The combinations, too, of these signs and symptoms are so infinitely diversified that many associations of them appear rarely to establish a definite disease; and to an unknown disease there cannot be an unknown remedy. Here, then, the judicious, the moral, the humane physician should stop. Having been so often a witness to the salutary efforts which nature makes to re-establish the disordered function, he should rather trust to their action than hazzard the intervention of that, and a greater derangement of the system, by conjectural experimentation on a machine so complicated and unknown as the human body, and a subject so sacred as human life.[9]

Thomas Jefferson, a true scientist himself, did not cease to have a great distaste for the medical practitioners of his time. Most of the doctors of his era had no background in physiology or in any other arm of medicine. The practice was purely empirical. We return here to Thomas Jefferson's letter of June 21, 1807, to Dr. Wistar: "One of the most successful physicians I have ever known has assured me that he used more red pills, drops of colored water, and water of hickory ashes, than all the other medications put together. The patient treated in the fashionable theory sometimes gets well in spite of the medicine. Medicine, therefore, restored him, and the young doctors seized new courage to proceed in his bold experiment."[10]

In spite of Jefferson's friendship with Dr. Benjamin Rush, one of the outstanding physicians of his time, Jefferson condemned Rush's drastic use of excessive bleeding and purging. He believed that such methods were killing more patients by far than they were curing. Jefferson said, "Our country is overrun with young lads from the Philadelphia school, who, with their mercury and lancet in hand, are vying with the sword of Bonaparte which shall shed the most human blood."[11]

Jefferson, though he was very critical of doctors in general, did on occasion practice a little of his own medicine. In one case he acted as an unlicensed surgeon. He found the Negro slave of a neighbor wounded and bleeding profusely, called for a needle and thread, and sewed up the wounds on this young slave. Nothing was related about the outcome or possible sterile technique used during the suturing. It is also related that he not only had himself inoculated but personally inoculated his own family against smallpox. In addition, Jefferson followed the advice of the progressive English physician Dr. Gem in treating his own ten-year-old daughter, Polly. He gave her one pint of madeira wine each day for several weeks, using this as his treatment for typhoid. He claimed to have saved the lives of several members of his own family and 20 to 30 of his friends and neighbors by the use of the madeira regimen. Jefferson very much opposed the use of catharsis and blood-letting on wasting diseases like typhoid.[12]

Throughout his life, however, Jefferson necessarily had many encounters with doctors. In 1781, soon after Jefferson retired as governor of Virginia in the latter part of June, he was thrown from his horse, sustained severe injuries, and became inactive for some time. During this period of inactivity he began writing his notes on Virginia. The injury was presumably a broken arm.[13]

In the summer of 1785, Jefferson, while still minister to France, became acquainted with Maria Cosway, the wife of a famous painter, Richard Cosway. After several days of discovering Paris together, they went out promenading the Seine. Ambassador Jefferson had apparently forgotten his age and the dignity which belonged to American chief diplomats in foreign countries! Not far from La Place de la Concorde, this animal energy sent him hurtling to disaster. He forgot that a Virginian born on horseback had not the same agility on his feet. When the ambassador tried to jump a fence, he crashed to the earth. When he rose to his feet, his right hand dangled uselessly. He pretended at the moment that it was nothing. They finished their walk and continued to talk. Only when he had reached his own house did he tell Mrs. Cosway that his wrist was injured. He sent her home in a carriage and called a surgeon.[14]

A different version is recounted by Nathan Schachner. In this account when the accident happened Thomas Jefferson was not with Mrs. Cosway but alone. Jefferson tried to leap over a large kettle which was in his courtyard. He fell heavily on his right wrist, which was then rendered useless. The surgeons attended him almost immediately and their diagnosis was a dislocation. They set the wrist, but set it so poorly that the injury never healed properly. It is felt that it must have been a fracture instead of a dislocation. Jefferson never recovered from the injury caused by this fall.[15]

It is felt that from the severe pain and the failure to recover that he certainly broke a bone, as his daughter, Martha, believed. Jefferson's daughter gave a third account in which Jefferson was not at home nor with Mrs. Cosway. He was walking, engaged in a conversation with an unidentified friend, when he fell and fractured his wrist. He neither jumped a fence nor a kettle, according to his daughter. The fracture was compound, poorly treated, and caused him trouble until he died.[16] For weeks the broken wrist remained swollen, painful, and useless. Jefferson was seen and examined by the leading doctors in Paris, and after the treatment by the Paris doctors failed to give relief he journeyed to Aix-en-Provence to try the mineral waters for the painful, deformed wrist.[17]

Although Jefferson's headaches have been labeled in many ways, in no way did they fit the diagnosis of migraine. Since they persisted for weeks at a time, one would have to rule out migraine. Jefferson himself gave a good description of a headache lasting for weeks and being absent at night, so we are persuaded to call this kind of headache a "cluster headache" of a variant sort.

The recurring reference to them as migrainous seems to have been caused by a much earlier biographer who referred to his headaches as migrainous, and many following authors made the same error.

In fact, in the second year of his presidency—1802—Jefferson developed a severe case of dysentery. He typically consulted no doctor about his affliction. He did, however, find that horseback riding relieved his dysentery. He also used the same remedy for his headaches, which would give credence to the idea that both problems were precipitated by tension.

In the late summer of 1794, after he had ended his tour as secretary of state, Jefferson returned to Monticello. On his return he found his estate debt-ridden and in poor condition. In spite of his crippled hand, he endeavored to do a lot of manual labor himself, and as a consequence he developed a backache which lasted two and a half months. The exact nature of his back disability is unknown. The only thing known for sure is that he was disabled almost totally for two and a half months. After this episode he suffered from repeated attacks of back pain. Jefferson suffered a recurrence of similar severe back pain in Monticello in 1797.

During the interval between his tenure as secretary of state and becoming vice president, 1793–97, Jefferson suffered a real ordeal. A mortgage on Monticello, the lack of productivity by his farm, his injured back, and the continued work on the house all served to injure his health. It was conjectured that perhaps he felt deeply trapped by his relationship to Sally Heming, his mulatto mistress, and the presence of her children at Monticello.

Jefferson's health was so bad that he began to think his death was near. He wrote to a friend: "My health has suddenly broken down with symptoms which give me to believe that I shall not have much to encounter in the tedium vita." There seems no doubt that the cumulative effects of domestic problems, financial woes, and illness had made Jefferson very depressed.[18]

Jefferson had become tired of the presidency and the multitude of problems which it brought to his doorstep. To add to his unhappiness, during the month of January 1808 he contracted a severe infection of his jaw, which confined him to his home for some time.[19] This infection was most likely due to a decayed and infected tooth. The dentists were as badly prepared to care for their specialty as were the doctors of their day. It is also known that Jefferson from middle age on had to wear glasses to read.

In the summer of 1811 Jefferson was incapacitated by a recurrence of his rheumatism. There are, unfortunately, not enough descriptive materials concerning Jefferson's rheumatism. The word rheumatism covered all sorts of bone, joint, and muscle problems, and hence we have no clue as to the true nature of his rheumatism except that he was disabled by it.

From 1816 to 1825 Jefferson was involved in the founding of the University of Virginia at Charlottesville. In August 1818 he met with James Madison and other Virginian notables to decide on a location of the new college. The meeting was at Rockfish Gap. He made the 37-mile trip to the gap in the Blue Ridge on horseback with no real difficulty. From there Jefferson rode to Warm Springs, where he spent three weeks. He had hopes that the famed waters would help his rheumatism. The springs did help his rheumatism, or at least eased for a while his symptoms, but while there he developed something equally if not more unpleasant. In the third week he developed some boils. The boils were on his rear and were likely due to some unsanitary conditions in the bath. This was a difficult problem for one who had to return home over mountain roads on horseback. According to all accounts, the journey home was no pleasant one. For several weeks he did his correspondence lying down and for several months he did not ride a horse. Jefferson always believed that this experience had greatly injured his health. This illness indeed somewhat set back his ability to work on his plan for the college.[20]

We have shown that Jefferson was a strong advocate for good health and physical fitness. In a letter addressed to Dr. Vine Utley, dated March 2, 1819, he expressed these views again. Apparently, Dr. Utley was conducting what we would now call a clinical survey. Utley had written to several leading citizens of his time, including Dr. Benjamin Rush, to learn what their views were on the same subject. This was very likely the first clinical survey ever conducted in this country. The letter, dated March 2, 1819, to Dr. Vine Utley, read as follows:

> Sir, Your Monticello letter of February 18 came to hand at the first instant and the request of the history of my physical habits would have puzzled me not a little had it not been for the model with which you accompanied it of Dr. Rush's answer to similar inquiry. I live so much

like other people that I might refer to ordinary life as a history of my own. Like my friend, the doctor, I live temperately, eating little animal food, and that not as an aliment so much as a condiment for the vegetables which constitute my principle diet. I double, however, the doctor's glass and a half of wine; but halve its effects by drinking the weak wines only. Ardent wines I cannot drink nor do I use ardent spirits in any form. Malt liqueurs and cider are my table drink, and my breakfast, like that also of my friend, is of tea and coffee. I have been blessed with organs of digestion which accept and concoct without any murmuring whatever that palate chooses to consign to them, and I have not yet lost a tooth to age. I was a hard student until I entered the business of life, the duties of which leave no idle time to those disposed to fulfill them; and now retired, and at the age of seventy-six, am again a hard student. Indeed, my fondness for reading and study revolts me from the drudgery of letter writing. A stiff wrist, a consequence of an early dislocation, makes writing both slow and painful. I am not so regular in my sleep as the doctor says he was, devoting to it from five to eight hours according as my company or the book I am reading interests me; and I never go to bed without an hour's previous reading of something moral, however, whereon to ruminate in the intervals of sleep, but whether I retire to the bed early or late, I rise with the sun. I use spectacles in the night but not necessarily in the day unless in reading small print. My hearing is distinct in particular conversation, but confused when several voices cross each other, which unfits me for the society of the table. I have been more fortunate than my friends in the article of health. So free from cold that I have not had one (in the breast, I mean) on the average of eight or ten years through life. I ascribe this exemption partially to the habit of bathing my feet in cold water each morning for sixty years past. And fever of more than twenty-four hours I have not had above three or four times in my life.

A periodical headache has afflicted me occasionally, once perhaps in six to eight years for two to three weeks at a time, which seems now to have left me; and except on a late occasion of indisposition enjoy good health; too feeble indeed to walk much but riding without fatigue six to eight miles per day, and sometimes thirty or forty. I may end these egotisms therefore as I began, by saying that my life has been so much like that of other people that I may say with Horace to everyone, "Nomina mutato narrator fabula de te." Translated, "With a change of name the tale could be told of you." I must not end, however, without due thanks for the kind sentiments of regard you are so good as to express toward myself; and with my acknowledgment for these, be pleased to accept the assurances of my respect and esteem.[21]

In this one letter Thomas Jefferson reveals much about his boldness, enterprise, and mode of living. We are told a considerable amount about his habits of the past and the way they have been modified by his advanced age.

In 1818, after he had completed and returned his plans on the university to the commission, he found that one of his close friends had defaulted on notes amounting to $20,000. Jefferson, therefore, after this disaster, had to mortgage everything and sell his cherished library. He was at this time stricken by the most severe attack of rheumatism he ever had. The rheumatism was accompanied by very obstinate constipation and indigestion. The severe constipation was even life threatening. In 1821, at the age of 78, Jefferson fell from a broken step on a terrace at Monticello and broke his left arm and wrist. During the healing process there was swelling and stiffness in this wrist, and he now had both wrists markedly crippled.[22] In a letter from Jefferson to John Adams, June 2, 1822: "It is very long, my dear sir, since I have written to you. My dislocated wrist has now become so stiff that I write slow and with pain, and therefore write as little as I can."[23] This letter was written several months after Jefferson's fall on the terrace. One can follow the downhill course of the physical state of these two giants, Jefferson and Adams, by reading their correspondence. Jefferson continued in the same letter to Adams: "I have ever dreaded a doting old age and my health has generally been so good, and is now so good, that I dread it still. The rapid decline of my strength during the last winter has made me hope sometimes that I see land. During the summer I enjoy the temperature, but I shudder at the approach of winter; and wish that I could sleep through it with the dormouse and only wake up with the spring, if ever. I am told that you walk well and firmly. I can only reach my garden, and that with sensible fatigue."[24]

We see here what appears to be a death wish expressed twice in this letter. Jefferson had seen so much grief in his family, had had domestic problems of his own and in his daughter's family, financial disaster, and now feebleness and pain. Again, Jefferson to Adams, January 8, 1825: "It is a long time since I have written to you. This proceeds from the difficulty of writing with my crippled wrist. Your hearing, too, is good as I am told. In this you have the advantage of me. This dullness of mine causes me to lose much of the conversation of the world and much a stranger to what is passing in it."[25]

It would not seem necessary to add to the multitude of medical problems which confronted Jefferson, but it is noted that during his last year he suffered from prostatic enlargement. The symptoms that he suffered due to this illness are not recorded in any detail, so we are left with only the statement that he did have prostatic enlargement.

Late in June 1826 the mayor of Washington sent an invitation to Jefferson to join in the celebration of the fiftieth anniversary of American independence. He replied in writing that his enfeebled state made his physical presence impossible. A short time later he was too feeble to get out of bed. On July 2 he sensed the end and summoned the family to his bedside. On July 3 at 9:00 P.M. the doctor came to give him his medicine and Jefferson shook his head. In a calm, distinct voice he said, "No, Doctor, nothing more." The medicine was laudanum and without it he became restless. Jefferson was conscious that July 4 was near and he had a great desire to live to that hour. He asked repeatedly if the Fourth was now present. Jefferson's withered chest continued to rise and fall as the clock passed midnight. As the clock passed midnight, he ceased to breathe. Jefferson died, according to his son Randolph, at fifty minutes past the meridian, or 12:50 A.M., July 4, 1826. "I closed his eyes with my own hands."[26]

References

1. Fawn Brodie, *Thomas Jefferson, An Intimate History*, pp. 65–66.
2. Alf J. Mapp, *Thomas Jefferson: A Strange Case of Mistaken Identity*, p. 28.
3. Brodie, *Thomas Jefferson*, p. 43.
4. Rudolph Marx, *The Health of the Presidents*, p. 56.
5. Brodie, *Thomas Jefferson*, pp. 252–53.
6. Page Smith, *Jefferson: A Revealing Biography*, p. 283.
7. Adrienne Koch and William Peden, editors, *The Life and Selected Writings of Thomas Jefferson*, pp. 690–91.
8. Brodie, *Thomas Jefferson*, p. 465.
9. Koch and Peden, *The Life and Selected Writings of Thomas Jefferson*, p. 584.
10. Ibid., pp. 550–51.
11. Marx, *The Health of the Presidents*, p. 48.
12. Ibid., pp. 48–49.
13. Marie Kimball, *Jefferson — War and Peace, 1776 to 1784*, p. 262.
14. Thomas Fleming, *The Man from Monticello*, p. 16.
15. Nathan Schachner, *Thomas Jefferson, A Biography*, 1:319.
16. Brodie, *Thomas Jefferson*, p. 208.
17. Marx, *The Health of the Presidents*, p. 57.
18. Smith, *Jefferson*, p. 242.
19. Schachner, *Thomas Jefferson*, 2:285.
20. Dumas Malone. *Jefferson and His Time, the Sage of Monticello*, 6:178–79.
21. Koch and Peden, *The Life and Selected Writings of Thomas Jefferson*, pp. 690–91.
22. Brodie, *Thomas Jefferson*, p. 459.
23. Paul Wilstach, editor, *The Correspondence of John Adams and Thomas Jefferson*, p. 179.
24. Ibid.
25. Ibid., p. 191.
26. Fleming, *The Man from Monticello*, p. 384.

4

James Madison

James Madison, the fourth president of the United States, was born in Port Conway, Virginia, on March 16, 1751. Madison, the smallest of all American presidents, never weighed more than 100 pounds. He was always a frail person, even in his youth, and his appearance was sickly from early infancy. Indeed, it was predicted that he would not survive long. Fortunately, his wealthy family was able to give him the best of care so that he was able to survive those early years.

When he was 18 his teacher found him ready for college, but his physician advised strongly that he should not go to William and Mary College, where he would be in the swampy tideland peninsula and therefore be exposed to malaria. At that time malaria was called bilious fever or ague, a disease strongly endemic in the land between the York and the James rivers. For this reason Madison was sent north to Princeton University. Madison earned his bachelor's degree from Princeton in two years, thus expending a lot of effort during his undergraduate days. When he graduated, he was in poor health, which his friends attributed to the doubled labor of taking his bachelor's degree in two years.[1]

After Madison finished his undergraduate degree he stayed on at Princeton for an extra six months to take further studies. His excuse for not going home was that he was too ill to travel. Throughout his life, in fact, Madison's physicians would recognize him to be very frail physically and made a great endeavor to increase his strength and stamina by various programs of riding horseback and walking. Madison at one time was sent to Warm Springs, a spa in the western part of Virginia, to recuperate.

His condition grew worse, however, after he returned home from college. At that time Madison suffered from a type of seizure, during which he became for a moment oblivious of his surroundings. His doctors labeled his affliction as epilepsy. Later, doctors and historians felt the episodes to be a manifestation of epileptoid hysteria. In psychoanalytic terms these seizures probably represented a conversion reaction.[2] From this great distance in time, however, the riddle will never be fully resolved. One can only indulge in speculation, though not totally informed speculation.

Madison himself described the disease as a "constitutional tendency to sudden attacks somewhat resembling epilepsy which suspended all intellectual function. . . . They continued through my life with prolonged intensity."[3] Years later his brother-in-law, J. C. Payne, would describe the attacks as of the nature of epilepsy—"of a character and effect which suspended his power of action."[4]

An entry for October 11, 1763, found among the papers of Madison's father, contains a list of medications presumed to have been used by James Madison. The list included drugs used at that time for seizures and designated as "for an epilepsy." There would still be controversy as to whether the malady was constitutional or was due to nervous or emotional problems. There is a great deal of biographical evidence that he suffered most from the seizures when he was under stress, which would tend to give weight to the idea that he suffered from an emotional disorder. However, by his own statement he had periodic recurrences of the problem throughout his life, which would persuade one to believe that it was not epileptoid hysteria—a condition associated with years at or about childhood and puberty. As Madison described the episodes, there were no convulsions, but what would seem to be periods when he had a physical and mental standstill. If organic, the seizures would seem to greatly resemble petit mal, which is characterized by the sudden cessation of conscious activity without convulsive muscular activity, or loss of postural control.[5] Perhaps some confirmation of the idea that Madison had petit mal might be found in Dolley's description of one episode: "I saw you in your chamber unable to move."

Some somatic symptoms noted in Madison are felt to be emotional in origin. This spectrum of symptoms would include pseudo-seizures. Conversion hysteria is a label which could easily apply. From Madison's own description of the seizures and the description of petit mal, one would be persuaded to think strongly of this form of epileptic disorder.

About three years after Madison graduated from Princeton he began to worry about the future prospects for his physical well-being. At one moment he wrote to his friend, William Bradford, "I am too dull and infirm now to look out for any extraordinary things in this world, for I think my sensations for many months past have intimated to me not to expect a long and healthy life, yet it may be better for me after some time, though I hardly dare to expect it, and therefore I have little spirit and alacrity to set about any thing that is difficult in acquiring and useless in possessing after one has exchanged time for eternity."[6]

Apparently, at this early age Madison was far from optimistic regarding his prospects for good health. However, Madison strangely never made clear just what specific ailments he suffered from in his youth. The Payne biography of James Madison gave the clearest statement made by Madison to anyone referring to his feeble health and the discouraging feebleness of his constitution.[7] In his early years, both before and after Princeton, his uncertainty about his physical state resulted in brooding, depression, inertia, hypochondria, and expectations of an early death.[8]

In 1775 an epidemic of enteric fever swept over the colonies. Madison, with his presumed frail constitution, would certainly be expected to succumb very readily; but he was one of the few members of his family who did not contract this deadly infection, which robbed him of a younger brother and sister.

A particularly interesting situation developed during his campaign for Congress against James Monroe in 1780. On one very cold, snowy day, Madison went to a Dutch church for a debate with Monroe. On the way home that night his nose and ears froze, leaving scars which he carried for the rest of his life.[9] Madison afterward pointed proudly to his scars as battle scars.

Of Madison's many health problems, one almost removed him from the Constitutional Convention, which began on May 3, 1787. Madison served there as a note-taking secretary. In August and September 1787 sheer fatigue and illness forced him to restrict his part in the debates and reduced greatly his note taking. However, he remained on the job exhausted and half sick.[10] In spite of his ill health and exhausted condition, Madison did not miss a single session. At the time of the critical debates Madison was suffering from a severe attack of malaria, the disease his family had attempted to prevent his contracting. Malaria was an illness which plagued him off and on for the rest of his life.[11]

In 1790, during his second year in the Congress, he suffered a severe attack of dysentery. After staying in Georgetown for a few days, he was cured of his dysentery but had a severe residual case of piles.

In 1800, during his tenure in the Virginia legislature, Madison had several health problems, including a severe attack of rheumatism.

After Jefferson was elected president on the thirty-sixth ballot in the House of Representatives, Madison was named secretary of state. At that time his health was very feeble and his father was also in very poor health. Madison's departure for the Capitol was delayed until after his father's death. The heavy duties as the secretary of state contributed to Madison's already poor health. He found work piled up for him, in "little accord with my unsettled health."[12]

In January 1807, while still secretary of state, Madison fell down his front steps and dislocated his ankle. It required several months for the ankle to heal.[13] In March he wrote to Monroe, "For the last year ... the weight of business has almost broken me down."[14] In early February 1808, during the time that Russia entered the war on Napoléon's side, Madison was involved in some very complex negotiations. In this interval he was very ill—too ill to go to his office—and he had to have meetings at his house.

A great deal of his problem was undoubtedly due to the problem which was so prevalent in Washington and the Tidewater area—malaria. In many instances his illness was labeled as bilious fever. The incidence of bilious fever (malaria) greatly increased in the summer when the Capitol was aswarm with mosquitoes, since Washington was to a large extent a swamp.

In June 1813, Madison, in his second term as president and at the end of a year of war disaster, was attacked again with malaria. On this occasion he was very ill, in fact, almost fatally. The three doctors attending him had not dared to give him "the bark" (quinine) during his period of high fever. He received quinine only beginning the third week of his illness.[15]

During this illness, when Daniel Webster called to deliver a congressional resolution, the president was too sick to receive him. After three weeks of round-the-clock nursing, Dolley wrote to a friend that Madison's fever had gone down: "He is taking bark every day."[16]

During this illness, when he lingered for weeks near death, Dolley attended him day and night. Dolley wrote to Albert Gallatin of her deep concern over her husband's illness: "You can have no idea of its extent and the despair in which I have attended his bedside for nearly five weeks."[17]

When Madison retired from the presidency in 1817, he was, for him, in relatively good health. But later, as early as 1821, he suffered a relapse of his malaria. He survived nearly 20 years after he left the White House, the last 9 of which found him greatly incapacitated with his numerous health problems.[18] For example, Madison had during his retirement several relapses of malaria. He was very ill in 1827 and again in 1829, just before he became a delegate to the Virginia state convention.

In the summer of 1827 Madison's health problems became much more severe, and in the fall he had an attack of illness labeled influenza. This episode of illness from which he needed several weeks to recover seemed to be the very beginning of a slow but rather steady decline in his health.

In the summer of 1828 Madison had another recurrence of malaria. In 1831 he suffered the beginning of a painful rheumatism in his hand. By midsummer 1831 his rheumatism had become so general that he had become almost incapable of continuing his correspondence. There is a great deal of resemblance between Madison's problem with arthritis and that of Jefferson, who in his later years also became so crippled with arthritis that he had a great problem in continuing his correspondence with his friend, John Adams.

Gradually, Madison's frame shrank, he became little more than skin and bones, and his arthritis continued to become worse. In 1831 he was confined to his bed by crippling arthritis in his arms and legs. Since he was unable to move his wrists, he could only use his fingertips to move his fine quill. His handwriting became smaller and smaller. "In explanation of my microscopic writing," he observed to Monroe, "I must remark that the older I get the more my stiffening fingers make smaller letters, as my feet take shorter steps."[19] By 1834 his eyesight also began to fail significantly, and at about the same time he became deaf in one ear.[20]

In 1834, due to illness, he had to resign his place as rector at the University of Virginia. From mid–1835 and to June 1836 he spent almost all of his time in bed or in his chair. At times he could hardly talk, but his mind and memory remained intact.[21]

In May 1836 the renowned Dr. Dungleson was summoned to Montpelier to see the ailing ex-president. Madison shared some recently arrived sherry with the good doctor, but regretted that his own palate was too vitiated to pass proper judgment upon it. The distinguished Dr. Richard Jones Dungleson pronounced the sherry "to be of the first chop," but he saw that the ravages of age had left his patient beyond help.[22]

As the spring of 1836 faded, Madison rapidly failed in health. He was the last survivor of the Virginia Convention of 1778 and the Constitutional Convention of 1787. On the morning of June 28, 1836, he was moved from his bed to his writing table, and his niece brought in his breakfast as usual. His niece left him, and when she returned a short time later she found him dead. Madison, who had had such misgivings about his prospects of surviving to old age and who suffered all his life from a great variety of illnesses, lived to the age of 85.

References

1. Robert A. Rutland, *James Madison: The Founding Father*, pp. 8–9.
2. Rudolph Marx, *The Health of the Presidents*, p. 70.
3. Ralph Ketcham, *James Madison, A Biography*, p. 51.

4. Virginia Moore, *The Madisons*, p. 38.

5. Mark A. Dictor, "Epilepsy and Convulsive Disorders," in *Harrison's Principles of Internal Medicine*, p. 2020.

6. Irving Brant, *The Fourth President: A Life of James Madison*, p. 105.

7. Ibid., p. 106.

8. Marx, *The Health of the Presidents*, p. 70.

9. Ketcham, *James Madison*, p. 277.

10. Ibid., pp. 224–25.

11. Marx, *The Health of the Presidents*, p. 72.

12. Brant, *The Fourth President*, p. 48.

13. Marx, *The Health of the Presidents*, p. 73.

14. Brant, *The Fourth President*, pp. 321–22.

15. Ketcham, *James Madison*, p. 561.

16. Moore, *The Madisons*, p. 290.

17. Ethel Arnett, *Mrs. James Madison, the Incomparable Dolley*, p. 214.

18. Homer F. Cunningham, *The Presidents' Last Years*, p. 34.

19. Brant, *The Fourth President*, p. 629.

20. Marx, *The Health of the Presidents*, p. 74.

21. Cunningham, *The Presidents' Last Years*, p. 35.

22. Ketcham, *James Madison*, p. 669.

5

James Monroe

James Monroe, the fifth president of the United States, was born in Westmoreland County, Virginia, April 28, 1758. Unlike Madison's, his childhood and youth were relatively free of health problems. At age 18 he enlisted in the Third Virginia Infantry. At that time Monroe was described as having a rugged constitution, standing a little over six feet tall with broad shoulders and a massive, raw-boned frame.[1]

Monroe was severely wounded in the battle at Trenton in 1776. His life was saved by a doctor, a resident of Trenton, who was with the troops purely by accident. Monroe and his captain, William Washington, led a charge on two British guns which barred their way. Captain Washington was wounded and Monroe took command. Monroe was also wounded. A bullet grazed the left side of his chest, buried itself in his shoulder, and injured the axillary artery, which bled profusely. The doctor was able to stop the bleeding and probably saved Monroe's life. His manner of treatment was a little different from the present-day technique used in treating gunshot wounds, but it was effective. The doctor applied pressure on the bleeding vessel by inserting his index finger into the wound and exerting pressure on the bleeding artery.[2]

Monroe, after the preliminary effort to stop the hemorrhage, was removed to a house nearby, where two surgeons were in attendance. These doctors used the method that was in use at that time for treating wounds — incidentally, a technique later used on James Garfield after he was shot on July 2, 1881. Apparently, little or no progress was made in the treatment of bullet wounds from the Revolutionary War until sometime after the Civil War. In treating Monroe the surgeons continued to exert pressure on the bleeding site and cleansed the wound with a sea sponge soaked in a basin. They then probed with their unwashed fingers in an effort to find the bullet, which they never found. It remained in Monroe's shoulder for the rest of his days on earth.

Dr. Hayes Agnew published in 1878 a textbook of surgery in which he described the treatment of bullet wounds and removal of foreign bodies. This was probably the state of the art at that time. Essentially, the treatment consisted of probing with the index finger for the bullet. No mention was made of any sterile technique. However, one innovation in the technique was added, "The fingernail should be guarded by scraping it over a piece of soap to fill up the space beneath the nail, so that no unnecessary violence may be done to the wound."[3]

Monroe was luckier than Garfield; if he suffered any infection it was slight. His recovery lasted a period of 11 weeks.

In 1783 Monroe was elected to the Congress of the Confederation and served until 1786. During this time he took trips into the swampy area of the Mississippi in order to study the possibility of free navigation on the Mississippi River. While in that mosquito-infested area he contracted a severe type of malaria and was very ill during 1785. Monroe had several episodes of febrile illnesses during his life, which were probably due to recurrence of his chronic malaria.

In March 1815, while Monroe was still secretary of state, the strain of the job over several months had put a very heavy burden on him. This time it required a full six months for him to regain his health. In 1814 he had added to his ordeal by assuming the Department of War, in addition to that of state. At that time John Armstrong, who was secretary of war, did not enjoy the confidence of President Madison or Secretary of State Monroe. The exact nature of Monroe's prolonged illness is apparently unknown except for the stress and strain of his wartime services and his recurrent malaria.

In the summer of 1815 he was freed of his War Department responsibilities, and soon thereafter began to regain his health. However, in spite of feeling better, he had not improved in appearance. In August his family physician, Dr. Charles Everett, prescribed a stay in the Virginia spas, Sweet Springs, White Springs, and Warm Springs. The respite improved his health. His strength came back, and he gained weight.[4]

Monroe succeeded Madison as president in 1817. During his presidency he had a number of serious illnesses.

It is likely that one of Monroe's illnesses was responsible for an undeclared war. Andrew Jackson in January 1818 wrote a confidential letter to President Monroe in which he urged that east Florida should be taken by force and held as indemnity for Spanish outrages on U.S. property in that area. "This can be done," wrote Jackson, "without implicating the government. Let it be signified to me through any channel, say Mr. Rhea, that the possession of the Floridas would be desirable to the U.S. and in a short time it will be accomplished."[5] Monroe did not acknowledge that such authority had been given to Jackson. Jackson, on the other hand, did claim that it had been given. But the Rhea letter, claimed to have been written with Monroe's approval, was never brought to light. Monroe stated, "In transcending the limits of your orders, . . . you acted on your own responsibility on facts and circumstances which were unknown to the government."[6] Apparently, Jackson did not want a clear statement from Monroe's government. He only wished a nod or a wink. Monroe finally conceded that the letter came but that he had never read it. He claimed that he gave it to John Calhoun, then secretary of war, who said that it concerned a plan for the proposed expedition against the Seminole Indians. But General Jackson stated that he soon thereafter got a letter from John Rhea, a congressman from Tennessee, saying that the president had given him approval for the expedition. It is felt that there must have been a massive general misunderstanding.[7]

Indeed, Monroe was bedfast during this time in early 1818 with a fever of undetermined origin, probably malaria, and may never have been aware of the presence or contents of the letter.[8]

In August 1825 Monroe had a convulsive seizure which was so severe that he was felt to be near death. There is no evidence that would establish the true cause of his seizure. The speculation suggests mushroom poisoning, a stroke due to cerebral hemorrhage, or cerebral malaria.

In addition, Monroe's general health and appearance suffered during his presidency. For example, when Monroe attended the meeting of the Board of Visitors of the University of Virginia at Charlottesville in July 1828, Madison was also present. A press reporter commented, "Mr. Madison, I think, looks very well — Mr. Monroe is the most perfect picture of woe I have ever seen. He is exceedingly wasted away and manifesting in his countenance the deepest and most fixed melancholy."[9]

When Madison left the presidency he was in a state of exhaustion. He seemed much older than his 67 years. His 8 years as president had made great inroads on his constitution. He attended the Virginia Constitutional Convention in 1829 and 1830, which was physically too much for him. He was forced, due to ill health, to leave the convention before it was over. John Quincy Adams, who saw him at the convention, noted that he looked emaciated and ill. After he arrived back home, his health seemed to improve.[10]

Monroe liked horseback riding, and after he left the presidency he engaged a great deal in this recreation. In 1829 he had a fall from his horse and injured his right wrist, which kept him from keeping up his correspondence for several weeks. Three presidents in a row, Jefferson, Madison, and Monroe, had problems with injury and arthritis which impaired their writing.

Monroe apparently made his last public appearance in New York on November 26, 1830, to help celebrate the dethronement of Charles X of France. He had developed a chronic pulmonary illness, which caused him to have a harassing cough, accompanied by a great deal of expectoration. His illness caused him to spend most of his time in bed. No specific diagnosis was ever made, but the doctor prescribed a rest at Saratoga. This prescription, along with his symptoms, would indicate his doctor suspected pulmonary tuberculosis.[11] Monroe was too weak to go to Saratoga, however. He said of himself, "I am free of pain, but my cough annoys me both day and night." Apparently, the only medication which he took was horehound syrup, which did not relieve the cough.[12]

In April 1831 Monroe wrote to Madison, "My state of health continues, consisting of a cough which annoys me night and day accompanied by considerable expectoration."[13] And when John Quincy Adams visited in the spring of 1831 he was much shocked by Monroe's emaciated appearance.[14] As time went by Monroe grew gradually weaker. Sometime before his death he was too weak to carry on a conversation. He got no better when summer came, and progressively grew weaker. He died July 4, 1831.[15]

There is no possibility of giving Monroe's last illness any precise diagnosis. It is known that the illness lasted for several months and involved his lungs progressively. He had a harassing, exhausting cough, and suffered from fever and severe night sweats. His cough was productive of much mucous and at times gushes of blood. As the disease involved more of his lungs, his breathing became more difficult.[16] The clinical picture is highly suggestive but is not diagnostic of pulmonary tuberculosis.

References

1. Harry Ammon, *James Monroe*, p. 7.
2. Rudolph Marx, *The Health of the Presidents*, p. 78.
3. D. Hayes Agnew, *The Principles and Practices of Surgery*, pp. 40, 286.
4. Ammon, *James Monroe*, p. 347.
5. W. P. Cresson, *James Monroe*, p. 304.
6. David C. Gilman, *James Monroe*, p. 145.
7. Gerald W. Johnson, *Andrew Jackson*, p. 196.
8. Marx, *The Health of the Presidents*, p. 85.
9. Irving Brant, *James Madison*, 6:460.
10. Homer F. Cunningham, *The Presidents' Last Years*, p. 39.
11. Cresson, *James Monroe*, p. 494.
12. Ibid.

13. Marx, *The Health of the Presidents,* p. 40.
14. Cunningham, *The Presidents' Last Years,* p. 40.
15. Ibid.
16. Marx, *The Health of the Presidents,* p. 88.

6

John Quincy Adams

John Quincy Adams, the sixth president of the United States, was born July 11, 1767, in Braintree (now Quincy), Massachusetts. He was the only son of a president ever to achieve the nation's highest office.

When Adams was three years old he had his right shoulder dislocated by a sudden jerk given to that arm by his nursemaid when he had wandered into the street against orders. There was also apparently some nerve damage, which resulted in subsequent muscle atrophy and weakness in his right upper extremity, an area which was thereafter weak and prone to re- injury and which interfered with his writing. On May 18, 1840, for example, while he was serving as a representative from Massachusetts, he was tripped up by the matting on the floor of the House of Representatives and fell forward, dislocating his right shoulder. The shoulder was set by Drs. Thomas and Maye. From this injury Adams suffered severe pain. Questioned then about any previous injuries, Adams recalled that he had been told by Abigail, his mother, about the injury which occurred when he was two or three.[1]

In addition, at the age of eight Adams fractured the index finger of his right hand, which was set by the family physician, Dr. Joseph Warren. This fractured right index finger, combined with the nerve damage to his right arm sustained when his right shoulder was dislocated, undoubtedly impaired his ability to write.

Adams was apparently inoculated for smallpox in 1775 at age eight.[2] The usual procedure during Adams's lifetime was to introduce infected material subcutaneously. It was not until July 1800 that Benjamin Waterhouse, an army surgeon, introduced Jenner's vaccine into the United States. The vaccine, made from material obtained from cowpox lesions, was placed directly on skin which had been scratched or abraded.

The year 1776 brought a number of health issues to the fore in the Adams family. In the summer a virulent episode of dysentery struck Braintree. Adams's mother and two of his brothers were stricken, but he escaped. In the fall Adams suffered from sore eyes which, however, did not prevent his writing to his father several times. During that winter Adams suffered from a severe attack of pleurisy, which he survived with no residual effect.[3] In addition, the family physician, Dr. Joseph Warren, died that year in the Battle of Bunker Hill.

Remarkably, in 1781, at age 14, Adams was in St. Petersburg, Russia, serving as private secretary and interpreter to the American minister to Russia; and two years later, at the age of 16, he was the U.S. secretary at the Treaty of Paris, which ended the American Revolution. Consequently, he was admitted to Harvard in 1785 as an advanced student, a junior. The president of Harvard did require of him further tutoring, however, which was supplied by his uncle, the Reverend John Shaw, a very exacting taskmaster. Under the strain caused by the intensity of the program of study Adams became tense and irritable, lost considerable weight, and had constant trouble with his sore eyes. His sore eyes seemed to follow somewhat the pattern of his father, John Adams, who was bothered with sore, inflamed, weepy eyes. It is likely that both father and son had an allergy.[4]

Early in his days at Harvard his Aunt Mary reported back to Abigail that Adams did not leave his studies long enough to maintain good health.[5] And a cousin reported that he found Adams in his quarters in an extreme state of dirt and neglecting his person.[6] It is obvious from these reports that Adams was not engaged in any exercise or sport while at Harvard.

Such inactivity apparently showed in his health. After spring vacation his senior year, for example, he suffered some heartburn and had a spell of dizziness. That year he also took a rest leave from his studies at Harvard and retreated to Braintree. Under considerable stress, he visited a doctor in Newberry Port to get an opiate to quiet his nerves. A week later he went to visit his Uncle Shaw, a doctor, in Haverhill, Massachusetts, for medical advice. His Aunt Eliza wrote to Abigail that Adams's nervous system seemed much affected. He was taking "the bark" that Dr. John B. Swett had recommended for him. The bark — Peruvian bark — whose effect was due to the quinine it contained, was used in many febrile illnesses at the time. There was considerable resemblance between John Quincy Adams's health problems and those of his father. Both had ailments which seemed to be precipitated by overzealous application to their work, but the older Adams's illnesses were more prolonged and more severe.

John Quincy Adams apparently inherited liberally of his father's genes of portliness, shortness, baldness, and a tendency to be gloomy. Adams even described himself this way: "I am a man reserved, cold, austere, and of forbidding manner. My political adversaries say a gloomy misanthropist, and to my personal enemies, an unsocial savage."⁷ His periods of depression, however, were never so severe nor so prolonged as his father's.

In the winter of 1789 Adams had the "flu." However, during that year something of much more import than flu occurred which left a permanent mark. The 22-year-old Adams wrote to a friend that all of his future happiness depended on possession of 16-year-old Mary Frazier. Both families disapproved of the relationship. Therefore, it was ended. Adams, however, was never entirely able to forget this love. At the age of 23, a broken-hearted young man, he opened his first law office in Boston. He wrote to his son, Charles Francis Adams, on March 15, 1838, 39 years later, that "these troubles of the heart were deep and distressing."⁸

In 1794 Adams was appointed by President Washington to be minister to the Hague. His departure for Holland, however, was delayed until September because he began to suffer from ill health. The illness was severe enough to require bleeding and the attacks continued throughout the summer of 1794, however nothing can be found that gives even a vague idea about the cause of the illness.⁹

In 1797, in his third year as diplomat to several European countries, Adams married Louisa Catherine Johnson. Louisa had 12 pregnancies and 7 miscarriages between her twenty-first and forty-second years. As a result, her health was poor a great deal of the time.¹⁰

Adams served as U.S. Senator from Massachusetts from 1803 to 1808. During this time Abigail, his mother, concerned herself greatly with his health. She was concerned that he had neglected his exercise program. She was also concerned about his not eating. Abigail felt that he was spending too much time in writing and studying, meantime neglecting his health. He was not seriously ill; but he did, like his father before him, have frequent colds and felt unwell most of the time.

Adams eventually developed habits of exercise as compulsive as his habits of reading and study—at least at times. It was his routine to take long periods of exercise each day, usually brisk walking, horseback riding, and swimming. When he was president, for example, his diary recorded hour-long swims in the Potomac against the tide. He also noted that he did his swimming in the nude.¹¹ However, it must be remembered that at times during his career he became so involved in his studies and his work that he totally neglected his exercise.

Adams had a short period of depression in 1814 when he was serving as minister to Russia. His poor mental state was brought on by a number of factors: the death of his infant daughter, the separation from his three sons, and worry about the course of the War of 1812 with England. He described his symptoms in his diary: "I am very unwell and have strong symptoms of jaundice; a lassitude which has almost, but not quite, depressed my industry; and a listlessness which without extinguishing the love of life, affects the mind with sentiment that it is nothing worth; a depression of the heart, which without being positive pain, is more distressing than the pain itself." His physician, Dr. Galloway, diagnosed his illness as jaundice, in spite of the fact that there were no distinct signs or symptoms of jaundice. Dr. Galloway had learned as early as 1800 what a lot of our contemporary doctors have learned, that is, that the average patient to escape vagueness and uncertainty likes to have a distinct diagnosis hung on his problem. Dr. Galloway prescribed for his illness a vial of "sacred elixir." Whether Adams took it or not is not known. He did share some of Thomas Jefferson's skepticism of doctors. Adams recovered in a few weeks and was able to travel to Ghent as the head of the U.S. peace commission.[12]

After he ended his ambassadorial duties in Russia, Adams was sent to England to help draw up a peace treaty with Great Britain, the Treaty of Ghent, which was concluded in December 1814. At that time he was 47 years of age and was still having eye problems. He also had what was probably arthritis in his right hand. The arthritis had struck him during his second year of his stay in Russia and had become much worse since. The arthritis only exacerbated his already weakened right hand, making the act of writing even more painful and difficult than it had already been. When he left Russia he was very thin, but later he became very rotund.[13]

In the summer of 1818, while secretary of state, Adams was involved in dealing with the Spanish envoy, Don Luis de Onís, about Andrew Jackson's war against the Seminoles in Florida. The discussions were long and arduous. During the difficult interactions between himself and Onís, Adams was greatly affected by a palsy of his right hand. Anxiety over the Spanish problem also caused him to have trouble with sleeplessness.[14]

Adams's years as president saw no remarkable health problems. Shortly after his retirement from the White House, though, in 1829 Adams was deeply affected by health problems experienced by two of his sons. Both sons, George and John, courted the same woman, Mary Catherine Heller. George lost the contest and under this and other pressures, including a domineering father, George became an alcoholic, became manic depressive, and neglected his law practice. On April 29, 1829, George boarded a steamer for New York City. He complained of a headache that evening, then told others on board ship that he was hearing voices and feared a conspiracy against him. He jumped or fell overboard and was drowned.[15] Only five years later, in October 1834, the other son,

John, died. He had been overworked and began drinking heavily; he suffered from fevers, stiff joints, and loss of memory. Adams reached his son's bedside four hours before his death.[16]

Adams's own health in retirement was generally good, although his diaries and correspondence revealed that he suffered from a number of minor ills during the last years of his life. In 1836 he did have a severe leg infection, the nature and duration of which are not known.[17] His eyes constantly gave him trouble; but he refused to wear glasses, whether from vanity or as a sign that he would not concede his infirmity. His eyes were described as "rumy." He had one very troublesome symptom — a harassing cough. From the frequency and duration of his colds one may conjecture that he had chronic bronchitis.[18]

Even so, at the age of 80 he was still exercising. In his last year as a representative from Massachusetts to the U.S. Congress and a few days after his birthday, he went for his last swim in the Potomac. The temperature was 74 degrees and there was a strong breeze. He shivered getting dressed and had to walk briskly to return home.[19]

Adams's decline dates from November 20, 1847. On that day Dr. George Parkman came to escort him on a tour of the newly established medical school at Harvard. As they started away together, Adams collapsed. Parkman was able to get him back to the house. Adams was pale and his legs were limp. Dr. John Bigelow, the family physician, determined that Adams had had a stroke. From that day he said, "I date my decrease and consider myself for being for every useful purpose to myself and to my fellow creatures as dead."[20]

For the last 18 years of his life Adams served as congressman from Massachusetts. He made himself unpopular with his colleagues because of his stand against slavery. During several years of his tenure as congressman he fought in particular to abolish the "gag rule," which forbade the discussion of the slave question on the floor of the House, and to try to abolish slavery in the District of Columbia. For his views he was assailed on every side. Due to this struggle he, an elderly man, was under much stress. He was even threatened with assassination. On February 21, 1848, there came from the floor of the House a proposal and motion to honor the generals of the Mexican War. Because he had feared the introduction of slavery into the territory conquered in that war and so did not wish to recognize the war by honoring its generals, Adams partially rose as if to address the House, grasped the arms of his chair, turned red, and collapsed to the floor. He lingered for two days in a coma, but until he died he was never removed from a little room off the old hall of the House. He died February 23, 1848.

References

1. Allan Nevins, editor, *The Diary of John Quincy Adams*, p. 510.
2. L. H. Butterfield, editor in chief, *Adams Family Correspondence, the Adams Papers*, 1:510.
3. Marie B. Hecht, *John Quincy Adams*, pp. 11–13, passim.
4. David C. Whitney, *The American Presidents*, p. 56.
5. Hecht, *John Quincy Adams*, p. 43.
6. Ibid., p. 67.
7. Robert A. East, *John Quincy Adams, the Critical Years*, p. 54.
8. Jack Shepherd, *The Adams Chronicles: Four Generations of Greatness*, p. 149.
9. East, *John Quincy Adams*, p. 171.
10. Paul F. Bolled, *Presidential Wives*, p. 55.
11. Nevins, *The Diary of John Quincy Adams*, p. 297.
12. Rudolph Marx, *The Health of the Presidents*, p. 92.
13. Hecht, *John Quincy Adams*, p. 263.
14. Ibid., p. 287.
15. Shepherd, *The Adams Chronicles*, pp. 311–12, passim.
16. Ibid., p. 322.
17. Homer F. Cunningham, *The Presidents' Last Years*, p. 45.
18. Ibid.
19. Leonard Falkner, *The President Who Wouldn't Retire*, p. 300.
20. Ibid.

7

Andrew Jackson

Andrew Jackson was born in the Waxhaw settlement of the Carolinas, March 15, 1767. Records from his schooldays indicate that he was tall, extremely slender, sinewy, and very agile. Finally, he reached a height of six feet, and remained very slender all of his life until his final illness, when he became very dropsical and bloated. His weight never exceeded 145 pounds. What remains of his clothing shows that his legs and his arms were extremely thin.[1] In Andrew Jackson's early youth his only recorded disease was an attack of something called "the big itch," during which he itched a great deal all over.

During the Revolutionary War there was considerable action in the Waxhaw area. Andrew Jackson and his brother joined in the fight against the British. Andrew and his cousin Lieutenant Thomas Crawford were fleeing from the British on horseback when Crawford's horse became mired in a swamp. Crawford was wounded and captured. Jackson got away and returned to inform Crawford's family of his capture.

A Tory informant had told the British of Jackson's whereabouts, so Andrew and his brother were surprised at breakfast by a file of dragoons. While his men wrecked the furnishings of the house, the officer in command ordered Jackson to shine his boots. Jackson refused, declaring that as a prisoner of war he was supposed to be immune from such treatment. The officer lifted his sword and struck a violent blow. Jackson fended the blow as well as he could with his left hand, which was cut to the bone. Andrew also received a gash on his head, leaving a scar which he bore till the end of his life.[2]

Andrew and his brother Robert with 20 other patriot soldiers were taken to Camden, South Carolina, on horseback, where they were jailed with 250 other prisoners. There were no beds, no medicine, and no dressings for their wounds. The brothers were exposed to smallpox, which they later contracted. Fortunately for them, their mother arrived just as an exchange of prisoners was being accomplished. She persuaded the British to include her own sons in the exchange.[3]

On the journey home to Waxhaw Jackson's brother Robert was so ill from smallpox, infected wounds, and lack of care that he had to be held on his horse. Jackson walked barefooted, bareheaded, and without a coat. Heavy rains drenched this small group on the way. Once home, Robert was put to bed, raving and terribly ill. In two days he was dead, and Andrew was delirious. For several weeks Elizabeth Jackson fought to save the life of her remaining son.[4]

In the summer of 1781 news came to the Waxhaws of the horrible condition of the British prison ships in Charleston. Among the prisoners was the son of Elizabeth Jackson's sister. As soon as Andrew had passed the critical state, his mother went to Charleston to see what she could do for those unfortunate prisoners there. Mrs. Jackson and two other women rode horseback to Charleston to deliver supplies and medicine. Not much can be found regarding the details of their expedition. It is known, however, that stopping at the home of a relative at or near Charleston, Mrs. Jackson was seized with "ship fever" and, after a short illness, died.[5]

Ship fever, or typhus fever, is an acute, infectious, and highly contagious disease, endemic and epidemic. Through ignorance and neglect of sanitation, the prison vessels were often pest houses, and outbreaks of typhus were common.[6] This infection was later found to be due to Rickettsia Mooreri, and transmitted to humans by fleas.

As Andrew lay recovering very slowly from his illness, he mourned for his mother. It was always a great sorrow to him that he never knew where she was buried.[7]

From 1781 until 1806 there is little to relate concerning the health of Andrew Jackson. In 1806, at the age of 33, he had been a member of the militia in the Revolutionary War, had been admitted to the practice of law in North Carolina, and had married Rachel Donelson Robards. The latter figured a great deal in Jackson's history.

On the morning of May 29, 1806, Jackson rose early, ate, and told his wife that he would be gone for a couple of days. In the meanwhile, he continued, he might have some trouble with a Mr. Dickinson. Jackson and Dickinson were involved in an exchange of words following a horse race. Jackson's horse, Truckston, was to run against Plowboy, owned by Joseph Erwin of Nashville, a horseman. Before the day of that race, Plowboy became lame; Erwin withdrew him, and paid the forfeit. However, Captain Patton Anderson circulated a story that Erwin and his son-in-law, Dickinson, had attempted to pay their obligations with notes that did not reflect the payment arrangements upon which they had agreed.

The relations between Jackson and Dickinson were strained already.

Mr. Dickinson had made a reference to Rachel Donelson's matrimonial history. Confronted by Jackson, he had apologized by saying that he was drunk when the statement was made. After the exchange of words, Jackson finally challenged Dickinson to a duel.

A place was chosen in Kentucky, just beyond the state line. The duel was fought at ten paces. Jackson wore a loose jacket which concealed the true width of his chest. Dickinson fired first. There was a quick flash and Jackson was seen to press his hand tightly to his chest. He had obviously been hit. Jackson then deliberately adjusted his aim. He pulled the trigger but there was no explosion. The hammer had stopped at half cock, which by the rules did not count as a fire, and Jackson was given another shot.[8] Jackson recocked his gun, deliberately took aim again, and fired. He gave his opponent a lethal wound, from which he was dead before 9:00 P.M.

Here some authors relate that Jackson's wound was an ugly one which had only broken a rib or two and raked the breastbone, not entering his chest.[9] Other accounts, which are more credible in view of his further history, state that the bullet, instead of grazing his ribs, actually entered his chest cavity. Jackson was more than a month in recovering enough strength to get around. The bullet lodged in his chest and remained there until he died. The wound was probably the cause of the worst of his illnesses.[10]

On September 4, 1813, Jackson fought another duel, this one with the Benton brothers, Thomas Hart and Jesse. Jackson had challenged the Bentons on the pretext that they had impugned his honor and that of his wife, Rachel. The duel was fought with pistols. According to those witnessing the battle, Jackson charged Thomas with a whip and demanded that he defend himself. Jesse came to his brother's defense, firing a pistol. The ball from the pistol shattered Jackson's left shoulder. Bystanders finally separated the combatants. Jackson was rushed to get medical care and he lay in Nashville Inn for three weeks, recovering from the wound and severe blood loss.[11]

The lodging of the pistol ball in Jackson's left shoulder was to cause him much trouble from the time the injury occurred until his death. The bullet practically destroyed the left shoulder joint and introduced infection which became chronic. The infection involved not only the tissues but the bone structure itself, causing osteomyelitis.

Despite this wound, on October 17, 1813, still pale and weak with his arm in a sling, Jackson took command of the West Tennessee Army.[12] Soon afterward, in the war against the Creek Indians, Jackson led about 2,000 men against 800 Creeks in the Battle of Horseshoe Bend on March 27, 1814. A few days later Chief Red Eagle surrendered and the war with the Creeks was over.[13] Ironically, the Creek War established Jackson's reputation as a general but permanently damaged his health. Already weakened by his dueling wounds, during the eight months of war Jackson became even more debilitated by chronic diarrhea and dysentery, natural accompaniments to war at that time. The food was not of the right kind and the medication was primitive. Even the slightest imprudence in drinking or eating would bring on an attack, during which he suffered greatly.[14] Jackson was of a very stoic nature, however, and bore his suffering with a seeming indifference.[15]

During the Creek War, while his paroxysms of abdominal pain lasted, he could obtain relief only by sitting on a chair with his chest against the back of it and his arms dangling forward. He had at times to remain in this position for hours. At times he was seized by abdominal pain while on the march at the head of his troops. In the absence of other relief, he would have a sapling half severed and bent over upon which he would hang with his arms downward until the agony had subsided. The only medicine he took (and his only beverage) was weak gin and water. He gradually learned to control his disease but through the Creek and New Orleans campaigns he suffered greatly.

Through the years until 1813, when he was 46, there were recurrent complaints which grew more frequent as time went on. "I have a very severe attack of fever and cold with pain in the chest and cough"; "severe attack of dysentery"; and "serious intermittent fever" (the last was probably malaria). By the end of the century he had "rheumatism, especially in the right arm." He was never very well, but, in his opinion, never very ill.[16]

His habits with regard to diet and medication were not very good for a man who had all of his health problems. Coffee and tobacco he used to excess—he both smoked and chewed tobacco. Bleeding was a remedy he relied on to stay his lung hemorrhages and calomel to check his diarrhea.[17] Jackson—unlike Thomas Jefferson, who distrusted doctors and all of their various treatments—apparently believed everything his doctors were telling him, even during the time that they were apparently killing him with their medications.

For example, in one letter to Rachel Jackson from headquarters near Washington, March 7, 1813, he wrote, "My Love, When I wrote you last mail, I was laboring under a distressing complaint proceeding from a violent cold which fell upon my lungs and had assumed inflammatory symptoms. A free use of the lance by William Butler relieved me, and I am now restored to my former health."[18] (By the free use of the lance he meant the free use of bleeding.)

A few days later, October 11, 1813, he wrote again, and it seemed to Rachel that he was trying to keep from her just how much he was suffering. The report on his health in this letter does not agree with other reports: "My Dear, I refer you to Col. Hayes for the news of the camp. My health is good and my arm mending fast. The little place on my shoulder gives me more pain than my arm. Both, I hope, will soon be well."[19]

On November 22, 1814, Jackson set out for New Orleans and summoned Rachel to meet him there. He needed her desperately because he was close to total collapse. He said before he left Pensacola, "I was taken very ill, the doctor gave me a dose of Jalap and calomel, which salivated me, and then I was eight days on the march that I never broke bread."[20] (Jalap is a potent laxative.)

By the time Jackson reached New Orleans on December 1, 1814, he was showing the ravages of the long campaign and his illness. His stomach was so reluctant to accept food that with all the wonderful Creole dishes in New Orleans he could only manage a tablespoonful of hominy and small amounts of milk.[21]

After Jackson arrived he was invited to the home of J. Kilty Smith. Smith, a bachelor, had as his hostess a Creole lady whose name has not been retained for posterity. She described Jackson this way: "A tall, gaunt man very erect with a countenance furroughed by care and anxiety. His dress was simple and nearly threadbare. A small leather cap protected his head, and a short blue cloak his body, whilst his high dragoon boots were long innocent of polish, or blacking. His complexion was sallow and unhealthy, his hair iron gray; and his body thin and emaciated like someone who had just recovered from a lingering illness. But . . . a fierce glare lighted his bright and hawk-like eyes."[22]

Dr. Frederick May, who accompanied Jackson on his expedition against the Creeks and to New Orleans, was asked on his return how the general had survived the trip. Dr. May's interesting but somewhat cryptic reply was that they had to stop frequently and wash the general all over with sugar of lead to keep down the inflammation.

Sugar of lead, believed at the time to have antiphlogistic (anti-inflammatory) action beyond its astringent powers, was Jackson's greatest support. He used it not only internally for his supposed tuberculosis and his chronically queasy stomach but externally for anything that bothered him. He even used it for an eye wash when his sight began to fail. Since his specific for dysentery was calomel, which he took in massive doses, it raises the question that whether after years of constant use some of his various discomforts might have been increased by lead or mercury poisoning. The only other drug that he would countenance was common salt for emergency use in pulmonary hemorrhages, which he backed up with the free use of the lancet for bleeding.[23]

May described Jackson in early January before the Battle of New Orleans:

> At 47 that long useful body shifting restlessly on the mound at New Orleans was dented within and without by enough ax scars to fell a whole forest of taller trees than himself. Over one eye was a sword gash that he had suffered at 13 for refusing to shine an Englishman's boots and in one breast was a duelist's bullet too close to the heart to be removed. In one shoulder was a scar from a wound due to a pistol shot that had let out enough blood, according to Mrs. Jackson, to soak through two mattresses. The rigors of border warfare had left him a perpetual indigestion which was starving him into a shadow, a case of chronic diarrhea that all but disemboweled him, a paralytic rheumatism that so disabled what he designated in writing as "my rist," that he could barely scrawl his reports, and the vanguard of tuberculosis was just finding its way into his lungs.[24]

Several biographers, including Holmes Alexander, have referred to Jackson as being tuberculous simply because he had all the symptoms of chronic tuberculosis. However, it seems more logical that his pulmonary problem arose from the bullet lodged in his lung with subsequent repeated infections, repeated scarring, and the final development of bronchiectasis. The above could readily explain his repeated attacks of severe pulmonary infection and repeated copious pulmonary hemorrhages.

On May 8, 1815, at the end of the War of 1812, Jackson and his wife Rachel returned to the Hermitage, their home in Nashville, Tennessee. He was hoping for a quiet life on his plantation. He was to remain there a few months, and during that time his health showed some temporary improvement. However, on December 26, 1817, John Calhoun, secretary of war under Monroe, ordered General Jackson to Georgia to take the proper measures to end the conflict with the Seminoles in Florida.[25] In 1818 he invaded Florida, defeated the Seminoles, and overthrew the Spanish governor. For several months after the Seminole War, he was allowed to retreat to the Hermitage.

After Jackson returned from the Florida campaign he was very weak and still troubled by his chronic dysentery. He felt at that time he would not live long and determined to retire permanently at the Hermitage. He was so ill that he did not expect to live until the house was completed. In 1821 Jackson served as provisional governor of Florida for slightly more than 11 weeks. As early as October he had notified President Monroe of his desire to return to Tennessee. He used as his reason the poor health of his wife, not mentioning that his health was far worse than Rachel's. Monroe accepted his resignation on December 1, 1821.[26]

Jackson returned to the Hermitage a sick, exhausted old man on the verge of collapse. From that time until his death he suffered pain practically every day. The bullet in his lung caused chronic infection with lung abscesses and frequent bouts of profuse lung hemorrhaging. He had a severe cough which at times was productive of purulent sputum. Besides his dysentery he had contracted malaria. He treated these illnesses with large doses of mercury and lead in the form of calomel and sugar of lead.

After his return from Florida to Tennessee he suffered a physical breakdown. For several months he suffered and he wrote, "I have been oppressed with a violent cough and costiveness" (constipation). This was followed by a severe attack of dysentery which made an invalid of him, and he then began to complain that his cough brought up "great quantities of phlegm." Jackson referred to the sputum as "great quantities of flime."[27] The surgeon Gardner speculated most logically that the tortured bronchi had responded to the perpetual inflammation by the establishment of a characteristic bronchiectasis which assured the patient, though he did not know it, that until the end of his days he would be harassed by "flime," cough, and hemoptysis (hemorrhage).[28]

Bronchiectasis is defined as a permanent abnormal dilatation of one or more large (greater than 2mm) bronchi due to the destruction of the elastic and muscular components of the bronchial wall. The definition is not completely satisfactory because bronchi are also abnormally dilated in clinical bronchitis. This chronic bronchitis merges into bronchiectasis. The two conditions frequently coexist. The origin of the destructive process is nearly always a bacterial infection. The hallmarks of the disease are chronic cough, sputum production, hemorrhages (lung hemorrhages), and recurrent pneumonia.[29] The description of symptoms and pathology fits aptly with those found in Jackson's case. The sequence was damage to the lung and bronchi by the bullet, recurrent local infection in the lungs, damage to the bronchi, and dilatation of the bronchial wall.

His life continued with gradually worsening health problems. In 1820 to 1821 his chest condition grew gradually worse. For four months in 1822 he was incapacitated with a severe cough and "costiveness." The period of costiveness suddenly ended and turned into his old enemy, dysentery, with attendant weakness and cramps. During one period he had 30 or more loose stools in 12 hours. Then his terrible refractory cough was attended with large amounts of sputum.

Despite these illnesses, however, Jackson was the U.S. senator from Tennessee from 1823 to 1825. In the fall of 1825 Jackson had one of his worst hemorrhages. This came at a time when he was obsessed with the corrupt coalition between John Quincy Adams and Henry Clay, which he was not able to fight because he was bedridden. He had a very bad fall, which kept him in bed for weeks, having torn apart the weakly healed shoulder wounded in both duels.[30]

He had a series of severe pulmonary hemorrhages during this prolonged episode of severe illness. Jackson apparently knew when he was threatened with pulmonary hemorrhages. When threatened with an attack he would bare his arm, bandage it, take his pen knife from his pocket, call his servant to hold the bowl, and bleed himself freely. Often during his presidency he performed this during the night without assistance.[31] During this severe illness he was at times unconscious. He did, however, find the strength to recover, though the hemorrhages were frequent throughout the rest of his life.[32]

At this period, 1822–25, Jackson's teeth were decaying with great rapidity, perhaps due to the calomel and his poor health. In the years 1826–28 he lost most of his teeth and he acquired some false ones, which he refused to wear. In those years he suffered a great deal from toothache and increasing headaches. In addition to his other woes, his vision was failing.[33] His health was at this low level when he won the presidential election of 1828.

Soon after Jackson became president, there were some marked changes in his condition. These changes came on rather gradually through the spring and summer of 1829. His feet and legs began to swell, and by December 1829 they were very swollen. He complained of pain in his chest; his shortness of breath was noticeable to anyone near him. His almost constant headaches were worse; and his eyesight continued to fail.

He tried a holiday and came back to work only to be felled by a fever caused by the "miasmia" arising from a sewer being dug. Of course, all of this was supposition. Gardner felt that Jackson had a true nephritis with nephritic headaches. He also conjectured that there must have been some early cardiac failure.[34] However, Jackson's edema could have been explained purely on the basis of nephritis, while shortness of breath could have been explained by the presence of chronic, extensive pulmonary disease.

The presidential election year of 1832 began badly for Jackson. He contracted influenza in addition to his political wars with Clay and Biddle. Then his left arm began to trouble him again. The bullet from the duel with the Bentons 20 years earlier was still lodged in his arm and shoulder and caused him intense pain at times. By 1831 the bullet had migrated downward and could be felt less than an inch below the surface of the skin. Months later the pain intensified to the point of interfering with his work. Since it was so near the surface, his family persuaded him to undergo surgery. Jackson agreed, and a doctor was summoned from Philadelphia to do the surgery, which was done without benefit of anesthesia, since there was none available. Jackson gritted his jaws, grasped his walking stick, and told his surgeon to proceed. The surgeon made an incision, squeezed his arm, and out came the bullet, which had been flattened by the impact on the bone. The wound was dressed and Jackson went back to work.[35]

In 1833 Jackson was invited to visit New England (June 8). While in Philadelphia Jackson planned to visit the famous Dr. Phillips Syne Physick to find out if this eminent physician could relieve him of his constant pain. The so-called "bleeding of the lungs" particularly troubled him.

After the removal of the bullet from his arm he still had the pain in his chest and side. Dr. Physick said that "cupping" would relieve the pain and that the bullet lying so close in his breast to his heart was of no consequence. (Cupping is the process of drawing blood from the body by application of a cupping glass to the body surface.) Physick did not, however, comment on the dysentery, the swelling, the pulmonary hemorrhage, or the other assorted ailments.[36]

The bullet in his chest, which was received in the duel with Dickinson in 1806, had lodged near his heart and could not be removed. Around the bullet was an area of chronic infection. Jackson had periods of quiescence followed by flare-ups of copious sputum. These attacks were interspersed with frequent bleeding from the lungs. A heavy coughing spell might trigger an onset of hemorrhaging. Chills seized him, and soon he was drenched in sweat. At times he collapsed. Finally, he would return to stability, greatly weakened and several pounds thinner.[37]

In spite of these multiple health problems, Jackson decided to make a trip through the middle Atlantic and New England states in the spring of 1833 to solidify his popularity.[38] By the time the Jackson entourage had passed through Connecticut, Jackson seemed refreshed by all the festivities extended to him. The arrival in Boston was attended by a continuation of the acclaim. However, on the fourth day of his visit to Boston Jackson developed a bad cold, followed by severe pulmonary hemorrhage. He was ordered to bed and the attending physicians resorted to bleeding. If Jackson had been as suspicious of his doctors as was Jefferson before him, he might have been much better off. Jackson somehow amazingly survived, and a few days later was sitting up drafting letters to the secretary of the treasury, William J. Duane, instructing him to transfer funds from the Bank of the United States to the State Bank. Soon he was up and around insisting on continuing the tour. First was the visit to Harvard where he was presented with an honorary degree — despite the disapproval of one of its most distinguished alumni, John Quincy Adams, who muttered that Jackson could hardly write his own name.[39]

Jackson's last months in office were times of great personal misery and pain. His feet had swollen so much that he had difficulty walking, while his headaches were so severe and so prolonged that he had difficulty in conversation. He was troubled by the old complaints of diarrhea, indigestion, hemorrhage, shortness of breath, and deep pain in his chest. Jackson had blindness in one eye, and dimness of vision in the other.[40]

After 1834 he rarely had an hour free from pain. Pain in his chest and his side, and his shortness of breath all kept him in great distress. He could eat nothing beyond rice and milk. His right eye blinded, he treated his remaining eye with a weak solution of sugar of lead. Jackson at this time could exercise very little due to shortness of breath.[41]

In this sad state of his health he traveled to New Orleans to attend a celebration in his honor. On the way there he hemorrhaged badly for many hours. When he finally arrived, he was so weak that he could make only a token appearance. Then after ten days in Vicksburg he somehow got back to the Hermitage. He reported that when he got there his health was as good as when he left. This was his last long trip.[42]

In the early part of 1838 Jackson hemorrhaged regularly, and had prolonged, severe headaches. He also had the continued severe pain in his side. Jackson was at times bled to prevent a hemorrhage. Usually, after the hemorrhage had subsided he was again bled, presuming that this would stop the bleeding! It is incredible that he could survive such great loss of blood by hemorrhaging and by lancet.[43]

During the six years after his retirement from the presidency, his health was not much worse than it had been in Washington. The attacks of pulmonary hemorrhage continued, each time taking some added toll on his already much debilitated frame. Every recovery period took longer. He remained very weak, and a cough harassed him day and night.[44]

By 1843 Jackson was almost a complete invalid. In his last years he suffered several additional illnesses, including erysipelas — which discolored his skin to a beet red — spells of delirium, and an enormous swelling of his head. In 1844, having lost all power of voluntary movement, he had to depend on others to lift him from his bed. His mind remained clear and he was able to write brief letters. In a letter to his foster son he wrote, "I am swollen from my toes to the crown of my head and in bandages to my hips."[45]

An artist from France went to the Hermitage to try to paint a portrait of the general in retirement. What he found was "a tall man, propped up in a chair, fighting for breath, his face a mask of swollen flesh crossed by the lines of pain; one eye was covered with a white scar, the other a glowering slit between puffed eyelids. Jackson was a gruesome sight."[46]

A cough tormented Jackson day and night. He had all the symptoms of consumption. Six months before his death certain dropsical signs which had been threatening for years were established and much worse; and from that time he was alternately swollen by dropsy and at others relieved of his swelling and prostrated by diarrhea. At times, to use his words, he was "one blubber from head to foot."[47]

His last words were, "What is the matter with my dear children? Have I alarmed you? Oh, do not cry—be good children and we will all meet in heaven." He fixed his eyes on his granddaughter, Rachel, as though invoking the blessing of heaven to her. He spoke with calmness, with strength, and indeed with animation. At 4:00 P.M., June 8, 1845, the general seemed to be sinking rapidly. His son approached the bed and took the old man's hand. "Father," he whispered, "How do you feel? Do you know me?"

His breathing was so gentle that it was difficult to know whether he was still alive. Major Lewis supported his head to help him breathe. At 6:00 P.M., after one slight convulsion, General Jackson, the seventh president of the United States, aged 78 years, 2 months, and 22 days, expired at the Hermitage.[48]

Much has been written about the health of Jackson by numerous biographers. The bullet wounds have been regarded by some as the cause of much pain but not a particularly great factor in his final illness. His pulmonary disease has been regarded by most of his biographers as the result of tuberculosis. In fact, Jackson referred at times to his pulmonary problems as "consumptions." Indeed, many of his symptoms fit tuberculosis quite well; his cough, sputum, weight loss, and hemoptysis are all characteristic. However, the course of his illness over several decades and certain aspects which were present the last few years of his life would leave a great number of questions in one's mind.

Gardner has used his medical knowledge, along with deductive reasoning, to give what would seem to be the most logical conclusion regarding his illness.

Contrary to the opinion of several biographers, including James Parton, who were of the opinion that the bullet lodged in his chest in the Dickinson duel had stirred up Jackson's latent pulmonary tuberculosis, Gardner stated doubt that Jackson had ever had tuberculosis at all. Gardner also felt that the recurrent fevers were due to malaria, dysentery, and the infection in the bronchi of his lungs. His dysentery was due perhaps to bacterial or amoebic infection. Emaciation and poor color could be attributed to his malaria and dysentery. Gardner reasoned further that when the bullet entered Jackson's chest, it carried with it bits of cloth, dust, and other foreign material. He deduced that the bullet immediately set up an inflammatory process and caused an abscess nearby. Gardner felt that good reasoning would prefer the theory of an abscess over other possibilities, even though Jackson had all the clinical signs and symptoms of pulmonary tuberculosis, so it was assumed then and later that he had tuberculosis.

Gardner states: "In all probability the man was becoming the victim of a series of unlucky illnesses, any one of which was formidable and which all together unhealed and unintelligently treated could lead inevitably to that dogged murderess follower of longstanding suppuration—amyloid disease."[49] Gardner concluded that Jackson had a chronic osteomyelitis from the wound inflicted in his left shoulder. Thus Jackson had two sites of chronic suppurative disease.

After Jackson became president, Gardner says, "The basic septic condition was yielding to an even greater sequel." Gardner assumed that the progression of the infectious process in the lung led to bronchiectasis with the attending severe cough, copious sputum, and hemorrhages. Gardner reasoned also that Jackson had true nephritis, subsequently the cause of his headaches.

According to Gardner, amyloidosis was the only condition that would account for the "grisly last years of the patient." Amyloidosis is a condition brought on by prolonged chronic infection and suppuration. Gardner concluded, "By 1845 this beautiful mind rested in a body which was nothing more than a decaying mass."[50]

After reading accounts of Jackson's illnesses in several biographies and then comparing them to Gardner, one is compelled to agree with Gardner. Biographers other than Gardner have depended on prevailing lore to make their conclusions, whereas Gardner, viewing the overall history of Jackson's illnesses, has analyzed them carefully using his knowledge of medical science and pathology.

References

1. Robert V. Remini, *The Life of Andrew Jackson*, p. 1.
2. Marquis James, *The Border Captain, the Life of Andrew Jackson*, p. 27.
3. Remini, *The Life of Andrew Jackson*, p. 8.

4. James, *The Border Captain*, p. 30.
5. James Parton, *Life of Andrew Jackson*, 1:88–89.
6. William Pepper, *A Theory and Practice of Medicine*, 1:134.
7. Ibid., p. 95.
8. John Spencer Bassett, *The Life of Andrew Jackson*, pp. 61–64.
9. Gerald W. Johnson, *Andrew Jackson*, p. 115.
10. Francis Tomlinson Gardner, "The Gentleman from Tennessee," *The Surgeon's Library — Surgery, Gynecology, and Obstetrics* 30 (March 1949): 404–11.
11. Samuel B. Smith, ed., et al., *The Letters and Papers of Andrew Jackson*, 2:408.
12. Remini, *The Life of Andrew Jackson*, p. 68.
13. David C. Whitney, *The American Presidents* (1990), p. 68.
14. Parton, *Life of Andrew Jackson*, 2:547.
15. Remini, *The Life of Andrew Jackson*, p. 84.
16. Gardner, "The Gentleman from Tennessee," p. 407.
17. Parton, *Life of Andrew Jackson*, 3:667.
18. Smith, *The Letters and Papers of Andrew Jackson*, 2:379.
19. Ibid., p. 515.
20. Remini, *The Life of Andrew Jackson*, p. 89.
21. Ibid.
22. James, *The Border Captain*, p. 216.
23. Gardner, "The Gentleman from Tennessee," p. 408.
24. Holmes Alexander, *The American Tallyrand*, p. 112.
25. James, *The Border Captain*, p. 320.
26. Remini, *The Life of Andrew Jackson*, p. 113.
27. Gardner, "The Gentleman from Tennessee," pp. 408–9.
28. Ibid., p. 409.
29. John F. Murray, "Diffuse Infiltrative Diseases of the Lung" in *Harrison's Principles of Internal Medicine*, p. 1539.
30. Gardner, "The Gentleman from Tennessee," p. 409.
31. Parton, *Life of Andrew Jackson*, 3:63–64.
32. Remini, *The Life of Andrew Jackson*, p. 154.
33. Gardner, "The Gentleman from Tennessee," p. 409.
34. Ibid.
35. Parton, "A Letter, Donaldson to Coffey, January 16, 1832," *Life of Andrew Jackson*, 3:63.
36. Gardner, "The Gentleman from Tennessee," p. 410.
37. John B. Moses and Wilbur Cross, *Presidential Courage*, p. 46.
38. Whitney, *The American Presidents*, p. 74.
39. Ibid., p. 57.
40. Moses and Cross, *Presidential Courage*, p. 64.
41. Gardner, "The Gentleman from Tennessee," p. 410.
42. Remini, *The Life of Andrew Jackson*, p. 339.
43. Parton, *Life of Andrew Jackson*, 3:668.
44. Moses and Cross, *Presidential Courage*, p. 65.
45. Ibid.
46. Parton, *Life of Andrew Jackson*, 3:668.
47. Remini, *The Life of Andrew Jackson*, p. 358.
48. Gardner, "The Gentleman from Tennessee," p. 407.
49. Ibid., p. 411.
50. Ibid.

8

Martin Van Buren

Martin Van Buren, the eighth president of the United States, was born December 5, 1782, in Kinderhook, New York. He was the first president to have been born under the American flag rather than under the British.

It appears that during his childhood and as a young man he enjoyed good health. No significant illness has been documented as occurring when he was a child or youth. By the age of 18 he had developed his full physical stature; he was five feet six inches in height, trim and slender. He was nearly 60 years of age before he put on enough weight to lose his trim lines. There was a suspicion around Washington in those later years that he wore a corset in an attempt to preserve the idea that he still kept his slender figure.[1]

Apparently, throughout his early career as a lawyer, U.S. senator, governor, secretary of state, and vice president Van Buren generally enjoyed good health, despite his heavy drinking.

As early as 1807, at the age of 25, Van Buren established a reputation for being able to drink great amounts of alcoholic beverages without the usual surface manifestations of being drunk. He later earned for this prowess in imbibing the title of "Blue Whiskey Van."[2]

It is interesting that in 1830 Van Buren wrote to his son, John, warning him against drink: "What you may regard as an innocent and harmless indulgence will take you years to overcome in the public estimate."[3] When Van Buren wrote the letter to John, he was undoubtedly trying to prevent him from having some of the same problems with alcohol that he had experienced.

When Van Buren was vice president he found his daily appearances in the Senate chamber to be very worrisome and distasteful—he was bored. Perhaps as a consequence, during his tenure as vice president he experienced more than the usual amount of colds and other ailments that caused him to seek bed rest for short intervals.[4]

In late September 1834, in his second year as vice president, Van

Buren returned to Washington. He and his sons were renovating the Paulding House for their future dwelling. When Van Buren had finished his new home and moved in, he was stricken with what he called influenza, with which he had been ill for several weeks in the previous summer. At this time in late September he was confined to his bed for several days.[5]

Soon after Van Buren was elected president in 1837, he was greatly troubled by the threat of impending financial panic. At this time he was under great stress and was apprehensive about the financial state of the nation. He was troubled more than he had ever been before with dyspepsia and was taking a mixture of water, soot, and powdered charcoal that was presumed to have given Van Buren some relief.[6] Charcoal has been used even up until recent years for the relief of gas. Van Buren apparently suffered from time to time with indigestion, especially when he was under stress.

Van Buren's health remained good, but his love for fine cuisine and fine wine led him to become much overweight. He developed gout in his fifties. Such a development was no doubt aided by the fine foods prepared by his French cook and the madeira and port wines he consumed.

In the summer of 1838, after having been in office for 20 months and having settled his problems with the cabinet, Van Buren took a working vacation at White Sulfur Springs. He assured the ex-president, Andrew Jackson, that he was quite well, but it was noted that he had lost weight and had for some time looked worried and pale. He was suffering a great deal from gout.[7]

During Van Buren's last year in the White House, early July to late September, he vacationed again at the famous spa in White Sulfur Springs. He was, while there at the spa, treated for gout.[8] His stay at the spa helped his gout, at least temporarily. Aside from his asthma and occasional difficulty with gout, Van Buren was not afflicted with any severe debilitating health problems. He went to New York for medical treatment in the spring of 1862.[9]

At the age of 71, 12 years after his retirement from the presidency, Van Buren went to Aix-les-Bains, France, for treatment of gout, on the advice of his doctor. Many years before, Jefferson had visited that same spa for treatment of his broken wrist. Jefferson's wrist had been broken in an accident, and he had received such bad treatment at the hands of his doctors in France that he was never free from pain again. Apparently, Van Buren's gout responded much better than did Jefferson's broken, maltreated wrist.

The year 1861 found Van Buren suffering from a severe attack of asthma which he had had for several months in late 1860. He recovered enough that he was back at full strength and was able to go horseback riding around his estate, but in the autumn of 1861 he had a sudden recurrence of asthma. He was counseled at that time by his physician to avoid all strenuous exertion.[10] Van Buren celebrated his seventy-ninth birthday and in early 1862 had recovered enough from his asthma to go to New York for treatment by Dr. Alonzo Clark, a noted physician of that day.[11]

Van Buren returned to Kinderhook in late May 1862, where he remained until he died. His lung disease was in the late stage, he suffered from extreme weakness, and he spent most of his days in bed. In mid–July he became terminal. His circulation began to fail him, and his skin became clammy and cyanotic. His son, John, was sent for, but when he arrived Van Buren was semicomatose. He went into a coma July 21 and died three days later. He was 79 years of age when he died on July 24, 1862.

Martin Van Buren's health problems became severe late in life. He lived many years beyond the normal life expectancy of his time. He became obese when he was past middle age, and this obesity and his excessive use of alcohol undoubtedly helped to precipitate the attacks of gout. Late in life he suffered from severe attacks of asthma. There is no evidence that he smoked or used tobacco in any way, so we are unable to say that his pulmonary disease was aggravated by smoking. When terminally ill he manifested signs and symptoms of circulatory failure. However, unless we are able to secure a detailed history and an accurate report of his physical findings, we could never make the exact diagnosis. Van Buren's weakness and shortness of breath may have been due to emphysema, secondary to his asthma; while his shortness of breath may have been due to right heart failure, secondary to emphysema.

References

1. Holmes Alexander, *The American Tallyrand*, p. 49.
2. Ibid., p. 75.
3. Denis Tilden Lynch, *An Epoch and a Man, Martin Van Buren and His Times*, p. 339.
4. John Niven, *Martin Van Buren*, p. 366.
5. Ibid., p. 379.
6. Ibid., p. 404.
7. Ibid., p. 435.
8. Lynch, *An Epoch and a Man*, p. 421.
9. Homer F. Cunningham, *The Presidents' Last Years*, p. 65.
10. Lynch, *An Epoch and a Man*, p. 540.
11. Ibid., p. 440.

9

William Henry Harrison

William Henry Harrison, the ninth president of the United States, was born on February 9, 1773, in Charles City County, Virginia. He was the youngest of seven children of Benjamin Harrison, who signed the Declaration of Independence. As a child Harrison, when not in school, spent his time riding, swimming, and shooting. His father had a very large plantation, which gave Harrison a wide range of freedom to engage in such sporting activities.[1]

Harrison's childhood and youth were essentially free from any remarkable illness. At least early in life he did not indulge in alcohol. His abstinence is thought to be due not to any virtue but to problems of digestion which were aggravated by alcohol. He also avoided roughage in his diet, which no doubt contributed to his chronic constipation. To relieve his constipation he used very strong laxatives.[2]

Harrison entered Hampden-Sydney College in Virginia at the age of 14 and left before graduation to study medicine under the famous Benjamin Rush of Philadelphia. The curriculum of medicine at the University of Pennsylvania at that time consisted of two 16-week series of lectures. His father died after he had finished one 16-week term, in 1791, and at that time Harrison gave up medicine to join the U.S. Army, where he was commissioned as an ensign.[3]

Harrison's military and administrative career was a steady string of successes. In 1793 he was appointed an aide-de-camp to General Anthony Wayne and was engaged in a campaign against the Ottawa, Chippewa, Shawnee, and Pottawatomie tribes. This war ended with the signing of the Treaty of Greenville, Aug. 3, 1795. He resigned from the army in 1798. He was then secretary of the Northwest Territory (1799–1800) and governor of the Indiana Territory (1800–1812). In 1811 Harrison led 950 troops against the Indian confederacy under the Shawnee brothers Tecumseh and the Prophet. The Indians were defeated in the Battle of Tippecanoe, where Harrison earned his nickname, "Old Tippecanoe." Harrison resigned in 1812 to take part in the War of 1812, during which he became a national hero. In May 1814 he resigned from the army to enter politics. He was a U.S. representative from Ohio (1816–19); an Ohio state senator (1819–21); a U.S. senator (1825–28); and the U.S. minister to Colombia (1828–29).

In Harrison's military career there is no record of his having suffered any significant illnesses nor any wounds. It is strange and unusual that he should have gone through the war against Chief Tecumseh and the War of 1812 without some illness, since most of the military at that time had at least a bout of malaria or dysentery.

The year of 1832 was a poor one financially for Harrison. At the age of 59 he had long since resigned from the military (having done so in 1814); and his political career too was seemingly over. The general was supporting two families besides his own, and he was entertaining great numbers of people in a lavish style. During February and March 1832 he was described as being dangerously ill, probably from malaria. At that time when a person was described as having ague and fever the usual cause was malaria. While the general was recovering from this acute illness, a devastating flood struck his plantation, destroying houses and flooding his farmland. Still not fully recovered from his illness, he nevertheless rode about his farm to direct the rebuilding of the fences and buildings. He overworked himself and had a relapse, which required him to return to his bed. Toward the end of April he had recovered enough to accept an appointment to the Board of Visitors attending the June examinations at West Point.[4]

During Harrison's campaign for the presidency in late 1840, he was a visitor at North Bend, the home of Judge John Cleves Symmes, where he received numerous callers. At that time there were widespread reports that he was feeble and sickly. These reports caused him to lead a very active campaign to offset the rumors.[5] When Harrison was elected to the presidency in 1841, he was, at 68, the oldest yet to reach that high office. Ronald Reagan would later be elected at age 69. Harrison arrived in Washington on February 9, his sixty-eighth birthday, and on that day took a stroll down Pennsylvania Avenue and, alone and unannounced, dropped into the Senate chambers. Senator Calhoun was surprised when he felt a tap on the shoulder and turned around to find the president-elect there. Calhoun thought Harrison did not look well and rightly doubted if he had the strength to encounter the heavy responsibilities which would soon be his.[6]

From the first day Harrison sank under the burden. He delivered an Inauguration Day speech which lasted for 1 hour and 40 minutes. The day was very cold, and he had worn no overcoat or hat.[7] When Harrison had finished his speech he felt quite ill, but he was forced by protocol to return to the White House and greet a host of Whigs and other admirers who wanted to wish him well and shake his hand. The ardent supporters were disappointed; they had to settle for a nod and a smile. Earlier throngs of admirers had shaken his hand so many times and so forcefully that it was too sore and swollen for him to continue.[8] To add to his discomfort, Harrison related to an aide that the business of being president-elect had so occupied his time that he had failed to find time to perform "the necessary function of nature." He was referring to his constipation.[9]

As president, Harrison tried to begin each day with an early morning walk. During one of these he was caught in a rain shower and became chilled. After a short interval he developed a fever, and on March 27 a physician was called. The illness was not at first regarded as being serious, and the initial treatment by the physicians was "mustard to the stomach, heat to the extremities, additional warm drinks, and additional bed-clothes."[10]

According to some reports his doctor did not, because of Harrison's advanced age, bleed him. Cupping, however, was applied to "drive out the poisons." (Cupping was a technique for drawing blood from the surface of the body. This was frequently done by first making several small lacerations in the skin and then applying a cupping glass to the incised area. The cupping glass was first heated and then placed over the scarified area. As the glass cooled a partial vacuum was formed inside to draw blood from the cut area. This was presumed to relieve congestion and inflammation of internal organs.) Cupping was used together with other treatments of that time. His fever increased, and there were some gastrointestinal problems. He was diagnosed as having bilious pleurisy.[11]

Phillip Hone related that part of the president's terminal problem was a "violent diarrhea," which came one month after he had confessed to an aide that he was badly constipated. His physician had given him harsh cathartics, followed by more of the same. He was also given ipecac to produce vomiting. The purging and vomiting completely exhausted the aged general. After they had performed these medical outrages, his physicians then resorted to opium, camphor, brandy, and finally to some Senaeca Indian remedies: crude petroleum and Virginia snakeroot. Virginia snakeroot was used for a tonic and as a cure for a snake bite.[12]

Dr. Thomas Miller, his physician, finally became quite concerned about the famous patient. In the sick room on the second floor of the White House he began his treatments, most of which were outmoded even in 1841. The president was bled, cupped, and given doses of calomel, laudanum, castor oil, and other items. In the week following, Dr. Miller resorted to opium, which was even more potent than laudanum. He also gave Harrison shots of whiskey which were provided at regular intervals.[13]

Politicians and officials moved in and out of the president's bedroom, staring at the sick man who lay there. In the coming and going of his consciousness he at times failed to recognize them.[14] Apparently, Harrison must have had a very strong constitution in order to be able to continue as long as he did while he was being treated in such a horrible manner. Had he been left alone he might have lived out his term. In fact, the August 1841 number of the *Boston Medical Journal* contained an article protesting the mode of his treatment, with authors intimating that the president's life had been sacrificed needlessly.[15] He died early on the morning of April 4, 1841.

After his death the attending doctors issued a statement about his illness. The diagnoses were pneumonic inflammation and hepatic congestion. Terminally ill, Harrison had developed jaundice and gastrointestinal irritation.

For years it was rumored that General Harrison did not die a natural death, but this allegation was not heard of until 1866, when John Smith Dye, in his historical work, *Crimes of the Great Conspiracy to Overthrow Liberty in America,* boldly asserted that the general had died from poison. This was presumed to have been administered under the direction of John C. Calhoun who, according to Dye, since he represented the powers of slavery, poisoned the president so that a friend of slavery might sit in the White House. Fortunately, this slander was never accepted by the American people.[16]

At least two other presidents, Zachary Taylor and Warren G. Harding, were alleged to have been poisoned—Harding by his wife and Zachary Taylor by the abolitionists because of his presumed Southern sympathies. Harrison was the first American president to die while in office.

References

1. Dorothy Burne Goebel, *William Henry Harrison, a Political Biography,* p. 15.
2. Rudolph Marx, *The Health of the Presidents,* p. 127.
3. David C. Whitney, *The American Presidents,* p. 85.
4. Freeman Cleaves, *Old Tippecanoe,* pp. 279–80.
5. Ibid., p. 307.
6. Norma Lewis Peterson, *The Presidencies of William Henry Harrison and John Tyler,* p. 33.

7. Homer F. Cunningham, *The Presidents' Last Years*, p. 68.
8. Page Smith, *The Nation Comes of Age*, p. 183.
9. Ibid., p. 185.
10. James A. Green, *William Henry Harrison, His Life and Times*, p. 398.
11. Cunningham, *The Presidents' Last Years*, p. 69.
12. Marx, *The Health of the Presidents*, p. 131.
13. William Seale, *The Presidents' House*, p. 233.
14. Ibid., p. 233.
15. Green, *William Henry Harrison*, p. 400.
16. Ibid., p. 401.

10

John Tyler

John Tyler, the tenth president of the United States, was born in Charles City County, Virginia, on March 29, 1790. In 1807 he graduated from William and Mary College and in 1809 was admitted to the bar to practice law. During his career he was a member of the Virginia legislature (1811–16); a captain of militia in the War of 1812; a U.S. representative from Virginia (1817–21); the governor of Virginia (1825–27); a senator from Virginia (1827–36); a member of the Virginia legislature (1838–40); the vice president (1841); and the president of the United States (1841–45). In December 1839 at the Whig National Convention in Harrisburg, Pennsylvania, he was nominated for the vice presidency as running mate for another military hero, William Henry Harrison. Within a month after he was elected vice president, he became president, due to Harrison's death.

Tyler was never in truly good health. He had recurring bouts of severe diarrhea, the etiology of which can only be guessed. He had frequent colds and was very thin all of his life. There is practically nothing that can be obtained to reveal anything about his health as a child.

At the age of 30, when he was a U.S. representative from Virginia, he had an illness which was very odd and difficult to identify. He wrote to his doctor from Washington, "I sustained a violent singular shock four days ago. I had gone to the house on Thursday morning before experiencing a disagreeable sensation in my head, which increased so much as to force me to leave the hall. It then visited in succession hands, feet, tongue, and lips, creating in each the effect that is produced by what is commonly called a sleeping hand, which all of us are subject to; but it was so severe as to render my limbs, tongue, and so forth, almost useless to me. I was bled and took purgatives which have rendered me convalescent. The doctor ascribed it to a diseased stomach, and very probably correctly did so. I am now walking about and I'm to all appearances well, but often experience a glow in my face and over the whole system which is often followed by debility with pain in my neck and arms."[1]

The presentation of Tyler's illness, as he described it, was a symmetric weakening of all of his limbs, which would be most unusual in a cerebral vascular accident. The onset and progression of his illness was so well described by Tyler as to reduce the differential diagnosis to those entities which produce symmetrical and generalized paralysis. These would include Guillain-Barre syndrome, myosthenia gravis, tick paralysis, diphtheretic paralysis, and others. The doctors ascribed the illness to a diseased stomach. The gastrointestinal involvement followed by the typical march of neurological symptoms would lead one to favor the diagnosis of botulism. He was slow in his recovery, and his convalescence was so slow and prolonged that he resigned his seat in Congress for two years.

Tyler's living conditions in Washington were very poor. The swampy condition of the land in and around Washington was an excellent breeding ground for mosquitoes. The town was very dirty with almost no provisions for sewage and garbage disposal. It was so hot and unhealthy in the summertime that those who were financially able fled to the seashore or the mountains. Tyler lived in a boarding house where the food was very bad.

Tyler must, however, have functioned quite well in some ways because he was the father of fifteen children—eight by his first wife and seven by his second wife, the former Julia Gardiner. Tyler had married Julia after his first wife died in 1842. An acquaintance, Phillip Hope, referred to Tyler in his diary as "the old fool." The reference was made apparently because Tyler was 30 years older than Julia. Fool he may have been, but sterile or impotent, never.

Tyler, unfortunately, became the aging father of a large brood of young children and the aging husband of a young wife. He found it difficult to keep up. During the last eight years of his life he had increasing health problems with numerous unspecified aches and pains, but as usual his health problems seemed centered in his digestive tract. After leaving the White House, Tyler retired to his estate in Virginia, where he suffered from repeated attacks of dysentery in the summer and frequent attacks of respiratory infections during the winter. Later he was prone to colds, arthritis, arthritic attacks, and kidney problems.[2]

Tyler, like Jefferson, had very little confidence in the medical profession. He felt that physicians' diagnoses and treatments varied too widely for illnesses that had the same signs and symptoms. Tyler regularly took the water, though, at the various spas in Virginia to ease his aches and pains. Tyler came to believe greatly in the efficacy of sulfur hydrotherapy. He also took frequent and massive doses of calomel, which may have contributed to his frequent, quite severe gastric upsets. In 1881 he complained,

"I have many aches and pains. They will attend on a sexogenarian, however, so be it, for I am convinced that it is all wisely ordained by providence."[3]

After the Civil War began, Tyler was elected to the Congress of the Confederacy in Richmond. Julia, his wife, had a dread that Tyler's life was in danger, and she hurried to Richmond to be near him. On her arrival she found him in good health. However, the next morning he became dizzy and vomited. He had had numerous such episodes before, so he chose to dismiss it. He further complained that he was having a chill and went down to the hotel dining room for a cup of tea. Soon thereafter he slumped to the floor, unconscious. Moved to a couch, he regained consciousness. The four doctors who attended Tyler at that time safely concluded that he had biliousness and bronchitis. The first label was placed on him because he had vomited bile, and the second one because he had coughed.

On January 16 his condition had not improved, and he was ordered to absolute bed rest. On the morning of January 17 he appeared to be improved, but toward evening he awoke, complaining of having a feeling of suffocation. He was given a cough medicine containing morphine. His personal physician, a Dr. Brown, ordered mustard plasters and brandy. Soon thereafter Tyler died, just after midnight, January 18, 1862.[4]

The clinical picture leads almost certainly to one conclusion: his terminal illness was due to a cerebrovascular accident or stroke. The pattern of dizzy spells occurring in past years is indicative of a series of "small strokes" which led up to the final stroke. "Little strokes" are more commonly called transient ischemic attacks (meaning a temporary deficiency of blood supply to an area of the brain). A full 60 percent of atherosclerotic strokes are preceded by transient ischemic attacks.[5]

References

1. Rudolph Marx, *The Health of the Presidents*, p. 134.
2. Robert Seager II, *And Tyler, Too*, p. 422.
3. Ibid., p. 423.
4. Homer F. Cunningham, *The Presidents' Last Years*, p. 76.
5. Jay P. Mohr, Carlos S. Kans, and Raymond D. Adams, "Cerebrovascular Diseases," in *Harrison's Principles of Internal Medicine*, section 356.

11

James K. Polk

James K. Polk, the eleventh president of the United States, was born November 2, 1795, near Pineville in Mecklenburg County, North Carolina, the oldest in a family of ten children. Polk was described as never being robustly well. A frail child and small for his age, he was said to have good features, dark hair, and grey eyes; but he was frail and often sick.[1]

His grandfather, Ezekiel, said, "The victuals just don't stick to his ribs." His mother, Jane, gave him herbal tea and kept a bag of asafetida around his neck. To the uninitiated, asafetida is a gum resin with a strong garlic odor taken from the roots of several plants. The little bag of asafetida worn on a string around one's neck was supposed to ward off many diseases.

Polk's gracile habitus and his poor health were later attributed to a chronic kidney condition caused by a stone in his urinary bladder with secondary infection of the urinary tract. The pain from the stone and chronic infection robbed him of his strength to such an extent that he was not able to enjoy the usual childhood activities. His father recognized the frailty in the child and made an effort to help him to build his strength and stamina by taking him on survey trips into the wilderness, but Polk was unable to maintain the pace in this environment.[2] His father took the young boy on several surveying trips, but each time his strength was not adequate for the physical requirements of surveying in the wilderness.

Finally, Polk's mother suggested that he be taken to see a doctor. Soon thereafter the future president made an arduous 250-mile trip on horseback to see Dr. Ephraim McDowell in Danville, Kentucky. Dr. McDowell made a diagnosis of urinary bladder stone and advised surgery.[3]

Dr. McDowell had had some training in Scotland and was brave enough to attempt surgery, a procedure no other doctor in the area dared do. He was widely known in the Midwest as an outstanding surgeon, having been the first in this country to successfully remove an ovarian tumor.

Polk was in very poor condition when he arrived in Danville, and his already weakened system had been further depleted by the arduous and painful trip. Dr. McDowell mandated that his patient rest for several weeks before surgery.[4]

Although a number of well-written and widely circulated biographies, including those by Martha Morrel and Charles Sellers, state that the chronic and debilitating illness referred to by Polk was due to gall bladder stones which were alleged to have been removed by Dr. McDowell, it seems that this was not the case. Dr. Samuel Gross, professor of surgery at the University of Louisville, in an address before the Kentucky State Medical Society on October 20, 1856, 40 years after Polk's surgery, described Polk's operation. Dr. Gross's description of Polk's surgery concerned itself with a cystolithotomy (stone removal from the urinary bladder). Medical history indeed would almost certainly have refuted the claim that Polk underwent a cholecystectomy (gall bladder surgery) by McDowell.[5]

Indeed, records show that the first cholecystectomy performed successfully in this country was done by Dr. John Bobbs in 1867, 50 years after Polk's operation.[6]

It seems important here to discuss something of the surgery which was performed on Polk. Brandy was used as anesthesia, while the patient was held down by assistants and restraining straps. The incision was made by a cut through the perineum, the area behind the penis and in front of the anus. The opening was then extended through the prostate and into the urinary bladder by means of a gorget (a gorget was a sharp instrument made for this purpose). The stone was then sought for and removed with forceps.

Polk apparently did not have any postoperative complications, such as fistula, infection, or hemorrhage. However, there is a fairly well-founded speculation that Polk may have been rendered impotent by this surgery. This speculation is based on the possible effects of surgery due to McDowell's technique and the fact that Polk was the only one of the seven married children of Sam and Jane Polk whose marriage was childless.[7]

In 1816 James Polk was enrolled at the University of North Carolina, where he so exhausted himself by his studies that he was very weak and had to spend several months regaining his health before he could return to Tennessee.[8]

After Polk's graduation from the University of North Carolina, he studied law and in 1820 was admitted to the bar to practice law in Tennessee. From 1823 to 1825 he was a member of the state legislature in Tennessee. From 1825 to 1839 he was the U.S. representative from Tennessee. In 1835 he became speaker of the U.S. House of Representatives, a job which he held until 1839. During his congressional campaign of 1835, after Polk had undergone a great deal of stress in the previous congressional session, the arduous campaigning put an undue pressure on his very frail constitution. When the election was over, he retreated to Beaver Dam Springs, where he rested. He was quite ill for a time and was not able to leave the spa until the end of August 1835. Apparently, Polk had not been completely well, and lived from one medical crisis to another.[9]

In 1839, after 14 years in the House of Representatives, Polk decided to run for governor. He resolved to run a very energetic campaign through Tennessee. The task of running for governor taxed his frail constitution to its limit. His voice became so weak that it was difficult for most of his audience to hear him. He had to leave the campaign in the latter part of September 1838 to recuperate before he could continue.

Polk twice failed to be reelected for governor (1841 and 1843). During his campaign in the summer months of 1843, his travels carried him into the unhealthy swampland near the Mississippi. He became very ill at Dyersburg and for several days was unable to continue. At one place he had to spend three days in bed before he could continue his campaign.

Soon after Polk became president in 1845 he was subject to continuous stressful situations which were related to being president at that time—threatened war with Mexico and the ever present wrangle over slavery. True to form, his frail constitution fell prey to pressures and he became ill. The first episode came a few weeks after his inaugural; and then later in June 1845 he was forced to keep to his bed for several days. At that time he was described as showing considerable debility and exhaustion.[10]

The threat of the onset of war put terrific strain on Polk in 1845 and 1846. However, he did not succumb in any major way until the fall of 1846, when he felt so weak and exhausted that he planned a vacation. However, he became very ill while he was on vacation. He described the illness: "My stomach was deranged and I felt a soreness and aching in my limbs."[11]

Following the congressional session of August 1846, Polk was completely exhausted and weak. The following week he went on a retreat to his vacation home in Fortress Monroe, but was not able to escape the public. He was carried to Norfolk where he was compelled to shake well-wishers' hands for hours on end during an extremely hot day. Later he returned to his beach retreat completely exhausted and had a miserable sleepless night. He was very ill by the next morning, but forced himself to entertain an invited guest. Later he was able to rest, relax, and recover some of his strength.[12]

In Polk's diary he refers to regular attacks of chills and fever. His illness at that time, with intermittent chills and fever, was undoubtedly due to malaria. He was most likely treated with quinine, since it was available at that time, and had been to some extent available during the Revolutionary War in the form of Peruvian bark.

When Polk retired from the presidency in 1849, he was physically drained. His return to his home state and to his home was by a difficult, arduous, and circuitous route—partially by boat and partially by rail. All along the way he was greeted by huge crowds and attended receptions. When he reached Charleston, South Carolina, he was in a very hot, humid atmosphere: such a contrast to the cold when he left Washington. On his arrival in Montgomery, Alabama, he was very ill and quite exhausted. His group reached New Orleans on March 21, 1849, and he stayed in the city, despite the rumor that cholera was rampant there. Polk was entertained in New Orleans as he had been in each place he had stopped. It was very hot and humid in New Orleans, and he was very ill with his recurrent diarrhea. When his boat finally arrived at Paducah a doctor came on board to treat him. The doctor ruled out cholera and treated him with a number of medicines, the natures of which are not known. When he arrived at Nashville, Tennessee, his home, he was greeted by a very large crowd.[13]

When Polk arrived in Nashville his diarrhea, which had been present recurrently for many years, was present again in a severe form. He took an opiate, which caused some improvement and he was better for a month or so.

As throughout his career, Polk remained a very frail man, lacking in stamina. When he was able to lead a relatively quiet life, his health was reasonably good. But when he was compelled to undergo a great deal of stress his old problems returned—malarial chills and dysentery.

On Sunday, June 3, 1849, Polk had a very severe recurrence of his diarrhea accompanied by vomiting. The illness did not respond as it had previously done to opiates. His wife noted that his face was ashen. The symptoms, coupled with the fact that he had been exposed to cholera in epidemic form in Nashville, led those attending Polk to assume that he had cholera. The president was attended by doctors who were called, and on the next day he seemed better, but Polk had no reserves to call on. Very quietly and with no struggle his breathing stopped at 4:40 on the afternoon of June 15, 1849.[14]

References

1. Martha McBride Morrel, *"Young Hickory," The Life and Times of James K. Polk*, p. 13.
2. Rudolph Marx, *The Health of the Presidents*, p. 140
3. Morrel, *"Young Hickory,"* pp. 16–17.
4. Charles Sellers, *James K. Polk*, 1:40.
5. Robert M. Ikard, "Surgical Operation on James K. Polk," *Tennessee Historical Quarterly*, 48, no. 3 (Summer 1984):128–29.
6. Ibid., pp. 121–22.
7. Ibid., pp. 129–30.
8. Paul K. Bergeron, *The Presidency of James K. Polk*, p. 10.
9. Sellers, *James K. Polk*, 1:283.
10. Sellers, *James K. Polk*, 2:304.
11. Milo Milton Quaife, ed., *The Diaries of James K. Polk*, 2:92–93.
12. Sellers, *James K. Polk*, 1:485–86.
13. Homer F. Cunningham, *The Presidents' Last Years*, pp. 80–82.
14. Ibid., p. 82.

12

Zachary Taylor

Zachary Taylor, the twelfth president of the United States, was born on November 24, 1784, in Orange County, Virginia. He was the youngest of three sons in a family of nine children. When Zachary was not quite one year old, his father, Lieutenant Colonel Richard Taylor, moved his family to a large area of land which had been granted to him for his service in the Revolutionary War.[1]

For one so prominent as Zachary Taylor it is surprising that little is known about his childhood and youth, except that he grew up in a frontier settlement near Louisville, Kentucky. Very little is known about his education, but his speeches and correspondence in later years seemed to confirm the idea that his education was very limited.[2] There is also surprisingly little—next to nothing—written about his health in his early years, so his early health history is rather obscure.

Some information about Taylor's health begins to emerge after he entered the army in 1808, at the age of 23, when he was commissioned as a first lieutenant. In late April 1808 he and some recruits left Kentucky by boat to join Brigadier General James Wilkinson's brigade at New Orleans. New Orleans at that time was a very unhealthy place because of its wet and swampy terrain. In this city with no sewage system, garbage was dumped in the streets where it remained until removed by rainstorms. When General Wilkinson and Taylor reached New Orleans, they found 733 sick men on the rolls, the victims of prostitutes and whiskey as well as the terrible sanitary conditions. There were only two army surgeons present to treat the desperately ill. Over 500 of those who were very sick were moved to barracks converted to a hospital, which was extremely short of medications and supplies.

In June of that year Wilkinson shifted his camp to Terre aux Boeufs, about 12 miles south of New Orleans. His army spent the summer there in an incredibly unhealthy situation. He camped on swampy ground about three feet below the level of the river. The army had no mosquito netting, and their food was very poor—only wormy bread and spoiled pork. By the time Wilkinson moved his troops to healthier and higher ground, nearly half had died from sickness contracted at Terre aux Boeufs. It is noted that Wilkinson, Taylor's superior, in spite of having had medical training (he was a medical doctor), was ignorant concerning the proper location of troops to prevent some diseases brought on by lack of sanitation, poor food, and exposure to mosquitoes.

Later in May and June 1809 Taylor, after leaving Terre aux Boeufs, temporarily commanded at Fort Pickering near what is now Memphis, Tennessee. It is not known whether Taylor returned to New Orleans or remained at Fort Pickering. It is recorded that he served as Wilkinson's aide until developing yellow fever and returning to Louisville, Kentucky, to recover. He was at Louisville in September and October 1809.[3]

Taylor had just recovered from his encounter with yellow fever and returned to his company when he developed dysentery and was quite ill. He had returned in the spring to a fly-infested camp where dysentery was rampant. He was so ill that he returned home to Virginia to recover.[4]

Taylor was made captain in 1810 and placed in command at Fort Knox, where in the summer of 1810 he contracted malaria. He was still suffering from the ague as late as September of that year when the fort was attacked by Indians. He survived both the battle and the disease.[5]

Taylor must have presented a very unusual appearance. He was described this way in his early military career: "He had a big head, thick unkempt hair, coarse features, and a short neck. His eyelids half closed, the heavy brows pulled down over nearsighted eyes in an instinctive attempt to sharpen the focus of vision; but giving the impression of a fierce scowl. At close range, and in reading, Taylor had to shut one eye to avoid double vision. His body was big and barrel shaped, supported by legs that were so short that he had to be helped into a saddle by an orderly."[6]

Taylor did not drink or smoke, but he did chew tobacco. He was very accurate in his aim when he shifted his quid and spat it out.[7]

Zachary Taylor's experiences with his recurrent episodes of fever and dysentery during his military campaigns are very similar to those endured by Andrew Jackson, who suffered greatly in his campaigns in Florida and New Orleans from fever and dysentery. In the second Seminole War, during November 1839, Brigadier Taylor fell a victim to the fever (probably malaria) "which confined me to my bed for near two weeks when so many was dying around me."[8] In July and August 1844, while stationed at Fort Jessup in Louisiana, Taylor commanded the First Department with headquarters at Fort Jessup. During this time he suffered from several attacks of "bilious fever" (malaria).[9] At that time he was reported by Captain D. W. Bliss, later surgeon general, as being in a dangerous condition.

he soon began to recover, and before many days was able to resume his duties. However, as a result of this illness he was weak for many months. This was when he began to show the effects of his 40 years of service, a great deal of which was spent under much less than ideal conditions. He was thereafter ill much more often than he had been in the past.[10]

In May 1846, while Zachary Taylor was poised with his army to cross the Rio Grande, he developed a fever which kept him in his tent for a brief time.[11] Such fevers, unfortunately, were quite common. In fact, in the Mexican War the deaths and disability from diseases far outnumbered the deaths due to instruments of war. After two battles against the Mexicans Taylor moved his base to Camargo on the San Juan River. This was one of the worst places that an army could be based. One of the regiments from Tennessee lost over half of its men to dysentery and malaria. In July 1846, after the Battle of Monterrey, the troops were moved to a healthy area, but the attrition rate among the troops still remained high, probably from infection already established earlier.

In the summer of 1849, having been elected largely on the popularity resulting from his swift victories in the Mexican War, Taylor decided to take a presidential tour through the north. He had an onset of illness only a few days after he left Washington, which caused him to cancel the last part of his trip. In Pennsylvania he was attacked by what was thought to be the beginning of cholera, but he showed rapid recovery and insisted on continuing his tour. However, in Erie, Pennsylvania, he had a relapse of his severe diarrhea, accompanied by high fever; and his physician feared for his survival. He again recovered and went by boat to Niagara Falls. After several days at Niagara Falls Taylor returned to the capital, and in about a month he seemed to have returned to his usual state of health.[12]

In the summer of 1850, during Taylor's second year in the White House, he was plagued both with ill health and a scandal which involved three of his cabinet members and the Galphin claim. Some members of the cabinet, especially Secretary of War Crawford, were guilty of raiding the Galphin estate. Crawford had acted both as counsel for the Galphin estate and as secretary of war. Although the Galphin estate after many years recovered its claim against the government, Crawford had in the meantime pocketed a large part of both principle and interest. All this caused the Democrats to raise an uproar, blaming Taylor's Whig Party in general for this scandal.[13] Taylor consequently underwent a great deal of anxiety in the spring and summer months of 1850, and his friends noted some deterioration in his appearance. He was showing signs of fatigue and appeared haggard.[14]

During this stressful period, on July 4, 1850, the president attended a

Sunday School recital early that morning, and either before or soon thereafter ate several green apples, which undoubtedly helped bring on his subsequent severe illness. During that summer the heat had been very oppressive, and this added greatly to his distress. Many of the prominent people of Washington were ill from dysentery—labeled by some as cholera.[15]

On the afternoon of July 4, Taylor went to a celebration at the Washington Monument. He sat in the blistering sun without a head cover, and when the long ceremony was over he took an extended walk along the Potomac River. When he arrived back at the White House, he was very thirsty and hungry, so he ate large amounts of raw fruit, said to be cherries, and drank a great deal of cold water and milk. At dinner that evening he again drank a great deal of cold liquids and ate a considerable amount of cherries. His doctor, Alexander Watherspoon, dined with him that evening; and during the meal he admonished Taylor for drinking so much cold liquid and eating so much raw fruit. Soon after dinner the president had some abdominal discomfort with nausea and cramps. He spent a very uncomfortable night but did not seem ill enough to alarm anyone. Considering that he was already in poor health and considering the events of the previous day, it would have been remarkable had he not become ill. On the next day he did not feel well but tried to perform his duties as usual. He was very uncomfortable that night, so on Saturday, July 6, Dr. Watherspoon was called to the White House.[16]

Dr. Alexander Watherspoon diagnosed the illness as cholera morbus. This was a scrape-basket diagnosis which covered a number of gastrointestinal complaints having diarrhea as a symptom. It was not at all related to Asiatic cholera.

Watherspoon gave him calomel and opium with some apparent alleviation of his discomfort. There were reports that the illness was due to something he had eaten. This was a reasonable presumption in view of his marked dietary indiscretion of July 4. According to all reports he had some intermittent fever. He had a great thirst and ate ice to alleviate it. On Monday, July 8, Taylor was depressed and predicted, "In two days I shall be a dead man." On that same day dysentery appeared and he had a worsening of his vomiting.[17]

On July 9 the president was obviously worse, and by 5:00 P.M. he was barely alive. Terminally, the doctors had resorted to bleeding and blisters. The blisters were produced by such counterirritants as the extract of the blister beetle of the genus cantharis. His physicians apparently contributed to his demise. At 10:35 P.M. on July 9 he died.[18]

But posterity was not content to let Zachary Taylor lie in peace. There was some suspicion that Zachary Taylor, a Southerner originally, had betrayed the South by his views and actions regarding the subject of slavery while he was president. More recently there have been some questions regarding the cause of his death. Was he poisoned by some disgruntled Southern sympathizer? There was agitation in some quarters to have the body of Taylor exhumed and tested for poison — notably strychnine.

The body of Zachary Taylor was exhumed on June 17, 1991 from its crypt in the Zachary Taylor National Cemetery at Louisville, Kentucky. The brief removal of the body was done so that the Jefferson County coroner's office could conduct tests to determine the presence or absence of toxic substances. The tests were requested by a historical novelist who felt Zachary Taylor may have been poisoned because of his antislavery views during his presidency. The tests performed on the tissues removed from Zachary Taylor's remains showed only a trace of arsenic — not enough to have killed him. Samples of hair, nails, and bone were examined in a nuclear isotope reactor. His death apparently was due to some form of gastroenteritis. Almost surely someone will eventually insist on digging up Andy Jackson in an attempt to determine whether or not his demise was due to amyloidosis as claimed by Dr. Francis Tomlinson Gardner.[19]

References

1. David C. Whitney, *The American Presidents*, pp. 100–01.
2. Brainerd Dyer, *Zachary Taylor*, p. 15.
3. Kay Jack Bauer, *Zachary Taylor*, pp. 6–7.
4. Rudolph Marx, *The Health of the Presidents*, pp. 149–50.
5. Ibid., p. 150.
6. Ibid., pp. 150–51.
7. Holman Hamilton, *Zachary Taylor, Soldier in the White House*, p. 23.
8. Ibid., p. 140.
9. Bauer, *Zachary Taylor*, p. 113.
10. Dyer, *Zachary Taylor*, pp. 129–30.
11. Ibid., p. 164.
12. Ibid., pp. 402–03.
13. Hamilton, *Zachary Taylor*, pp. 398–99.
14. Ibid., pp. 352–53.
15. Elbert B. Smith, *The Presidencies of Zachary Taylor and Millard Fillmore*, pp. 155–56.
16. Homer F. Cunningham, *The Presidents' Last Years*, pp. 86–87.
17. Bauer, *Zachary Taylor*, pp. 315–16.
18. Smith, *The Presidencies of Zachary Taylor and Millard Fillmore*, pp. 156–58.
19. Francis Tomlinson Gardner. "The Gentleman from Tennessee," *The Surgeon's Library — Surgery, Gynecology, and Obstetrics* 30 (March 1949): 405.

13

Millard Fillmore

Millard Fillmore, the thirteenth president of the United States, was born January 7, 1800, in Cayuga County, New York. Fillmore was one of nine children born into a very poor family. At the age of 14 he was apprenticed to a clothmaker. He later bought his freedom from his apprenticeship and for a while taught school. Later, while still a youth, Fillmore was taken into a law firm to study law and was admitted to the bar in 1823.[1]

Fillmore was described as immaculately groomed and impeccably dressed, one whose polished manners concealed a background of severe poverty. He grew up semi-illiterate, physically powerful, and thoroughly accustomed to backbreaking labor.[2] In 1826 he married Abigail Powers, who had taught him to read and helped him to prepare to take the bar exam.

He was a member of the New York state legislature, 1828–31; a representative from New York, 1833–35 and 1837–43; comptroller of the state of New York, 1848; and vice president of the United States, 1849–50.[3] He was the second vice president to reach the presidency through the death of an incumbent, this time Zachary Taylor.[4]

Fillmore was one of a series of eight presidents of lesser stature, after Jackson and just before Lincoln, who are best known for their mediocrity. Fillmore was mediocre even in his illness. Some of the rest, Pierce and Van Buren, for example, had at least some bad habits that one could write about, such as excessive drinking. Fillmore neither drank nor smoked, and he restricted his diet to milk and simple foods. At the age of 54, during his vice presidency, Fillmore was described this way: "The heavy blond hair had whitened prematurely, but his massive frame remained athletic, and his pink complexion radiated vitality."[5] However, his overconsumption of even simple foods led to his being considerably overweight. Outside of his obesity, though, Fillmore had no remarkable health problems until his last years and final illness.[6]

Fillmore's wife, Abigail, did not fare as well as her husband with regard to her health. She was, during his presidency, ill most of the time. Fillmore's daughter, Mary Abigail, a talented young woman, was able to fill in as hostess in the White House for her mother.

One anecdote illustrates well the regard in which Fillmore was held in his time and how he has been viewed by history: The new president felt his position required that he have a carriage. Edward Moran, a White House attendant for many administrations, took Fillmore to see an imposing outfit, whose owner was leaving Washington and was willing to sell it at a much reduced price. "That is all very well, Edward," Fillmore said, "but how would it do for the President of the United States to ride around in a second hand carriage?"

"But sure," replied Moran, "Your Excellency is only a second hand President."[7]

When Fillmore left the White House in 1853 he was still in good health. His only problem at that time was obesity. He was much overweight and had an obvious paunch, but there was no painful or enfeebling illness.

In March 1853, within a month of leaving the White House, Fillmore was visited by tragedy. On a very cold day Abigail attended with her husband the inauguration of Franklin Pierce. She, due to the severe cold and her frail constitution, developed pneumonia and died on March 30, 1853. To add to the ex-president's grief one year later his daughter, Mary Abigail, died of cholera. Fillmore, except for a mentally ill son, was left without family.[8]

Millard Fillmore's health continued to be excellent until 1874. Fillmore had finished shaving on early February 13, when he suddenly lost the use of his left arm.

Soon thereafter the palsy extended to the left side of his face and the muscles of speech and swallowing. He showed some slight improvement, but two weeks later the paralysis involved the entire left side of his body. He was never again able to leave his bed. With the loss of his muscles of swallowing, he had some problem with food intake. On Sunday evening, March 8, he became unconscious, and shortly after 11:00 that night he expired.[9]

It is almost certain that a man of 74, presenting with paralysis of sudden onset spreading from his upper extremity to the left side of his face and thence to the larynx and pharnyx, was suffering from a cerebrovascular accident — or stroke. The sudden onset of his terminal illness would label it as being of cerebrovascular origin. One would strongly suspect that there was a major cerebral artery, affected by atherosclerosis, which was occluded by a thrombus.

References

1. David C. Whitney, *The American Presidents*, p. 106.
2. Elbert B. Smith, *The Presidencies of Zachary Taylor and Millard Fillmore*, pp. 43–44.
3. Whitney, *The American Presidents*, p. 106.
4. James Morgan, *Our Presidents*, p. 109.
5. Charles M. Snyder, *The Lady and the President, from the Letters of Dorothy Dix and Millard Fillmore*, pp. 16–17.
6. Rudolph Marx, *The Health of the Presidents*, pp. 157–58.
7. Morgan, *Our Presidents*, p. 109.
8. Homer F. Cunningham, *The Presidents' Last Years*, p. 92.
9. Ibid., p. 98.

14

Franklin Pierce

Franklin Pierce, the fourteenth president of the United States, was born November 23, 1804, in Hillsboro, New Hampshire. One of a family of nine children, Pierce was, according to his biographers, a roistering youth who did not let his studies interfere with his pleasures. In fact, in his second year at Bowdoin College in Maine he was at the bottom of his class, and at that time he almost decided to leave. He was persuaded by his friends to change his mind, though, and he then devoted himself to his studies and finished third in his class.[1]

As well as can be determined from the literature, Pierce did not have any significant health problems early in life. At the age of 16 he described himself: "Being thin and very small, slight, and an apparently frail boy of sixteen."[2] It is noted, however, that Pierce's mother was a heavy drinker, perhaps an alcoholic, and that Pierce at an early age developed a thirst for alcohol and a lack of ability to tolerate it.[3]

Pierce's earliest recorded illness occurred in the spring of 1825. While studying law at Portsmouth, New Hampshire, he noted a cough he thought in the beginning to be a "chin cough," which was to trouble him often in later years.[4] Then in 1833, while he was visiting with some friends in Boston, Pierce became very ill—so ill that there was fear that he might not survive. The illness was diagnosed as a "bilious attack."[5] Unfortunately for those interested in medical history, the diagnosis of bilious attack means nothing. It is very nonspecific terminology which refers to problems of the biliary tract and, indeed, to others that weren't even related to the biliary tract.

On November 10, 1834, before his thirtieth birthday, Pierce married Jane Means Appleton, daughter of the president of Bowdoin College. Jane suffered from what was diagnosed as chronic pulmonary tuberculosis and for that reason refused to continue to live in the unhealthy surroundings of Washington. She did not accompany Pierce when he returned to Washington in 1835. Consequently, he lived as did a lot of other congressmen in bachelor's quarters. Surrounded by other hard-drinking bachelor congressmen, Pierce lived a boisterous life. It is reputed that he competed with his fellow imbibers to determine who could drink the most. During those years he apparently suffered from great hangovers,[6] and he fought the battle of alcoholism for the rest of his life.[7] He succumbed in his tendency to the excessive use of alcohol.

On February 18, 1835, while Congress was still in session, Pierce awoke with a very violent "bilious attack," similar to the one he had had in 1833. While visiting in Boston he was so ill that he rang the bell to summon a servant. He was seen by a physician who gave him a dose of calomel.[8]

On February 2, 1836, Pierce received word of the birth of his first son. Soon thereafter he received further word that his newborn son had died. This grief was added to the fact that he had been undergoing a great deal of mental stress during the debates on slavery. He was also being verbally assailed by John Calhoun over the slavery issue.

Congressional life at that time was not at all suitable to one of Pierce's temperament. Many of the congressmen lived in boardinghouses and hotels without their families. Drinking and rowdying was common. Pierce was noted for his lack of tolerance to alcohol, and his convivial nature was due to being surrounded by friends who had a greater tolerance for alcohol than he. He tried to keep up with these companions, but as a consequence he became intoxicated and out of control before his friends could get started.

In late February 1836 Pierce, Wise of Virginia, and Hannigan of Indiana became involved in a fight in a theater. They had been drinking heavily before they arrived at the theater. Soon after this incident Pierce was awakened at night with a severe pleuritic pain and a high fever. Dr. Sewell visited Pierce and removed 16 ounces of blood from him. On the next visit, 24 hours later, the doctor removed 10–12 more ounces of blood by cupping. To this treatment was attributed his recovery. He gradually improved both mentally and physically. During the second week in March he was well enough to resume his work in Congress.[9]

When Pierce was only 33 years of age he was elected to the Senate. In his third year as a senator his wife lost her second child, and in 1842 she left Washington for good because of her fear that the third child, yet unborn, might bear the same fate if exposed to the unhealthy atmosphere of the capital. Pierce himself decided to change his mode of living, retired from the Senate in 1842, and left Washington. Some attributed his leaving the Senate to his overuse of alcohol.

For a period of time he apparently drank much less until he was involved in the Mexican War in 1846. He was a volunteer who was appointed colonel and brigadier. In that conflict Pierce distinguished himself for his bravery and coolness under fire. At the Battle of Contreras, August 1847, Pierce was thrown from his horse onto a lava bed and sustained a fractured pelvis and dislocation of his left knee. The doctor reduced the dislocated left knee and bandaged his pelvis. There could be some question about the fracture of the pelvis since he almost immediately remounted his horse, with help, and remained in the saddle for several hours thereafter.

Another account of this event was that when his horse stumbled, Pierce sustained his injury and lost consciousness, but that he soon thereafter regained consciousness. When he was helped to his feet, it was found that he had sustained injuries to his pelvis and left knee. Soon thereafter Dr. Ritchey, brigade surgeon, gave first aid and Pierce continued into battle after he had found another horse. He presumably stayed on his horse until late that night. Pierce was unable to continue the next day and turned his command over to Colonel Truman P. Ransome. During the Battle of Molino del Rey and the storming of Chapultepec Pierce was suffering both from his injuries and from a severe case of diarrhea.[10]

In another report it was related that on the day after the Battle of Contreras he had collapsed from pain while leading his horse across a ravine. He was then related to have spent a great part of September in a military hospital where he suffered from his injury and from a severe dysentery and a febrile illness, presumably malaria.[11]

After the Mexican War Pierce returned to his law practice (1848) in Concord, New Hampshire. He was very successful at his profession. During the presidential campaign of 1852 Pierce was asked by his friends to become a candidate on the Democratic ticket. He was a desirable candidate from their standpoint because he had been out of politics for ten years and could not be tied to any controversial issues such as slavery and he was also a war hero. Pierce at first refused to run. However, when the convention became deadlocked, Pierce was persuaded to accept the nomination. He became the Democratic nominee on the forty-ninth ballot.

Two months before he was inaugurated, the Pierce family was involved in a railway accident. Pierce and his wife were unharmed, but their 11-year-old son, Benjamin, was killed before their eyes. This tragedy and the problems of the presidential office caused him to resort again to an overindulgence in alcohol. Neither Pierce nor his wife ever recovered from this tragic loss of their son. This terrible happening cast a pall over his entire administration. He drank so much that some members of his party expressed a regret that he was ever made president.

In the summer of 1853, the first year of his presidency, Pierce traveled to New York to attend the World's Fair. On his way to New York he developed a severe respiratory infection, which caused him to cancel some of his speeches. At one dinner and reception he suffered from severe pleuritic pain. In Philadelphia he appeared in a parade followed by a dinner. He tried to say a few words but each word was like "a pain in his lungs." The illness was called a severe cold but from his symptoms must have been considerably more than a cold—probably pneumonia. When the presidential tour finally arrived in New York, Pierce made a long speech at a reception in Castle Garden which was followed by a parade. During the parade there was a storm and Pierce was drenched. He was to make a speech at the Crystal Palace after the parade, and when he finally appeared on the platform he looked "tired and old." The next day, after attending several festivities the night before, he arrived back in Washington so ill that he had to take to his bed, tired and ill. It was noted at that time that he appeared "broken and wretched" from heat, malaria, and the political troubles in Kansas. John W. Forney, who had been with the president on the trip, wrote to Buchanan and implied that "the place overshadows him and he is crushed by his great duties and seeks refuge in. . . ."[12] Forney was implying that Pierce had returned to his excessive use of the bottle. In November 1866 Pierce suffered from neuralgia (not recorded where). The pain was so severe that he had to cease work, and one may speculate that he suffered from neuralgia brought on by low intake of food and high intake of alcohol. Peripheral neuritis is not uncommon in such cases.

During the second year of Pierce's presidency, in the summer of 1854, he became ill again with chills and fever—undoubtedly malaria. This illness was followed by a recurrence in the fall of 1856. There is reason to believe that he had attacks of malaria from the Mexican War until he died. Pierce failed to be renominated for a second term and this failure caused him a great deal of distress. The death of Pierce's wife in 1863 crushed Pierce so much that he returned to a marked overuse of alcohol. He had for a while during his presidency placed some restriction on his consumption of alcohol, but now he made no attempt to curb this addiction.

Pierce's overuse of alcohol apparently gave him a chronic gastritis, which in turn interfered with proper nutrition. He apparently suffered some liver damage also, another result of his great overindulgence.

Pierce also suffered from a chronic cough which some writers have thought to be tuberculous in origin. Part of this assumption is due to the fact that Pierce was exposed to his wife, who was presumed to have had tuberculosis. His doctors blamed his chronic cough on the dampness and poor heating in the White House.[13] While a clinical diagnosis of tuberculosis in the lifetime of Pierce was probably fairly good, the disease could be similar to many other chronic pulmonary diseases. The tubercle bacillus was discovered some time after Pierce died by Robert Koch, a German bacteriologist. We can only say for sure that Pierce and his wife suffered from chronic debilitating pulmonary disease. General Andrew Jackson's biographers attributed Andy's chronic pulmonary disease to tuberculosis. There could be no specific diagnosis because Jackson lived much before Koch discovered the tubercle bacillus. Francis Tomlinson Gardner, a surgeon, examined the fragments of Jackson's health problems in a precise and masterful way, and concluded that his pulmonary problem was due to bronchiectasis secondary to a chronic infection. Bronchiectasis is a disease which might simulate tuberculosis in many ways.[14]

In 1865 Pierce, who had never before been religious, became very devout and was baptized in the Episcopal church. Pierce at that time abstained completely from alcohol but, unfortunately, his giving up of his lifetime habit came too late. The ex-president was in the terminal stage of liver cirrhosis. In Pierce's final years he suffered from weakness, loss of appetite, nausea, and abdominal pain. During his last few months he developed what is common in late liver cirrhosis, a very large accumulation of fluid in his abdominal cavity. Alcoholism occurs in a very high percentage of patients who have cirrhosis, so we must conclude that alcohol was the causal agent in Pierce's case. Terminally Pierce became comatose, which is a common end-point symptom of cirrhosis. He spent his last summer in Little Boar's Head by the sea. He died in a coma October 8, 1869.[15]

References

1. James Morgan, *Our Presidents*, p. 117.
2. Roy Franklin Nichols, *Franklin Pierce*, p. 16.
3. Rudolph Marx, *The Health of the Presidents*, p. 161.
4. Nichols, *Franklin Pierce*, p. 30.
5. Ibid., p. 63.
6. Marx, *The Health of the Presidents*, p. 162.
7. David C. Whitney, *The American Presidents*, p. 112.
8. Nichols, *Franklin Pierce*, p. 69.
9. Ibid., pp. 86–87.
10. Ibid., pp. 165–66.
11. Marx, *The Health of the Presidents*, pp. 162–63.
12. Nichols, *Franklin Pierce*, pp. 282–83.
13. Marx, *The Health of the Presidents*, p. 165.
14. Francis Tomlinson Gardner, "The Gentleman from Tennessee," *The Surgeon's Library — Surgery, Gynecology, and Obstetrics* 30 (March 1949): 404–11.
15. Homer F. Cunningham, *The Presidents' Last Years*, pp. 103–04.

15

James Buchanan

James Buchanan, the fifteenth president of the United States, was born on April 23, 1791, near Mercersburg, Pennsylvania. He was the only president who never married. As a youth he showed a rebellious streak. He was expelled from Dickinson College at the end of his first year for insubordination, but later he was reinstated and allowed to complete his college education.[1]

Nothing of note was recorded about the health of Buchanan in his childhood and youth, except that he was always in good health.

Buchanan's life was marked by the peculiar habit of tilting his head to one side. The condition is presumed to have been caused by abnormalities of his eyes. One abnormality was the divergence of the pupils, the left placed slightly higher than the right due to a congenital flaw in the eye muscles. The other abnormality was nearsightedness in one eye and farsightedness in the other. He had a habit of closing one eye or the other in order to compensate according to the distance of the object he was scanning. The permanent twist of his neck was felt to be due to his efforts to make correction of his vision by turning his neck.[2]

Buchanan's adult life was also marked by heavy drinking of hard liquor. No single-bottle man, he would dispose of two or three bottles at a sitting, beginning with a stiff jorum of cognac and finishing off with a couple of glasses of old rye. According to one source, there were no after-effects. He was as calm and watchful as before.[3] The press often commented upon his "resisting power against the fumes of intoxicating drinks." He performed feats that would have startled the statisticians. One friend commented, "The madeira and sherry that he had consumed would fill more than one wine cellar."[4]

Buchanan also had very frequent attacks of "biliousness." It was also recorded that when he faced a hard political fight he suffered from nausea, violent headaches, diarrhea, and vomiting.

Toward the end of his term as secretary of state in 1849 under Polk, Buchanan developed a nervous tic in his leg and painful tumors in his nose. Removal of the tumors, presumably polyps, required a series of operations spread over a year and a half.[5]

When Buchanan became president, he was almost 66 years of age. He was described at the time of his election in 1856 as a hopeless, inept old man who was unable to cope with the tremendous demands made on him by the crucial times in which he came to office. His face was drawn and flour-pale, swollen, and furrowed. His black silk suits seemed to swallow his fleshy, puffy physique.[6] He had been violently ill for several months while the presidential campaign was on. At times he had very severe attacks of nausea, vomiting, and diarrhea. These attacks kept him near the slop bucket into which he would vomit until he was empty.[7]

Soon after Buchanan was elected president, but not yet in office, he attended a large dinner given in his honor at the National Hotel in Washington. The party was attended by many of his friends and supporters. Buchanan and a large number of those attending came down with a severe attack of dysentery. There were two theories about the cause of the outbreak. One contended that rats had fallen into the attic reservoirs of the hotel and drowned. The water from the attic reservoirs was used for cooking in the hotel. Others believed that during the very cold winter the water pipes in the kitchen had frozen and that sewage had backed up into the room where the food was prepared. Whatever the cause, several dozen people became extremely ill. One of Buchanan's favorite nephews, who was attending the party, died. The president suffered terribly for several weeks and may have had his judgment affected while preparing his inaugural speech.[8]

Remarkably, Buchanan contracted dysentery again, this time on the eve of his inauguration. He attended a preinaugural ball on the night before given at the same hotel, the National Hotel, which was owned by one of Buchanan's good friends and supporters. He had allowed the party to be held there to show his confidence in his old friend. Buchanan suffered for several weeks after the inauguration from this second bout of dysentery. He was so sick the next day that he was not sure he would be able to give his inaugural address. Many other guests were also very ill with the same disease. One guest later died of his illness. This endemic outbreak of severe dysentery was thereafter called "National Hotel Disease."[9]

After Buchanan ended his term as president in February 1861, he hoped for a quiet, peaceful retirement at his beautiful estate, Wheatland. He was, however, not permitted this luxury. He was persecuted as a traitor. The southern sympathies that he had shown added strength to the accusation that he had been responsible for the fall of Fort Sumter. He received many insulting and threatening letters. Buchanan's ills were at times precipitated or exacerbated by the vast amount of calumny piled on his head. At first the attacks made the ex-president violently ill, but he later became more immune to the insults and began to prepare to defend himself.[10]

The "violent illnesses" were headaches, vomiting, and diarrhea, in addition to gout. In a letter to a Mr. Capen, dated September 23, 1867, from Wheatland, Buchanan wrote, "I have had another attack of my old enemy, the gout, in a very severe form, which I am just now recovering from."[11] And again, in a letter to Mr. Johnson, dated November 14, 1867: "I fear that I shall not be able to pay you a visit for months to come. Like all old men, I feel a great reluctance to leave home. The idea of becoming dangerously ill away from home deters me from going abroad. Although relieved from acute pain in my left hand and arm, yet my hand is still so weak and swollen that I cannot carve. And to add to all this, my left eye is now as black as if I had been fighting with Shillelaghs at Donnybrook Fair. On Saturday last, supposing that I was at the head of the steps on the front porch, I took a step forward as if I were on the level, and fell with my whole weight on the floor, striking my head against one of the posts."[12]

Buchanan's death came on June 1, 1868, in his seventy-eighth year. In a letter addressed to George Tichner Curtis, Annie Buchanan wrote: "In his last year he began to feel that he was very old and looked forward to death and spoke as if he expected it constantly. He had attacks of gout, more or less severe up to the time of his death."[13]

Toward the end of 1867 Buchanan developed shortness of breath on mild exertion, and profound fatigue — symptoms suggesting heart failure. Without a doubt his chronic illnesses — gout, dysentery, and heart failure — made Buchanan susceptible to these illnesses which claimed him terminally on June 1, 1868, at the age of 77. He died of pneumonia.

References

1. David C. Whitney, *The American Presidents*, pp. 119–20.
2. Rudolph Marx, *The Health of the Presidents*, p. 169.
3. Philip S. Klein, *President James Buchanan*, pp. 210–11.
4. Ibid.
5. Ibid., p. 192.
6. William Seale, *The Presidents' House*, 1:333.
7. Klein, *President James Buchanan*, p. 69.
8. Elbert B. Smith, *The Presidency of James Buchanan*, p. 23.

9. Klein, *President James Buchanan,* pp. 22–23.
10. Smith, *The Presidency of James Buchanan,* p. 195.
11. George Tickner Curtis, *Life of James Buchanan,* 2:659.
12. Ibid., p. 660.
13. Ibid., p. 665.

16

Abraham Lincoln

Abraham Lincoln, the sixteenth president of the United States, was born February 12, 1809, near Hodgenville, Kentucky.

He was born at a time and lived under such conditions that life was most precarious. The presence of isolated illnesses was obscured and made to seem almost insignificant by the prevalence of frequent epidemics that sometimes erased whole families and even entire communities. When Lincoln was nine years of age, for example, an epidemic of milk sickness struck the Indiana community in which his family lived. Lincoln's mother, Nancy Hanks, was killed by that disease along with many others of that prairie community. Milk sickness, or "milk sick," was an illness common among settlers of the Midwest and was caused by a poison transmitted by the milk from cows fed on poisonous plants such as snakeroot.

At any rate, no record of Lincoln's specific childhood illnesses has survived. And although much has been written about Lincoln's health problems, organic and emotional, most of it is about his emotional health and a great deal of it is highly speculative in nature.

For instance, some biographers feel that Lincoln's morbid thoughts, and at times deep depression, were conditioned by his many close encounters with death: his mother, his sister, many of his friends and neighbors, and almost himself. Among Lincoln's memories of his early years in Kentucky was a time when as a child he almost drowned in Knob's Creek. While Abe was struggling in the water, a neighbor's boy went into the water and kept him from drowning.[1] The doctrine of fatalism instilled in him by his mother led Lincoln to believe that he was saved from drowning by divine providence.

One of Lincoln's dreams, which seemed most prophetic, occurred only a few weeks before his assassination. This dream was related by Lincoln to Ward Hill Lamon, a friend of Lincoln. The dream possibly occurred following his return to the White House after seeing a performance of Gounod's *Faust* and about the time he was so physically depleted that he held cabinet meetings in his bedroom. Abe dreamed that he was awakened by the sound of sobs from many weeping people. He wandered down the stairs and went from room to room all lit, but empty of people. He kept on until he reached the East Room. When he entered he saw there a catafalque on which there was a corpse in funeral dress. There were soldiers around the catafalque on guard, and there were many people around the corpse mourning. The face of the corpse was covered. "Who is dead in the White House?" he asked a soldier. "The President," was the answer. "He was killed by an assassin."[2]

In fact, it is apparent that Lincoln believed in the signs, myths, and superstitions of his time. A single confirmation of Lincoln's belief in the supernatural came when he believed so much in the potency of the "madstone" that he took his young son, who had been bitten by a dog, to Terre Haute, Indiana, to have the magic stone applied.

Pierce Clark felt that even though Lincoln's bent toward mysticism and superstition were essentially a part of his inheritance, this did not account for all of it. Again Clark noted that Lincoln derived pleasure from reading mystical and philosophical works. In his happy moods he occupied himself with wit and humor and love of the comical. But for the most part he was inclined to ponder over works with a gloomy content.[3]

Clark also seemed convinced that Lincoln believed in the supernatural. At times Lincoln professed not to believe in superstitious dreams, but one notes that Lincoln's whole mood, his very attitude about his dreams shows that whatever may be his logical conscious opinion, the unconscious is not so disposed. In other words, Lincoln did believe in the supernatural.[4]

Once, too, Lincoln suffered a dangerous blow to the head. As a youth one of Lincoln's chores was driving an old horse to turn a grist mill. Lincoln once lost his patience with the old nag and struck him with a whip. Abe was caught unawares when the animal let fly her unshod hooves and caught him square on the head. He was knocked unconscious, suffered a concussion, and was out for a day.[5]

The young Lincoln did undergo one interesting preventive treatment. When his family moved to Pidgeon Creek in Indiana, the area was described as being on a hill surrounded by swamps. The region was infested by mosquitoes which carried malaria, and the children had to take Peruvian bark to ward off the disease.[6] (Peruvian bark, or Jesuit's bark, contained the drug quinine, which was effective against malaria. This remedy had been in use in some South American countries for 150 years before being introduced to this country).

Most interest about Lincoln's organic health, however, centers on his great height and angularity. As early as 11 years of age he started a growth spurt which presaged his great height of later years. When he was 16 he was more than 6 feet tall, and at 17 he towered at 6 feet 4 inches. At 17 he weighed 160 pounds. His head was small, and his arms and legs were disproportionately long compared to his trunk.[7] Disproportion between limb and trunk length became most apparent when he sat and then rose to his full height. When sitting he did not seem tall, but when he got up slowly it seemed that he would never reach full height. According to Stephen Oates, "Parts of him did not seem to fit. His head appeared too small for his height, and his chest was narrow and thin in contrast to his long arms and legs and his huge hands and feet."[8]

From his general habitus as described by his close friend and law associate William Herndon, we would be tempted to speculate on the possibility that he suffered from Marfan's Disease, a congenital illness characterized by abnormal body proportions. In Marfan's Disease the extremities are long and thin, and almost all who suffer from the disease are tall; the distance from the top of the pelvis to the sole of the feet is increased in proportion to the upper half of the body. Extremely long, thin fingers (arachnodactyly), or spider fingers, are found in most patients, as is a dislocation of the lens of the eye. There is no question that Lincoln had a great number of these characteristics, but all we can do is speculate. No one ever subjected Lincoln to an examination which would have proved such a diagnosis. In his late teens Lincoln nevertheless developed tremendous strength in his legs, chest, and arms. Abe, according to his biographers, became recognized as the best all-around athlete in the Centerville neighborhood.[9]

If Gore Vidal's historical novel *Lincoln* is to be believed, however, Lincoln was engaged in more than just wholesome outdoor activity. According to Vidal, Lincoln, while practicing law in Springfield, before his marriage, had visited a brothel. Vidal was presumably quoting Herndon, Lincoln's old law partner. Vidal further wrote that in 1835, at age 24, he had visited a girl in Bargetown and there had contracted syphilis.[10] Vidal even speculates that the syphilis accounted for Lincoln's periods of depression; that Lincoln infected Mary Todd Lincoln, who died of central nervous system syphilis; and that Lincoln infected three of his children, who died prematurely. Stephen Oates stated, "Such prattle tells us more about Vidal than about Lincoln, for there is not a shred of truth in it."[11]

Although Lincoln did have some organic illnesses, more by far of Lincoln's medical history is concerned with his mental malady—depression—which he apparently suffered from childhood on in varying degrees. It is said that he suffered greatly from his mother's death, and that the winter immediately following was the winter of a deep depression.

Apparently, the second greatest tragedy in Lincoln's life was the loss of his betrothed, Ann Rutledge, who had consented to become Lincoln's wife in the spring of 1839. Her death apparently was a tremendous calamity for Lincoln. He grieved for a long period of time. He went many times to weep over her grave; and at that time to some of his close friends he seemed to be on the brink of madness. Abe recovered gradually over several months. There was, after his recovery from the more profound depression, a recurrence of less severe episodes of depression which had no apparent cause, and he himself termed them unreasonable.

Lincoln had a third great period of anxiety and depression following his engagement to Mary Todd. It is stated by some and denied by others that when the time for the wedding came the Reverend was there, the guests were there, the refreshments were on hand, the bride was there in veil and beautiful gown, but there was no Lincoln. Hours passed and the groom had not appeared. The guests gradually left, greatly puzzled. The stricken bride retreated to her room. Lincoln was found after several hours by his friends in a state of agitated depression. His state was such that those close to him were afraid he might do himself harm, and they chose not to leave him alone. He was watched night and day, and all instruments of possible self-destruction were removed. Ninian Edwards, brother-in-law to Mary Todd, and his wife, Elizabeth Edwards, were not hesitant in declaring Abe insane. Clark wrote that Lincoln's profound depression came on due to the fact that he was unable to adapt himself to the full requirements of marriage itself: "This despondency was as deep as that seen in the depressive psychosis. There was retardation of thought and action, periods of extreme silence, listlessness, indifference, loss of appetite, and insomnia; all alternating with moods of anxious restlessness. He had gloomy forebodings and thoughts of suicide."[12]

Another version of the same story mentioned nothing regarding preparations for a wedding and a failure of the groom to appear: Lincoln had become engaged to Mary Todd, but in January 1841, while serving in the Illinois legislature, he broke off his engagement. Following the breaking off of the engagement came a profound depression. As his melancholy became deeper, he called on Dr. Anson Henry, who labeled Lincoln's state as "hypochondria." Dr. Henry said that Abe's depression was due to extreme anxiety, overwork, and exhaustion. After a week of deep despair, insomnia, and loneliness, he returned to his seat in the legislature. His colleagues were shocked by his appearance. "He looked emaciated," said James Concklin, "and seems to have barely enough strength to speak above a whisper."[13]

Which version is nearer the truth is really not too important. The first was related by Herndon, who was given to questionable hyperbole. Herndon wrote, "Lincoln was crazy as a loon and did not attend the legislature in 1841 and 1842." He wrote further that Lincoln had to be watched constantly. However, according to the records of the legislature, Lincoln was in his seat on the first day of January and thereafter his attendance was regular. His attendance to the close of the session on the first of March was as good as or better than average.[14] However, the important aspects agree in both stories. Essentially, Lincoln became estranged from Mary Todd and suffered a long period of depression.

Even after his marriage to Mary Todd, though, his depression recurred periodically. In 1847–48, while the U.S. representative from Illinois, Lincoln became involved in a controversy over which country was the aggressor in the Mexican War. Lincoln felt that the war was unjust and that the United States was the aggressor. Apparently, his view got few supporters, and it was essentially ignored by the Congress and the president. The president did not condescend to answer and this lack of attention to Lincoln caused him to respond with a deep depression and to cease to fight for this cause. He then suffered in silence. In some of his letters to Mary there are hints of a period of depression in April 1848.[15]

When Lincoln left Washington in 1849 and returned to Springfield to practice law, he felt his days as a politician were over. During the next five years he frequently fell into fits of depression marked by occasional manic outbursts in which he seemed totally withdrawn and filled with some self-pity.[16] Lincoln was described as being markedly fascinated with madness, obsessed with death, and troubled with recurring bouts of melancholy.[17]

One of Lincoln's very severe periods of depression came after he received news of the terrible Union and Confederate losses at the battle of Chancellorsville. Lincoln had entrusted the Army of the Potomac to General Hooker. After the armies were engaged, Lincoln was in such a state of tension that he was unable to sleep. The battle lasted for three days. It was early on the third day that the bad news began to come in from the battlefield. The whole day Lincoln was in great distress and was unable to sleep or eat. On the evening of the third day of that battle he went to the War Department where he stayed with Edwin Stanton to receive news from the battle. Finally, the news of Hooker's retreat and the story of the dreadful losses came in from the field. Lincoln was extremely depressed at the news. He started to leave the War Department, but Stanton felt his state to be so low that he was afraid to leave him alone. Stanton persuaded the president to remain at the War Department with him. Stanton told Lincoln that he should remain there, try to get a few hours of rest, and the next morning visit the battlefield. Stanton related that the idea of visiting the battlefield acted like a tonic to the president, who acquiesced immediately. The next morning Stanton and Lincoln went to the battlefield. On the trip back to Washington Lincoln, according to Stanton, confessed to him that on the night before when he started to leave the War Department he had fairly made up his mind to go immediately to the Potomac and there to end his life by drowning. This is yet another episode when Lincoln had entertained suicidal thoughts during a time of depression.[18] Lincoln's family was described by many as sad and gloomy. His mother and sister both had very melancholy dispositions. Nancy Hanks was described as having eyes like "pools of sadness." Lincoln remembered Nancy Hanks, his mother, taking him and his sister to the grave of her youngest child. The brother and sister had scarcely known the infant, but the mother's grief was so great that Lincoln never forgot the scene.[19] It was natural that Abe himself after his exposure to so much disease, death, and hardship would also have a gloomy outlook.

There was another period of depression in Lincoln's life related to the unexpected death of his son, William. This particular time of depression was different from others in its duration. From his history one would have expected the great loss to have been accompanied by a very long period of depression. The intensity was as marked as usual for such circumstances, but the duration — the severe state — was only a few days. It is contended by some writers that Lincoln at this time had a religious experience, that he made a full reconciliation with God, and from that time on it was seen that a calm and peace entered into his attitude toward life.[20]

It is alleged by others that Lincoln was able, especially in later years, to depend on wit to assuage his bleak, despairing moments. He is supposed to have said that he could not survive without wit and humor. Lincoln's need for wit and humor at times to expel his periods of deep despondency may be likened to that of Mark Twain, who once said the "secret source of humor is not joy but sorrow."[21]

Pierce Clark, in his *Lincoln: A Psychobiography,* outlined Lincoln's emotional life as a series of melancholic episodes. Edward Kempf felt that the president's depressions were due to the concussion caused by being kicked in the head by a horse. Others, such as Herndon and Vidal, alleged that his emotional problems were due to cerebrovascular syphilis. The latter idea is generally discounted.

Psychobiologists have also proposed that Lincoln was an undersexed man, that he preferred the company of his male friends to that of women. It is also said that Lincoln married without the slightest sexual intent; he entered marriage for social reasons and perhaps political ones.[22]

They have alleged that Lincoln was afraid of dentists perhaps due to the one dentist who broke off a piece of his jawbone while pulling a tooth without anesthesia. Rudolph Marx wrote that in 1862 Lincoln had a very severe toothache and consulted his dentist, Dr. G. S. Wolf, who had offices near the White House. When Dr. Wolf prepared to pull the tooth, Lincoln waved the instrument off. "Just a minute, please," he said, and took a container of chloroform from his pocket, inhaled it deeply, and sleepily gave the signal for the dentist to proceed with his work.[23]

Lincoln did, though, encounter a number of organic illnesses during his adult life. For example, when Lincoln was campaigning for the presidency in 1860 he developed a sore throat, headache, and fever. His son, Willie, at the same time, was in bed with scarlet fever. Lincoln felt that he himself had a different form of the same disease. He was probably right, since scarlet fever and a form of sore throat are both due to the same organism, streptococcus-A. Lincoln had a temporary malaise which lasted only a few days.[24]

After Lincoln gave his immortal address at Gettysburg, during his trip back to Washington, he was almost completely exhausted. He became ill after he returned to the White House with what the doctor called "varioloid," a less severe form of smallpox. Lincoln joked, "Where are the office seekers?" Now he had something he could give everybody and nobody wanted it. Lincoln was confined for only a short time with this illness.[25]

Lincoln's eyes are of some interest. His eyesight remained good until he was 45–48 years of age. He was 47 when he required glasses. On a shopping tour to Bloomington, Indiana, he purchased his first pair of glasses for 37 cents, which helped him with small print. The glasses, still preserved, are six and one-half diopters strong. These were about three times stronger than Lincoln actually needed. The use of these extraordinarily strong glasses might help to explain why Lincoln had severe headaches after reading for long periods of time. Lincoln was also color blind. He was unable to enjoy the sight of beautiful flowers or the colorful clothes that his wife wore. In addition, Lincoln suffered from an imbalance of his eyes. Some photographs of Lincoln show the left pupil to be higher than the right and closer to the eyelid. This muscular imbalance of the eyes was probably aggravated by fatigue. Under the condition of eye fatigue the eyes may diverge widely in the vertical direction, and there may be double vision. One image may be shown sharp and clear and the other blurred.[26]

It is possible also that he may actually have had Marfan's Disease, which could have interfered with his sight due to a dislocation of the lens which may occur in this disease.

The ending of Lincoln's story has been told and retold many times, and there were so many witnesses to his assassination and its sequel that it need not be retold here. Extraordinary bad luck and careless guards allowed the assassin to penetrate the presidential box at Ford's Theater and fatally wound Lincoln with a pistol shot in his head from behind. John Wilkes Booth temporarily escaped by theatrical flourish, but within a few days Booth was overtaken and slain. Lincoln died on April 15, 1865, the victim of assassination.

However, there are those intruders in the dust who feel that the remains of Lincoln, at this remote time, must be probed to determine the presence or absence of Marfan's Disease. The interest in Marfan's was increased in late 1991, when a researcher requested the National Museum of Health and Medicine to permit the removal of Abe's blood, bones, and hair to determine whether Lincoln had that genetic disorder. A panel met to advise the museum on how such a study might be conducted. Dr. Victor McKusick, an expert in Marfan's Disease, was adviser.[27]

However, the committee which was convened by the National Museum of Health announced on Wednesday, April 16, 1992, that there was not at present enough known about the genetic role in Marfan's Disease and that improvements in the ability to recover and analyze DNA from historical material were anticipated.[28]

So the residue of this immortal man may remain undisturbed for a while longer.

References

1. Stephen B. Oates, *With Malice Toward None*, p. 5.
2. Rudolph Marx, *The Health of the Presidents*, pp. 177–78.
3. Pierce Clark, *Lincoln: A Psychobiography*, pp. 531–32.
4. Ibid., p. 537.
5. Marx, *The Health of the Presidents*, p. 180.
6. Emil Ludwig, *Lincoln*, p. 11.
7. Edgar Lee Masters, *Lincoln the Man*, p. 21.
8. Stephen B. Oates, *Abraham Lincoln, the Man Behind the Myth*, p. 34.
9. Benjamin B. Thomas, *Abraham Lincoln, a Biography*, p. 14.
10. Gore Vidal, *Lincoln, a Novel*, pp. 288–90, passim.
11. Oates, *Abraham Lincoln*, p. 21.
12. Clark Pierce, "Unconscious Motives Underlying the Personalities of Great Statesmen," *Psychoanalytic Review* 8, no. 1 (January 1921): 13.
13. Oates, *With Malice Toward None*, p. 62.
14. Ida Tarbell, *The Life of Lincoln*, 1:180.
15. Gabor S. Boritt, editor, and Norman O. Farness, associate editor, *The Historian's Lincoln*, p. 231.

16. Ibid., p. 262.
17. Oates, *Abraham Lincoln*, p. 54.
18. Clark, *Lincoln: A Psychobiography*, pp. 383–84.
19. Tarbell, *The Life of Lincoln* 1:26.
20. Ibid., 3:92.
21. Justin Kaplan, *Mr. Clemens and Mark Twain*, p. 124.
22. Masters, *Lincoln the Man*, p. 147.
23. Marx, *The Health of the Presidents*, p. 184.
24. Oates, *With Malice Toward None*, p. 200.
25. Ibid., p. 397.
26. Marx, *The Health of the Presidents*, p. 178.
27. Journal of Facts on File, May 2, 1991, p. 587.
28. *Greensboro News and Record*, April 16, 1992, p. A-10.

17

Andrew Johnson

Andrew Johnson, the seventeenth president of the United States, was born in poverty in Raleigh, North Carolina, on December 29, 1808. He never had a day of formal schooling and was largely self-taught except for the tutoring by his wife, Eliza McCardle, who taught him the three R's.[1] However, Johnson built on this foundation and became a well-educated man.

Johnson's frequent references in later years to his poverty-stricken childhood were accurate. His father died when Andrew was just three. His mother tried to feed and clothe her two sons, but her earnings from taking in washing were inadequate. Andrew never forgot, nor chose to let others forget, his background of grinding poverty. In later years Andrew would say, "I have grappled with the gaunt and haggard monster called hunger."[2]

Despite a youth marked by stark poverty and hunger, there is no record of his having any childhood illness. In those days, however, childhood diseases were taken for granted and no public record was kept.

Johnson worked as a tailor's apprentice, 1822–24; married Eliza, May 17, 1827; was alderman of Greeneville, Tennessee, 1828–30; was mayor of Greeneville, Tennessee, 1830–33; was a member of the Tennessee House of Representatives, 1835–37 and 1839–41; was a member of the Tennessee Senate, 1841–43; was a U.S. representative from Tennessee, 1843–53; was governor of Tennessee, 1853–57; was a senator from Tennessee, 1857–62; was military governor of Tennessee, 1862–64; and was vice president of the United States, 1865.

In 1843 Johnson became a U.S. congressman from Tennessee. He was still a congressman in 1847, but he was at odds with his own party and had a strained relationship with President Polk and with his own constituents in Tennessee. Needless to say, Johnson was not happy. He was in poor health and according to other biographers suffered problems with his legs, arms, and heart.[3] The exact nature of these problems, however, is not known.

In January 1857, during Johnson's last year as governor of Tennessee, he went to Washington on an official visit. The Tennessee legislature had voted to buy Andrew Jackson's home, the Hermitage, and to offer it to the United States, on the condition that it be used as a western military academy. Johnson delivered to President Pierce the property, the resolution of the Tennessee legislature, and the draft of a bill to be presented to Congress asking that the Hermitage be accepted. The bill did not pass, however, and on the return trip Johnson had a near fatal accident. His train was derailed, and he was severely injured.[4]

The train in which he was traveling met with an obstruction, and the car in which he was passenger went down a bank nearly 30 feet high. His right arm was severely injured. Johnson had to wait until he arrived in Nashville to get medical attention—a distance of several hundred miles. In Nashville surgeons were called and made an attempt to reset the fractured bones. After Johnson suffered for several weeks, it was discovered that the bones had not been properly set. The surgeons were called again, and their decision was that the only possibility of restoring normal function would be to break the arm again and reset it. His arm was rebroken and reset, followed by several weeks of great pain. Another examination revealed that the efforts of the surgeons had restored no function in his arm. Johnson offered to submit to yet another operation, but his surgeons felt that the damage to his arm was not reversible. Johnson was thereafter unable to write without pain, which probably accounts for the fact that so many of his papers are not in his own handwriting.[5]

In 1862, while Johnson was serving in the Senate in Washington, Confederate soldiers raided his home in Greeneville, Tennessee, and drove out his wife and eight-year-old son, both of whom had pulmonary tuberculosis. After great difficulties the two were able to reach the home of relatives several miles away. The young son recovered from his illness, but Mrs. Johnson remained an invalid as long as she lived.[6] Further grief visited Johnson in 1863 while he was serving as military governor of Tennessee. His son, Charles, a physician, was thrown from a horse and killed.[7]

Even without these family misfortunes, Johnson's term as military governor of Tennessee (1862–64) was a very stressful one.

For years he struggled to contain the rebellion in his state and to return Tennessee to the Union. He was consequently hated by the South. When he finally returned to Washington in March 1864, he was exhausted and suffered from a fever which was labeled variously as typhoid and malaria. The illness was so severe that his doctor kept him in bed for several weeks. Whatever illness was involved, it was severe and left him very debilitated.[8]

He was just beginning to recover from this severe illness when the time came for his inauguration as vice president. Lincoln had been appreciative of Johnson's efforts during the war to help hold the Union together, so much so that he asked for him as running mate. The illness had left Johnson in such a weakened condition that he felt unable to go through the ceremony. To add to his problem he had attended a party on the night before the inauguration and had drunk a great deal of wine, which aggravated his condition.[9] Johnson did not wish to attend the ceremony, but Lincoln insisted.

Just before entering the Senate chamber, while waiting with Vice President Hamlin and others, Johnson felt nauseated and faint, too ill to go ahead with the inaugural ceremony and speech. Johnson requested some whiskey, and since there was none in the Senate chamber, Hamlin sent a page to get some. Johnson drank too much and during his speech was obviously under the influence. The scene embarrassed Lincoln and others attending the ceremony. This slip provided future ammunition for those who were opposed to Johnson and gave a handle to the radicals, who began to speak of him as the "drunken tailor." Papers all over the country printed the accusation and spoke of his special train as a traveling barroom.[10]

In spite of the unfortunate incident at the inauguration, there is no evidence that Johnson was a drunk; and, in fact, Lincoln came to his defense asserting that Johnson was not a problem drinker. There is no record that after his election to vice president that he was ever again inebriated during his presidency.

Throughout his vice presidency and, especially, his presidency, Johnson did, however, suffer from chronic dysentery — recurring attacks of intestinal cramps. He also had a problem with kidney stones and renal colic, which occasionally gave him great pain.[11]

These recurring problems came notably during the June 1865 trial of Mrs. Surratt, one of the individuals supposedly involved in Lincoln's assassination. Her case was a touchy one; the members of the court who sat in judgment apparently wished to see Mrs. Surratt executed but wished to be absolved from any responsibility for her death. Accordingly, Secretary of War Edwin Stanton and others worked out an arrangement whereby Mrs. Surratt would be found guilty and sentenced to hang but a recommendation would be added that President Johnson commute the penalty to a life sentence. At that time, however, Johnson was sick in bed and was denied all visitors. He was under excessive strain and emotional stress and he also had several medical problems — renal colic produced by kidney stones, and malaria.

The recommendation for clemency never came to Johnson's attention, and Mrs. Surratt was hanged. Stanton is accused of having plotted to withhold the request to the board to reduce Mrs. Surratt's sentence to life imprisonment. But many other petitioners for clemency besides Mrs. Surratt were unable to present their petitions to Johnson, due to his illness.[12] Never at that time nor later, was the president made aware that the trial board had made a recommendation for clemency.[13]

The execution of Mrs. Surratt troubled Johnson greatly, and for weeks after he suffered from severe headaches. After this there emerged a rumor that the president had refused to see those who wished clemency because he was drunk.[14]

Stanton was central also in the attempt to impeach Johnson. In the spring of 1867 Johnson removed Secretary Stanton from office, a radical Republican who had been an obstructionist in Johnson's cabinet. In order to try to impeach Johnson, the radical Republicans invoked the 1867 Tenure Office Act which forbade the president to remove from office any federal official who had been appointed with the advice and consent of the Senate. The trial lasted two months and imposed great stress on President Johnson. During this period of great stress, Johnson continued to have severe pain, due to kidney colic.[15]

Johnson, at age 62, finally left the White House in 1869 and returned to his home in Tennessee. Soon thereafter he suffered a recurrence of his malaria and had to deal with the suicide of his son Robert, a very sensitive young man, who could not face life in the way his tough-minded father had been able to do. Robert was a chronic alcoholic who suffered from depression and sought solace in the bottle.

In 1871 there was an epidemic of cholera in Tennessee. Johnson chose to remain in Greeneville to help those afflicted with the disease. He finally contracted the disease himself. This illness was complicated by the fact that he had, through his chronic gastrointestinal problem, a greater susceptibility to the epidemic than others. For a time he was near death and never completely recovered.[16]

In 1875 (elected in 1874) Johnson returned to the U.S. Senate and was as active a representative of Tennessee in the Senate as his health would allow. After the first session was over, he returned to his home in Greeneville, Tennessee, to take care of private matters. Since his prostration by cholera two years before, however, his health had not been good. In addition to his other problems he was also having some difficulty with his heart.[17]

On July 28, 1875, he went to visit his daughter, Mary Stover, at Carter Station, Tennessee. He reached his daughter's home about an hour before noon. After lunch he retired to his room, and as his granddaughter was leaving the room she heard a thud. Johnson had fallen to the floor. He had suffered a stroke.

His left side was paralyzed. He remained conscious and able to speak and forbade anyone to summon a doctor. He was put to bed, but he remained restless. His mind wandered as he reviewed his past — his struggles and triumphs. The next day he had a second stroke that left him totally paralyzed, and he lost consciousness. He lingered until 2:30 A.M., July 31, 1875, and expired.[18]

References

1. David C. Whitney, *The American Presidents*, p. 142.
2. Thomas Lately, *The First President Johnson*, p. 11.
3. Hans L. Trefousee, *Andrew Johnson*, p. 66.
4. Lately, *The First President Johnson*, p. 107.
5. Leroy P. Graf, and Ralph W. Haskins, editors, *The Papers of Andrew Johnson*, 2:525.
6. Rudolph Marx, *The Health of the Presidents*, p. 197.
7. Ibid.
8. Lately, *The First President Johnson*, p. 189.
9. Albert Castel, *The Presidency of Andrew Johnson*, p. 9.
10. Howard K. Beal, *The Critical Years: A Study of Andrew Johnson and Reconstruction*, p. 13.
11. Marx, *The Health of the Presidents*, p. 199.
12. Ibid., p. 200.
13. Lately, *The First President Johnson*, pp. 350–51.
14. Ibid., p. 352.
15. Castel, *The Presidency of Andrew Johnson*, p. 36.
16. Marx, *The Health of the Presidents*, p. 202.
17. Robert W. Winston, *Andrew Johnson*, p. 506.
18. George Fort Milton, *The Age of Hate*, p. 693.

18

Ulysses S. Grant

Ulysses S. Grant, eighteenth president of the United States, was born April 27, 1822, in Point Pleasant, Ohio. He was really christened Hiram Ulysses Grant. Through some error when he was registered at West Point he was registered as Ulysses S. Grant. He did not later call the mistake to anyone's attention.[1]

Very little can be found regarding Grant's health as a child or youth. The cadet from a little town of southern Ohio was strikingly unnoticeable. His slight frame did not invite the taunts of the worst hazers. James Longstreet called Grant "delicate" and recalled that he had been too small (5' 1", 117 pounds) to excel in any sport save riding, which he did well.[2]

When Grant graduated from West Point he was 6 inches taller at 5 feet 7 inches but not in good health. When he arrived home, he was down to the 117 pounds he had weighed 4 years earlier. He was suffering from a respiratory ailment that made him fear tuberculosis, since there had been some in his family. The illness, however, proved to be of no importance. Some of his biographers later stated that he probably had tuberculosis, but this doesn't seem to be borne out in the overall picture.

Not much more was heard about Grant's health until the Mexican War. This war began when Grant was serving as a second lieutenant, first under Zachary Taylor and then under Winfield Scott in 1845. Fellow officers remembered Grant at this time as being "careless about his dress, wearing hair and whiskers long and ragged." "He chewed tobacco," they said, but at that time never drank to excess nor indulged in the profligacy so common in Mexico.[3] When the Mexican War was over, Grant got a leave of absence and returned to St. Louis where on August 22, 1848, he married Julia Dent.

Grant was first posted to Sackets Harbor, New York, where he, apparently on his wife's insistence, joined the Sons of Temperance and discoursed on the evils of rum. "There is no safety from the ruin of liquor," he declared at that time, "except by abstaining from it altogether." At Sackets Harbor he had hardly anything to do, so under the strain of idleness the temperance pledge was forgotten.[4] During the 1850s he was assigned to the military post of Fort Vancouver on the West Coast. He left his wife and children in St. Louis, feeling he could not afford to take them west, but while living alone on a dull army post he began drinking heavily. Finally, in 1854 he was forced to resign his commission.[5]

He had begun to use whiskey in Mexico, and he was always a solitary drinker. When he was under the influence of whiskey he was morose and downcast. It was felt by one biographer that it was plausible to believe his bitter distaste for the military life started him on his drinking habits.[6]

One careful observer noted that Grant actually drank "far less than other officers whose reputations for temperance were unsullied, but with his peculiar organization a little did the fatal works of a great deal." A Fort Vancouver regular army man insisted that Grant was not by any means a drunkard but merely indulged in two to three sprees per year. Grant was always open to reason, and when rebuked on the subject would own up and promise to stop drinking—which he did. Grant hated to be alone, and whiskey was his solace. He hated the military, and he needed the presence of Julia, who was always able to reduce his drinking a great deal.[7]

In fact, it was discovered that when Julia was around, Grant drank much less, so great efforts were made in later days, if possible, to have Julia near him.

Grant was promoted to captain in 1853 and was transferred to Fort Humboldt, in California. There, without Julia, he was melancholy, silent, gloomy, and he got the reputation for being a souse. He drank in a peculiar way, holding his little finger even with the bottom of the tumbler and holding his other three fingers above the little one, and then filling the whiskey to the top of his first finger. He took it without water, and he often drank every day.

Perhaps it gave him courage for, in addition to his military work, he went on with a new business project, a billiard room in Frisco, which did not pan out. He continued to drink. Lieutenant Colonel Robert Buchanan liked Grant, but when Grant turned up for paymaster duty drunk, Buchanan told him to fill out an unsigned resignation. Another binge and Grant would sign that resignation, Buchanan said.[8]

Grant's problem was that he essentially had nothing to do. At Humboldt he was away from his wife and two sons. He was lonely and depressed, so he responded by drinking. There are markedly different reports concerning the manner in which he at that time concluded his army life. One writer, William McFeely, wrote, "Grant did not leave the Army because he was a drunk. He drank and left the Army because he was profoundly depressed." Another account of his manner of leaving was given by McFeely,

"On April 11, 1856, while listed on the Company roll as sick, U.S. Grant wrote two letters, one formally accepting promotion to Captain, a permanent rank. The second letter read, 'I very respectfully tender my resignation of my commission as an officer of the Army!'"9 Another version was that after Colonel Buchanan's warning, he drank again at a party. The next day Grant reported to Buchanan's office. Buchanan took out the unsigned resignation and asked Grant what he thought his proper course was now. Grant signed it. It was on April 11, 1854. He was now a civilian.10

After leaving the army in July 1854, he rejoined his wife and children at St. Louis to settle with his family on a small farm. Charles Dana reported "He threw aside completely the habits of Army life and went to work bravely with his own hands to better his family."11 Dana was wont, however, to greatly understate Grant's failings.

Grant felt that he had done well until 1858, when he was attacked by fever and ague, undoubtedly malaria. He stated then, "I had suffered very severely from this disease while a boy in Ohio." Apparently, although the biographers haven't mentioned it much, he did have malaria back in Ohio. This attack of malaria lasted over a year, and while it didn't keep him in the house it did interfere greatly with the amount of work he was able to perform.

It would have been unusual for malaria to have lasted a year when it was treated with quinine. He may have either been treated inadequately with quinine, or he may have formed a resistance to the medication.

In a letter to his sister, Mary, September 7, 1858, he wrote of much sickness in his family. His son, Freddie, at first had bilious fever and then typhoid fever. Julia and he were both sick with chills and fever.12

Marx speculated further that Grant may have reactivated the tuberculosis in his lungs.13 However, it is felt that protracted malaria and poorly treated malaria were enough to explain his debility. Besides, there is not enough evidence in any of the studies of Grant's life to indicate that he ever had tuberculosis in the first place. Grant spent four years trying to succeed as a farmer. His failure seems to have been due to his illness in the last year of that endeavor. After his failure as a farmer he tried selling real estate in St. Louis.

All the evidence points to his being a failure in that venture also. "His clothes became ragged, his shoulders drooped more than usual; poverty found him pawning his watch the night before Christmas in order to bring cheer to his family."14

There is evidence also that he continued to drink. Perhaps he was not drinking as much as he did in the army, but it is recorded that he did drink with his old army comrades when they visited him.

After his failure as a real estate salesman he moved his family to Galena, Illinois, where he worked in his father's leather store. He was 39 years old, penniless, and discouraged.

The onset of the Civil War signaled an abrupt change in Grant's fortunes. Here was a trade that he did not particularly like, but it was at least a trade that he knew. His history of alcoholism was a great barrier to Grant, although he was a West Pointer and had 11 years of service. Four days after Beauregard fired on Fort Sumter, the president issued the call for 75,000 volunteers. Four days later a company was enrolled at Galena, Illinois, and Grant, being the only man in town who knew anything about the military, became responsible for drilling this company. Four days later he went with the company to Springfield and reported to the governor for service.[15]

Grant's rise in the military was rapid, and this was due partly to the fact that there was such a small reserve of men who knew much about military science. Also helpful was Congressman Elihu Washburne from Illinois, who was responsible for nominating a new brigadier general. Washburn nominated the only colonel among his constituents who had military experience—U.S. Grant.[16]

Another person who influenced Grant's career was John A. Rawlins, a lawyer from Galena. Rawlins was an admirer of Grant and was a "fanatic teetotaller." Grant didn't drink in Galena, and his conquering of rum made him a hero to Rawlins. Rawlins himself was a former alcoholic who had reformed, and like other reformed individuals he became very obsessed with the idea of reforming others. Rawlins later became a member of Grant's staff and a self-appointed guardian of Grant's conscience.[17]

The man who recommended him to Grant's staff was Congressman Washburne. Washburne knew a great deal about Grant's reputation with the bottle. He felt that since Rawlins was such an avid abstainer that he might be a good one to keep an eye on Grant.[18] Rawlins wanted so much to be admired by Grant that he could test their friendship by admonishing Grant not to indulge in alcohol. Sometimes these warnings were listened to; sometimes they were ignored.[19]

Once when rumors came to Washburne that his protégé was drinking heavily at his headquarters in Cairo, Rawlins responded with "a cordial and telling letter." Rawlins wrote, "I would say unequivocally and emphatically that the report that General Grant is drinking very hard is utterly untrue. When I came to Cairo, General Grant was as he is today, abstinent, and I have been informed by those who knew him here, that such has been his habit for the last five or six years." Rawlins went on to detail every drop of wine, beer, or spirituous liquor that he had seen Grant consume in the three months he had been at Cairo. Of course, Grant was an alter ego to Rawlins; and it is reasonable to assume that he was as protective of Grant's reputation as he was of his own, or more so. Perhaps he had built his own expectations consciously or unconsciously upon Grant. He apparently saw a great future for Grant, and he expected his fortunes to be interlinked with those of Grant.

There are reports from many sources that Grant gave his word to Rawlins that he would drink no more for the duration of the war.

After the fall of Fort Donaldson there was a new outbreak of rumors that Grant, after the battle, had resumed his old habits. General Henry Halleck sent a telegram to Major General George McClellan which stated, "Word has just reached me that since the taking of Fort Donaldson General Grant has resumed his bad habits." It seems that his former reputation remained an albatross.[20]

Grant, a few days before the Battle of Shiloh, suffered a very painful injury to his ankle. On the morning when the battle started at Pittsburg Landing on the west bank of the Tennessee River, his ankle was painfully swollen. At the beginning of the battle Grant was nine miles away at Savannah, Tennessee. He heard the sound of the guns while he was eating his breakfast. Grant said to his staff, "Get the boat ready at once and let's be moving."

Late in the day of the battle stragglers and prisoners brought to the Union Army a rumor that Albert S. Johnston was dead. This rumor was soon followed by the cessation of the Confederate offensive.[21] The loss of Johnston to the Confederacy perhaps contributed more to the Union cause in winning than did Grant's skill.

After the Battle of Shiloh, where the federal arms had sustained horrible casualties, and following the celebration, Grant's past again pursued him. "Grant was pilloried, charges of cowardice and drunkenness filled the newspapers, Grant was wearied and depressed."[22] Grant was accused by journalists of being drunk on the field of Shiloh, not being on the field at all, and of running away.[23]

During the time when Grant was maneuvering to get his army into position to attack Vicksburg, he claimed to be in good health, but he was suffering from indigestion and a painful case of boils. His mouth was sore, his servant threw away his only set of false teeth, and Grant had to chew without teeth. He also was having attacks of severe sick headaches. These headaches were in other places labeled as being migrainous in nature. Julia was there administering vinegar water and mustard plaster. In June 1863, after Grant had crossed the Mississippi from the west side and approached the town of Vicksburg from below and behind, he became restless and impatient. Vicksburg was surrounded and was being shelled from all sides. Grant had little to do. Sherman reported he was complaining of "illness," and a few days later Charles Dana, the correspondent, noted that Grant was "ill." Apparently with Dana and William T. Sherman and others, "ill" was a euphemism for a resort to the bottle by Grant.[24]

What transpired may have been comical had the times not been so tragic and the main actor in the scene so important in the play. Three weeks after the fighting had turned into a dull seige, the man who was more able than anyone else to control him under such circumstances was away. On June 5 Rawlins found a box of wine in front of Grant's tent and had it removed. Grant protested, but to no avail, that he was saving it to celebrate the fall of Vicksburg. Rawlins learned also that Grant had accepted a glass of wine from an army doctor. These were danger signs, and Rawlins sat down after midnight and wrote Grant a letter: "The great solicitude I feel for the safety of the Army leads me to mention what I had hoped never again to do, the subject of your drinking."[25]

Grant, however, left early the next morning, apparently before the letter reached him, on a tour of inspection up the Yazoo River to Satartia, where he had posted a division should the Confederate General Johnson come that way. The day trip without his conscience, Rawlins, became a two-day spree.[26] In what became one of the most celebrated scandals of the war, on June 6 he apparently got very drunk.

Charles Dana, who accompanied Grant on this spree, and protected him as well as he could, related 25 years later that the episode really happened. On the way upriver from Haines Bluff they met the steamboat *Diligent* coming down. Grant hailed the vessel, whose captain was a friend of his, transferred to her, and had her turn back upstream to Satartia. On board was Sylvanus Cadwallader, a *Chicago Times* correspondent, on the prowl for news. The bender lasted for two days and for Cadwallader it was more like a two-day nightmare. "He made several trips to the bar room of the boat in short time and became stupid in speech and staggery in gait." Cadwallader secured him in his stateroom, locked the door, and commenced throwing Grant's supply of whiskey through the window and into the Yazoo River. Grant protested, but to no avail. The reporter gently but firmly persuaded him to remove his coat, vest, boots, and lie down. After much resistance, finally Grant went to sleep.[27]

Shortly before dark when the *Diligent* came near Satartia, a naval officer came aboard to warn Grant that Confederate troops had been sighted and it was unsafe to proceed. Charles Dana knocked on the stateroom door to ask Grant whether the boat should turn back. Grant, he reported later, was "too sick to decide," and told him, "I will leave it to you." Thus, under strange circumstances, we have a civilian with no portfolio whatever making decisions for a two-star general. Grant was awake then and decided that he would dress and go ashore. This was in spite of the warning that it was not safe. Once more Cadwallader was able to persuade him to go back to bed. While he slept, the boat made its way south to Haines Bluff.

The next morning, according to Dana, Grant was "fresh as a rose, clean shirt and all, quite himself." When he came to breakfast he observed, "Well, Mr. Dana, I suppose we are at Satartia."[28] Apparently, he was totally oblivious of all that had happened. He truly didn't know his whereabouts.

Cadwallader, in spite of Grant's marked error in geography, relaxed his vigilance. He was greatly shocked, a while later, "that Grant had procured another supply of whiskey from on shore and was quite as much as intoxicated as the day before." Finally, Cadwallader and his escort loaded their horses for the five-mile ride back to the army headquarters.[29]

Cadwallader, by his help at this time, saved Grant from what might have been a total disgrace. After this caper Rawlins gave Grant a severe tongue-lashing, reminding him of his pledge not to drink anymore. The remorseful Grant very solemnly repeated his pledge.[30]

Soon after the capture of Vicksburg, Grant was invited to New Orleans to celebrate. He was lavishly entertained by his army of friends. It was in New Orleans that Grant's new pledge to Rawlins was broken. His more generous biographers, including Dana, reported that he seemed to have "fallen ill on several occasions," that is, he was intoxicated.

On this same trip to New Orleans, while he was returning from a review given in his honor, his horse ran away from him, dashed against a carriage, and fell with its whole weight on Grant's leg. He was carried on a stretcher to the St. Charles Hotel, and there he lay for two weeks, until he had at least partially recovered.[31]

The next rumors of Grant's indulgence in heavy drinking came during and after the Battle of the Wilderness with its terrible loss of life. The newspapers throughout the United States were full of stories of his drinking.[32] It is written that on the first day of the second Battle of the Wilderness Grant wore white cotton gloves, and that he was visibly nervous for the first time during the war. Horace Porter said that Grant smoked 20 cigars from nightfall and had whittled sticks all day.[33]

It is indeed strange that considering the confusion, slaughter, and horror of that campaign that someone could have the time for such a trivial pursuit as counting the general's cigar butts. Horace Porter was on Grant's staff so he must have been in a position to make this observation.

Grant apparently throughout the Wilderness campaign suffered from boils and migraine headaches. He was still suffering from boils after the Battle of Spotsylvania and Cold Harbor. It was related that he treated his migraine headaches with chloroform.[34] The enemies of Grant reported that he was drinking when he ordered the murderous assaults on Cold Harbor, but there is no proof of this.[35]

During the days of the Union siege of the fortification at Petersburg, the assaults were stymied and it appeared that the offense ought to be put off until spring. Grant, apparently, at this time fell off the wagon at least once, and disgraced himself during a "bibulous trip to visit General Ben Butler at Norfolk." Predictably, he became "ill" again in the reports, presumably a long drunk, and during December took to his bed.[36]

On the day before Lee's surrender and before the meeting at Appomattox Grant was suffering from an excruciating migraine headache. The headache was still severe six hours before he met Lee. Grant's aide went to wake him on April 9. He found him outdoors pacing, and clutching his head in both hands. The pain was apparently relieved to some degree by coffee.

From the time the Civil War was over and until he became president there was very little written about his drinking habits. Presumably, he drank much less during this time. During his presidency coffee was apparently the only drink which he regularly used. Opponents continued to accuse him of indulgence in drink and actual drunkenness. There is no firm evidence that he drank to any extent while he was president more than a glass now and then of wine. The records in the White House show some wine was ordered for use there, but not an excessive amount.[37]

His eating habits were most unusual. The president would eat only beef, and if the beef were cooked rare he would not touch it. In fact, he preferred his meat very well done — almost charred. It was said that Grant would not eat anything that walked on two legs. Many of the foods he liked were difficult to digest, but there is no record of his having suffered greatly from gastrointestinal upsets except rarely during the war itself.[38]

There is some evidence that throughout the late years of Grant's life he was a very heavy smoker of cigars. Grant was interviewed by the editor of the *Lewiston Journal,* a Washington publication, on May 12, 1866. The correspondent spent an hour in conversation with Grant, and Grant was quoted as saying: "I am breaking off from smoking. When I was in the field I smoked 18 to 20 cigars per day, but now I smoke only nine or ten per day."[39]

Grant's health when he assumed the presidency was relatively good. He did later develop a paunch which was not present at the time of the

Civil War. Much good food and good wine supplied by cronies were the cause of this. He ceased to ride horseback and took up buggy racing. There is no word anywhere that he took any form of regular exercise.

After Grant's political career was closed, he trusted the wrong people and suffered great financial reverses which left him almost destitute. He had been appointed by President Arthur as the commissioner to draw a Treaty of Commerce with Mexico. After this he invested all or a great deal of his money in Brand and Ward, who were in the banking business. Before his financial failure came a physical injury on Christmas Day, 1883. Grant was returning home from a social call, and when he turned to pay the cabbie he slipped on the ice and severely injured his thigh. For several weeks he was unable to walk. While still confined by his thigh injury he developed an attack of pleurisy, which kept him in bed for several weeks. One wonders here if Grant's thigh injury and his prolonged confinement in bed may have resulted in a blood clot in his leg, followed by a pulmonary embolism. This would have easily explained his pleuritic pain. Just when he had recovered enough to walk on crutches, his financial disaster struck.[40]

When Grant was 62 years old, 30 pounds overweight, and lame, his recent injury to his thigh was still troubling him. And then one day while eating a peach he experienced a severe pain in his throat.[41]

His wife, Julia, at the time wondered if he had been bitten by an insect which was concealed in the peach. Grant felt at first that the discomfort was due to an ordinary sore throat, but the pain persisted. A Philadelphia doctor was asked to examine Grant's throat, and immediately, after taking a look, he advised Grant to see his own doctor as soon as possible. Grant delayed such action for several weeks. He had hoped the pain would go away on its own. Finally, on October 22, 1884, he saw his own doctor, and was on the same day sent to see a throat specialist, Dr. James H. Douglas. Douglas knew at once what he was dealing with. Grant asked, "Is it cancer?" Douglas answered, "The disease is serious, epithelial in character, and sometimes capable of being cured."[42]

In late February 1884 a group of specialists diagnosed the growth as an epithelial cancer of the malignant type, that was sure to end fatally.[43] Only a short time before the discovery of the malignancy Grant had contracted to write his memoirs. What followed was nearly 12 months of agonizing pain. This 12 months and a struggle to finish his memoirs was probably the most courageous battle of Grant's entire life. For some time after the discovery of the cancer Grant went to Dr. Douglas's office almost every day. Douglas expended his efforts trying to reduce the size of the lump that went "from the size of a pea to the size of a plum." Dr. Douglas painted the area with hydrochlorate of cocaine to relieve the pain. The cancer spread over the palate. The patient gave up cigars not too reluctantly. He stated that his cigars were indeed giving him much less satisfaction of late.[44]

In January 1885 he had some easing of his symptoms and his writing progressed. By mid–February the ulceration began to increase rapidly. The lump grew so that he had the problem of swallowing. In late February the patient had frightful pain in one ear. In early March he suffered nausea, headache, and sleeplessness. It was an agony to drink anything. "If you could, imagine what molten lead would be like going down your throat," he told George W. Childs. "This is what I feel like when I swallow."[45]

In April his suffering was so great that brandy was injected into his veins. For months he suffered from great pain and sleeplessness. He was unable to lie down, but in the daytime he continued without ceasing to write.

Grant sat at a large table and worked with remarkable steadiness, mornings and afternoons. On March 28, 1885, his doctors expected him to die. On April 7, 1885, an artery in his diseased throat ruptured, causing him such severe hemorrhage that it seemed certain he would not endure through the night. With the help of digitalis, cocaine solutions, and morphine solutions, he was saved temporarily.[46]

One painful problem at this time was severe coughing and vomiting. His condition was so poor that it was hard to determine why some improvement in his feelings occurred. It was speculated by one medical expert that "he bled into his tumor, the tumor cells died, and were sloughed away." There must be some truth in this, since the tumor was smaller and less painful.

After this, for a short while, he was able to dine, go for drives, and work on his book. He had a sense of urgency because he wished to finish the book before he died. He wished for the completion of the book to financially insure his wife.

Grant was very factual and realistic. On June 17, 1885 he wrote a memorandum to his physician, Dr. Douglas, in which he told Douglas that he would die of "hemorrhage, strangulation, or exhaustion." He did, however, let Douglas know that he dreaded more doctors, more treatment, and more pain.[47]

In June Grant had been moved to Mount McGregor, New York, to try to escape the heat. He and his family occupied a cottage there on the top of the mountain. By June 15, 1885, the summer heat had begun to aggravate his already poor condition. His cancer had become rooted in deeper tissue, his neck was swollen, his speech difficult, and his pain was great.[48] On July 22 Grant wrote on his pad that he wanted to lie down. "Does it seem good to lie down in bed?" someone asked, leaning over him. "Yes," he whispered, "so good." As the evening came on, his feet were very cold and his breathing very labored. On the morning of July 23 he died.[49]

He had displayed such courage that his physician paid him perhaps his finest tribute. "Nine months of close attention have only endeared him to me. I have learned to know him as few have known him. The world can know him as a great general, and as a successful politician; but I know him as a patient, self-sacrificing, gentle, quiet, uncomplaining, sufferer, looking death calmly in the face and counting almost the hours he had to live, and the hours were studied by him that he might contribute something of benefit to some other fellow sufferer. If he was great in his life, he was even greater in death."[50]

References

1. David C. Whitney, *The American Presidents*, p. 150.
2. William S. McFeely, *Grant: A Biography*, p. 14.
3. Nancy and Dwight Anderson, *The Generals, U.S. Grant and Robert E. Lee*, p. 87.
4. W. E. Woodard, *Meet General Grant*, p. 104.
5. Whitney, *The American Presidents*, p. 152.
6. Woodard, *Meet General Grant*, p. 86.
7. Anderson, *The Generals, U. S. Grant and Robert E. Lee*, p. 121.
8. Gene Smith, *Lee and Grant*, p. 65.
9. McFeely, *Grant*, p. 55.
10. Smith, *Lee and Grant*, p. 65.
11. Charles A. Dana, *U. S. Grant, General of the Armies of the U.S.*, p. 30.
12. U. S. Grant III, *Ulysses S. Grant, Warrior and Statesman*, p. 106.
13. Rudolph Marx, *The Health of the Presidents*, p. 207.
14. William B. Hesseltine, *Ulysses S. Grant: Politician*, p. 16.
15. Dana, *U. S. Grant, General of the Armies of the U.S.*, p. 42.
16. Hesseltine, *Ulysses S. Grant: Politician*, p. 21.
17. Anderson, *The Generals, U. S. Grant and Robert E. Lee*, p. 170.
18. Ibid., p. 205.
19. McFeely, *Grant*, p. 87.
20. Anderson, *The Generals, U. S. Grant and Robert E. Lee*, p. 231.
21. Woodard, *Meet General Grant*, p. 250.
22. Anderson, *The Generals, U. S. Grant and Robert E. Lee*, p. 240.
23. Ibid.
24. Ibid., p. 303.
25. Shelby Foote, *The Civil War*, 2:417.

26. Ibid.
27. Ibid., p. 418.
28. Ibid.
29. Ibid., p. 419.
30. Marx, *The Health of the Presidents*, p. 214.
31. Woodard, *Meet General Grant*, p. 301.
32. Hesseltine, *Ulysses S. Grant: Politician*, p. 41.
33. Woodard, *Meet General Grant*, p. 320.
34. Anderson, *The Generals, U. S. Grant and Robert E. Lee*, p. 396.
35. Marx, *The Health of the Presidents*, p. 215.
36. Anderson, *The Generals, U. S. Grant and Robert E. Lee*, p. 417.
37. Hesseltine, *Ulysses S. Grant: Politician*, p. 310.
38. Ibid., p. 301.
39. John Y. Simon, editor, *The Papers of Ulysses S. Grant*, 16:257.
40. Hesseltine, *Ulysses S. Grant: Politician*, pp. 446–47.
41. McFeely, *Grant*, p. 495.
42. Smith, *Lee and Grant*, p. 349.
43. McFeely, *Grant*, p. 303.
44. Smith, *Lee and Grant*, p. 350.
45. Ibid.
46. John B. Moses, and Wilbur Cross, *Presidential Courage*, p. 105.
47. McFeely, *Grant*, p. 505.
48. Ibid., p. 507.
49. Woodard, *Meet General Grant*, p. 502.
50. Moses and Cross, *Presidential Courage*, p. 106.

19

Rutherford Birchard Hayes

Rutherford Birchard Hayes, the nineteeth president of the United States, was born October 4, 1822, in Delaware, Ohio. He was the beneficiary of a political bargain aimed at ending what seemed an oppressive rule of the Southern states by the North during the Reconstruction days.

Hayes's father died three months before Hayes was born, from an infectious disease, the exact nature of which is not known.[1]

From his birth and early childhood "Rud" led a sheltered existence, due in part to his feebleness at birth. When he was one year old he was so frail and emaciated that his uncle, Sardis Birchard, feared that he would always remain in this feeble condition. Until Hayes was seven he was not allowed to play with other children, and he was nine before he was allowed to play games with other boys. Rud was not allowed to do the easiest physical tasks; and he was, for several years, not allowed to attend the district school. His mother taught him at home to read, spell, and write.[2]

It is probable that his mother really coddled him, for his illness seemed to have ended when he was about four years of age. However, his mother continued to be very protective for several more years. Part of his mother's overprotectiveness was due perhaps to the fact that he had no father.

Rud spent a great part of his youth at the home of a wealthy maternal uncle, where he worked as a farmhand. The vigorous activity of farming allowed him to grow much stronger. Besides farming, he engaged in hunting, fishing, swimming, and skating. It is probable that he, like Teddy Roosevelt, felt a physical inadequacy and sought to remedy it. After some time he became a very strong, broad-shouldered young man with a fine physique.

Rud entered Kenyon College, Ohio, in 1838 at the age of 16. He was a good student and, in addition, he found time for outdoor sports. He was actually a champion runner at Kenyon. While in college he also played baseball, but after a hand injury he had to give up that sport. His engagement in sports increased his strength greatly. Apparently, Hayes had inherited the courage of the pioneer stock, for when he broke through the ice one day while skating, he felt no panic but remained calm until his companions rescued him.[3]

Hayes entered Harvard Law School in 1843 at the age of 21, receiving his bachelor of law degree in 1845. During the time he was a student in Cambridge he apparently remained in good health.

Hayes started his law practice in Lower Sandusky, Ohio, where he was described as "a strong young man, good to look at, and well groomed, his auburn hair and blue eyes exuding health and determination."[4] Later in Hayes's law practice in Sandusky he fell in love with a young maiden named Fannie Perkins. He was deeply involved emotionally and had great difficulty in trying to decide just how he should pursue the young woman. This romance failed, however, deep depression resulted, and Hayes fell into a state of mental and emotional confusion.[5]

Rutherford's failed love and the routine work of his law practice at Sandusky all combined to undermine his health to such an extent that his friends became concerned. Hayes was so restless and depressed that he finally decided that a change might be good for him, and the Mexican War seemed to promise just such a diversion.

On June 1, 1847, he decided to volunteer for service in the Mexican War. However, he decided to seek medical advice before he made his final commitment. His doctors, R. D. Mussey and Dresbach, advised against such a venture. It was felt by his doctors that the Mexican climate might further erode his already poor health. After Hayes received this advice from his doctors, he withdrew from a company that he had already joined. His doctors at this time advised bleeding, cod liver oil, snakeroot, and a Northern climate.[6]

Hayes's medical problem before and during the Mexican War was recurrent tonsillitis. This was apparently the problem which kept him out of the conflict. In 1849 he developed quinsy, "a peritonsillar abscess," which was treated with rest, purges, and cod liver oil. There was no incision or drainage. The abscess was allowed to drain on its own.[7]

In December 1846, Hayes was feeling desperate. He had failed in his awkward pursuit of Fannie Perkins and he was on the verge of a nervous breakdown. Physically, he was troubled with bloodshot eyes and a chronic cough so severe that at times he coughed up blood. He had difficulty in concentrating, and lost interest in his work and everything else. Hayes had some fear that he was becoming mad. He feared that he might finally have to go to a lunatic asylum. Hayes consulted doctors about his cough and blood spitting, which suggested tuberculosis, but his doctors decided that he did not have pulmonary tuberculosis.[8]

It is, however, indeed probable that he did have pulmonary tuberculosis. His symptoms were very suggestive of it. There were, however, no X rays at that time, and Wilhelm Röntgen, the man who discovered X ray, was born only in 1845. Robert Koch, the great German bacteriologist who first isolated the tubercle bacillus, was born in 1843, only three years before. Also, it is fairly well established that the best physical diagnostician may fail to diagnose tuberculosis, even in a fairly well-advanced stage, unless he has all the laboratory and X-ray techniques at his command.

For some time Hayes's health followed a series of improvements and declines. Having abandoned the idea of going into the Mexican War, for example, he took a trip to New England. In the mountains and at the seashore he recuperated during the summer months, and in September 1845 he returned to his law practice, much improved in health. However, after another year his health problems recurred, and he was compelled to rest again. In December 1848 Rud and his uncle, Sardis Birchard, went to Texas. The trip and his stay in Texas lasted until the spring of 1849. He was apparently much refreshed, but during the summer of 1849 he closed up his law practice in Sandusky and moved to Cincinnati. The move was made due to his health since Hayes and his doctors felt that the climate in Cincinnati was better than in Sandusky. At the time of his change in residence Hayes suffered from chronic throat trouble and a chronic cough. He still feared that he might develop tuberculosis.[9]

R. B. Hayes was one of five U.S. presidents who served on the Union side in the Civil War and became generals. However, Hayes was the only one of these five generals who was wounded. His most serious wound was sustained at the Battle of South Mountain on September 14, 1862. The Battle of South Mountain was really a prelude to the Battle of Antietam. The battle was fought by Lee as a delaying action to hold the passes over the mountain long enough so that Jackson might rejoin him. Jacob D. Cox was the commander of the Kanawaha Division in which Hayes served as colonel commanding the 23d regiment. The 23d regiment attacked over Foxes Gap, and after Hayes's attack began he forced the defenders to retreat to a position behind a stone wall. The Federal advance seemed to be going well, and Hayes ordered another advance. Just at the time he gave the order to advance, he felt a severe blow to his left arm. He had been struck by a musket ball just below his left elbow joint.[10]

Hayes's first concern was that the bullet may have severed an artery, so he had one soldier apply a handkerchief as a tourniquet above the point where the bullet had entered. The ball had splintered one of the forearm bones and lacerated a large blood vessel. After the injury Hayes felt so weak and faint that he lay down on the ground and from that position continued to give orders for the battle. Before Hayes was removed from the battlefield, he transiently lost consciousness. After he was removed, he was taken to the regional surgeon who gave him opiates for his pain and some brandy. After the brandy he felt well enough to walk half a mile to the private residence of a Mr. Kugler. An ambulance finally arrived and carried him to Middleton where a Dr. James Webb saw Hayes and informed his family that his compound fracture would require a prolonged recovery period.[11]

Hayes was fortunate on that battlefield in the choice made not to amputate. In the Civil War the usual thing to do when someone had a bullet wound with a compound fracture was to amputate. Stonewall Jackson, who suffered a similar wound at Chancellorsville, had his arm amputated and he subsequently died. Such surgery was done at that time under almost primitive conditions with unsterilized instruments and unsterile hands. The patient could die of shock or infection, and a very high percentage did just that. The surgeon at times held the knife between his teeth while he was using his hands to help the patient onto the operating table. "The surgeon snatched the knife from between his teeth, wiped it rapidly once or twice on a blood-stained apron, and the cutting began."[12]

After several weeks Hayes returned to his regimental command. Following his wound at South Mountain, he remained in good health until the Battle of Cedar Creek, which was fought in the Shenandoah Valley when General Jubal Early caught the troops under General Philip Sheridan in an unwatchful state. During this battle Hayes commanded a division. In the flight of Hayes's division before the advancing rebels his horse was struck by a bullet, and Hayes was thrown to the ground so forcefully that he temporarily lost consciousness. When he awoke, he was not aware of how long he had been unconscious. However, he was aware that he had a pain in one of his ankles but found that he could walk in spite of it. At that moment some Confederate soldiers arrived and demanded that he surrender, but Hayes escaped into a dense area of woods. Before he was able to return to his division, he was struck by a spent bullet, which only stunned him momentarily. Eventually, Hayes caught up with his staff, borrowed a horse, and was finally able to regain his division near Middleton. Hayes's injuries, while painful at the time, were not severe, and there was no permanent disability.[13]

While Hayes was still fighting, the people back home nominated him for Congress in 1864. Elected, he took his seat in Congress in December 1865. He was nominated for governor of Ohio in 1867 and reelected to a second term in 1869. After leaving the governorship, he ran without success for U.S. Congress in 1872. He retired to his home in Spiegel Grove, where he believed himself to be through with public life. However, three years later, in 1875, he was again nominated governor. One year later Hayes was nominated and elected to the presidency of the United States. The decision was greatly resented by the Democrats, who felt the election had been stolen.

While president, Hayes received a number of threatening letters. He ignored the threats until one evening while the family was eating, a bullet came through a window, passed through two walls and lodged in the wall of the library. Thereafter, he took greater precautions.

Hayes, like Teddy Roosevelt, became very aware of weakness and frailty at an early age and strove mightily to maintain a state of physical fitness. When he became president at the age of 54, he was still in good physical condition. He exercised each day, and on days when the weather was bad he did his walking on the piazza. He was careful of his health and made efforts to see that the public was made aware of it. Through a correspondent of the *Cincinnati Commercial,* he outlined his daily routine: "I rise with the sun both winter and summer, and seldom use the gas to dress by. This makes me get up early on the long days of the year, but in the winter I sometimes lie in bed as late as 7:00. I do all of my disagreeable work before breakfast, and I solve my most knotty problems at that time. I walk at least six miles a day and often more."[14]

In regard to Hayes's habits: he drank only one cup of coffee for breakfast, and it is not recorded that he at any time used tobacco or alcohol—at least socially. It is stated that later in life he used some alcoholic beverages as a tonic.

Hayes retired from the presidency in 1881 to his home in Spiegel Grove. After his retirement he was quite active for a few years in various civic endeavors. However, in his late sixties he began to show signs of deterioration. In an attempt to stay healthy and physically fit, he had spurned such vices as alcohol and tobacco and had adhered rather rigidly to a program of physical exercise.

In his late sixties it appeared that the element took over that one cannot control—his genes. He progressively began to be visited by some infirmities of age. He gradually lost his memory for recent events, he gained weight, and he lost his vigor.[15] These late health concerns of Hayes would lead to the conclusion that he was suffering from some arteriosclerotic changes. At this time he also developed some nerve deafness, which progressed until he had difficulty in carrying on a conversation. The loss of hearing led to social isolation. The less he understood what people were saying the more suspicious he became that they were talking about him.[16]

On June 25, 1889, at the age of 67, there came to him a very devastating emotional blow when his wife, Lucy Ware Webb, aged 57, died of a stroke. Hayes never overcame the grief that he experienced at this great loss.[17]

At the age of 70, on January 9, 1893, Hayes traveled to Columbus to attend a board meeting of Ohio State University. Afterward, he personally visited with ex–President McKinley and some others. He walked in very cold weather to the depot accompanied by Alexis Cope, secretary of the board at Ohio State University. When he came to the station, he had to wait for half an hour for the train, and Cope noted that as Hayes waited he seemed to be extremely nervous and depressed. When Hayes returned to Cleveland, he went to the Linus Austin home. On the next day, when there was a deep snow and a temperature near zero, he went by foot and by streetcar to visit, among other things, Western Reserve University. Afterward, Hayes went to the station with Joseph B. Webb, and after he arrived at the station he experienced some severe chest pain which did not go away. He was given some brandy which gave him some partial relief. Dr. Webb tried to get him to return to the Austin home, but Hayes refused, saying, "I would rather die at Spiegel Grove than to live anywhere else." When Hayes arrived back at his home he was put to bed immediately.[18] After he arrived at Spiegel Grove, he lingered for three days. At first his doctors were optimistic for his recovery but soon gave up hope. On Tuesday, January 17, 1893, he died.[19]

It was apparent from his past history and the prolonged chest pain which began at the station that he had sustained a myocardial infarction as the terminal condition. The evidence that he suffered from arteriosclerosis would lend great support to the diagnosis of arteriosclerotic heart disease and myocardial infarction.

References

1. Rudolph Marx, *The Health of the Presidents,* p. 228.
2. Harry Barnard, *Rutherford B. Hayes and His America,* pp. 73–74.
3. H. J. Eckenrode, *Rutherford B. Hayes, Statesman of Reunion,* p. 7.
4. Barnard, *Rutherford B. Hayes and His America,* p. 142.
5. Ibid., p. 155.
6. Ibid., p. 150.
7. Marx, *The Health of the Presidents,* p. 228.
8. Barnard, *Rutherford B. Hayes and His America,* p. 156.
9. Charles Richard Williams, *The Life of Rutherford B. Hayes,* 1:55.
10. T. Harry Williams, *Hayes of the 23rd,* pp. 137–38.
11. Ibid., p. 140.
12. Marx, *The Health of the Presidents,* p. 223.

13. T. Harry Williams, *Hayes of the 23rd*, pp. 302–4.
14. Eckenrode, *Rutherford B. Hayes, Statesman of Reunion*, p. 327.
15. Homer F. Cunningham, *The Presidents' Last Years*, p. 147.
16. Marx, *The Health of the Presidents*, pp. 231–32.
17. Cunningham, *The Presidents' Last Years*, p. 147.
18. Barnard, *Rutherford B. Hayes and His America*, p. 522.
19. Cunningham, *The Presidents' Last Years*, p. 149.

20

James Abram Garfield

James Abram Garfield was born in Orange, Cuyahoga County, Ohio, on November 19, 1831. The majority of individuals, when they think of the twentieth president, think first of his assassination. James Abram Garfield was sworn in on the Capitol steps on March 4, 1881. He was shot and wounded on July 2 of the same year, and died of his wound on September 19, 1881. The country had little time to evaluate him as a president.

Not a great deal has been recorded about his health except to say that early in life it was generally good. A friend at that time, Corydon Fuller, wrote: "My first impression of him as a young man . . . about six feet in height, powerfully built, with a head of bushy hair, and weighing about 185 pounds."

He decided at age 17 to become a sailor, but later left sailing and got a job as a "towboy," driving horses and mules pulling boats on the Ohio Canal. He fell off the narrow towpath many times, and, as he later said, "had fourteen almost miraculous escapes from drowning."[1]

The canal experiment was brought to a halt when he developed malaria on October 3, 1877. In his journal he wrote, "I was confined to my bed for ten days and on the tenth broke the ague. It stayed off about three weeks, and then it came again. I employed Dr. Butler, but his medicine had little or no effect. I continued to have the ague every day until January 30, 1849. I commenced doctoring with Dr. Vincent and Dr. Harmon of Chagrin Falls, and since that time I have not had the ague, although not able to work any."[2] He was attended, he wrote, by physicians of the "old school" and "was treated after the old style. I was given terrible doses of calomel, and only my powerful constitution could have saved me."[3]

In the winter of 1852–53, after he had thought that he was deeply in love, he discovered that he did not wish to marry the young lady after all. This discovery seemed to disturb him greatly. A painful explosion followed: letters, an interview, an outburst of gossip, and savage criticism from friends of the injured girl. With this he sank into a depression that lasted for months, until he could regain his composure.[4] It would seem that Lincoln and Washington were not the only presidents who became depressed over their failed love affairs.

For most of his later life Garfield was susceptible to gastrointestinal complaints, presumed to be due to his army life. Among the great plagues of our army and all of its wars before World War I, after malaria, the chief was dysentery. The army camp life under war conditions with questionable sanitation was very conducive to this problem. It is apparent that Garfield had recurrent dysentery, sometimes severe, throughout his army life.

In 1862, and again in the summer of 1863, while serving as brigadier general and chief of staff to General William Rosecrans in Tennessee, he was subject to severe attacks of dysentery and camp fever.[5] The attack in Tennessee was one of his worst, and came after his brigade had occupied the Confederate entrenchments. "I have fancied," he wrote to a friend on June 10, "that the two weeks breathing the breath of the great Rebel camp and all its sickness and offal has half poisoned my system."

On July 17 he wrote from Athens, Georgia, a more cheerful note regarding his health, but a week later Garfield endured a violent relapse of his chronic illness. He wrote in a letter on July 24, "I tell you, Harry, it is far from pleasant to toss on a bed of pain alone in a hot, sweltering room, hundreds of miles from those who care especially for your life and comfort, but I am better now, though weak."[6] There is a record that in August 1863 he was taken violently ill and lay sick at headquarters.

From the time Garfield was shot, July 2, 1881, until September 19, 1881, almost 11 weeks, was a period of great anxiety for the entire country. On the morning of July 2, 1881, President Garfield and Senator Blaine were entering the Baltimore and Potomac railroad station, where the president was to board a train to attend the twenty-fifth reunion of his class at Williams College, when a mentally disturbed, unsuccessful office seeker, Charles J. Guiteau, fired two shots. One struck the president in the arm, the other in the back.[7]

Garfield had paid scarcely any attention to his surroundings as he walked toward the train platform, deep in conversation with Blaine. This path took them by the ladies' waiting room, close to the spot where Guiteau was lurking. They were no more than halfway across the room when Guiteau came up from behind the president, extended his pistol at arm's length and fired into Garfield's back from less than a yard away. The president's hat flew off his head, he threw up his arms in the air, and cried, "My God! What is this?" Guiteau said nothing, but took two steps forward and fired once more as Garfield fell. With the second shot the president crumpled to the floor and Guiteau wiped off his pistol and put it back in his pocket.[8]

As the assassin's victim lay on the floor of the railroad station, his blood started to form a pool; the shock to his system caused him to vomit. The matron of the waiting room rushed over to place his head on her knee.[9]

The bullet entered four inches to the right of the spine, broke his eleventh rib, pierced the spine, but not the spinal cord, damaged the splenic artery, and lodged 2.5 inches to the left of the backbone below the pancreas. The other bullet grazed his left arm.[10]

To ascertain the track and location of the bullet, the doctors probed the wound with their unwashed fingers and instruments. They felt that the bullet had probably entered the liver. He was placed on a mattress and carried upstairs in the depot. The wound was dressed. There were a score or more of doctors milling about suggesting remedies, but no one took the initiative.

The first impression was that the wound was fatal. The president was not bleeding a great deal, and seemed to be in shock. Revived by a bit of brandy, Garfield suggested that he be removed to the White House and was carried from the station to the White House on an improvised litter.[11]

After he was removed to the White House, the sick room was number 18, a corner room on the south side of the second floor, overlooking the Potomac. It also overlooked the city's mosquito-laden canal, and concern over the president contracting malaria led them to give him regular doses of quinine.[12]

In the White House he was seen by a number of doctors who consulted together. From the wound and his symptoms it was agreed that he was experiencing internal hemorrhaging and would not last the night. During the rest of the day, the group of physicians did little more than watch the symptoms. After superficial examination of the wound and giving stimulants, they were under the impression that an attempt to extract the bullet would be fatal.[13]

As it transpires, it is highly likely that Garfield would have fared much better had they continued the mode of harmless nonintervention.

At about 7:00 P.M. Garfield asked Dr. Bliss, the surgeon general, to tell him frankly what his condition was. The doctor said to him, "Unless there is a reaction, you cannot live long." At 8:00 P.M. Garfield's mind was still clear.[14]

The doctors, from their statements, did not expect the president to live until morning. They were anticipating a rupture of the liver. Garfield had frequent spells of nausea and vomiting during the night. Late in the evening, however, his symptoms somewhat abated, and Dr. Bliss was hopeful.

The next morning the president was resting and free from symptoms. The nausea and vomiting had abated, and he had taken milk and lime water. Garfield chose Dr. Bliss, the surgeon general, for his chief physician. Drs. Joseph K. Barnes, Underwood, and Robert Reyburn were retained as consultants. Dr. Frank Hamilton of New York and Dr. Hayes Agnew of Philadelphia were also called in. Susan Edson, former army nurse, took over as head nurse.[15]

Some sources describe Susan Edson not as a nurse, however, but as a female homeopath from Cleveland, Ohio. Dr. Reyburn was described as a prominent surgeon and teacher of medicine. Dr. Bliss was almost 60 years old, partially bald, with flowing sideburns. He was described as being an able physician and a member of the District Board of Health, but his tendency to talk too much and his pompous air became a burden to the Garfield family in later days.[16]

At this time there was no possibility of Garfield performing any of his duties as president. He was in constant pain, except when relieved by an analgesic.

After Sunday morning, July 3, the bulletins about the president's condition were more encouraging. Day after day, as in the case of Dwight Eisenhower's heart attack in 1955, the public was given very minute clinical details about Garfield's condition.[17]

The Capitol returned to work on Tuesday, after a solemn July 4. The nation at that time had no executive head, but the members of the cabinet were determined to carry on. They were forbidden by the doctors to present any administrative problems to the president. Mrs. Garfield was the only member of the family allowed in the sick room. The next morning, July 6, it was reported that the president had slept well. Morphine was administered each night to induce sleep. To offset the heat, the president was allowed cracked ice and ice water.[18]

During July days both the temperature and the humidity soared into the upper 90s. The discomfort was great. Suggestions of cooling the room came in from all over the country. Most of these involved either the punkah, a fan used in India, or large blocks of ice. Ice was tried, but this only added to the humidity without appreciably lowering the temperature of the room.

The problem was brilliantly solved by a group of navy engineers who, with the aid of scientist Simon Newcomb, invented and installed what may have been the world's first air conditioner. The device consisted of a blower which forced air over a large chest containing six tons of ice. The cool air was then passed through a large cast iron box filled with cotton screens. The end of this box was connected to the sick room heat vent, from which poured a steady flow of air that averaged 20 percent cooler than the outside temperature, and was less humid.[19]

During the early days and weeks there was a regular Dodge City scenario with "Doc probing for the bullet." The doctors seemed most concerned about the location of the bullet. Apparently, since there was little that could be done, they felt that they must do something. During the first few days and weeks the president apparently improved, and the bullet had done all the harm it could do. It was also obvious that any surgery to remove the bullet would have been fatal. Perhaps they felt that the removal of the bullet would have made a sensational press release. However, they continued to poke dirty fingers and unsterile instruments into the wound, concluding that finally the bullet had gone to the right after hitting the ribs, and finally lodging in the muscle under the right groin. This seemed to be confirmed by the fact that a flexible catheter passed through the wound would drop unobstructed for a distance of almost 12 inches in a direct line to the supposed location of the bullet.[20]

The bullet wound was washed and drained daily with a mild antiseptic solution, yielding considerable quantities of a "healthy pus," "laudible pus." On July 6, with the president's life seemingly in the balance, Alexander Graham Bell's astronomer friend, Simon Newcomb, suggested to the attending physician the possibility of locating the bullet through some sort of electrical or magnetic effect, such as retardation of a rapidly revolving magnetized needle, though Newcomb doubted that such an effect would be detectable. Bell read of Newcomb's suggestion in the newspaper, and promptly wired him an offer of assistance.[21]

After an exchange of telegrams with Simon Newcomb, Bell, and Sumner Tainter — an associate of Bell — a Washington correspondent wrote, "Professor Graham Bell and Professor Tainter came here from Boston today for the purpose of making, under supervision of attending surgeons, a series of experiments intended to test the practicability of ascertaining by electrical means the location of the bullet which lies embedded in the president's back, they were driven at once to the executive mansion, and are now together with Professor Newcomb in the surgeon's room."[22]

Early in the afternoon of July 26, Bell and Tainter brought their apparatus to the White House. Garfield being asleep, Bell surveyed the sick room to see how wires might be brought in. Bell described the scene later.

Garfield looked so calm and grand he reminded me of a Greek hero chiseled in marble. He has a magnificent intellectual looking head, as you know, with massive forehead. As I remember him of old, his florid complexion rather detracted from his appearance, giving him the look of a man who indulged in good living and who was accustomed to work in the open air. There is none of that look about him now. His face is very pale, rather, and is of an ashen gray color, which makes one feel for a moment that you are not looking at a living man. It made my heart bleed to look at him and think of all that he must have suffered to bring him to this.[23]

The attempt to use the apparatus on July 22 to find the bullet was a failure, due to a malfunction of the apparatus. There were, as it turned out later, some faulty connections. The doctors agreed to a new trial on the morning of August 1.

Although the official bulletins treated the test as successful, Bell felt that nothing positive had been ascertained. He was puzzled by a faint buzzing sound noticed over a wide area. This was felt to be due in all probability to the metal springs in the bed, which the doctors had failed to remove. Bell persisted in his effort to perfect the apparatus. August was in its third week when the president had a relapse, and by the time the instrument improvements had been made in the exploring coil, Garfield's condition was too grave to allow further tests. His death on September 19 and the subsequent postmortem examination revealed that the bullet was too deeply embedded to have affected the balance of the tests made.[24]

In the third and fourth weeks of August it was evident that the battle was a losing one. Another relapse occurred on August 15. He collapsed after a period of vomiting. On Thursday, August 18, swelling of the parotid gland was noted. On August 20 there was another relapse. He became weak and delirious. On Wednesday, in the fourth week of August, pus was noted to be forming in his right parotid gland, and it was decided to drain the gland by surgery. An incision was made by Dr. Hamilton below the right ear.[25] Typically, suppurative parotitis occurs in debilitated, chronically or very seriously ill patients, so the appearance of this complication was a bad omen. The surgery on Garfield's parotid gland left the right side of his face paralyzed. On September 6, 1881, Garfield was moved to Elberon, New Jersey, where a track had been laid up to the seashore cottage which had been offered for Garfield's use by Charles Franckly. He rested well that first night after his arrival, and the doctors reported that he was better. On Thursday morning, September 7, his pulse was slower, and the president felt hungry. Cool weather came. Four physicians, Drs. Edson, J. J. Woodward, Barnes, and Rayburn, were let go.

At about this time the weakened splenic artery gave way, and blood emptied into the abdominal cavity. Garfield was hoarse, and evidence of bronchial pneumonia was noted. On Sunday, September 11, the fifth day after arriving at the seashore, there was a high pulse rate and a high temperature. Another relapse came on September 15. Evidence of septicemia was pronounced, and at times his mind wandered. On Saturday, September 17, he had a severe chill, and pulse, temperature, and respiration rates rose alarmingly, accompanied by delirium. The stomach could not retain anything. The cabinet was summoned.[26]

On the night of September 19, the anniversary of the Battle of Chickamauga, at the hour when 15 years before Garfield had been writing dispatches for Rosecrans, the blow fell. Only the attendant and one other person were with him. He woke up and cried out, "How it hurts here!" pressing his hand upon his heart. "Swain, can't you stop this? Oh, Swain!" He then became unconscious. Dr. Bliss came, followed by Mrs. Garfield, who immediately saw the end had come.[27]

After Garfield was shot, in the 80-day period that the president lingered, Chester A. Arthur made no attempt to assume the duties of the presidency. He is presumed by some to have hesitated to make any such move after Guiteau's assertion that the motive of the crime was to make Arthur president so that the stalwarts might be in power.[28] Even if Arthur had been energetic in trying to find out if such a succession were possible, he would have been frustrated — there was no such mechanism. After the president was shot the nation had no actual chief executive. The members of the cabinet were, however, determined to continue, but they were forbidden by the doctors to communicate with the president any executive problems. Thus, for 80 days the country was essentially without a president.

An 1878 textbook of surgery written by Dr. Hayes Agnew, which was just about the state of the art in Garfield's time, gave some instructions on the removal of foreign bodies:

> Removal of foreign bodies: This, of course, involves the examination of the wound, which should be made at the earliest possible moment in order that a correct diagnosis may be made. The patient at this time is in the best condition for the examination. The sensitivity of a wound is not acute, and there is no inflammatory alteration of the adjoining parts.
>
> That the examination may be conducted in the most favorable circumstances it is essential that the patient be placed as nearly as can be ascertained in the position corresponding to that which he occupied at the time of receiving the wound. This often gives the clue to the position

of the ball. A soldier during the late war [Civil], while standing at a height and his rifle being a muzzle loader, was shot in the back by a person occupying a lower position. The ball lodged under the skin at the back of his wrist, from which it was extracted. It had consequently passed the whole length of the back, over the shoulder and along the arm to the hand. The behavior of the ball was entirely inexplicable until it was discovered that the man was loading his rifle at the moment of receiving the wound.

And in the same text under removal of foreign bodies:

The best instrument for exploration of a gunshot wound is the index finger. The information which it communicates is accurate and conclusive. The fingernail should be guarded by scraping it over a piece of soap to fill up the space beneath the nail, so that no unnecessary violence may be done to the wound. If the finger is too short, we can sometimes, by making counterpressure with the other hand, bring the foreign body sufficiently near to be touched.

When the finger is too short to reach the full extent of the wound, it must be supplemented by instrumental prolongation. For this purpose we have recourse to probes. [In none of this discussion by Agnew is there any mention of sterile technique, or even washing one's hands before probing.][29]

The attempt by John W. Hinckley, Jr., a 25-year-old ne'er-do-well from a wealthy family, who fired six rounds from a .22 Rohm RG-14 revolver at Ronald Reagan on March 30, 1981, produced a much more deadly wound than received by James Abram Garfield in July 1881, just 100 years earlier. The difference in the results achieved in treatment were vastly different. The great strides in improving sterile technique, the development of methods in treating shock, and modern anesthesia, all made the difference between a president who survived and one who didn't.

References

1. David C. Whitney, *The American Presidents*, p. 165.
2. Theodore Clarke Smith, *The Life and Letters of James Abram Garfield*, pp. 25–26.
3. Ibid., pp. 25–27.
4. Smith, *The Life and Letters of James Abram Garfield*, pp. 56–57.
5. Ibid., p. 215.
6. Ibid., p. 219.
7. Whitney, *The American Presidents*, p. 169.

8. Allan Peskin, *Garfield: A Biography*, p. 596.

9. Richard O. Bates, *The Gentleman from Ohio*, p. 346.

10. Ibid., p. 338.

11. Peskin, *Garfield*, p. 597.

12. John M. Taylor, *Garfield of Ohio, the Available Man*, p. 271.

13. Smith, *The Life and Letters of James Abram Garfield*, p. 271.

14. Ibid., p. 1181.

15. Bates, *The Gentleman from Ohio*, p. 343.

16. Taylor, *Garfield of Ohio*, p. 272.

17. Peskin, *Garfield*, p. 600.

18. Bates, *The Gentleman from Ohio*, pp. 343–44.

19. Peskin, *Garfield*, pp. 601–02, from U.S. naval reports on ventilation and cooling.

20. Ibid., p. 602.

21. Robert C. Bruce, *Alexander Graham Bell in the Conquest of Space*, p. 344.

22. Katherine McKenzie, *Alexander Graham Bell: The Man Who Contracted Space*, p. 235.

23. Bruce, *Alexander Graham Bell in the Conquest of Space*, p. 346.

24. McKenzie, *Alexander Graham Bell*, p. 239.

25. Bates, *The Gentleman from Ohio*, p. 347.

26. Ibid., p. 349.

27. Smith, *The Life and Letters of James Abram Garfield*, p. 1200.

28. Whitney, *The American Presidents*, p. 173.

29. D. Hayes Agnew, *The Principles and Practice of Surgery*, pp. 383–84.

21

Chester Alan Arthur

Chester Alan Arthur, the twenty-first president of the United States, was born October 5, 1829, in Fairfield, Vermont. Arthur, known as the "Gentleman Boss" of the Republican Party in New York, held no elective office until he became vice president of the United States. He was nominated to the vice presidency as a henchman of Roscoe Conkling. Two years before becoming vice president, Arthur was dismissed by President Hayes from his post as collector of the Port of New York, presumably because of corruption—not of Arthur himself but of some of those who worked under him. The public concern for President Garfield during the few months he survived after he was shot and until he died was accentuated by the fear that Arthur would succeed to office after Garfield's death.[1]

Arthur was the eldest of seven children of the Reverend William Arthur, a Scotch-Irish Baptist minister. There is no record of any significant illnesses during his childhood and youth.

Arthur entered Union College at Schenectady, New York, at the age of 15. He was said to be an excellent student and was admitted to the National Honorary Fraternity Phi Beta Kappa. He graduated from Union in 1848 at the age of 18.[2] Union apparently, however, had neither intramural nor intercollegiate sports (its "sport" was debate), so it is reasonable to say that Arthur played no college sports. There is no record that Arthur ever enrolled for the debating team, either.[3]

After finishing college, Arthur taught school part-time while studying law at Ballston Spa, New York. He finished his law studies in the office of E. D. Culver in New York City and was admitted to the bar in 1854.[4]

As a young man, Arthur was trim, weighing 175–85 pounds, and stood about 6 feet, 2 inches tall. However, his sedentary life-style and his love for rich foods, fine wines, and after-dinner liqueurs eventually added much bulk.[5] His presidential portrait reveals a man with a heavy build, markedly overweight, with pale flesh.[6] Arthur was described as a "high liver who ate and drank excessively." His sedentary living combined with

131

his love of good foods made him much overweight. He gained weight—weighing 220 pounds—and lost strength during his White House years.[7]

Individuals of Arthur's day were not exposed to the idea of risk factors. Rich foods, obesity, and lack of exercise were not regarded as being any great deterrent to longevity. The words "cholesterol" and "low density lipoproteins" were not yet part of our working vocabulary. Two other presidents of that era, Cleveland and Taft, were also excessively overweight. They, too, had not yet gotten the message that obesity was a bad thing.

To escape the horde of office seekers who crowded the White House trying to procure a sinecure, Arthur—during the summer and whenever else it became possible—lived on the grounds of the Soldier's Home in a comfortable house provided for the president. There he pursued a lavish social life, entertaining some of his friends smoking, drinking, and conversing.[8] It was stated that no human being could withstand the stress produced by such socializing combined with the extreme pressures of his official office. As the winter of 1883-84 passed, his associates noted that late at night while socializing his face was lined, his eyes dulled, and his mind much less acute than it had been.

During the second year of Arthur's administration, in October 1882, the surgeon general was reported to have examined the president and found that he was suffering from Bright's Disease. Afterward, the president was seen in consultation by New York specialists, who confirmed the diagnosis but were able to offer no more than advice for rest and relaxation.[9]

Bright's Disease is a term which at present belongs to medical history. It was first described in 1789 by Richard Bright, an English physician. It was actually not a specific disease but a syndrome related to other severe diseases of the kidney which terminally manifests several signs and symptoms connected with renal failure and hypertension. Just what specific pathology was present in Arthur's kidney is not known. In William Osler's *The Principles and Practice of Medicine* it is stated: "Chronic Bright's Disease is an incurable affection and the anatomical conditions on which it depends are quite as much beyond the reach of medicine as wrinkled skin and gray hair."[10]

During the year of 1882 Arthur was noted to be fatigued, irritable, and physically ill. In August of the same year a physician, and relative by marriage, wrote, "The President is sick in body and soul."[11]

Arthur's administration was the first to systematically mislead the public about the president's health, and some of Arthur's successors may have learned something from him about covering up their illnesses—for example, Grover Cleveland, Franklin D. Roosevelt, and John F. Kennedy. The report in the *New York Herald* of Arthur's Bright's Disease was systematically and emphatically denied. A friend, one in authority under the president, denied entirely the allegation that Arthur suffered from this affliction. He stated that the president had merely suffered from a mild attack of malaria during the past summer and was now fully recovered.[12]

Arthur's spokesman stated: "The President has returned to this city in excellent health. The reports which have been circulated that he has Bright's Disease are pure fiction." The reports gathered some credence, however, and the president was constantly in receipt of letters on the subject, some expressing sympathy and hope for his recovery.[13]

In the *New York Tribune,* October 10, 1882, under "Points about Folger and Arthur," it was written: "I have it on authority of the President himself—that Mr. Arthur is not troubled with Bright's Disease or any other kidney complaints as far as he knows. When he left Washington he was troubled with malaria but not in severe form. His physician advised him to go inland to get rid of it. This was the reason for his trip to the Thousand Islands."[14] This episode reminds one of Robert Kennedy's denial of the report that JFK suffered from Addison's Disease.

Arthur's worsening health status was one of the best kept secrets of his presidency. Part of this secrecy persisted almost to the present. At the present time his fatigue, irritability, depression, and lethargy are ascribed to his illness—chronic renal disease.[15] By March 1883, during the third year of Arthur's presidency, his illness was steadily becoming worse. A statement made by his physician three years later brought to light that Arthur was a victim of hypertensive cardiovascular disease, which was secondary to his renal failure.[16]

Arthur's campaign of 1879-80 was reported to be vigorous, but by March 1882 he was far from well, and from that time on he became progressively worse. He was at that time suffering a great deal from indigestion, which was at times accompanied by colicky abdominal pain. This has been felt by some to be due to gallstones. By January 1883, when Arthur paid a visit to New York, his physical appearance aroused comment: "He has grown thin and feeble," a reporter noted: "His cheeks are emaciated and he has aged in appearance."[17]

The president from time to time made fishing trips, and almost daily sought to escape the stress of his office by walking and horseback riding. In April 1883 Arthur sought relief in a full-scale vacation, a train trip to Florida. The trip progressed in a hot, sweltering, and very dusty atmosphere. Besides the heat, humidity, and dust, there were occasional delays. A broken coupling at one point left his car siderailed for two hours in the hot countryside. On April 6 he was greeted in Jacksonville, Florida, by a temperature of 99 degrees and a large, cheering crowd.[18]

Arthur had doubts about the wisdom of his trip when he began to suffer from fatigue and the severe heat. This fatigue and exposure to the heat were followed by increased irritability. Arthur found a hotel at Sanford, Florida, so comfortable that he would have liked to remain there but did not. He was stated to be irritable, sullen, and very out of sorts. While the train was stopped at Maitland to visit some orange groves, Arthur refused to go to a picnic and instead sat indignantly inside his stuffy, hot railway car while the train was stopped. He was seen "not to be himself."[19] Those near to Arthur finally found out about his declining state of health. Arthur stated for public consumption that after he retired from the presidency he intended to return to his law practice in New York. He realized, however, that due to the state of his health he could not count on remaining in that practice for long.[20]

He tried to return to his law practice in New York, but he had not been well since his Florida trip and found, in fact, that his health was actually getting worse. His nervous indigestion, which was worse at times, did not improve. After a year had elapsed with no improvement in his health, he was advised by his physician to retire permanently.

In early 1886 he was recognized as having heart trouble, a natural sequel to his renal disease and hypertension.[21] One may assume that the sequence of progression in Arthur's illness, as in the usual case, would be acute renal disease, chronic renal disease, hypertension, cardiac enlargement, and finally heart failure. Terminally the ex-president was in unrelieved misery. He was short of breath and had to sleep with his head elevated. He was able to sleep only if aided by opiates. Due to his loss of appetite he was losing real body weight but was more than replacing it with edematous fluid. He tried changing in June 1886 to the cooler climate of Connecticut, but this did not help; he became steadily worse. After he returned to his home in New York, he despondently told a friend, "After all, life is not worth living. I might as well give up the struggle for it now as at any other time and submit to the inevitable."[22]

On the morning of November 17, 1886, his nurse found Arthur unconscious. He died early on the following morning of a massive cerebral hemorrhage.[23]

Determining just how long Arthur had been suffering from his illness would be very difficult since the disease or syndrome labeled as Bright's Disease may be insiduous in onset. It seems probable, however, that Arthur was quite ill when he first entered the White House.

References

1. James Morgan, *Our Presidents*, p. 209.
2. David C. Whitney, *The American Presidents*, p. 171.
3. George Frederick Howe, *Chester A. Arthur*, p. 9.
4. William A. Degregorio, *The Complete Book of U.S. Presidents*, pp. 308–09.
5. Ibid., p. 309; and Rudolph Marx, *The Health of the Presidents*, p. 248.
6. William Seale, *The Presidents' House*, 1:530.
7. Howe, *Chester A. Arthur*, p. 174.
8. Thomas C. Reeves, *Gentleman Boss: The Life of Chester Alan Arthur*, p. 274.
9. Ibid., p. 317.
10. William Osler, *The Principles and Practice of Medicine*, pp. 741–55.
11. Justus D. Doenecke, *The Presidencies of Garfield and Arthur*, p. 80.
12. Reeves, *Gentleman Boss*, p. 319.
13. *New York Herald*, "The President's Health," October 21, 1882, p. 3.
14. *New York Tribune*, "Points about Folger and Arthur, October 10, 1882, vol. 41, no. 13.
15. Doenecke, *The Presidencies of Garfield and Arthur*, p. 80.
16. Reeves, *Gentleman Boss*, p. 355.
17. Ibid., p. 318.
18. Ibid., p. 356.
19. Howe, *Chester A. Arthur*, pp. 244–45.
20. Seale, *The Presidents' House*, 1:50.
21. Howe, *Chester A. Arthur*, p. 286.
22. Marx, *The Health of the Presidents*, p. 251.
23. Homer F. Cunningham, *The Presidents' Last Years*, p. 159.

22

Grover Cleveland

Grover Cleveland, the twenty-second and twenty-fourth president of the United States, was born March 18, 1837, in Caldwell, New Jersey. He was the only president in U.S. history to serve a term, lose an election, and then be reelected. His father was a Presbyterian minister who moved often. Cleveland remembered little about his birthplace. His best, most pleasant recollection was of Fayetteville, New York, where he engaged in such sports as were available. He swam in the swimming holes along Limestone Creek, and early in life he developed a love for fishing.[1] In fact, it is alleged that he fished in Green Lake in spite of the fact that a ferocious panther roamed the woods nearby.[2]

When Grover was a boy he was said to be a great prankster. His father recounted that Cleveland received an injury to his leg while engaged in one of his pranks. He and another boy climbed through the window of the academy and up the stairs to the belfry. The episode was in the dark of night, and their intent was to awaken the whole village by ringing the bells. Indeed, the clanging of the bells did awaken the village, but the terrific din in the narrow confines of the belfry terrified the invaders. They felt that they were being pursued. They slid down a rain pipe that ran beside a nearby window. In the act of sliding down the rain pipe, Cleveland cut his leg on a projecting piece of metal.[3]

Despite such active pranks and other sports, however, Cleveland was recalled as being chubby and large for his age. For most of his life, in fact, he had a tendency to be obese. In the 1870s he became so large that some of his family—nephews and nieces—referred to him as "Uncle Jumbo." At that time he was in his early and middle thirties. By the time he was elected president, his weight exceeded 280 pounds. He drank large amounts of lager beer, which undoubtedly abetted his obesity, and he apparently never thought of restricting his diet to hold his weight to a reasonable level. He had a huge beer belly.

Cleveland suffered one serious illness in his youth, typhoid fever when he was aged 18, and came very near to dying. At that time he was in

Buffalo working a temporary job. He was extremely ill for several weeks. The treatment consisted of bed rest and a starvation diet of low calorie liquids.

Cleveland did not attend college, but he studied law and worked as a law clerk and then as a lawyer in Buffalo, New York (1855–62). He was then successively assistant district attorney of Erie County, New York, 1863–65; sheriff of Erie County, New York, 1871–73; mayor of Buffalo, New York, 1882; and governor of New York state, 1883–84. When he was elected governor of New York, and when he gave his inaugural address, Cleveland wanted to present the proper image. However, because of his size, he had no illusions that he could appear both dignified and handsome.[4] Cleveland, like the twenty-seventh president, Taft, was very corpulent and the butt of a great many jokes about obesity.

In 1885, when Cleveland had been elected president for the first time, he developed a crippling arthritis. He was observed at the funeral of General Grant to be limping on his right foot. His life-style undoubtedly had all the classical characteristics that one would find in a patient with gout: obesity, large intake of alcoholic beverages, and lack of exercise. And again during his second campaign for the presidency in 1892 he was, due to the severity of his gout, able to make but few public appearances.[5]

It is mentioned from time to time that Cleveland loved to smoke cigars and that he was a heavy smoker. It has also been noted that he inhaled deeply and held the smoke for a long time in his lungs. He and Ulysses Grant were noted for their cigar smoking. Grant, by the count of another, smoked 20 cigars from sunup to sundown during the first day of the Battle of the Wilderness. It is also remembered that Grant died of throat cancer and that Cleveland was operated on for a malignancy of his oral cavity.

In 1893, during the first year of his second term as president, Cleveland was faced with two crises: a severe national financial crisis, one of the worst in our history; and a severe health problem for himself. One crisis alone would be of great concern; for both to happen at once was potentially catastrophic. The first crisis was the financial panic of 1893, given the name "Black Friday," when prices on the stock market plummeted, banks began to call their loans, credit dried up, and business failures were increasing week after week.[6]

The second crisis, the problem of Cleveland's health, emerged also in June 1893. While Cleveland was shaving, he discovered a rough spot in the roof of his mouth. After about six weeks' delay, he had the spot examined by the White House physician, Dr. Robert M. O'Reilly, who called Dr. Bryant, a capable surgeon, into consultation. A biopsy specimen was sent to Dr. William H. Welch of Johns Hopkins University. Dr. Welch found the tissue to be malignant. Dr. Bryant advised immediate surgery.[7] There was considerable concern in the physicians' minds about the president's malignancy, yet there was also great concern that if the news leaked out about Cleveland's health problems it would intensify the financial crisis which faced the nation. The president agreed that the surgery must be done but insisted that it must be done in absolute secrecy.

It was decided that the surgery would take place on Commodore E. C. Benedict's yacht, the *Oneida*. Since Dr. Bryant felt that the president would be recovered enough to return to work in five weeks following surgery, Cleveland prepared a proclamation summoning Congress to meet in special session on August 7 to repeal the Sherman Act. On the day of the proclamation, June 30, 1893, under closest secrecy he joined his physicians on the *Oneida* in New York harbor.[8] What followed is truly bizarre. It is almost beyond comprehension that either patient or doctors would be so foolhardy as to place themselves in such a position. The thing which most baffles one is just how the doctors, should the outcome be fatal, explain the whole thing to the American public. Discounting the fact that there were no malpractice suits in those days, a result less than good would have meant disaster to Cleveland, to the country, and to the doctors' careers. The surgeons on the *Oneida* were Dr. W. W. Keen of Philadelphia, a famous surgeon and medical writer; Dr. E. G. Janaway, a general physician; Dr. Ferdinand Hasbrouck, a dentist; Dr. John F. Urdman, Bryant's assistant; and Dr. Joseph D. Bryant, a surgeon. What followed the meeting of Cleveland and his surgeons on the *Oneida* bears telling in some detail.

After a night's sleep (one can only guess at how good that night's sleep was) the tremendously obese president was strapped upright in a chair against the mast on deck of the *Oneida* and given anesthesia, beginning with nitrous oxide and followed by ether. The anesthesia itself even without surgery was far from a good risk. Dr. Janaway had examined Cleveland prior to surgery, and his examination had revealed the obvious: his obesity, a strong pulse, and a suggestion of arteriosclerosis. One wonders if he was not also hypertensive. Cleveland was a good candidate for a medical catastrophe coming from a number of different directions.

Dr. Hasbrouck removed two left upper bicuspid teeth, and then Dr. Bryant made the incision in the roof of the president's mouth.[9] Dr. Bryant used surgical hammer, chisel, and bone-cutting instruments. He removed the greater part of the left upper jawbone. The bleeding was checked by a battery-driven cautery, the left antrum was opened, and a mass of cancerous material was removed. All of the surgical approach was from within Cleveland's mouth. When the surgery was completed, the extensive wound was packed with antiseptic gauze, and after he awakened he was given opium for his pain. In this way the 56-year-old obese, sedentary president who drank too much, smoked too much, and ate too much survived the surgery. The operation lasted 41 minutes, and on July 5, 1893, Cleveland left the yacht and went ashore to his summer home, Gray Gables. But on July 7 Dr. Bryant examined the wound and decided that further surgery was needed to remove what seemed to be residual cancer. The same cast—the president and the surgeons—reassembled on board the *Oneida* on July 17, 1893. A second operation was done, the surface cauterized, and the wound repacked. The second surgery was in no way as extensive as the first.[10] An artificial device made of rubber replaced the palate and filled the cavity made by the surgery.[11] The dentist, Dr. Kasson C. Gibson, also made a temporary artificial upper jaw for him. This gave a normal appearance to his face and helped to restore a more normal sound to his voice.[12]

After the surgery Dr. Bryant prescribed some medication for pain and sedation. In a letter to Colonel Lamont, Dr. Bryant complained of the president's tendency to disobey orders regarding the medication prescribed for him: "I found him grunting as you know full well, suffering from an excess of medication rather than the lack of it. He almost believes that if a little will do some good a bottle full must be a great advantage indeed. On that theory he had received the full effects of the medication sent him as well as some after effects."[13]

Attorney General Richard Olney was admitted during the recovery period in order to discuss the upcoming message which Cleveland was supposed to deliver on silver:

> After a fortnight more or less during which I made frequent attempts to see Mr. Cleveland, I succeeded in having an interview. He had changed a great deal in appearance, lost a great deal of flesh, and his mouth was so stuffed with antiseptic wads that he could hardly articulate. The first utterance that I understood was something like this: "My God, Olney, they nearly killed me." He did not talk much, was very much depressed, and at that time acted, and I believe he felt, as if he did not expect to recover. He was very depressed about the progress he was making and complained that his mind would not work.[14]

One is inclined to believe that the side effects of Cleveland's medication would have been the same as in any other patient taking an overdose of medication—oversedation and slurred speech.

The secret of his surgery was kept for two months before the story leaked to the press. Cleveland and his doctors flatly denied it, and it was

1917 before the full truth was known. During his recovery, however, he was successful in preventing the Sherman Silver Act from becoming law, and he continued to perform his duties.[15] In fact, Cleveland is alleged to have said that he had done more lying in the period just before his surgery and the period immediately thereafter than he had ever done in the remainder of his life.

By September 5, 1893, Cleveland had recovered enough from his surgery and had become adapted well enough to his artificial jaw prosthesis that he was able to open the Pan-American Medical Congress in Washington. His voice was clearer and more easily understood than it had been since the surgery. The operated area was so well healed in October 1893 that it was possible for Dr. Gibson to fit him with a permanent prosthesis made of hard rubber, which Cleveland wore for the rest of his life.[16]

In his latter years Cleveland continued to be afflicted with gout. His affliction was called rheumatism, but all of its features were those associated with gout. With this illness, the problem was worse from time to time and finally became so severe that he was obliged to spend weeks in bed and caused him to cancel his most beloved recreation—fishing. Cleveland was also troubled with indigestion and frequently used a stomach pump.[17]

One later president adopted the use of a stomach pump—Woodrow Wilson. Wilson also suffered from indigestion. The precise nature of Cleveland's gastrointestinal complaint, and that of Wilson, has been subject to speculation, but no exact diagnosis was ever made. In 1899–1900 Cleveland's gastrointestinal problem became worse. He used his stomach pump quite often. One may guess that he suffered from a duodenal ulcer and that the removal of acid by the pump perhaps gave him relief. At that time he was urged by certain influential Democrats to run for a third term. Cleveland, to his credit, did not feel—as did the two Roosevelts and Wilson—that he was indispensible, although his health was comparatively better than either Wilson's or FDR's when they aspired to run for a third term.[18]

In early 1908, suffering from arthritis (gout) and heart failure, he had to become a bed patient. In June 1908 his condition became so much worse that Bryant, his personal physician, summoned other consultants. On June 23 Cleveland seemed to rally, but on the morning of June 24, 1908, he lapsed into a coma and died at the age of 71.[19] The probable cause of Cleveland's death was coronary occlusion.

References

1. Allan Nevins, *Grover Cleveland: A Study in Courage*, p. 11.
2. Denis Tilden Lynch, *Grover Cleveland*, p. 18.
3. Ibid., p. 17.
4. Richard E. Welch, *The Presidencies of Grover Cleveland*, p. 20.
5. Rudolph Marx, *The Health of the Presidents*, p. 266.
6. Welch, *The Presidencies of Grover Cleveland*, p. 116.
7. Nevins, *Grover Cleveland*, p. 529.
8. Robert McElroy, *Grover Cleveland*, 2:28.
9. Nevins, *Grover Cleveland*, pp. 530–31.
10. Welch, *The Presidencies of Grover Cleveland*, p. 120.
11. William Seale, *The Presidents' Home*, 2:606.
12. Marx, *The Health of the Presidents*, p. 260.
13. McElroy, *Grover Cleveland*, 2:29.
14. Ibid., pp. 30–31.
15. Kenneth R. Crispell, and Carlos F. Gomez, *Hidden Illness in the White House*, p. 204.
16. Ibid., p. 261.
17. Homer F. Cunningham, *The Presidents' Last Years*, p. 165.
18. Nevins, *Grover Cleveland*, p. 763.
19. Marx, *The Health of the Presidents*, p. 267.

23

Benjamin Harrison

Benjamin Harrison, the twenty-third president of the United States, was born August 20, 1833, in North Bend, Ohio. Harrison had the distinction of being one of several American presidents, all Republicans, who served as officers in the Union Army and were from Ohio. He was named for his great-grandfather who was a signer of the Declaration of Independence.[1] Harrison's grandfather, William Henry Harrison, was the ninth president of the United States.

Harrison grew up as a slender, wiry child who gradually became chubby with square shoulders. The young Harrison engaged in schoolboy sports and enjoyed fishing, hunting, and swimming. Often he half walked and half ran to school in order to get there early enough to play bullpen for half an hour before school began.[2] Congressman Butterworth, who was raised on a farm in southern Ohio, said of Harrison's youth, "Ben had the usual number of stone bruises, stubbed toes, and the average number of nails in his foot that fell to the portion of the rest of us."[3]

Harrison got his early education from tutors in a one-room log schoolhouse. He was said by his first teacher to be the brightest of his family. From 1847–50 he attended Farmer's College, a preparatory school in Cincinnati. In 1850 Harrison was admitted to the Miami University of Ohio and graduated near the top of his class in 1852. He studied law, 1852–54, in the law offices of Storer and Gwynne and was admitted to the bar in 1854.[4]

Harrison acquired the habit of smoking cigars while at Farmer's College. When his father learned of this, he wrote a letter which was calculated to persuade young Harrison to end the new habit: "It will be sufficient for you to remember that a sainted mother once made you this request to make the sacrifice for her, to induce you to say, 'I have smoked my last cigar,' and adhere to it with the same steadfast resolution that you would in carrying out the wishes of your mother when she was still living."[5] An entry in his diary New Year's Day, 1858, was this resolution: "Stop use of tobacco in every form."[6]

In 1862 Harrison aided in forming the 70th Indiana Infantry and was the colonel of this unit. He received no wounds in the Civil War. However, in the Battle of New Hope Church in 1864, when the regimental surgeon could not be found, he set up a first-aid station to care for the hundreds of wounded in that battle. "He rolled up his sleeves," according to Rudolph Marx, "he went to work in the light of flickering candles, bandaging wounds, applying and loosening tourniquets, and giving opiates until the regimental surgeon arrived."[7]

Harrison did suffer some ailments which were almost incidental to the military during the Civil War. On November 24, 1862, when his brigade was being ordered to Gallatin, Tennessee, he was quite ill. Harrison had eaten some fresh pork, which caused him to have what was called ptomaine poisoning. The term ptomaine poisoning belongs to medical history. It is a general term which covered food poisoning caused by bacteria or by bacterial toxins. It was manifested by nausea, vomiting, diarrhea, and cramps. Near the end of the Civil War, Harrison developed also a severe case of scarlet fever and was ill for three weeks, but fortunately he developed no sequelae. And during the campaign with Sherman at Atlanta, just after Harrison had been made brigadier general, he developed a poisoning of his hands, making it necessary for him to wear gloves all the time. This susceptibility, probably a contact dermatitis, remained with him the rest of his life and eventually worked to his political disadvantage. In 1870 when he was campaigning for the governorship of Indiana, he was called the aristocratic "Kidgloves Harrison."[8]

In 1867 Harrison, at the end of two years' work as Supreme Court reporter and lawyer, suffered a near physical breakdown from overwork. His wife, Carrie, nursed him to recovery; but he very sensibly decided for his health's sake to lighten his work load in the future. He gave up his court reporter's job and to went on his first vacation in three years, hunting and fishing in and around some lakes in Minnesota. In the fall of 1867, much improved, he returned to his law practice in Indianapolis.[9]

Except for this near breakdown, Harrison's health from the Civil War up until he became president was good. He was described this way: "Only 5' 6" in height. He had a big torso supported by short legs. His bearded face was plain and square with white skin that never tanned. Although he was a short man he was strong and muscular."[10]

In August 1886, after Congress adjourned, Senator Harrison returned home to take an active part in his state campaign. At the end of August he returned to Washington absolutely "used up" and had to spend two weeks under the care of his doctor. "A diet of iron, strychnine, and quinine helped to bring him to physical health."[11]

However, during his candidacy for the presidency in the summer of 1888, there were reports of a near nervous collapse. Despite the fact that his friends grew uneasy, the *Republican Journal* declared him to be in robust health. The opposition paper, the *Democratic Sentinel,* reported that Harrison "is physically and politically played out." The truth was probably somewhere in between.[12]

There is no record that Harrison had any definite organic illness in 1888. It was his lack of stamina which plagued him during the presidential campaign. Although he was at the time only 56 years of age, the stress of the campaign so demonstrated his lack of endurance that he was persuaded to pace himself during the four years of his presidency.

Harrison as president never exerted strong leadership. He only carried out the laws enacted by Congress. He thus conserved his health, and at the end of his term in 1893 his health was as good as or better than it was at the beginning of his term.

President Harrison helped to maintain his health by walking when- ever the weather was suitable. To James Blaine, friend and supporter, he wrote on February 1, 1889, during his first year in office: "My health is good. I get out twice a day for a walk — a hurried one to be sure — to give me air and exercise.[13] Harrison maintained his regimen throughout his term. He took his evening walk around the District of Columbia and pre- ferred walking out on Connecticut Avenue or Massachusetts Avenue. While he did enjoy walking, these outings were taken largely because he wished to escape the confines of the White House. On returning to the White House, Harrison once commented, "This is my jail."[14]

Again, during Harrison's second year in office on August 2, 1891, Harrison wrote to Blaine, "Grand Union Hotel, Sarasota Springs, New York, Dear Mr. Blaine, I expected to have written you yesterday according to promise, but the fatigue of the reception was such that I could not well do so. On my way to Bennington I contracted a cold, probably by speaking in the rain in Albany, which first affected my bowels and then settled in my face affecting two molars, and giving me a bad time of it for two days. I had hard work to get through the exercises at Bennington, and reached here in an unhappy condition. Today I feel somewhat better."[15]

That any individual, the president included, survived the unhealthy atmosphere of Washington in Harrison's day is indeed remarkable. Much of the land in the District of Columbia and Washington was a swamp, breeding clouds of mosquitoes and flies during the summer months of the year. It was only in 1901 that real efforts were made to drain the swampy areas of the Potomac basin. The more affluent who could escape Washing- ton in the summer did so. They fled to their part-time residences in the mountains or at the seashore. Another unpleasant occurrence during Harrison's presidency was the Johnstown flood of 1889, causing the Potomac River to flood Washington and deposit sewage in the low-lying areas of D.C. Most of Washington for a time was covered with diluted sewage.

After Harrison retired from the White House in 1893, at the age of 59, he remained in good health for eight years. Three years after he retired from the presidency he married the niece of his deceased wife, Carrie. His new wife, Mary Dimmick, presented him with a daughter when he was 64 years old. This feat bore some witness to the state of his health. His late marriage, however, caused some unhappiness for his children. Russell Benjamin Harrison and Mary Harrison McKee were concerned that some part of their inheritance might go to the new wife. Harrison, however, declared his independence in the matter of his marriage because he was concerned that by himself he would be very lonely. He also pointed out that his children did not live near him, nor probably ever would. His children never became reconciled to their father's second marriage.[16]

Harrison, after he left the presidency, enjoyed many years of practicing law. He also wrote articles for several national magazines. In March 1901, at the age of 67, he developed what seemed at first to be a severe cold but later developed into flu. Two days after the onset of this illness he developed a severe chill, high fever, and generalized aches and pains. The ex-president was treated with bed rest, pain relievers, and steam inhalations. Forty-eight hours later he developed pleuritic left chest pain, with shortness of breath and rapid pulse. By physical findings it was determined that he was suffering from pneumonia. His personal physician called in several other doctors in consultation. In Harrison's time, before the sulfas and other antibiotics were discovered, the doctors employed such drugs as camphor and digitalis to treat pneumonia. Oxygen inhalation through a gas mask was also used, but none of these treatments was of any avail. Benjamin Harrison died in the afternoon of March 13, 1901. He died in the arms of Mary, his beloved second wife.[17]

References

1. David C. Whitney, *The American Presidents*, pp. 189–90.
2. Harry J. Sievers, *Benjamin Harrison, Hoosier Warrior*, 1:23.
3. Ibid.
4. William A. Degregorio, *The Complete Book of U.S. Presidents*, p. 353.
5. Sievers, *Benjamin Harrison, Hoosier Warrior*, 1:53.
6. Ibid., p. 129.

7. Rudolph Marx, *The Health of the Presidents*, p. 260.

8. Sievers, *Benjamin Harrison, Hoosier Warrior*, 1:236.

9. Ibid., p. 18.

10. Marx, *The Health of the Presidents*, p. 276.

11. Sievers, *Benjamin Harrison, Hoosier Statesman*, p. 294.

12. Ibid., p. 372.

13. Albert T. Volwiler, editor, *The Correspondence Between Harrison and Blaine*, p. 51.

14. Homer E. Socolofsky, and Allan B. Spetter, *The Presidency of Benjamin Harrison*, pp. 161–62.

15. Volwiler, *Correspondence Between Harrison and Blaine*, p. 181.

16. Homer F. Cunningham, *The Presidents' Last Years*, pp. 178–79.

17. Ibid., p. 171.

24

William McKinley

William McKinley, the twenty-fifth president of the United States, was born January 29, 1843, in Niles, Ohio. He was the third president to be killed by an assassin. McKinley became president 16 years after Garfield, who was also shot by an assassin.

As a child, McKinley was described as a serious, delicate lad, not interested in sports or games, although no record of any serious childhood illness exists. He was graduated from the Poland Academy at the age of 17 and entered Allegheny College, Pennsylvania, that fall. McKinley had to leave Allegheny at the end of his first term due to illness.[1] The nature of his illness cannot be determined.

McKinley's adult life was equally healthy, and we are not aware of any severe illness that he had prior to his assassination, apparently due to temperate living. A religious person, McKinley was very strict in his habits. His rigid Methodist upbringing forbade drinking and smoking. He rode horseback and walked for his exercise, but took no part in competitive sports. He wrote to his nephew, James, in wording which reminds one of Polonius's speech to Laertes in *Hamlet*. It also reminds one of Jefferson's letter to his nephew, Peter Carr. He wrote: "Look after your diet and living, take no intoxicants, indulge in no immoral practices. Keep your life and your speech both clean and brave." In four years of army life, McKinley did not learn to drink, smoke, or swear.[2]

McKinley saw much action during the Civil War but managed to avoid being wounded. He was cited for bravery after the Battle of Antietam and was given a battlefield promotion, dated September 24, 1862. During the war he was reported to have suffered the usual ailments incidental to camp life, but he went through the entire war without any marked health problems. This fortunate outcome was attributed to his strong constitution. He was said to have become a hardened veteran by 1863 with a slim, muscular build: "He carried himself straight and walked at a rapid pace." By 1863 he had become an excellent horseman.[3]

Apparently, however, especially in his later life, McKinley drifted away from his earlier habits of abstinence from smoking and drinking. Although McKinley ate simply and never drank intemperately, he did become a heavy smoker of cigars. His conscience was never completely clear about it though, and when he became president he did not smoke while being photographed: "We must not let the young men of this country see their President smoking." He was said to have liked good scotch, but he was a moderate social drinker and drank moderate amounts of wine with dinner.[4]

Most of his biographers devote a great deal of space to the assassination and the moments which followed it. The ordeal was not nearly as great and as prolonged as that of Garfield, who survived for 11 weeks after he was shot.

Early in McKinley's second term he left Canton, Ohio, to make an address at the Pan-American Exposition at Buffalo, New York, on September 5, 1901. His speech in Buffalo was to be his last address to the American people. On September 6, 1901, a day following his speech, McKinley stood in the exposition's Temple of Music, greeting and shaking hands with innumerable admirers, when he was approached by a demented man named Leon Czolgosz, who had been recently in the acute phase of schizophrenia. Czolgosz had waited for his opportunity, and it came in that long reception line. He approached McKinley with a short-barreled .32 revolver, concealed in a handkerchief wrapped around his right hand. Czolgosz fired two bullets at point-blank range into the body of McKinley. The president, showing a great look of disbelief on his face, then slumped into the arms of his secretary. McKinley was helped to a chair; he put a hand on his chest, and it came away covered with blood. McKinley was almost immediately moved by an electric ambulance to an emergency hospital on the exposition grounds.[5] Before McKinley was moved, he saw that the assassin was being roughly handled and called out, "Don't let them hurt him."[6]

McKinley arrived at the emergency hospital on the exposition grounds at 4:18 P.M. He was at once taken to the operating room and placed on an operating table. He was conscious but in dire shock. While he was being undressed, the bullet fell from his clothing. This bullet, fired at his chest, had only grazed his ribs. The bullet had been deflected by a button on his clothes. However, the bullet fired into McKinley's abdomen was of a much more serious nature. Dr. Roswell Parks, the medical director of the exposition, was away in Niagara Falls. The doctors who were available judged the surgery to be so urgent that it was decided to go ahead immediately. Dr. Matthew D. Mann, a prominent Buffalo surgeon, had arrived and settled the question of whether to operate immediately. There was later speculation that they should have waited for Dr. Parks and moved the president from the ill-equipped emergency hospital to the Buffalo General Hospital. At 5:30 P.M. the anesthesia was started with ether dripped through a gauze mask. The surgery was performed by Dr. Mann and three assistants, who sterilized their hands and forearms by scrubbing with soap and water. The doctors then placed their hands and forearms in a solution of bichloride of mercury. The surgery was done with bare hands, since rubber gloves were not available at that time.[7]

Dr. Pressley M. Rixey, McKinley's private physician, used a looking glass to reflect the late evening sun onto the operative site. They succeeded later, after the sun had gone down, in using an electrical light which was found somewhere on the exposition grounds. No use was made of X rays, though such an apparatus was available on the fairgrounds.[8]

When the anesthesia was started, the patient was asleep in nine minutes. His belly was shaved and scrubbed with green soap and then washed with ether and bichloride of mercury. The doctors and nurses wore steam-sterilized gowns, and the surgical area was draped with sterile towels. Dr. Mann made the incision, four inches long, downward from the ribs and across the bullet wound. In the incised area the surgeon found a piece of cloth from the president's clothing. The incision was made through three inches of fat, fascia, and peritoneum.[9] Dr. Mann found the stout president's abdomen so protruding that he was operating at "the darkened end of a big hole."[10] Dr. Mann found that the bullet had passed through both front and back walls of the stomach. The surgery performed was the closure of the bullet wounds in the stomach wall and an attempt to cleanse the abdominal cavity. Due to McKinley's precarious condition, no attempt was made to probe for the bullet.

After Dr. Mann had closed the rent in McKinley's stomach, he introduced his hand and forearm into the peritoneal cavity to his elbow in order to try to palpate the structures posterior to the stomach, but he had to abandon this effort because the president's pulse, already fast and weak, showed some further weakening. The surgical wound was closed without draining, and the wound was covered with an antiseptic dressing.

The surgery had gone forward under several handicaps. The best surgeon in the area and the one who had had special training in treating bullet wounds was Dr. Roswell Parks, but he was occupied at that time with surgery on another patient at Niagara Falls. The surgery was done in the small, poorly equipped exposition hospital instead of Buffalo General Hospital. In addition, the patient's large, obese abdomen was another surgical obstacle, as well as the fact that there were no retractors available to better expose the abdominal contents.[11]

The president had shown some evidence of shock during the surgery, but seemed to have recovered well from this when, after the surgery, he was removed to the Milburn home. This removal of the president to the Milburn home seems astonishing. Why was he not left in the hospital or moved to Buffalo General Hospital? His doctors were optimistic and felt that there was a fair chance of recovery. On the following day, September 7, the president seemed to be doing well and the *New York Times* announced that the physicians and friends were hopeful of recovery.[12]

Why, then, did McKinley die? His death could have been attributed to many things that have been previously mentioned, but the real clues may be found in his autopsy report and in the scrapbook left behind by one of McKinley's attending physicians. This scrapbook was given to Dr. Selig Addler, who published excerpts of it in the March 1963 issue of *Scientific American.*[13] Much of the information obtained by Addler came from a scrapbook kept by one of the physicians who cared for McKinley, Dr. Charles G. Stockton. "It was my great privilege," Stockton said, "in his last illness he was the best patient I ever had. I am not a surgeon, but I was called to care for the medical aspects of the case." Stockton praised the emergency operation done on the president, but explained that because the bullet had damaged the president's pancreas, he was doomed from the beginning. This information was obtained from Stockton by a local reporter.[14]

After McKinley was shot, he survived for eight days. During the first 24 hours his pulse was as high at times as 140 and his rectal temperature was as high as 102.5 degrees. He was given morphine for his pain and digitalis for his heart. No intravenous fluids were given, but he was given retention enemas of saline solution to maintain his fluid. Dr. Charles McBurney, the famous New York abdominal surgeon, saw him on the morning of the third day postoperative and gave a favorable prognosis. The president was given enemas to maintain bowel movement, and was given strychnine by hypo and digitalis by mouth in an attempt to slow his pulse. The strychnine was used as a stimulant. The primary effects of strychnine are on respiration centers and on the spinal cord. There is little or no direct effect on the heart. The use of this drug is now largely outmoded. He was given small amounts of warm water by mouth and retention enemas with egg white. His renal output became quite low. On the following two days the president seemed to be improved and had a TPR at a low level.[15]

McKinley rallied during the weekend and on Tuesday, September 10, his condition seemed so good that Vice President Roosevelt was told that he need no longer keep vigil with McKinley. Roosevelt left that evening for a vacation with his family in the Adirondacks. His family was awaiting him there in a mountain cabin. On the morning of the seventh day, McKinley was seemingly so improved that he was fed chicken broth and toast with a cup of coffee, which he seemed to enjoy. However, about noon of that day he developed an alarming elevation of his pulse rate. His doctors began again the treatment with strychnine and digitalis. McKinley complained that afternoon of headache, nausea, and complete exhaustion. He was then given whiskey, water, and beef juice, but could not take soft-boiled eggs and toast. The doctors felt that the cause of his worsening condition might be attributed to intestinal toxemia, for which they gave him calomel and castor oil, followed by an enema of oxgall. In spite of, or on account of, all the heroic measures, his pulse became faster and weaker.[16] To give calomel and castor oil to a patient in McKinley's condition would seem very drastic, both medications being harsh purgatives.

During the time following Vice President Roosevelt's departure from Buffalo on September 10, at 1:25 P.M., to 1:25 P.M. on September 13, Roosevelt was in as remote a spot as could be found on the continent. The report of McKinley's death came to him by a mountain ranger who arrived on foot.[17] When McKinley's condition worsened, the Secret Service had no idea where in the Adirondacks the vice president was to be found. When the ranger did find him, Roosevelt rode down the mountain at a great speed, using a fresh team of horses at each stop, to take him to his train bound for Buffalo.

The autopsy done on McKinley provided as many questions as answers. The postmortem was done by a local pathologist in the presence of physicians appointed by the government. Mrs. McKinley halted the procedure before it could be completed, however, and the bullet was not found.

The notes on the autopsy were made by James T. Wilson and read as follows: "William McKinley, President of the United States, died of gangrene of both walls of the stomach and pancreas following gunshot wounds." The autopsy lasted four hours but left a number of questions unanswered. The surgical wound showed infection. There was no free pus in the peritoneum, but there was gangrene in the bullet track behind the stomach. The left kidney and the left adrenal gland had been injured by the bullet. However, the finding considered most important was the damage to the pancreas and the sequela of leakage of pancreatic juice into the abdominal cavity.

After the fact, there was a great deal of disagreement among the doctors about the surgery and the possible causes of President McKinley's death. Dr. Parks stated that the injury to the pancreas with subsequent release of pancreatic secretions had resulted in terminal toxemia. Another physician who did not participate in the surgery, Dr. Eugene Waldin, was present during the surgery and the postmortem examination. Dr. Waldin made a public statement, declaring that a poisoned bullet tip would have been required to produce such massive necrosis of the tissue.[18] From careful reading of the autopsy report one would have to feel that Dr. Waldin's conclusion was due to a powerful imagination.

Strangely, a few weeks after McKinley's death, Dr. Roswell Parks performed surgery on a young woman who had an almost identical wound to McKinley. She had heard of McKinley's wound and his surgery, had marked a spot on her abdomen, and had fired a bullet into her abdomen which followed almost the same track as that in the case of McKinley. This bullet fired into her abdomen also damaged her pancreas and caused leakage of pancreatic juice into her peritoneal cavity. However, as opposed to McKinley's surgery, Dr. Roswell Parks used aseptic technique and drainage. The young woman survived. Of course, one case should not cause anyone to argue too strongly that the absence of such technique may have contributed to McKinley's death.[19]

Both Garfield and McKinley were shot by men who were demented. However, their wounds were quite different. In the case of McKinley, the doctors did not, as in the case of Garfield, probe for the bullet with dirty fingers. Instead, they were apparently motivated by the relatively fresh memory of Garfield's case, which caused them to do immediate surgery. It is true that, in retrospect, had McKinley been admitted initially to Buffalo General Hospital and had Dr. Roswell Parks, the only one in the area who was trained and had experience in treating bullet wounds, done the surgery, the result may have been different. A crucial fault in the conduct of his surgical procedure was the absence of drainage to divert the pancreatic secretions from the abdominal cavity.

References

1. Margaret Leech, *In the Days of McKinley,* pp. 6–7.
2. Ibid., p. 10.
3. H. Wayne Morgan, *William McKinley and His America,* p. 23.
4. Ibid., pp. 315–16.
5. Ibid., p. 521.
6. Charles Olcott, *The Life of William McKinley,* 2:316.
7. Rudolph Marx, *The Health of the Presidents,* p. 275.
8. Leech, *In the Days of McKinley,* p. 596.
9. Marx, *The Health of the Presidents,* p. 276.

10. Selig Adler, "Operation on President McKinley," *Scientific American* (March 1963), p. 128.

11. Homer F. Cunningham, *The Presidents' Last Years*, p. 178.

12. *New York Times*, September 7, 1901.

13. Adler, "Operation on President McKinley," p. 118.

14. Ibid.

15. Marx, *The Health of the Presidents*, p. 278.

16. Ibid., p. 279.

17. Edmund Morris, *The Rise of Theodore Roosevelt*, pp. 740–45.

18. Adler, "Operation on President McKinley," p. 123.

19. Ibid.

25

Theodore Roosevelt

Theodore Roosevelt, the twenty-sixth president of the United States, was born October 27, 1858, in New York City during Buchanan's presidency.

Thedore Roosevelt would probably be a classical case for students of psychosomatic medicine. His signs and symptoms appeared more often when he was under stress. He was reported to stress not only himself but everyone around him. The illnesses most often referred to in his biographies were asthma and cholera morbus (an acute gastroenteritis occurring in summer and autumn marked by severe cramps, diarrhea, and vomiting). The cholera morbus seemed to be related to stressful situations. Asthma, which is mentioned most frequently, was, if not due to stress, precipitated by it.

He was referred to as a bright, hyperactive baby, who had early problems with severe asthmatic attacks. The attacks occurred frequently and kept him from resting at night. There are frequent references in the writings about TR's asthma. TR referred to himself in his autobiography, "I was a sickly, delicate boy who suffered much from asthma and frequently had to be taken away on trips to find a place where I could breathe."[1] He was awakened at night with a feeling of suffocation, gasping for breath, and cyanotic (the blue coloring of the skin which goes with lack of oxygen). His asthma persisted throughout adolescence. The attacks were frequently associated with diarrhea.

All kinds of medications were tried. One of the most effective treatments was caffeine contained in a cup of strong coffee. This was effective in relieving his asthma but caused him to lose sleep.[2] His parents also arranged for him to inhale the fumes of stramonium, from jimsonweed, found in Jamestown, Virginia. This drug acts as a bronchodilator and was very frequently—at least until recent years—smoked in a pipe for the relief of asthma.

Roosevelt in his diaries related after his father's death his grief for his father and the wonderful, loving care he gave his son: "I remember so well when I was a very weak asthmatic child, he used to walk up and down with me in his arms for hours together night after night. . . . I owe everything I am or have to Father. . . . I was a sickly, timid boy. He not only took great and untiring care of me, but some of my earliest remembrances are of nights when he would walk up and down with me for an hour at a time in his arms when I was a wretched little mite suffering acutely from asthma."[3]

In 1869, when Theodore was 11 years of age, his family, hoping to alleviate the asthma problems of Teddy and his sister, went to France, Italy, Austria, and Germany. During the journey Teddy had recurring and frequent asthmatic attacks and diarrhea. There was relief of his symptoms when they visited some mountain resorts where the rarified atmosphere contained less dust and pollen. A second trip, to Egypt and the Holy Land, where the climate was dry, also gave some relief.[4]

Teddy also had the usual childhood diseases, including chicken pox, mumps, and measles. His asthma and gastrointestinal problems seemed to have retarded his growth. He was a pale, thin boy, small for his age, with skinny legs.[5] Theodore was remembered by one of his fellow travelers on the steamer as a tall, thin lad with bright eyes and legs like pipestems, who developed rapidly in mind but whose asthma still tormented him and threatened to make a permanent invalid of him.[6]

Very early in life Roosevelt learned that his vision was poor. When he was about 13 he was given his first gun and was puzzled that his friends could see targets that he could not. One day someone read aloud some large letters on a distant billboard but Teddy could not even see the letters. Teddy recognized that there was something wrong with his vision, told his father, and was fitted for his first pair of glasses. Roosevelt stated that before he had gotten his spectacles he had not realized just how beautiful the world was. He concluded that his previous clumsiness and awkwardness were at least partially due to the fact that he could not see.[7]

Teddy's father was pleased with his mental development, but was not satisfied with his progress physically. Roosevelt, Sr., outfitted their New York home with a small gymnasium and told Teddy, "You have brains but you have a sickly body. In order to make your brains bring you what they ought, you must build up your body—it depends on you." Teddy became determined to become strong and he did his gymnasium exercises religiously.[8] To compensate for the humiliation brought about by his weakness as a child, he became obsessed with the idea of excelling in sports, which called for strength and stamina, such as boxing, wrestling, and mountain climbing. He even became an acceptable tennis player.

In his autobiography TR cited an incident which spurred him to

develop himself physically in order to be able to defend himself. This occurred when he was about 14 years of age.

> Having an attack of asthma, I was sent off by myself to Moosehead Lake
> in the stagecoach. Two boys who were about my age, much more con-
> fident and also much more mischievous, were also in the coach. I have
> no doubt they were good-hearted boys, but they were boys. They found
> that I was a predestined victim and industriously proceeded to make life
> miserable for me. The worst feature was that when I finally tried to fight
> them, I discovered that either one singly could not only handle me with
> easy contempt but handle me so as not to hurt me much, yet prevent
> me from doing any harm whatever in return. That experience taught me
> probably what no amount of advice could have taught me. This one in-
> cident occurred which did me real good. I made up my mind that I must
> try to learn so that I would not again be put in such a helpless position.
> I decided that I would try to supply its place by training. Accordingly,
> with my father's hearty approval, I started to box. I was painfully slow
> and awkward and certainly worked two to three years before I made any
> perceptible improvement.[9]

After being fitted with thick-lensed glasses, he practiced with his rifle
until he became a crack shot.[10] In his early teens Roosevelt was very much
involved in hunting and taxidermy. Along with these interests he began
to develop more stamina. His asthmatic attacks occurred less frequently
and his physical energy seemed almost inexhaustible.[11]

Roosevelt entered Harvard at age 18. At that time he was described
as "thin chested, bespectacled, and frail." Richard Welling, who at that
time was the strongest student in the records of Harvard's gymnasium, had
the impression that "Theodore was a youth in the kindergarten stage of
physical development, drearily swinging between vertical poles."[12] Later,
however, Welling was amazed to find what remarkable vitality TR possessed.

In his days at Harvard in the class of 1880 he did not smoke or drink.
He was happy to learn, he wrote in one of his letters home, that of the
11 young men at his dinner table, no fewer than 7 did not smoke and 4
drank nothing stronger than beer.[13]

While still a freshman, he was engaged in numerous activities including boxing, wrestling, body building, and his daily hours of recita-
tion.[14] "I did a good deal of boxing and wrestling at Harvard," he wrote,
"but never attained to the first rank in either, even in my own weight.
Once in a big contest in the gym, I got either into the finals or semi-finals,
I forgot which. I was fond of horseback riding, but took to it slowly and
with difficulty, as with boxing. It was a long time before I became a re-
spectable rider."[15]

In spite of his modest statement in his autobiography about his prowess as a boxer while at Harvard, he wrote his family that by the middle of his freshman year he worked daily with the boxing master at the college gymnasium and that the following year he hoped to win the undergraduate lightweight championship. He entered the competition, but after winning the first bout was defeated by a contestant who, according to an item in the *New York Times,* spent most of the match punishing Roosevelt severely.[16]

In February 1877, during his freshman year at Harvard, he had a bout with measles. He did not allow this illness to cause him to lose time. He canceled his Easter vacation in New York and spent the time on a friend's farm where he completed in five days the parts of several classics.[17]

In March 1880 TR, in the spring of his last year at Harvard, had a physical examination by the school physician, Dr. Dudley A. Sargent. The physical findings were: 5 feet 8 inches and weight 136 pounds. Dr. Sargent listened to his breath sounds and his heart and followed up with some advice. The doctor told him that his heart had an irregular beat and it would be wise for him to select a career of a sedentary type, avoid undue excitement, and never run up stairs.[18] It is likely that no more futile advice than this was ever given anyone. His beloved father had advised a vigorous life and his inclination was exactly opposite to that of Dr. Sargent.

When TR finished at Harvard he had, due to his unrelenting efforts, become much stronger physically. He still had some bouts with asthma but not of the severe disabling kind that he had endured in earlier years. He still craved activity and the craving grew stronger as his body strength grew.[19]

The summer of 1880, after his graduation from Harvard, he spent completely ignoring the advice of Dr. Sargent by taking long rowboat excursions around Oyster Bay and climbing mountains in Maine, followed by a week's hunting trip with his brother, Elliott.

The next summer, after studying law at Columbia for an academic year, he took a four months' honeymoon tour with his bride, Alice Lee. The climax of the tour was Switzerland where, after climbing a few of the lesser Alps, he climbed Pilatus and Jungfrau. He then tried the most difficult, the 15,000 foot Matterhorn. TR hired a guide and climbed to an icy cave near the peak where they spent the night. They got up the next morning at 3:45 so as to be able to see the sunrise from the summit.[20]

Viewing the truly awesome Matterhorn from high on an opposite mountain is enough to make one wonder why one did not just spend his time admiring its splendor rather than clawing and scratching one's way to the top of a mountain—a climb which is fraught with great danger. The danger involved is manifest when one visits the small graveyard near Zermatt, which is filled with those who failed in their attempts. Perhaps if we understand what motivated Roosevelt to climb the Matterhorn, we would better understand the man. Roosevelt was always testing certain qualities in his life. Sir Arnold Lunn wrote that, while trying to explain the climbers' motivation, "I understand our verdict on a particular sport is necessarily influenced by the values we attach to the qualities it tests."[21]

During this summer of strenuous mountain climbing, there was no reference to sickness. He never once mentioned asthma or cholera morbus, his chief afflictions. He seemed to have won his battle to achieve good health.[22]

During the summer of 1883, however, TR had a return of asthma and cholera morbus. The illness was perhaps precipitated by some nervous strain of the past winter, plus the prospect of becoming a father. He was at that time very ill. In early July 1883 his doctor prescribed for him a stay at a spa, Richfield Springs in the Catskills. In a letter to Corinne, his sister, he described the experience. "Under directions of a heavy jowled idiot of a medical man whose tender mercies Dr. [William M.] Polk has entrusted me, I am rapidly relapsing."

At Richfield Springs he was forced to drink prescribed mineral water. "I don't mind drinking the stuff," he said. "You can get an idea of the taste by steeping a box of sulfur matches in dishwater and drinking the delectable compound tepid from an old kerosene oil can. At first the boiling baths were rather pleasant; but for the first time in my life I came in an ace of fainting when I got out of the bath this morning. I have a bad headache, a general feeling of lassitude, and am bored out of my life by having nothing to do."

Roosevelt married Alice Lee soon after his graduation from Harvard. Four years later his wife died of complications which occurred at the birth of his daughter. Roosevelt's asthma had improved in the four years of his marriage and his attacks were much less frequent, but after his wife died he had a severe recurrence of his asthma, associated with a chronic persistent cough. TR feared that he may have begun to develop tuberculosis. His doctor advised him to go west to live, so Teddy bought a ranch in North Dakota and became a cowboy.

His life in North Dakota was one of vigorous activity.[23] Roosevelt said, "In that land we led a free and hardy life with horse and with rifle. We worked under the scorching mid-summer sun, when the wide plains shimmered and labored in the heat, and we knew the freezing misery riding night guard around the cattle in the late fall roundup. In the soft springtime, the stars were glorious in our eyes each night before we fell asleep, and in the winter we rode through blinding blizzards when driving snowdust burned our faces."[24]

In 1882 he became a New York assemblyman and on January 24 made his first speech to the assembly. During the delivery of this speech he was noted to have some respiratory problems. Apparently, there was some difficulty with his old problem — asthma. The reporters also noted some slight stammer.[25]

In early 1885 his months of writing had left him physically and emotionally drained. And, as usual, when he was under great stress he was visited by cholera morbus and asthma which delayed his return to the Badlands until April.[26]

In June 1885, after another winter and spring in the Badlands, TR returned to New York. He was there largely to see about the publication of his book, *Hunting Trips of a Ranchman,* and to oversee the building of Sagamore Hill, his future home. He returned to the Badlands to attend a meeting of the stockholders' association of which he was president. TR returned to New York in September to take part in the Republican state convention. He continued his vigorous activities on Long Island, riding with the Meadowbrook Hounds. On one ride he sustained a broken arm and other injuries when his horse missed a jump and rolled on top of him. After the fall he immediately remounted and returned to the hunt and that night attended a dinner.[27] TR's stay in the Badlands resulted in a net loss of $20,000 but more importantly, there was a great increase in his physical strength and stamina. He liquidated his financial interests in the Badlands in the spring of 1887.[28]

In 1891 while TR (age 33) was still a civil service commissioner he had a severe attack of bronchitis. His doctors warned him of the possibility that the illness might develop into pneumonia. He improved for a short time but became worse in December. His second wife, Edith, insisted that he go to bed for eight days. This was his longest confinement since childhood. His bronchitis recurred again in 1897.[29]

In 1897, his last year as police commissioner of New York, he was 38 years of age. He was said to have the strength of an ox, quick in movement and tough in endurance.[30]

In 1898 TR resigned his position as assistant secretary of the navy to become part of the Expeditionary Force in Cuba during the Spanish-American War. TR determined that if there was to be a war he would be a part of it. Just before the advance on Santiago and the charge on San Juan Hill, his regiment came under fire from the Spaniards. According to

Teddy, "One of the shrapnel bullets fell on my wrist and raised a lump as large as a hickory nut, but did not break the skin." Apparently this was his only very close encounter with instruments of war.[31]

In the Spanish-American War many more soldiers died of dysentery, yellow fever, and malaria than from bullets. As for TR, from all accounts he developed what was called Cuban fever—undoubtedly malaria. Apparently, there was some confusion about TR's health in Cuba since there were many later references to his having contracted malaria during that miniwar.

After the fighting ceased and he had returned to the United States, his popularity was at an all-time high. Three months of terrible food, unbearable heat, and mosquitoes had not caused him to lose weight. He looked heavier and stronger than he had at the onset. He almost immediately became involved heavily in politics. In November 1898 he was elected governor of New York. TR's health was undoubtedly good while he served as governor of New York and was vice president of the United States.

In regard to his habits, we know that TR consumed a moderate amount of wine and occasionally there is a reference to mint juleps. Archie Butt, in a letter to Clara, wrote on December 15, 1908, "While he does not smoke himself, he says that the host can give his guests the finest meal in the world, yet undo everything by offering an indifferent cigar after dinner."[32]

During his presidency, aside from the ordinary demands of the office, Roosevelt set aside two hours each day for strenuous exercise. He still did some boxing. There was a young army captain acting as his sparring partner who did not pull his punches, and hit TR in the left eye. The blow resulted in intraocular hemorrhage and detachment of the retina. Roosevelt stopped boxing and took up jujitsu.[33]

During the coal strike of 1902, which idled 140,000 miners, Roosevelt became very active in trying to bring about a just settlement. On September 3 he was being driven toward Pittsfield when his carriage was struck by a street car. A Secret Service operative was killed. The president was thrown from his carriage, and at first it appeared that his injuries were minor. He had some facial contusions and walked with a limp, but with his usual bravado he chose to ignore the injury and continued with the tour. The injury was much more severe than was first thought and the extent of it was not made public at that time. The tour was halted in Indianapolis and an abscess on his leg was drained. There was apparently some bone involvement with early osteomyelitis. After his return to Washington he was confined to a wheelchair for some time.[34]

In a letter to Grover Cleveland, dated October 10, 1902, TR wrote, "My dear Mr. Cleveland. Will you excuse me for not writing? It is almost impossible for me to write in my present position. I am sincerely sorry to have to say that the doctors tell me that in all probability it will be impossible for me to go to Princeton on the 25th. The wound in my leg is healing rapidly, but I shall have to exercise great care because I have narrowly escaped serious trouble with the bone."[35]

This leg injury plagued him off and on for the rest of his life, with periodic worsening of the condition. Three times during 1904 he suffered an injury to his leg. On one occasion he injured a muscle in his thigh with the formation of a large muscular hematoma.[36]

In the latter part of TR's second term Archie Butt wrote a letter to his mother, dated September 25, 1908, in which he noted, "He [TR] has not taken any exercise since he came to Washington this time. He is suffering from an old wound he received several years ago in a trolley accident. At that time it was thought that the bone of his leg was injured, but he apparently recovered. He told me yesterday that whenever he gets tired or takes a jar it pains him again. I am afraid he is going to have trouble with it in Africa, for I have seen cases like this—one developed most seriously in the tropics. It would not surprise me if he had to have part of the bone taken out later."[37]

One curious medical incident of Roosevelt's presidency concerns a cryptic reference to yellow underwear. In a letter to Clara, November 19, 1908, Archie Butt related that TR told him, "Wood [General Leonard Wood] has persuaded me that the new yellow underwear which the army is getting out will prevent the actinic rays from eating my spinal cord. Will you look into this matter and tell me what it means?"[38]

No one else, we are sure, has had any idea what Leonard Wood had in mind. We suppose he was referring to the possible evil effects of the sun rays. Just how yellow underwear would help, no one knows.

The most remarkable event of his presidency, however, is undoubtedly his amazing behavior after being shot by a would-be assassin. On October 14, 1912, when Roosevelt was running for a third term on the Progressive ticket, there was an attempt at an assassination of Teddy by a crazed fanatic, John Schrank. TR was standing in an automobile, taking the adulation of a friendly crowd, when the assassin at almost point-blank range fired the shot. Ebert E. Martin, one of TR's secretaries, forced the would-be assassin to the ground. Martin was a former football tackle and his intervention may have saved the president's life. In spite of being hit, TR insisted on going ahead.

One of his secretaries suggested that TR be taken at once to a hospital.

TR said, "You get me to that speech. It may be the last one I shall deliver, but I am going to deliver this one." Three physicians who were found in the audience examined his wound and said the bullet had penetrated his breast but that they could not tell how serious the injury was. However, in their opinion, he should be taken at once to a hospital. He refused absolutely to allow such a move: "I will make this speech or die; one or the other." When TR got to the platform, the presiding officer said: "I have something to tell you. I hope you will receive it with calmness. Colonel Roosevelt has been shot and he is wounded." Roosevelt stepped to the front of the platform and said, "I am going to ask you to be very quiet and please to excuse me from making a very long speech. I will do the best I can; but, you see, there is a bullet in my body but it is nothing. I am not hurt badly." TR talked for an hour and when asked how he felt, he answered, "I am as strong as a bull moose." The party was thereafter called the Bull Moose party.[39]

The bullet had passed through his clothes, the manuscript which he had in his pocket, and his metal spectacle case. He finished his speech and was taken by train to Chicago, arriving at 3:30 A.M. TR refused to be carried to the ambulance — he walked there — and also refused to be carried from the ambulance to the hospital. It was determined by examination, which included an X ray, that the bullet had entered his breast at the right and below the nipple, was lodged in a rib, but had not entered the chest cavity. Other sources say that the bullet fractured the fourth rib on the right, but did not enter the chest cavity.[40]

The surgeon, John Murphy, did not attempt surgical removal of the bullet for fear of infection. TR received a shot of tetanus antitoxin. His chest was strapped, and he was given mild sedation and bedrest. He recovered uneventfully.[41]

By early 1909, when TR had left the presidency and was contemplating a hunting trip to Africa, his health had deteriorated somewhat, and some of his friends had great reservations regarding his ability to make the trip. "A touch of Cuban fever was still in his blood. He was totally blind in one eye and the sight in the other was imperfect. Although only 50 years old, he was considerably overweight."[42] However, at the end of the expedition in March 1910 at Khartoum, there had been only five days of illness due to the fever contracted while in Cuba.[43]

At the time of TR's defeat as candidate for the presidency for the third term, he was 54 years of age. His arthritis — apparently of a generalized inflammatory nature, which added to his leg injury sustained in 1902 — so crippled him that he could not engage in the vigorous exercises that had been his wont in earlier days. As a result, he gained considerable weight and became thick around his middle. He could not or did not control his appetite. His friends related that "he ate like a trencherman." It was not unusual for him to consume a whole chicken with trimmings all by himself and wash it down with four glasses of milk.[44]

Nevertheless, Teddy opted to go on another hunting expedition — this time to South America. He wished to go to the region of central Brazil, at that time unexplored, and reach the wildest regions bordering on the Amazon. He was, by the route he had chosen, to encounter the River of Doubt — Rio de Duvido — by which he would descend to the Amazon. The trip was attempted with much difficulty. The group's provisions shrank rapidly, and there were almost no game animals for them to shoot. They were glad to shoot a monkey or a great lizard for fresh meat. Insects bit them day and night and caused inflammation and infection.

Roosevelt wounded his leg on a rock while wading in the water, and the wound became so infected that he had to be carried over the portages. Finally, fever attacked TR, and the expedition was delayed for a few days because he was too weak to continue. Meanwhile, the provisions were so low that they seemed to be facing starvation. Roosevelt begged the others to leave him behind and continue without him. He felt that if they delayed further they would all die of starvation. Of course, they refused to leave him. He determined to shoot himself unless he soon became better.

Eventually, 48 days after the trip down the River of Doubt they saw a peasant rubber gatherer, the first human being they had encountered. Where the River of Doubt flowed into the River Madeira, TR took a steamship which carried them to Manáos on the Amazon. This steamer then carried Roosevelt to New York. On the voyage home TR regained some of his strength.[45]

However, on June 29, 1914, five months after his return to New York from his expedition to Brazil, TR wrote to Arthur Hamilton Lee, "I'm not in good trim. Five minutes after you left me on the tugboat — and thank heavens you did not leave me before it happened — I, without any warning, had an attack of fever, which lasted intermittently for some days. I am not over it now and my voice is naturally worse than ever."[46] From descriptions which recur throughout the literature on TR, it seems his intermittent fever was due to a quinine-resistant malaria.

Moreover, the deep cut he had received on his leg on the voyage down the River of Doubt developed an abscess which never completely healed.[47] He obviously developed osteomyelitis, since he had repeated recurrences of sinuses draining purulent material, and from time to time some fragments of bone which separated and were extruded. Fistulas closed from time to time and had to be drained surgically.[48]

In fact, TR would never regain the health he enjoyed before the expedition to Brazil, as he himself confessed. In a letter to Dr. Pressley Marion Rixey, dated Oyster Bay, February 21, 1919: "As for me, my dear doctor, I am practically through. I am not a man like you who keeps his youth almost to the end, and I am now pretty nearly done out. I would not say this except to my old friend, who was also my old physician. Because it is rather poor business to speak about one's personal ailments; but the trouble is that I have rheumatism or gout and things of that kind to a degree that makes it impossible for me to take very much exercise; and then in turn the fact I cannot take exercise prevents my keeping in good condition."[49]

It is apparent that TR had contracted malaria in Cuba, which was referred to as Cuban fever, and that his problems with the fever persisted throughout his life. Inflammation of his joints, which was referred to as rheumatism, was at times very painful and disabling. The general description of his joint ailment corresponds more to rheumatoid arthritis than anything else.

In February 1918 he was hospitalized for several days with a flare-up of the abscess in his leg. At the same time he developed an infection in his left ear, which deafened him permanently.[50]

At the age of 60 TR was deaf in his left ear and blind in his left eye. Following his ear infection, in addition, he had a case of chronic mastoiditis.

Surgeons, for reasons not clear, did not operate on his mastoid, but decided to treat conservatively with irrigations. After TR's acute ear trouble, his health did show some moderate improvement.

There are some contradictions in the accounts of William Thayer about TR's later illnesses. Thayer related that in the winter of 1918 TR's mastoid infection was so severe that surgery was done and that his life hung on a thread for several days. That fall he had another outbreak of his ear infection and had to be hospitalized in Roosevelt Hospital. He remained there until Christmas Eve. At that time he was also suffering from an inflammatory type of rheumatism.[51]

Roosevelt remained at home after his discharge from the hospital and spent the evening of January 5, 1919, with his family. He retired at 11:00 P.M. and at that time gave an order to his attendant to put out the light. At about 4:00 A.M. the next morning James Amos, his attendant, noted that Roosevelt's breathing pattern was greatly changed and called the nurse, but when they reached his bedside, he was dead.[52]

References

1. Theodore Roosevelt, *Theodore Roosevelt: An Autobiography*, p. 13.
2. Rudolph Marx, *The Health of the Presidents*, p. 284.
3. Noel F. Busch, *T. R.: The Story of Theodore Roosevelt*, pp. 15–16.
4. Marx, *The Health of the Presidents*, p. 285.
5. Ibid.
6. William Roscoe Thayer, *Theodore Roosevelt*, p. 11.
7. Roosevelt, *Theodore Roosevelt: An Autobiography*, p. 14.
8. Thayer, *Theodore Roosevelt*, p. 11.
9. Roosevelt, *Theodore Roosevelt: An Autobiography*, pp. 26–27.
10. Marx, *The Health of the Presidents*, p. 286.
11. Stefan Lorant, *The Life and Times of Theodore Roosevelt*, p. 116.
12. Edmund Morris, *The Rise of Theodore Roosevelt*, p. 84.
13. Henry F. Pringle, *Theodore Roosevelt: A Biography*, pp. 28–29.
14. Edmund Morris, *The Rise of Theodore Roosevelt*, p. 87.
15. Roosevelt, *Theodore Roosevelt: An Autobiography*, p. 28.
16. Lorant, *The Life and Times of Theodore Roosevelt*, p. 152.
17. Edmund Morris, *The Rise of Theodore Roosevelt*, p. 89.
18. Busch, *T. R.: The Story of Theodore Roosevelt*, pp. 33–34.
19. Thayer, *Theodore Roosevelt*, p. 25.
20. Busch, *T. R.: The Story of Theodore Roosevelt*, pp. 34–35.
21. Sir Arnold Lunn, *Matterhorn Centenary*, p. 17, insert from top and right side of page.
22. Carleton Putnam, *Theodore Roosevelt, a Biography*, 1:236.
23. Marx, *The Health of the Presidents*, p. 287.
24. Roosevelt, *Theodore Roosevelt: An Autobiography*, p. 59.
25. Edmund Morris, *The Rise of Theodore Roosevelt*, p. 168.
26. Ibid., p. 300.
27. Lorant, *The Life and Times of Theodore Roosevelt*, p. 205.
28. Ibid.
29. Edmund Morris, *The Rise of Theodore Roosevelt*, p. 445.
30. Thayer, *Theodore Roosevelt*, p. 108.
31. Roosevelt, *Theodore Roosevelt: An Autobiography*, p. 133.
32. Archibald Butt, *Taft and Roosevelt: The Intimate Letters of Archie Butt*, 1:246.
33. Marx, *The Health of the Presidents*, p. 290.
34. Pringle, *Theodore Roosevelt*, p. 269.
35. Ellen Morris, editor, *The Letters of Theodore Roosevelt*, p. 346.
36. Marx, *The Health of the Presidents*, p. 290.
37. Butt, *Taft and Roosevelt*, p. 101.
38. Ibid., p. 182.
39. Homer F. Cunningham, *The Presidents' Last Years*, p. 182.
40. Joseph Bishop, *Theodore Roosevelt and His Times*, pp. 338–39.
41. Marx, *The Health of the Presidents*, pp. 292–93.
42. Pringle, *Theodore Roosevelt*, p. 508.
43. Ibid., p. 510.
44. Marx, *The Health of the Presidents*, p. 294.
45. Thayer, *Theodore Roosevelt*, pp. 390–95.
46. Ellen Morris, *The Letters of Theodore Roosevelt*, 7:769.

47. Cunningham, *The Presidents' Last Years*, p. 183.
48. Marx, *The Health of the Presidents*, p. 295.
49. Ellen Morris, *The Letters of Theodore Roosevelt*, 8:903.
50. Cunningham, *The Presidents' Last Years*, p. 189.
51. Thayer, *Theodore Roosevelt*, pp. 448–49.
52. Ibid., p. 449.

26

William Howard Taft

William Howard Taft was born September 15, 1857, in Cincinnati, Ohio. He was the only American who was both president and chief justice of the Supreme Court. Always a good student, he was admitted to Yale University at the age of 17; graduated in 1878, second in his class; and gave the class oration. In 1880 he received his law degree from the Cincinnati Law School and was admitted to the Ohio bar.

His health as a child and youth were very good, although he had one fairly serious accident at age nine. He was riding downhill in a horse-drawn wagon when the horses got out of control and ran away. The wagon was overturned, and Taft was thrown out, landing on his head. His scalp was badly lacerated, and he had a slight fracture.[1]

Not much can be said about Taft's health, however, without saying a great deal about his size. Apparently, there was never a time when he did not have a struggle with being overweight, for even as an infant he was labeled as being fat and cherubic in appearance. His mother wrote to a friend, "He is very large for his age and grows fatter every day." This trend continued throughout his life. At age 20 he weighed 220 pounds, and when he was 32, as solicitor general, Taft was already having quite a problem with obesity. In fact, his weight kept him out of the military in 1898.[2] When he was 53, in the second year of his presidency, his weight peaked at 350 pounds.[3]

Taft, almost the antithesis of Theodore Roosevelt's doctrine of stren-uosity, exercised only to try to control his weight. In 1900, for example, at the age of 43, Taft was made president of the U.S. Commission to the Philippines. On the voyage to the Philippines Taft worried about his bulk and exercised by tramping around the deck. His efforts were futile, how-ever, and his bulk, which grew year by year, became the basis for many jokes throughout his life. His journey took him through Japan, for in-stance, where his first ride in a ricksha occasioned much amusement.[4]

During the first decade of the century, a legend developed that Taft was large, fat, and always smiling. A great many individuals added to the legend, including Taft himself to some degree. He had encouraged the publication of Elihu Root's witty inquiry cable to the Philippines concerning the health of the horse which had borne his tonnage.[5] An associate justice of the Supreme Court added to this legend in an address at Yale: "Secretary Taft is the politest man alive. I heard that recently he arose in a streetcar and gave his seat to three women."[6]

In September 1902, while Taft was governor-general of the Philippines, he became ill. In the beginning the illness was diagnosed as dengue. He was taken from the Malacanan Palace to the army hospital, staying for two weeks before it was decided that he had an abdominal abscess.[7] Since it is known that Taft had amebiasis while in the Philippines—really amebic dysentery—and, since amoebic infection is frequently accompanied by abdominal abscesses, it is most likely that this was an amoebic abscess. That the abscess was in the perineum makes an amoebic abscess even more likely. There was some apprehension lest gangrene set in. After the surgery any immediate danger was over, but he was still far from well. A second operation was performed on Thanksgiving Day, and Taft made plans to return to the United States for recuperation.[8]

During his return to the United States on Christmas Eve, 1901, the civil governor was very weak, and even after weeks in Washington Taft's health was still poor. His gastrointestinal problem was still with him. At that time it appeared that another operation would be necessary, and during the visit to the United States in 1902 Taft had his third operation for the perineal abscess. After a period of recuperation Taft returned to the Philippines by way of Europe.

In early 1903, while Taft was still in the Philippines, his health was still not good. The abscess which had caused so much trouble seemingly had healed; but in January 1903 he attended a Filipino christening and came down with indigestion. In March he was suffering from amebic dysentery again, a disease which was prevalent in the Philippines. By the end of the month the members of his family were alarmed by his illness. Taft, refusing to give in to his illness, made a trip to Baguio, a mountain resort, the last part of the journey being on horseback. He sent a cable to the secretary of war, Elihu Root: "Stood trip well, rode a horse back twenty-five miles to five thousand feet elevation." Root, reassured, and with the picture of the 300-pound Taft flashing through his mind, called a stenographer and dictated a reply: "Referring to your telegram, how is the horse?"[9]

Taft was subsequently secretary of war under Teddy Roosevelt for four years, 1904–8, and in 1908 he succeeded Teddy Roosevelt as president of the United States.

When president, Taft normally began his day with exercise at 7:00

A.M. Generally free by 5:00 P.M., he would sometimes go for a walk or drive before going home. Later in life he gave up riding horseback to exercise and took up walking in order to keep his weight down. He then became almost addicted to golf, at which he became adept.[10]

Archie Butt, military aide to Taft, wrote some very revealing things about the health and habits of Taft and Roosevelt. "In contrast to brisk, bouncy Teddy Roosevelt, who called men to follow him, the heavy—indeed immense—Taft poured over them affectionately, like a huge pan of sweet milk."[11]

On April 4, 1909, Butt wrote, "He eats a hearty breakfast, and invariably remains in his office from 8:30 A.M. until 5:00 P.M., when he goes riding or walking. Sometimes he breaks his fast by eating an apple, but seldom anything more."[12] Butt continued:

> I do not think the fast does him any good, for he eats a correspondingly larger dinner. He has a tremendous appetite, and does not control it as did his predecessor, Roosevelt. . . . I could not help laughing at him one evening at dinner; he had finished dinner and we were sitting around the table smoking. There was a large bon bon cordial fruit before him, and every now and then he would take a piece, apparently unconscious that he was doing it. Before we rose from the table he had eaten every piece there was in the dish. He never smokes, and in consequence has to do something.[13]

Of course, after he became president the Taft legend grew. The witty sayings about his obesity continued. (William Allen White described him as "a big blond man who is molded between two six foot parentheses.") Anecdotes, jokes, and cartoons inspired by Taft's weight were innumerable. All Washington talked, for example, about the bathtub—reputed to be the size of a small swimming pool—which had to be installed for him in the White House. Several times it was said he had become stuck in the regular bathtub, and had to be assisted by several individuals in order to get out.[14]

Many of his friends and associates delighted in teasing him about his tremendous size. James Watson was present one day to observe an exchange between the president and Chauncey Depew, the senator from New York from 1899–1911, in which Taft for once got the upper hand. "Mr. Depew stepped up to Taft and taking liberties that I wouldn't have thought of taking with the President, said to him, putting his hand on Mr. Taft's big frontal development, 'What are you going to name it when it comes, Mr. President?' It was just about at that time that Taft was beginning to have some difficulty with Roosevelt, and he quickly responded,

'Well, if it's a boy, I'll call it William. If it's a girl, I'll call it Theodora; but if it turns out to be just wind, I'll call it Chauncey.'"[15] Taft often joked about himself. For example, after a state visit to Mexico to discuss relations between the United States and Mexico with the Mexican president Díaz, Butt and John Hays Hammond (also in the party) returned to the special train with the president, who suggested that they seemed very nervous and that a highball might steady their nerves. "Thank God we're out of Mexico," Hammond said, as he drank one, "and the day's over. We've been half crazy for fear someone would take a shot at you." "Oh, so that's what's been bothering you," the president replied, "Why should you worry about that? If anyone wanted to get me he could not have missed such a large target."[16]

Taft at times liked to attend a baseball game, but on account of his size special preparation was needed. On April 19, 1909, Archie Butt reported in a letter to Clara, his usual correspondent: "We rode for an hour and a quarter. He then changed his clothes and we took the big touring car for the ballpark. I had gone earlier in the morning with Tom Noyes to select a box, and there later to bring a big chair for him to use, and finally secured one at Moses."[17]

After becoming president, Taft ate as never before. Apparently he was reluctant to forego the one sure source of comfort while suffering in the White House. He sensed that the heavy responsibilities of the presidency were the cause of his weight problem. Mrs. Parks, the White House housekeeper, described "one little meal" that the president enjoyed, which included lobster stew, salmon cutlets with peas, roast tenderloin with vegetables, salad, roast turkey with potato salad, cold tongue with ham, frozen pudding, cake, fruit and coffee.[18]

On May 2 and 3, 1909, Archie Butt reported a severe attack of upper respiratory infection in the president. Then on May 8 a bug flew into Taft's eye and injured it so badly that he had to wear a bandage for several days.[19]

Taft did play golf and ride horseback with Archie Butt, who was proud to have done something in the way of keeping him from lapsing into a semicomatose state. Occasionally, however, Taft would not go out. Butt states, "The President didn't play golf this A.M. He is laid up with gout, looking a picture of woe." Butt had suspected for some time that the president had grown gouty, and Taft resented the suggestion that he had such a disease. Dr. Jackson, his physician, when called to examine Taft's feet, began to laugh. The president grew red, but finally forced a smile, saying, "It is, is it?" "It certainly is," answered Jackson, "and as good a case of it as I ever saw."[20]

As his military aide while Taft was president, Archie Butt summed up Taft: "I have found three things he [the president] does well. He dances well, he curses well, and he laughs well. . . . On the other hand, his corpulency made him sensitive to heat and increased his natural lethargy. Often after a meal his head would fall on his chest, and he would go fast asleep for ten to fifteen minutes, awaken, and then continue the conversation where he left off. Almost invariably he fell asleep in church."[21] Taft's excessive weight actually impaired his ability to carry on the function of the presidency. Butt reported several occasions when in the middle of the affairs of state he closed his eyes and took a catnap. "Even though Taft was aware of the humiliating consequences of his drowsiness, he was happy to escape in slumber." Nellie, his wife, dubbed him "Sleeping Beauty."[22]

In a letter from Butt to his most frequent correspondent, May 12, 1909, he wrote: "Dear Clara. The death of Mrs. Dalzell is very sad. Chairs were provided for the President and myself, and other chairs were there for the Vice-President and Mrs. Sherman, the speaker, and other men of note. I gave my chair next to the President to Justice White. In the midst of the service I saw the President fall asleep, and I stood there horrified when I heard an incipient snore. I could not wake him up — I was not near enough to him, and just as I had made up my mind to walk over to him and arouse him for fear he would fall into a heavy snore, Justice White fell asleep also; and I let them remain so, for had either snored loudly I had made up my mind to lay it to the Justice when comment was made of the incident."[23]

Dr. Sidney Burwell, of Harvard Medical School, noted the resemblance between the somnolent, wonderfully fat boy in Dickens's *Pickwick Papers* and certain of those patients who came under his clinical observation who were also very somnolent. The complex symptoms and signs were called the Pickwick syndrome. The syndrome is characterized by marked obesity, somnolence, impaired arterial oxygen saturation, and markedly reduced vital capacity. All these findings are brought about by the impaired mechanics of respiration due to obesity. A characteristic of such patients is an extraordinary degree of somnolence in which sleep may overcome the patient while he is sitting up or even while he is engaged in conversation or other muscular activity. The reference here is to extreme obesity associated with alveolar hypoventilation, or Pickwick's syndrome.[24]

It seems possible that Taft did have Pickwick's syndrome, and his untoward somnolence can thus be explained on the basis of his obesity. He apparently made no great effort to lose weight, though, so we shall never know if he would have been improved by weight reduction.

Different biographers, including Judith Anderson, ascribed his periods of great overweight to stress and a tendency to overeat while under stress. After his years as president he was offered the chair of constitutional law at Yale University, and within 18 months after accepting the appointment Taft, free from stress, reduced his weight from 350 pounds to 270 pounds.

When Taft became chief justice in 1921 he no longer golfed or rode horseback and, although he still walked some, he had reason to be worried about his health. He had lost some weight but he was still vastly overweight. Taft was a temperate man in all ways but one. He neither smoked nor drank; his only excess was in overeating. When he was serene, his weight went down; when he was plagued with problems, his weight went up. He congratulated himself a year before his death that he weighed only 244 pounds.

In December 1922 the chief justice told his relatives and friends about a hospitalization during which a stone was removed from his bladder.[25] During the last decade of Taft's life he suffered from chronic genitourinary difficulties. He had prostatic hypertrophy which obstructed the flow of urine from his bladder so much that he was at times reduced to a dribble of urinary flow and was unable to empty his bladder completely. When Taft developed stones in his bladder, the "gravel" was removed with a cystoscope which was invented in 1920, just two years before he was operated for "gravel" in 1922.

In 1923, at age 66, Taft suffered from digestive and heart problems. The heart problem could have been heart failure, which at times is a sequel to Pickwick's syndrome. The heart problems, called "heart attacks" by his biographers, were of course not then separated into any definite categories of heart disease. The most logical conclusion again is that these episodes were due to right heart failure secondary to his obesity. It has been related by several different biographers that in the 1920s Taft was rapidly losing his memory. In March 1928, in response to a request for information regarding some person he had known, Taft said he could not remember. "My memory is growing poorer and poorer," he said.[26]

In March 1929 Taft, as chief justice, administered the oath of office to incoming President Herbert Hoover. This was the first presidential inaugural ever broadcast over the radio. Taft forgot some of his lines and had to improvise. From different references to his loss of memory at that time it is apparent that, had he been living now and consulting a modern neurologist, he could not have escaped without the diagnosis of Alzheimer's disease.

When Taft's brother, Charles, died in December 1929, Taft insisted on attending the funeral against his doctor's advice. He returned home so weak that he had to be hospitalized and subsequently declined into an all but helpless state from cardiovascular collapse. Robert, his son, returned to Washington in February 1930 to announce his father's retirement from the Supreme Court.[27]

Taft did live to be 77 years of age, which was several years beyond the life expectancy of his day. He was always overweight and he took very little exercise. Several biographers refer to his daily walks, but others attest that his walks were brief and short. During his last decade of life he was plagued with serious genitourinary problems, hypertension, and heart disease. At the time of Taft's resignation as chief justice his doctors issued a bulletin, saying that "for some years Chief Justice Taft has had a very high blood pressure, associated with general arteriosclerosis and myocarditis."[28]

It is safe to say that Taft, suffering as he did from severe hypertension, general arteriosclerosis, myocardial failure, and prostatic obstruction must also have suffered from renal failure. During his last days he hallucinated, and at times he failed to recognize visitors whom he knew well. He lingered, gravely ill, during February 1930, and died March 8, 1930.

References

1. Rudolph Marx, *The Health of the Presidents*, p. 299.
2. Henry F. Pringle, *The Life and Times of William Howard Taft*, 1:155.
3. Judith Icke Anderson, *William Howard Taft: An Intimate History*, pp. 29–31.
4. Pringle, *The Life and Times of William Howard Taft*, 1:166.
5. Ibid., p. 334.
6. Herbert F. Duffy, *William Howard Taft*, p. 5.
7. Ibid., p. 139.
8. Ibid.
9. Pringle, *The Life and Times of William Howard Taft*, 1:135–36.
10. Paolo E. Coletta, *The Presidency of William Howard Taft*, p. 2.
11. Archibald Butt, *Taft and Roosevelt: The Intimate Letters of Archie Butt*, 1:233.
12. Ibid., p. 37.
13. Ibid.
14. Anderson, *William Howard Taft*, p. 28.
15. Ibid.
16. John Hays Hammond, *The Autobiography of John Hays Hammond*, 2:259.
17. Butt, *Taft and Roosevelt*, 1:58.
18. Anderson, *William Howard Taft*, p. 29.
19. Butt, *Taft and Roosevelt*, 1:78.
20. Anderson, *William Howard Taft*, p. 30.
21. Coletta, *The Presidency of William Howard Taft*, p. 2.

22. Anderson, *William Howard Taft*, p. 31.

23. Butt, *Taft and Roosevelt*, 1:85.

24. C. Sidney Burwell, et al. *The American Journal of Medicine* 21 (November 1956): 811.

25. *Letter: Taft to J. C. C. Black*, December 25, 1922. (Relates to Black about surgical removal of bladder stones.)

26. *Letter: Taft to Robert A. Taft*, February 15, 1925. (Taft tells son, Robert, about newly invented cystoscope.)

27. Anderson, *William Howard Taft*, p. 27.

28. Marx, *The Health of the Presidents*, p. 306.

27

Woodrow Wilson

Woodrow Wilson, the twenty-eighth president of the United States, was born on December 28, 1856, in Staunton, Virginia. The history of his health is just as complex and obscure as that of Franklin Roosevelt and John Kennedy, and for the same reason—a conspiracy of silence.

(Thomas) Woodrow Wilson grew up in a Presbyterian manse. When his family lived in Augusta, Georgia, and his father's church was there Wilson was described this way: "Tommy Wilson grew from a fat, healthy infant into a sickly little boy. . . . In physique he resembled his mother. Tommy had pale gray eyes and dull blond hair. He was thin, sallow, and weak. His eyes were exceptionally deficient. He had just shed baby skirts when he put on spectacles. The onset of indigestion, which harassed him all of his life, began at a very early age."[1]

Woodrow Wilson received most of his tutoring from his father and lived his childhood almost in isolation.

Since his indigestion persisted, he had many days of headache and stomach pain. He was so frail and sickly that his parents kept him out of school. Tommy did not begin to learn the alphabet until he was age 9 and could not read until he was 11. Here was a very intelligent young boy who had a reading problem so severe that he could not read until he was 11. One must believe that he had dyslexia.[2]

Many of the biographers describe Wilson's early childhood as frail, sickly, and prone to childhood illness. When he finally entered school for the first time at the age of 13, he was described as a rather pathetic little boy: weak, sickly, nervous, and retarded in his development. His eyesight was defective, and he suffered almost constantly from indigestion and headaches.[3] Others, however, say that Wilson, as a child, was engaged in a full complement of sports, including horseback riding and baseball. One prominent biographer, Edwin Weinstein, who was interested more in the psychological aspects, stated, "There is no evidence of any illness in childhood, and no record of any behavior that would indicate that he was frail or sickly."[4]

In 1873, at the age of 16, he attended Davidson College. He was there for only a year. His record during that year was no more than average. He debated and played a little baseball, but in May 1874 his indigestion became such a problem that he left Davidson for good.[5] It has been added by some biographers that the food at Davidson at that time was very poor, and that there were no provisions for physical exercise. "Frustrated aggression added to malnourishment resulted in nervous indigestion, with discomfort, heartburn, nausea after meals, and bowel dysfunctions."[6]

During Wilson's first year at Princeton, he kept a diary. In that diary a recurring theme was his concern with his health. He felt that it was not possible for him to take an active part in sports, but he took exercise in the gymnasium. Besides, he felt that his well-being depended on some physical fitness, and his journal showed that by the end of his freshman year he was engaged actively in sports such as baseball. At times he played catch, and went for a walk with a friend; and if the weather was bad he went to the gym.[7]

His four years at Princeton seemed to have been accompanied by relatively good health. He had apparently adapted himself to being away from home. This period, 1876–79, was a period free from the sorts of physical incapacity which occurred before and after.

After Wilson finished at Princeton in 1879, he enrolled at the law school of the University of Virginia, where he became involved in about everything: debating, special reading, oratory, public speaking, and so forth. The activities were added to the very rigorous and demanding law curriculum. The sum of these activities proved too much for his frail constitution, however. He was overwhelmed and had a total collapse in the winter of 1880.[8]

Soon after he had retreated to the safe haven of his father's manse, his health improved for a short period until confronted with the idea of facing his bar exam. As the time drew nearer, his problems with indigestion began again.[9]

The problems which beset him at the University of Virginia in 1880 — his indigestion and severe, prolonged headaches — were complaints which pursued him most of his life. He left the University of Virginia Law School without a degree and returned to his father's manse — his favorite place — to recover. His father was his alter ego, who gave him a sense of security.

His breakdowns at Davidson and the University of Virginia were part of a pattern which followed him throughout his career. According to Sigmund Freud and William Bullitt, his breakdowns were merely periods of greater nervousness during which he had more severe indigestion and more prolonged periods of severe headaches. These authors, who wrote a psychological study of Wilson, listed at least 14 times during his career when his nervousness, dyspepsia, and headaches became severe enough to interfere with his work for periods as long as six to eight months.[10]

The same source noted that his physical weakness and his periods of breakdown coincided with periods when he was under great stress. "I conclude that his nervousness and intensity were caused by the conflict between his femininity and his exalted super ego, which demanded that he should be all masculinity."[11]

Wilson did pass the bar, of course, and in the early part of 1882 he went to Atlanta to establish a law practice. After only a few months engaged in the practice of law, he realized that he really had a distaste for it. He had apparently decided that his happiness lay in pursuing an academic career. He applied for and got a fellowship to study at Johns Hopkins University. In 1883 he became engaged to his future wife, Ellen Louise Axson.

When Wilson sought refuge in academia, first at Johns Hopkins University where he received his Ph.D., and then later as a teacher at Bryn Mawr and Wesleyan University, his life in general was better, healthier, and happier. His wife seemed to have a lot to do with the change. He did, however, continue to have some gastrointestinal complaints, but of a less severe nature.[12] And in the spring of 1885 he worked so hard on his academics that he came close to another breakdown of his health.[13]

In 1890 he left Wesleyan University and returned to teach at his alma mater, Princeton University. Then in 1902 he was elected president of Princeton University. In his early years at Princeton he did not experience unusual health problems. However, during Wilson's fifth year as teacher there he was again overworked with teaching and writing. He began again to have severe gastrointestinal complaints, and with his gastrointestinal problems the pain continued to be severe. He saw a doctor in New York City who prescribed a stomach pump. His doctor felt his stomach problem was due to excess acid. Wilson was instructed to irrigate his stomach with water and siphon out the stomach contents. The pain, in spite of this most unusual treatment, continued until the end of 1895. His doctors were simply unable to relieve his problem.[14]

In January 1896 he had a sudden worsening of his stomach problem. He had "a sudden sharp attack of indigestion which forced him to take to bed." The doctor who had ordered the stomach pump advised its discontinuance. The pain, however, continued and he was in bed most of January 1896. The stress of his schedule added to his stomach pain began to affect his behavior but he refused to take an extensive leave. Wilson was described as looking worn, haggard, and of having developed a nervous tic.[15]

Other health problems plagued him as well. In the summer of 1904, while he was on a vacation in Ontario with his family, he strained himself portaging a canoe, and early in 1905 he had to be operated on for a hernia. After the surgery he had to stay in the hospital for several weeks with phlebitis.[16] The most serious problem, however, was blindness.

In May 1906 Woodrow Wilson awoke and found that he was blind in his left eye. For the month prior to that he had increased pain in his left shoulder and left leg. The blindness was due to hemorrhage in his left retina. This was, according to Freud and Bullitt, caused by arteriosclerosis. His overwork was credited for his blood pressure elevation. And, adding presumption to presumption, the authors assumed that the artheriosclerosis may have been to blame for his odd behavior prior to the hemorrhage.[17]

Wilson, after the sudden problem with blinding in his left eye, went to Philadelphia to consult the famous Dr. George DeSchweinitz. Wilson was examined closely by two doctors. He was informed by Dr. DeSchweinitz that he had arteriosclerosis, and that henceforth he should live a quiet and retired life.[18]

There is a great deal of controversy about how Woodrow Wilson's illnesses may be distributed between psyche and soma. Weinstein claimed to have divided his illness conveniently into three stages. The first period came before 1896 when his health problems were largely psychosomatic with "nervous stomach and tension headaches." The second stage began in 1896, when he was first presumed to have cerebrovascular disease, and extended to March 1919, when he had his massive stroke. The third took up the remainder of his presidential time, when Weinstein explained some of Wilson's bizarre behavior on changes in the cerebral hemisphere following his stroke.[19]

Michael Marmor, in an article in 1982, strongly contested Weinstein's view that Wilson had a stroke in 1896 followed by a series of small strokes. Marmor stated: "To fit Wilson's chronic hand and arm pain into a stroke syndrome is to struggle unreasonably against the evidence. To attribute Wilson's behavioral quirks at times of crises to reactions to stroke or encephalopathy is to ignore the fact that Wilson, like all of us, reacted to fatigue and stress. Finally, to think of carotid embolism when a person has retinal hemorrhage is unquestionably to think of zebras." Here Marmor refers to one who, hearing hoofbeats in the distance, thinks first of zebras. Strokes may be a theoretical possibility, but Wilson's signs and symptoms are far more commonly associated with other conditions.[20]

Weinstein related that Wilson, on the advice of Dr. Charles Mitchell, planned a vacation trip to England to help restore his physical well-being. Here Weinstein differs from other medical biographers: the first clinical

evidence of structural damage to his nervous system came in late May
1896, while he was spending a weekend in Princeton. He developed suddenly a weakness and pain in his right arm and numbness in the fingertips
of his right hand. Dr. Weinstein felt that he had had a stroke.[21]

Weinstein leaned heavily on what he felt was rapid onset of the weakness and numbness, while Marmor denied the suddenness of the onset
and felt that there was no clear evidence of a stroke.

The illness which incapacitated Wilson in 1906 for six months was
followed by similar incapacity throughout the years until his massive
stroke in 1919.

During the latter part of Wilson's stay at Princeton he was surrounded
by controversy. He was involved in a running feud with Andrew West and
other members of the faculty about some things which seem trivial — such
as where they should build a boarding house for graduate students — at
least not important enough to upset the entire university. It is suggested
that his behavior at this time, which seemed at times bizarre, may have
been an early indication that he was having some changes in his cerebral
arteries, which altered his mood and action.[22]

In December 1911, at the end of his first year as governor of New
Jersey, Wilson had another bout of what seemed to be neuritis in his left
extremities accompanied by cramping and pain in his right hand. At
about the same time he began to suffer from prolonged, excruciating
headaches which at times incapacitated him entirely. In the same period
of time Wilson had a spell of dizziness while delivering a public speech.
The fact that all of his symptoms came in a cluster caused Weinstein to
believe that Wilson was suffering from TIAs, or small strokes.[23]

When Wilson became president in 1913, Cary T. Grayson, a young
naval officer, became his doctor. Grayson, in an intimate memoir, related
that after an official luncheon on March 4, 1913, Mrs. Ann Howe, Wilson's
sister, fell on a staircase and lacerated her forehead. Grayson was a guest
only, but he had his equipment ready. He sewed up the cut and attended
her for a short time thereafter. The president was pleased at a job well
done and later at a luncheon with the president and Josephus Daniels
Grayson found himself assigned to be Wilson's physician.[24]

Grayson had been Taft's private physician in the White House so the
new appointment was just a continuation of the old.

Only a few days after the appointment Grayson was called by Mrs.
Wilson to see Woodrow. The president was in bed, suffering from his old
problems — gastrointestinal upset and headache. Grayson found that the
president was following a barbaric medical practice which he had done for
years — using a stomach pump. Grayson discontinued the pump plus

various other medications which Wilson was currently taking. Grayson advised fresh air, plenty of sleep, regular games of golf, and daily motor rides.[25]

It is odd that a man of Wilson's intelligence and with his history of very serious health problems should have chosen a physician simply because he was personable and had successfully sewn up a laceration. Grayson really had no special qualifications. He found that his new charge had suffered for many years from neuritis, respiratory problems, a retinal hemorrhage in May 1906, an operation for phlebitis, and for many years had chronic gastrointestinal problems and had been troubed with severe headaches for which he dosed himself freely with various powders.

Grayson put the president on a diet of raw eggs and orange juice. The president protested, but Grayson insisted that he remain on the diet. Grayson also put him on a schedule of 18 holes of golf every day. Sometime thereafter Wilson was allowed a more palatable diet of oatmeal, chicken, steak, and country ham. Overall, this would not seem to be the best of diets for one who had been diagnosed before as having arteriosclerosis. However, Wilson's health improved on this particular regimen.[26]

In August 1914 Woodrow Wilson's first wife, Ellen Axson, died of renal failure; and in December 1915, he married Edith Galt, a widow. After his marriage to Edith Galt, Wilson was in reasonably good health. Mrs. Galt saw to it that he kept to his diet and that he had a program of relaxation — theater, vaudeville, automobile rides, and so forth. He did continue to have his headaches and gastrointestinal disturbances, but they became less severe.[27]

His health remained fairly good, in fact, up to the Armistice of 1918. It was the battle of the treaty-making that altered the course of his health. Wilson, after the Armistice, set off to Paris to settle the peace with a staff of only Dr. Grayson, two secretaries, and Mrs. Wilson. He distrusted Joseph Tumulty, his faithful White House secretary — the most unjustified distrust of Wilson's whole life.[28]

At the present time such an endeavor would demand a huge staff with innumerable secretaries and advisers. Wilson was apparently afraid to trust anyone and took on an impossible task practically alone. Colonel Edward M. House felt that Wilson could do more to accomplish his purpose if he stayed at home and did not become personally involved in the treaty-making. But Wilson, as he had done on many occasions, felt that only Woodrow could do it.

At the time Wilson, his wife, and the peace commissioner went on board the *George Washington,* he was physically and emotionally drained; but the voyage revived him to some degree.[29]

After he had made his triumphant tour through victorious European countries, the peace conference began on January 18, 1919. Soon thereafter began again his usual pattern of working a long, exhausting schedule. He handled even the piddling details of the negotiation himself without consultation. Wilson, working without an adequate staff, worked hours alone sifting out the details of other proposals and then himself typing out the American response.[30] Wilson, who was frail to begin with, after a short time under this new and tremendous load began to show some noticeable changes.

In early April 1919 Wilson was laid up by an unspecific illness. Grayson's notes, found after his death, described an attack of influenza that was followed by severe cough and dyspnea. Grayson also mentioned vomiting and diarrhea in a letter to Wilson's secretary. Later his personal staff were confirmed in their view that this so-called attack of influenza marked the beginning of an abrupt change in his personality. His behavior was labeled by some as bizarre. Ike Hoover, chief usher of the White House, thought that Wilson had become mean and suspicious.[31]

Wilson worked hard for several weeks in Paris, and then he returned to the United States to try to gather support for the treaty and the League of Nations. When he got on board the *George Washington* to return to America, he was on the verge of collapse both physically and mentally. On his arrival in the United States with the unratified covenant, he began to try to find support for it. He found that with the covenant in its present form there was little support, and Wilson was adamant that there should be no change. After a fruitless battle with Henry Cabot Lodge in the Senate, Wilson returned to France, arriving March 14, 1919.

Wilson became exhausted by his labors. He worked for 18 hours each day—he wished to have the covenant of the League of Nations inserted in the peace treaty. The strain tightened up the muscles in his neck, and his features became drawn and haggard. In April 1919 Wilson broke down with a fever, severe diarrhea, cough, congestion of the lungs, and difficulty breathing—diagnosed by Grayson as flu. He began to have loss of sleep, for which Grayson ordered a barbiturate, and he was also troubled by recurrent attacks of severe asthma.[32] The diagnosis of flu at that time would seem reasonable since there was a flu epidemic going on. However, in his memoirs, Ike Hoover stated that he was told by Dr. Albert Lamb, a physician to the American delegation in Paris, that Wilson suffered from an infection of the prostate and bladder.[33]

During this illness his face became gaunt and thin. Wilson, although still very weak, was determined to continue to work as soon as possible. He invited Lloyd George, Clemenceau, and Orlando of Italy to come to his bedchamber to resume the conference. He was, according to Grayson, working too hard in the face of his illness. Wilson soon thereafter developed a burning fever and was compelled to have a respite from his labors. He slept for three days, and when he woke up he determined that his work was fruitless. He decided to go home and asked Grayson to order the captain of the *George Washington* to make ready to sail immediately for the United States.[34] When the Allies heard that he was leaving, they rushed to declare that they would desert their stubborn position and Wilson was persuaded to stay in Paris.[35]

He stayed, but those who surrounded him — the American delegation — were perplexed by his behavior. He became convinced in his own mind that the French servants at the embassy were spies who spoke perfect English and reported everything he said. He also felt that the French servants were stealing from the delegation. His feelings were so strong in this direction that he asked for a full inventory. Ike Hoover, the White House usher, wrote: "These were very funny things, and we could but surmise that something queer was happening in his mind."[36]

John Moses and Wilbur Cross described his situation this way: "Blotches of perspiration sprouted on his sallow clean-shaven cheeks as much from inner agitation as from physical exertion. Over and over he kept muttering to himself and to distraught companions something about French spies at work and forces of evil conspiring against him."[37]

His associates wondered why the most powerful man in the world, when he literally seemed to be holding the fate of the world in his hands, should be obsessed over such trivia. In some of his actions one would have to conclude that he was paranoid. He at one time began to be concerned with what he considered improper use of the delegation's automobiles. Whereas before he had been most liberal and insisted that the cars be used freely for recreational purposes, he now ordered that they be used for official business only.[38]

The work continued until the draft of the treaty was finished and the covenant of the League of Nations was completed. Wilson and his American delegation then sailed for the United States.

Soon after his return the feud with Lodge and the Republican Senate began again. There were certain proposals which tied the United States firmly to come to France's aid in time of war. To this portion of the treaty many of the Senate were firmly opposed, but Wilson was adamant in his stand that no change be made. He insisted that the treaty should remain as it stood. Wilson made no progress in his struggle with the Senate, so he finally decided in late August 1919 to take his case to the people. He was warned by Grayson that the strain of a long speaking tour might endanger his life. Wilson observed, "I cannot turn back now, I cannot put my personal safety, my health, in the balance against my duty—I must go."[39]

With disregard for the counsel of Grayson and others, Wilson and his staff departed from Washington on what to him was a "holy pilgrimage." The trip was wide-ranging and exhausting. Wilson drove himself to fulfill his commitments in spite of severe headaches, severe asthmatic attacks, and sleeplessness. The pilgrimage was terminated on September 23, 1919, in Pueblo, Colorado. Before Wilson started his speech there, he stumbled on a step and practically had to be carried up to the platform.[40] "Much of his speech was mumbled; he mouthed certain words as if he had never spoken them before. There were long pauses, and he had difficulty following the trend of his thoughts. It was a travesty of his usual brilliant delivery and fine logic."[41]

After his train left Pueblo, Mrs. Wilson found the president moaning beside his bed. He was resting his head on the back of a chair. Dr. Grayson was summoned, and when he arrived he noted some sagging of the left side of Wilson's face, and uncontrolled saliva trickling out of the corner of his mouth.[42] These were definite signs of a stroke. It became clear to Grayson that to continue the tour would be fatal. In spite of Grayson's advice, Wilson pleaded with him and Tumulty to let him continue. He was rushed back to Washington.

Those persons who observed Wilson before he started on his Western trip related how very ill and worn he appeared. When it became known that he had had a stroke, it came as a great surprise to no one who had seen him. When Wilson arrived at the White House, he made a futile effort to start his usual routine, but after a day or two he had a further collapse, this time a complete stroke.[43]

The weakness of the left side of his face had progressed to a completed stroke. When he awakened on the morning of October 2, his arm and hand hung limp and useless. The progression was rapid, and the paralysis soon involved his left leg. When he was helped to the bathroom he collapsed and became unconscious. The specialists who were called agreed in their diagnosis that he had had a cerebral thrombosis which had produced an infarct in the right hemisphere of his brain and subsequent left hemiplegia.[44]

Dr. Francis Dercum, the head consultant, ordered that all bad news and visitors should be kept away from the president. Following Dr. Dercum's orders and their own inclinations, Grayson and Mrs. Wilson kept all visitors away and no news found its way either in or out of the sickroom.[45]

Ike Hoover was asked into the room to help rearrange the furniture. Ike looked at the president, who was lying on Abe Lincoln's bed, and thought that Wilson looked as if he were dead. There was no sign of life. Hoover also noted a cut above Wilson's temple and on his nose and felt that he had probably had a fall.[46]

Grayson issued a bulletin, his second: "The President is a very sick man. His condition is less favorable today and he has remained in bed throughout the day. After consultation with Dr. Dercum of Philadelphia and others in which all agreed as to his condition it was determined that absolute rest is essential for some time." There was in this bulletin no hint whatever of what Wilson's condition really was.[47]

For three weeks he lay with absolute bed rest. He then developed a very much uninvited complication — urinary obstruction due to an enlarged prostate. He suffered so much from being unable to void that Dr. Hugh Young, a urologist, was called. The urologist tried very hard to place a catheter in Wilson's bladder to relieve the pressure and drain his bladder, but there was such spasm of the bladder sphincter that it was not possible. The urologist thought of trying to operate to relieve the obstruction, but Wilson was so ill and so weak that it was felt likely he would not have survived the surgery. However, the surgery became unnecessary when the obstruction cleared on its own and the president was able to void.[48]

All those around Wilson — Grayson, Mrs. Wilson, Tumulty, and others — were strictly charged to maintain absolute secrecy about his illness. When Robert Lansing, secretary of state, held his first cabinet meeting after Wilson's catastrophic illness, he called for Grayson to instruct the cabinet regarding the nature of the illness. Grayson lied that the president was suffering from a nervous breakdown, indigestion, and a depleted system. Grayson gave a guarded prognosis and said that the scale might be tipped against him if the president were harassed by official business. Even Thomas Marshall, the vice president, was not admitted to the inner council and was kept ignorant of the true nature of Wilson's illness.

After the episode with urinary obstruction the president improved at a very slow pace. By the end of October he was able to read the newspaper and by November he was dictating three or four letters a day. A letter sent to the sickroom was not answered — not even an emergency communication. Bills became law without his signature.[49]

When Wilson finally recovered enough to go for a ride in a car, he showed some strange behavior. Whenever a car passed the White House vehicle, he thought it to be going dangerously fast, although the White House limousine was not going over 15–20 miles per hour. Wilson would order the Secret Service men to overtake the car and bring back the driver. The Secret Service would simulate a chase of the other car and return with the story that they were unable to catch the other driver. Wilson even wrote to the attorney general, Mitchell Palmer, asking if the presidency carried with it the power of a justice of the peace. If it did—he told his staff—he was going to make sure the speeders were caught and himself try their cases at the roadside.[50] The Secret Service killed the idea by telling him that it was beneath his dignity. This behavior was somewhat reminiscent of his behavior in Paris when his staff felt that there must be something queer happening in his head.

During these months of slow recovery Wilson was in a poor mental condition. His attention span was short, he was forgetful, and repeated himself a lot.[51] Mrs. Wilson and Grayson continued to keep the president's illness clouded in secrecy. Mrs. Wilson kept presidential aides out of the sickroom for several months, and at times gave her own answer to policy questions by writing on the margin of documents, as if they were the response of Wilson himself.[52]

Edith Wilson's biographers denied any such activity by Mrs. Wilson. One wrote, "Those notes in shaky handwriting went up and down the sides, bottom, and tops of the white spaces on official letters. They were also along the backs of envelopes. Decisions were made in some matters, not the best, but they were his own."[53]

After several months the president finally was able to walk. His gait was shuffling, he had to have support of a person on either side, and leaned forward on a cane in his right hand. He also recovered some of his thinking and reasoning power. However, he remained emotionally unstable. When he finally became able to attend some of the cabinet meetings, some of the members were so upset by his emotional outbursts that they left the cabinet.[54]

On election day, November 2, 1920, the president strove to mount two or three steps that his doctor had built for him. He tried but could not lift his leg.[55]

In his last few months his health was good enough to permit moderate work and recreation. After the end of his second term he moved to a new house at 2340 South Street, where he lived the life of a severe invalid. He and Mrs. Wilson took automobile rides and saw old friends, but only once did he go to a public function—the burial of the Unknown Soldier at Arlington Cemetery on November 11, 1921.

He formed a law partnership with Bainbridge Colby after he left the White House, but was never able to practice.[56]

The ex-president and Mrs. Wilson celebrated a good Christmas in

1923, but both Mrs. Wilson and Dr. Grayson felt that the president's physical condition was further deteriorating. The end was described as just a gradual weakening, further loss of vision, poor appetite, a short attention span, and less awareness of his surroundings. The end came at 11:00 A.M., February 3, 1924.[57]

References

1. Sigmund Freud and William C. Bullitt, *Thomas Woodrow Wilson, Twenty-Eighth President of the United States; A Psychological Study*, p. 5.
2. Ibid.
3. Ibid., p. 70.
4. Kenneth R. Crispell and Carlos F. Gomez, *Hidden Illness in the White House*, p. 17.
5. Freud and Bullitt, *Thomas Woodrow Wilson*, p. 16.
6. Rudolph Marx, *The Health of the Presidents*, p. 310.
7. Henry Wilkinson Bragdon, *Woodrow Wilson: The Academic Years*, pp. 22–23.
8. Ray Stannard Baker, *Woodrow Wilson, Life and Letters*, p. 120.
9. Crispell and Gomez, *Hidden Illness in the White House*, p. 22.
10. Freud and Bullitt, *Thomas Woodrow Wilson*, p. 80.
11. Ibid., p. 81.
12. Crispell and Gomez, *Hidden Illness in the White House*, p. 24.
13. Bragdon, *Woodrow Wilson*, p. 118.
14. Crispell and Gomez, *Hidden Illness in the White House*, p. 23.
15. Ibid., p. 26.
16. Bragdon, *Woodrow Wilson*, p. 310.
17. Freud and Bullitt, *Thomas Woodrow Wilson*, p. 119.
18. Baker, *Woodrow Wilson, Life and Letters*, 2:201.
19. Edwin A. Weinstein, "Woodrow Wilson's Neurological Illness," *Journal of American History* 47 (1971): 325.
20. Michael F. Marmor, "Woodrow Wilson, Strokes and Zebras," *New England Journal of Medicine* 309, no. 9 (August 26, 1982): 581.
21. Weinstein, "Woodrow Wilson's Neurological Illness," p. 333.
22. Bragdon, *Woodrow Wilson*, p. 382.
23. Crispell and Gomez, *Hidden Illness in the White House*, p. 46.
24. Cary T. Grayson, *Woodrow Wilson: An Intimate Memoir*, p. 1.
25. Ibid., p. 76.
26. Jean Smith, *When the Cheering Stopped*, p. 8.
27. Marx, *The Health of the Presidents*, p. 314.
28. Freud and Bullitt, *Thomas Woodrow Wilson*, p. 69.
29. Arthur S. Link, *Woodrow Wilson: A Brief Biography*, p. 141.
30. Crispell and Gomez, *Hidden Illness in the White House*, p. 60.
31. Hugh L'Etang, *The Pathology of Leadership*, p. 49.
32. Marx, *The Health of the Presidents*, p. 316.

33. Crispell and Gomez, *Hidden Illness in the White House*, p. 62.
34. Smith, *When the Cheering Stopped*, p. 29.
35. Ibid., p. 49.
36. Ibid.
37. John B. Moses and Wilbur Cross, *Presidential Courage*, p. 131.
38. Smith, *When the Cheering Stopped*, p. 49.
39. Link, *Woodrow Wilson*, p. 164.
40. L'Etang, *The Pathology of Leadership*, p. 51.
41. Edmund W. Starling, *Starling of the White House*, p. 152.
42. Marx, *The Health of the Presidents*, p. 318.
43. Edith Gettings Reid, *Woodrow Wilson: The Caricature, the Myth, and the Man*, p. 223.
44. Marx, *The Health of the Presidents*, p. 319.
45. Ibid.
46. Smith, *When the Cheering Stopped*, p. 96.
47. Ibid.
48. Crispell and Gomez, *Hidden Illness in the White House*, p. 68.
49. Marx, *The Health of the Presidents*, p. 320.
50. Smith, *When the Cheering Stopped*, p. 147.
51. Moses and Cross, *Presidential Courage*, p. 164.
52. Crispell and Gomez, *Hidden Illness in the White House*, p. 70.
53. Tom Shachtman, *Edith and Woodrow: A Presidential Romance*, p. 233.
54. Marx, *The Health of the Presidents*, p. 321.
55. Smith, *When the Cheering Stopped*, p. 168.
56. Link, *Woodrow Wilson*, p. 179.
57. Homer F. Cunningham, *The Presidents' Last Years*, p. 208.

28

Warren Gamaliel Harding

When one thinks of Warren Harding, one thinks of tragedy in every aspect of his life — in society, politics, his family, and his tragic end. He was born on November 2, 1865, to Phoebe Harding, at Blooming Grove, Ohio.

As a baby he was described by his aunt when he was dressed up to go to church: "His big, fat, white face looked very pretty under a blue and white hat."[1] His infancy, childhood, and youth were not marked by any remarkable episodes of sickness.

It is apparent from reading various biographies that Harding was very hardworking as a child and as a youth. Some acquaintances remembered that he may have been too hardworking for his health. His younger sister, Charity, wrote after her brother's death: "He was large and strong, and thought himself able to carry out anything he would undertake. The chores of the family fell upon him as he was the oldest and a boy. He worked hard every day, in fact, too hard for one so young."[2]

As a youth Harding played scrub baseball and associated with a group of boys who swam in Whetstone Creek. He rode his father's horse at a gallop whenever he had the opportunity.

In 1878 Harding first experienced tragedy when his brother Charles and his sister Persilla died of a disease which caused them to be jaundiced, probably a form of infectious hepatitis.[3]

In 1880, at the age of 14, Harding attended Ohio Central College, in Iberia, Ohio. He studied Latin, math, history, and chemistry; however, he excelled in debating and composition. He edited the school newspaper, played the alto horn in the brass band, and graduated with a bachelor of science degree in 1882.[4] In all accounts of Harding's college days nothing is ever mentioned about his participation in any sport or physical exercise, although he later played much golf.

From the time he was a young man Harding had mysterious bouts with indigestion which seemed to be related to nervous tension. Five times in his presenatorial days he went for treatment to Battle Creek Sanitarium, a vegetarian establishment sponsored by the Seventh Day Adventists and run by Dr. J. H. Kellogg, the inventor of peanut butter and cornflakes.

The first of Harding's visits occurred just after the election of Benjamin Harrison in 1889. Harding suffered what he later called a nervous breakdown. On October 6 the *Daily Marion Star* reported that its editor, Harding, was "indisposed to such an extent that he is unable to attend to any newspaper duties, being scarcely able to reach the office one half an hour each day."[5] Urged by his father, he left for Battle Creek on November 7, 1889. After some weeks of Battle Creek's spartan regimen, Harding returned in early 1890 to Marion renewed in spirit and 20 pounds lighter.[6] In between, his medical problems were handled by his father, a homeopathic doctor, but as soon as the signs and symptoms disappeared, Harding returned to eating too much and sleeping too little.[7]

Harding also used too much tobacco, in four forms — cigarettes, cigars, pipes, and chewing tobacco. At times when his wife nagged him about chewing tobacco, he would surreptitiously break open a cigarette and chew its contents.[8]

Harding's marriage apparently contributed to his nervous tension in a number of other ways as well. In 1891, at the age of 26 he married Florence Kling DeWolfe, "Duchess," a divorcée who was described as a dowdy woman. The marriage was an unhappy one. Duchess nagged Harding without cease. He was so repelled by her that he sought solace playing poker with his pals and having affairs with other women.[9]

In February 1897 Harding and his wife made a trip to Florida where he came down with the "flu" and had to stay in bed for several days. After his return from Florida, he again went to Battle Creek for a short stay. As state senator, Harding continued to have health problems. During a session of the state senate in 1901 he developed an ear problem and had to have mastoid surgery. During his campaign for reelection to the state legislature of Ohio in the fall of 1903 Harding underwent a great deal of stress and soon after his reelection he returned to Battle Creek where he stayed for only one week. This was his last stay at the sanitarium.[10]

It is apparent that Harding had significant symptoms related to his heart over at least a 25-year period before he died in 1923.

One significant episode occurred in the fall of 1918, while he was a U.S. senator from Ohio. Harding was on a Chatauqua lecture tour. It was in Plattsburg where, during his speech, he was struck by a spell of dizziness and was barely able to finish his lecture. The significance of this attack is not clear. It could have been vascular, either cerebral or cardiac. There was no immediate sequela to this attack.[11]

By the spring of 1922, however, Harding was becoming much more easily exhausted and was complaining of chest pain, which by description would fit angina pectoris. Both he and his physician, Dr. Carl W. Sawyer, continued to tell themselves that they were dealing with indigestion, but later they suspected angina. The problems of his administration and Mrs. Harding's illness were wearying. The president's blood pressure soared above 180 systolic. At about this time Dr. Emmanuel Liebman, a famous New York heart specialist, happened to see Harding at a dinner party. The next day he confided to a friend his private opinion that the president would be dead of heart disease in six months.[12]

The observation that Harding had a history of pressure and pain in his chest was, in view of future events, very significant. There is no evidence whatever that he had a cardiac consultation or that an EKG was done, then or later. The possibility of cardiac disability was confirmed by a lay observer, Edmund Starling, his bodyguard, who found that Harding was short of breath when lying flat and could only sleep when propped up with pillows.[13]

From our perspective, Harding's physical decline seems rather obvious, but in January 1921, when Harding succeeded Wilson as president, no physician would have been rash enough to suspect that Wilson with all his severe physical problems would outlive Harding who was strikingly handsome and apparently healthy. Harding made the crippled Wilson look even more pathetic.[14]

At the beginning of Harding's presidency, his wife was elated. She was to be the First Lady. She had been informed of this succession earlier by a medium. Harding, however, was less elated. "A dark mood would supervene. He would droop physically and psychologically. A worried supporter, William Boyce Thompson, was shocked by Harding's depression and speculated whether he would not survive his term."[15] At times it seems Harding had omens of what the future might bring.

In January 1923 Harding suffered a severe attack of "flu" which also affected most of his cabinet. Harding refused to remain in bed for more than a week and consequently returned to work too soon. He had not recovered his strength by March. From March 9–19 Harding recuperated with friends on the Inland Waterway of Florida, stopping at golf courses along the way. However, he was not recovered fully when he returned to Washington.[16]

Harding's regular golf partners noted some deterioration of the president's game around this time. At the end of nine holes, or even earlier, lassitude overtook him. Not infrequently he would give up on the twelfth or thirteenth green. His fellow players attributed this to worry. They were mistaken because it was physical. Harding's heart was playing out.[17]

That uncanny diagnostician, Dr. Emmanuel Liebman, who had met Harding at a dinner party in the fall of 1922 and had privately told friends that within six months the president would be dead of a coronary illness, realized how already far advanced his condition was.[18] However, nothing is known of just how much Harding knew about his illness, except that he did cut down on parties and other social events. The attack of "flu" which Harding sustained in January 1923 apparently was the beginning of a rapid worsening of his health condition.[19] One medical expert later claimed that this "flu" attack was actually accompanied by an undiagnosed coronary thrombosis, followed by massive myocardial infarction. Thereafter, Harding did experience great difficulty in sleeping unless propped up on pillows. At this time he gave up drinking but could not give up smoking.

By the late spring of 1923 it was obvious to those around him that Harding was ill. His normal ruddy color had become a pallor, and his energies were always at low ebb. He told Justice Charles Evans Hughes that his blood pressure was consistently above 175 systolic.

Despite his apparent illness, however, in mid June 1923 Harding suddenly decided to make a trip to Alaska. The trip was much publicized. Harding apparently felt that he needed to get away from the seat of power with the rapidly mounting problems and the threat of impending scandal.

His physician, Dr. Charles Sawyer, did approve of the trip. Sawyer felt — wrongly, it turned out — that the trip might provide some degree of relaxation.[20] When Harding arrived in Seward, the town was suffering from an unusual heat wave. Harding, his face drawn with exhaustion, instead of landing directly, invited the mayor and the welcoming party aboard ship, explaining how exhausted he was, and asked to be excused from speeches and public appearances.[21]

As the *Henderson,* Harding's ship, moved south along the glacier- and mountain-edged coast, a naval seaplane caught up with her bringing a long coded message to the president from Washington. After reading the message, Harding suffered something like a collapse. For the rest of the day he seemed half stunned.[22] At Fairbanks, when the president had reached the most northern part of the trip, he seemed even more exhausted than before. By the time the *Henderson* reached Vancouver, the porters remarked on his condition. One of them stated: "The President is not just tired, worn out, he is beyond being merely fatigued. He is an entirely exhausted man, and the rest he requires is not that of a day or two or three."[23]

Serious trouble apparently began after an official luncheon in Vancouver, when Harding went to the golf course for some relaxation. He played the first six holes but became so tired that he moved over to the seventeenth and finished out the eighteenth so that there would be no suspicion. He returned to the hotel and lay down for about an hour before attending a formal dinner given by the Canadian government. He ate little and made only a 15-minute speech without the usual force. Returning to the ballroom, he stood for 25 minutes shaking hands, but excused himself long before the line had passed and returned to the *Henderson* where he went to bed.[24]

On July 27, after his arrival in Seattle, Harding went to the University of Washington's stadium for a speech. Under a fierce sun, without a hat, Harding delivered the speech listlessly. He had a slip of the tongue, calling Alaska Nebraska, and his voice fell several times. It was not until around 7:30 P.M. that he arrived at his private car and went instantly to bed. Later that night, as the train continued, Harding called for Dr. Sawyer, complaining of nausea and pain in the upper abdomen.[25] Sawyer blamed the midnight snack of crabmeat and released a bulletin that the president was suffering from some bad seafood and would take two days to recover.[26] The diagnosis, however, was in error. Sawyer claimed that crabmeat was the cause of the problem, but no crabmeat was on the president's menu. Also, of the party who had dinner with the president and ate the same dishes, no other person became ill.[27]

Harding had planned other speeches in Portland, San Francisco, and Los Angeles. But now, with his acute illness, the train was ordered to run straight through to San Francisco. During the trip Dr. Joel T. Boone took Herbert Hoover aside and related to him that the president was having more problems than alleged by Dr. Sawyer. Boone, with Dr. Herbert Work a former practicing physician, had examined the president and found his heart greatly enlarged. When Hoover learned this, he telegraphed ahead to have Dr. Ray Lyman Wilbur, the famous cardiologist, meet the train in San Francisco.[28]

At the San Francisco station, on Sunday, July 29, Harding rejected a wheelchair. But his skin, grayish and flabby, and his gait, torpid and lifeless, were testimony that only courage sustained him. Reporters noted that the president looked "old and worn." A chance news photograph — his last — showed "an aging, flabby faced man with a slack chin and puffy eyes."[29] Cardiac enlargement and high blood pressure were signs which alarmed Dr. Boone and Dr. Work, although Dr. Sawyer still insisted that Harding was suffering from acute indigestion.[30] Harding did not fully realize just how sick he was. After his symptoms lessened from the so-called "digestive complaint," he felt better. Unhappiness and worry, however, had taken their toll; his system was unable to fight back.[31]

Harding was driven to the Palace Hotel and put to bed at once. By nightfall he was much worse. It was obvious to his doctor that he had had a cardiac collapse. Blood counts and a chest X ray revealed that he also had bronchial pneumonia. Through Monday and Tuesday Harding was given digitalis and caffeine, and by Tuesday he was better. The president's pneumonia was clearing and the doctors were encouraged.[32] After the improvement on Tuesday, Dr. Sawyer decided to take a vacation. On Wednesday the president was so much improved that he was able to sit up in bed, eat solid food, and read the newspaper. His temperature was normal and his pulse was under 100. Drs. Wilbur and Charles Minor Cooper left Harding orders to cancel future appointments and to take a two-month rest.[33]

At least three different versions of Harding's death exist. According to one biographer, Robert Murray, on Thursday there was so much apparent improvement that Harding was allowed to sit up in bed. At about 7:30 P.M., propped up by pillows, he was listening to his wife read an article from the *Saturday Evening Post*. Sue S. Denver, a night nurse, was standing by at that moment while the day nurse had gone for his medicine. Mrs. Harding interrupted her reading to straighten his pillows when Harding remarked, "That's good, read some more." As she began to read again, the president twisted convulsively.[34]

Another biographer, Frances Russell, has a different version. After Mrs. Harding finished the article, she left and went to her room across the corridor. Harding's day nurse, Ruth Powderly, had gone for a glass of water to give him his night medicine, and as she came in out of the bathroom she saw his face twitch sharply and his mouth drop open. Then at that moment his body slumped and his head lolled to the right. In that instant she knew that he had died. She rushed from the room and called Mrs. Harding, who shrieked, "Get Dr. Boone, get Dr. Boone!"[35]

A third version of what happened at that moment was supplied by Gaston Means, a man to whom no credence whatever may be attached. He claimed, in a cleverly worded account, to have had a private conversation with Mrs. Harding following her husband's death in which she strongly implied, but did not admit, that she herself had killed her husband.[36] Means implied in the strongest terms that President Harding was killed by his wife to prevent the breaking of a scandal involving Harding's administration. Means also implied that the attack of indigestion was due to foul play. Means completely ignored the presence of organic disease being present prior to the trip to Alaska. Means was later totally discredited after he had been involved in another scam in connection with the Lindbergh kidnapping case in March 1932. Means went to Evalyn McLean, persuading her that he had made contact with the kidnappers, and that for

$100,000 plus expenses he was the one person who could recover the kidnapped child. It was not until later that Mrs. McLean realized that she had been swindled.[37]

The second story, that of Harding's nurse, Ruth Powderly, reentering the room at the moment of his death, seems the most plausible.

Dr. Work and Secretary Hoover arrived seconds later, followed by Dr. Sawyer. They found the nurse standing by the door and Mrs. Harding sitting by the bed, sobbing. It was 7:30 P.M.

Dr. Sawyer diagnosed the cause of death as cerebral hemorrhage, but the other doctors, after they arrived, disagreed. Mrs. Harding refused to permit an autopsy. In the anteroom, the doctors — Sawyer, Wilbur, Cooper, Work, and Boone — after a debate finally signed an official bulletin that death was apparently due to some brain involvement, probably a stroke.[38]

There were many things which contributed to the confusion surrounding the possible cause of Harding's death. The confusion began when Dr. Sawyer stated that Harding's illness was due to bad food, "crabmeat," when the president ate no crabmeat. The confusion and uncertainty were made worse when the faulty diagnosis was publicized and Sawyer persisted in his statement that Harding had "indigestion." It is additionally very difficult to understand why no electrocardiogram was done. Willem Einthoven had developed the EKG machine in 1903, and it had been in use for many years in this country. Also it seems most curious that the group of doctors, other than Sawyer, had been convinced by their findings that his problem was due to hypertension and coronary artery disease, but in their postdeath conference had agreed, or said they agreed, on a diagnosis of stroke. This final diagnosis was probably made to save face for Dr. Sawyer. The final and perhaps the greatest bar to a complete resolution of the mystery was Mrs. Harding's refusal to permit an autopsy.

However, in the presence of a history of typical angina, extreme shortness of breath, hypertension, and marked cardiac enlargement, there can be little or no doubt about the diagnosis of arteriosclerotic heart disease, hypertension, congestive heart failure, and anginal syndrome.

References

1. Frances Russell, *The Shadow of Blooming Grove*, p. 33.
2. Randolph C. Downes, *The Rise of Warren G. Harding*, pp. 7–8
3. Russell, *The Shadow of Blooming Grove*, p. 473.

4. William A. Degregorio, *The Complete Book of U.S. Presidents*, p. 433.
5. Russell, *The Shadow of Blooming Grove*, p. 80.
6. Ibid.
7. Robert K. Murray, *The Harding Era*, p. 4.
8. Russell, *The Shadow of Blooming Grove*, p. 446.
9. Degregorio, *The Complete Book of U.S. Presidents*, p. 434.
10. Russell, *The Shadow of Blooming Grove*, p. 156.
11. Ibid., p. 304.
12. Murray, *The Harding Era*, p. 41.
13. Hugh L'Etang, *The Pathology of Leadership*, p. 57.
14. Ibid., p. 54.
15. Samuel Hopkins Adams, *The Incredible Era: The Life and Times of Warren G. Harding*, p. 192.
16. Murray, *The Harding Era*, p. 423.
17. Adams, *The Incredible Era*, p. 333.
18. Ibid.; and "Profiles," *The New Yorker*, April 8, 1939, p. 24.
19. Murray, *The Harding Era*, p. 438.
20. Ibid., p. 439.
21. Russell, *The Shadow of Blooming Grove*, p. 584.
22. Ibid., pp. 586–87.
23. Murray, *The Harding Era*, p. 447.
24. Ibid., p. 448.
25. Ibid.
26. Russell, *The Shadow of Blooming Grove*, p. 580.
27. Adams, *The Incredible Era*, p. 373.
28. Russell, *The Shadow of Blooming Grove*, p. 589.
29. Ibid., p. 590.
30. Adams, *The Incredible Era*, p. 374.
31. Ibid., p. 375.
32. Murray, *The Harding Era*, p. 449.
33. Russell, *The Shadow of Blooming Grove*, p. 590.
34. Murray, *The Harding Era*, p. 457.
35. Russell, *The Shadow of Blooming Grove*, p. 591.
36. Gaston B. Means, *The Strange Death of President Harding*, pp. 264–65.
37. Russell, *The Shadow of Blooming Grove*, p. 641.
38. Ibid., pp. 591–92.

29

Calvin Coolidge

Calvin Coolidge, the thirtieth president of the United States, was born on July 4, 1872, in Plymouth Notch, Vermont.

Coolidge was described as a skinny, red-haired, freckle-faced child with a frightened look. He had occasional attacks of sneezing and coughing and was afflicted with numerous allergies, which caused congestion in his nose and sinuses and in turn produced an unusual quacking quality to his voice. His nasal twang was one of his trademarks. Even so, Coolidge was an active youth who enjoyed fishing, scouting in the woods, bobsledding, skating, and hayriding. When he was three, he fell from a horse and broke his arm.[1]

Although Coolidge did not really have a great deal to offer in the way of pathology, at least in his early years he witnessed plenty with his mother, an invalid, who died when he was 12 years old. Soon after her marriage to John Calvin Coolidge, she had developed a chronic respiratory disease and was, until she died 17 years later, a chronic invalid. She was diagnosed in those days as having pulmonary tuberculosis.[2]

Coolidge had to delay his college entrance for a year due to a severe respiratory illness he developed while attempting an entrance examination. He had to wait a full year to sit for the next exam. He did pass, though, and attended Amherst College 1891–95. He was for the first two years just an average student, but during his last two years his grades improved markedly. While there Coolidge did not engage in any sports, and took little part in extracurricular activities.

After graduation Coolidge's career developed steadily. He studied law in the office of John C. Hammond and Henry F. Field. Admitted to the bar in 1897, he opened his own law offices in Northhampton where, until 1910 when he became mayor of Northhampton, he was practicing law and involving himself in local politics. He was a Massachusetts state senator (1912–15), the lieutenant governor of Massachusetts (1916–18), and finally, in 1919 the governor of Massachusetts. During this time Coolidge's health was unremarkable. After 1919, however, it began to suffer.

As governor Coolidge greeted many people, attended many ceremonies, and made innumerable speeches. He rarely refused to participate in any event which could be graced by the governor. However, this load, as it has done to many other high government officials, imposed a great deal of stress which Coolidge thought was injurious to his health. He felt too cold in winter and too warm in the summer. He quite often appeared tired. Coolidge "had a chronic cough which caused him to fear that he, like his mother, might have tuberculosis. He was troubled greatly by the allergies which affected his nose and throat."[3] As a consequence, he developed a habit of taking pills of every description to relieve his ails. He was obviously hypochondriacal.[4] Coolidge never responded to his condition of frailty as did Theodore Roosevelt, who strove manfully to build up his weak body until he became powerful. In fact, Coolidge spent a great deal of his time asleep. After his noon meal, if nothing official kept him from it, he took a nap, at times for more than two hours. He rarely retired later than 10:00 P.M. —frequently earlier. He often slept 11 hours per day.[5] Coolidge remained physically awkward all of his life, and his awkwardness was accompanied by a feeling that he was being watched or observed. The fear of appearing ridiculous prevented him from engaging in games and exercise where skill, agility, and grace were required.[6]

Coolidge did not indulge in spiritous drink, gambling, and swearing; but he was a very heavy smoker of cigars.[7] In smoking cigars Coolidge was indulging the habit most likely to aggravate his allergies and worsen his chronic cough. It would have been much better to have traded his cigars for a couple of cocktails at dinnertime. However, at the time there was no hue and cry about the health problems associated with smoking.

The patterns Coolidge developed while governor continued after he became vice president, elected on the Republican ticket with Warren Gamaliel Harding, and then president, after Harding's tragic death on August 3, 1923. Coolidge served the remainder of that term and was re-elected in 1924.

Coolidge experienced three great periods of grief in his lifetime which may have shaped him a great deal emotionally. The first episode of grief came when his mother died. She had received very severe injuries in a fall from a runaway horse, and the wounds never healed. The injury was compounded by the fact that she had chronic pulmonary tuberculosis. The second came in the death of his sister, Abigail (Abbey), whom he adored. When Calvin was 18, Abbey was stricken by what was undoubtedly appendicitis. In those days the clinical syndrome which she experienced was called typhlitis. The doctors in cases such as hers at that time did the worst thing they could have possibly done—they purged the patient. Such action would hasten the rupture of an acutely inflamed appendix and precipitate peritonitis. There was no surgery at the time, and after the appendix ruptured the only thing a physician could do was keep a bedside vigil until the patient died. Coolidge's third episode of great grief came when his young son, Calvin, died of septicemia. Calvin, Jr. was the favorite son. In the summer of 1924 Calvin, Jr., developed a blister on his foot while playing tennis on the White House grounds while wearing sneakers without socks. The blister became infected, and, when the 16-year-old boy became febrile and listless, he was moved to Walter Reed Hospital where he lingered from July 3–7, when he died.[8] Coolidge took this especially hard: "When he went the power and the glory of the Presidency went with him. I don't know why such a price should be exacted for occupying the White House."[9]

One can reflect that had these three persons, so dear to Coolidge, lived in the present day, their survival would have been almost assured by the miraculous changes made since that time in medicine and surgery. His mother's tuberculosis would most likely have responded to modern antibiotics used for such illness. The same would have been true for Calvin, Jr. Antibiotics would most certainly have saved his life. The first successful appendectomy in the world was done in this country by George Morton of Philadelphia in 1887. Abbey died of acute peritonitis three years later. Apparently, the skill and technique for doing such surgery had not spread in those three years from Philadelphia to Ludlow, Vermont.

In 1927 Coolidge made the terse and, to most, a cryptic statement: "I do not choose to run for President in 1928." Many were distressed, but Mrs. Coolidge was relieved to see him end his days of public office. Both Calvin and Mrs. Coolidge were in poor health.[10]

Four years into his retirement, Coolidge was described by Gamaliel Bradford, a psychologist, as having the pinched, drawn face of a man who is perpetually confronted by problems too big for him. In the summer days of 1932 Coolidge, according to Bradford, was haggard. Age was chiseling out the curve from his jaws, gaunting his neck, and straightening the soft lines of his face. The man of 59 looked like his father looked at 70.[11]

During that summer Coolidge had severe hay fever which his doctors felt at the time might have left a lasting weakness upon his heart. In that fall Mrs. Coolidge recalled that scarcely a night passed when he was not compelled to use a spray for his allergy. He suspected many foods had contributed to his discomfort and because of this he was insufficiently nourished. In addition, he exercised very little, always conserving his energy and rarely allowing himself to become over-fatigued.[12] Grace

Coolidge said, "He lost weight and seemed very tired for he was not of a rugged constitution." Then she added, sadly: "The death of our younger son was a severe shock and the zest of living was never the same to him afterwards."[13]

Coolidge's personal physician, however, could detect no evidence of heart disease. And Coolidge kept some of his symptoms to himself. Grace Coolidge did note that on the sly he would frequently check his pulse. He, like his Vermont ancestors, trusted in home remedies and patent medicines; and he did not tell Dr. Edwin Brown all of his symptoms.[14]

In December 1932 Coolidge made his last trip to New York. In his usual state of health, he wrote his last love letter to Grace Coolidge: "Who has borne with my infirmities for years, and I have rejoiced in her grace. I thought we were made for each other."[15] On New Year's Day 1933 he saw his old friend, Charles Andrews, treasurer of Amherst, who inquired about his health. Coolidge answered: "I am comfortable because I am not doing anything of real account. But any effort to accomplish something goes hard with me. I am very old for my years."[16]

On January 5, 1933, a cold, clear day in Northhampton, Coolidge arose at the usual time. He neglected to shave, ate his breakfast, and left for the office at 9:00 A.M. He worked at his desk for an hour, then told his law partner that he was not feeling well but did not state especially what the complaint was. Harry Ross, his secretary, drove him home. There he read for a while, then went to the basement to get something. When he came back, he told his secretary that he had forgotten to shave and was going upstairs to do so. When Grace came home, she went to the room and found him lying on the floor of their dressing room in his shirt-sleeves.[17]

There was no autopsy, which is regrettable. It was the consensus of his doctors that "Cal died of a 'silent coronary.'" The coronary seems evident, but silent coronary is in question. It is more likely that Coolidge had symptoms but denied them, not only to himself but also to others.

References

1. Donald R. McCoy, *Calvin Coolidge: The Quiet President*, p. 8.
2. Claude Fuess, *Calvin Coolidge: The Man from Vermont*, p. 22.
3. Ibid., p. 99.
4. Ibid.
5. Ibid., p. 326.
6. Rudolph Marx, *The Health of the Presidents*, p. 340.

7. Homer F. Cunningham, *The Presidents' Last Years*, p. 220.
8. McCoy, *Calvin Coolidge*, p. 251.
9. Calvin Coolidge, *The Autobiography of Calvin Coolidge*, p. 190.
10. Isabelle Ross, *Grace Coolidge and Her Era*, p. 223.
11. William Allen White, *A Puritan in Babylon: A Story of Calvin Coolidge*, pp. 434–35.
12. Fuess, *Calvin Coolidge*, p. 458.
13. White, *A Puritan in Babylon*, p. 434.
14. Fuess, *Calvin Coolidge*, p. 458.
15. White, *A Puritan in Babylon*, p. 438.
16. Ibid., p. 440.
17. Cunningham, *The Presidents' Last Years*, pp. 226–27.

30

Herbert Hoover

Herbert Hoover, the thirty-first president of the United States, was born in West Branch, Iowa, on August 10, 1874. Hoover's Aunt Agnes recalled "Bertie's" birth: "He was a sweet baby that day. Round and plump and looked about very cordial at everybody." Hoover apparently remained this way, for his first grade teacher recalled him as "a sweet little boy, plump and with rosy cheeks; who learned easily and never made any trouble."

At age two Hoover almost died. He was so strangled by croup that his father called in the two village doctors. "We all thought he was dead," wrote Agnes: "The eyes of the infant were pressed closed with pennies; and a sheet was drawn over his body; but after resuscitation by his uncle, John Minthorn, Herbert stirred to life."[1]

Additionally, Hoover's childhood was marked by a variety of less serious accidents and illnesses. When he was very young, he ran into his father's blacksmith shop and, barefoot, stepped on some hot iron which burned his foot badly. At another time, while playing with a hatchet he nearly chopped off the index finger of his right hand.[2] He also had measles, mumps, diphtheria, earache, and chicken pox. Later the chubbiness of his childhood gave way to the tall, muscular, leanness of young manhood.[3]

His father died of typhoid when Herbert was six years of age, and two years later his mother died of pneumonia, said by some to be complicated by typhoid, so he grew up an orphan. The children were given homes by various relatives, who truly wanted them rather than feeling an obligation to take them. He was at first taken in by his uncle, Allen Hoover, who lived on a farm outside West Branch.

With almost no exception in his early life Hoover was blessed with robust health and almost endless stamina. He worked his way through college, for example, and in addition engaged in about every possible extracurricular activity. He learned to dance, took an occasional social drink, and learned to enjoy a good cigar; but later he would not allow himself to be photographed smoking a cigar. In his freshman year he went out for baseball, and made the team. However, he sprained a finger so badly that he had to abandon his athletic career.[4]

Hoover's career as a mining engineer lasted 18 years, 1896–1914, and there is no record that he had any health problems in this interval. In fact, his health was reported to be excellent during this period.

In addition to good health, Hoover possessed the physical vitality for immense exertion.[5] During World War I, for example, Hoover gained great national and international fame through his work as head of the American Relief Commission, head of the Commission for the Relief of Belgium, 1914–18, and director of the American Relief Administration, 1919–20, when he distributed millions of tons of food, clothing, and supplies to war-ravaged European countries. Hoover also served as secretary of commerce with distinction in the administrations of Harding and Coolidge. These tasks were monumental in nature, but apparently he suffered no ill health during this time.

Two activities in particular contributed to Hoover's mental and physical well-being. One was his great love for fishing. The literature on Hoover cites many stories about his fishing exploits. Indeed, late in life he wrote a book *On Fishing,* this in 1962 when he was 88 years of age.[6] The other activity was his use of the medicine ball. Hoover discovered this outlet for physical exercise while traveling by ship to Latin America just prior to his inauguration.[7]

Hoover took to the sport with great relish, enlisting several aides and cabinet members to participate. A great deal of exercise was obtained by passing an eight-pound medicine ball over a ten-feet net. The game was faster and required more exertion than tennis, but required less skill.[8] Hoover's working hours were so long and arduous that he had little time for recreation except for his early morning medicine ball game with his associates. This game became a ritual which went on six days a week, regardless of season or weather. He only missed playing his game of medicine ball one day during his entire presidency and, perhaps consequently, was reported to have never missed one day from work during his presidency on account of illness. Hoover felt that medicine ball gave the most exercise with the least loss of time. Lillian Parks, a maid at the White House, wrote, "The only time Mrs. Hoover would see her husband in the morning was after breakfast when she walked to the office with him. Before breakfast he would have his own form of recreation — a workout with his medicine ball. This was his only form of recreation."[9]

About the only threat to the sturdy Hoover's health came from the demands of protocol. During the White House annual reception Hoover had to shake hands with thousands of visitors. In addition to being an exhausting ordeal, his hand was at times swollen so much that he could not write for days. At one reception his hand received such a bad cut from a diamond ring which was turned inward that the reception came to a sudden halt.[10]

Hoover's postpresidential years were quite healthy and active as well. On August 14, 1949, at the age of 75, while returning to New York from a speaking tour, he did have a gallbladder attack. But when reporters queried him about the attack, he said characteristically, "It was much ado about nothing."[11] Also, during Hoover's work with the Truman Commission, he developed a case of shingles, which caused much pain but did not slow him down.[12]

More typical of his retirement was the vigor with which he pursued his leisure activities and aided his successors in the White House. After attending the inauguration of Eisenhower in 1953, for example, he retreated for his winter stay in Florida, where there were bonefish to catch, books to write, and a cottage set aside at the Key Largo Anglers clubhouse for his comfort.[13] And during Truman's administration Hoover was called on for various tasks, including a mission to Germany and Austria on President Truman's economic mission. Truman also called on Hoover in an attempt to curb and organize the vast governmental bureaucracy. At that time Hoover's personal physicians advised him to limit his activities, but he didn't know how. His usual day, according to his secretary, was begun with a brisk walk. He then began work, which continued to the so-called quitting time, 10:00 P.M., but it was common for him to continue to midnight.[14] In 1958 Hoover attended the Brussels' World Fair. At that time, suffering from abdominal pain, he was diagnosed as having cholecystitis, and his gallbladder was removed. At that time Hoover said, "A sound doctor must be opposed to exercise and in favor of tobacco." Later he kept at work on his projected book, *Freedom Betrayed,* in spite of the fact that he was deaf and nearly blind.[15] Nine years after his gallbladder surgery, when he was 86, a *New York Herald Tribune* reporter described him as "relaxed, jaunty, and vigorous."

In Hoover's eighty-eighth year, however, he developed abdominal pain, and a malignant tumor was removed from his intestines. Ten months later he developed massive gastrointestinal bleeding, and seemed almost terminally ill but made some improvement. In early 1964, near his ninetieth birthday, he was convalescing in his quarters at the Waldorf in New York. He was then noted to be frail, but he seemed to be increasing in strength. His spirits were good, his mind unclouded, and he kept up a great deal of correspondence.[16]

Hoover's last illness began in February 1964, with a recurrence of gastrointestinal bleeding complicated by pneumonia. He lingered until October 16, when he suffered a massive gastrointestinal hemorrhage. He refused at that time to be hospitalized. Hoover was in a coma when he died on October 20, 1964.[17]

The 90-year-old Hoover was buried near his birthplace in West Branch, Iowa. Only one other president, John Adams, lived longer. Adams survived to be 91 years of age.

References

1. David Burner, *Herbert Hoover*, p. 6.
2. Will Irwin, *Herbert Hoover*, p. 9.
3. Eugene Lyons, *Herbert Hoover*, p. 13.
4. Ibid., p. 25.
5. Ibid., p. 218.
6. Richard Norton Smith, *An Uncommon Man*, p. 418.
7. Ibid., p. 106.
8. Harold Wolff, *Herbert Hoover*, p. 165.
9. Lillian Parks, *My Thirty Years Backstairs at the White House*, p. 226.
10. Dorothy Horton McGee, *Herbert Hoover*, p. 228.
11. Wolff, *Herbert Hoover*, p. 432.
12. Homer F. Cunningham, *The Presidents' Last Years*, p. 235.
13. Wolff, *Herbert Hoover*, p. 403.
14. Cunningham, *The Presidents' Last Years*, p. 235.
15. Burner, *Herbert Hoover*, p. 378.
16. Lyons, *Herbert Hoover*, p. 438.
17. Cunningham, *The Presidents' Last Years*, p. 240.

31

Franklin Delano Roosevelt

Someone said of Franklin Delano Roosevelt, "In spite of his splendid physical appearance, he was always getting sick." Thus any attempt to recount the various health problems of FDR is a prodigious undertaking. For not only did he have a great variety of prolonged and severe health problems, but systematic attempts were also made to sustain the illusion of that splendid appearance. The health history of three other presidents presented this same problem of serious illnesses and attempts to keep these illnesses secret: Cleveland, Wilson, and Kennedy.

Franklin D. Roosevelt, the thirty-second president of the United States, was born on January 30, 1882, in Hyde Park, New York.

Giving birth to FDR was the major achievement in Sarah Delano Roosevelt's life. She wanted no more children; and, indeed, she had no more physical relations with her husband for the remaining years of their marriage. On Sarah Delano and James Roosevelt's honeymoon, which lasted ten months, Sarah enjoyed the traveling. What she liked less was the physical side of marriage. She would have preferred, it has been said, a "virgin birth."[1]

And no wonder, the birth of FDR was difficult and drawn out. Mrs. Roosevelt was given an overdose of chloroform, which almost asphyxiated the infant. He was born livid, blue, and in respiratory standstill. This infant in such a dire state was given mouth-to-mouth resuscitation. After a short while he reacted and rewarded the resuscitator with a cry. FDR weighed ten pounds at birth.

After careful nursing, Franklin grew into a healthy child. He was the only child of a domineering mother and an older father. James Roosevelt was about twice the age of his wife, and it was said of him that he was not the assertive type, at least not in his own household. FDR's mother was possessive, overprotective, and domineering. Perhaps domineering is too forceful a word but there was a tendency on her part to control his life. Perhaps this was a subconscious effort on her part. In order to avoid hurting his mother in this struggle of wills FDR resorted to the tactics of evasion and deception. There are those who feel that many of the tactics which he adopted in this struggle of wills were used to his advantage later in the White House.

From early infancy Franklin seemed to be more than normally suscep- tible to respiratory ailments, or perhaps his mother was more than normally responsive to his symptoms. At any rate, his childhood letters and his mother's diaries are full of references to his colds and sore throats, though he escaped most of the common childhood illnesses.[2]

Although he did have a number of attacks of upper respiratory infec- tions as a child, his most serious problem was an attack of typhoid at age seven.

On one of his European trips he went on board the tour ship with a fever. His physician thought the illness was due to malaria, but the epi- sode was declared typhoid by the ship's surgeon. Franklin was put in a room in the captain's cabin. Upon arrival at Liverpool he was taken by am- bulance to the eminent Dr. Gemmell. Franklin convalesced while his par- ents continued the tour.

When he was 11 years old he had a very frightening experience. His father had taken him to Superior, Wisconsin, to witness the launching of a large oil carrier. As the ship hit the water, it raised a large wave which washed Franklin over the pier into the bay. He was promptly pulled out.[3]

During Franklin's prep years in Groton his health was considered fairly good. He did, however, continue to have frequent spells of res- piratory infections; and he had at least one serious bout with the grippe which left him weak and depressed for several days. He was seriously ill with scarlet fever in the spring of his fourth-form year and with a normally light case of mumps at the close of his fifth-form year. In the spring of his last year at Groton he was found to be nearsighted. In addition, FDR had considerable trouble with his teeth, in consequence not only a childhood injury, but also of having inherited the irregular, uneven teeth characteristic of the Delanos. The injury to his teeth occurred on Campo- bello when he was 14 years old, when he was accidentally hit in the mouth with a large stick wielded by his friend, Joe Lovering. One tooth was broken off, another chipped, and he sustained a severe gash to his lip.[4]

When FDR was 16 he had an attack of measles and was kept by this attack from running away to join the navy in the Spanish-American War. He had all the signs and symptoms usually accompanying the disease such as sneezing, coughing, and a rose-colored rash.

His undergraduate years at Harvard were among the healthiest of FDR's life. In the fall of his freshman year he went out for football and succeeded only in making one of the scrub teams. He was battered and bruised as one would expect while playing football. After the football season he went out for the rowing team. He failed to make the varsity but did row on the intramural team. He rowed on the intramural team again in his sophomore year and was apparently engaged in rowing throughout his days at Harvard. Besides the bumps and bruises in football, there is no evidence that FDR had any serious health problems while there.

In 1904, during FDR's first year at Columbia Law School and after he had become engaged to his distant cousin, Eleanor Roosevelt, he fell ill. The problem seemed at first due to a cold; but after three days without improvement, his overanxious mother called in the family physician, Dr. George Draper. The doctor was unable to make any definitive diagnosis, but the eventual conclusion was that it was jaundice (perhaps hepatitis). The illness lasted several weeks, and during this illness a public announcement was made of his engagement to Eleanor.

Eleanor's family was not generally enthusiastic about the coming union. Corinne Robinson Alsop remembered, for example, that her first thought on hearing the news of the engagement was that Eleanor had lived through too much unhappiness to plan to marry a man with a mother like cousin Sally: "A more determined and possessive woman than I have ever known."⁵

On March 17, 1905, Franklin and Eleanor were wed. After some delay, while he took his law school exams, they sailed on the *Oceanic* for a three months' honeymoon. One night on that honeymoon he started to sleepwalk. At Eleanor's suggestion he quietly returned to the bed. There were other sleepwalking episodes, however, in the early years of their marriage. Once Eleanor woke up to find Franklin standing at the foot of the bed turning an imaginary crank as hard as he could and saying "The damn thing won't work." She calmly told him to get in the "car," whereupon he got back into bed and held an imaginary steering wheel while she had to pretend to do the cranking.⁶

A great deal has been made of FDR's sleepwalking. Naturally, it was of intense interest to the psychobiographers who saw a great deal of significance, both in the fact that he sleepwalked and in the content of his dreams. Somnambulism is a psychological disorder in which the sleepwalker in a dream of fantasy reenacts an early trauma.⁷ More specifically, a study evaluating a group of naval personnel found universally among somnambulists an inadequate identification with a male figure.⁸ On the whole, the somnabulists' mothers were "domineering, controlling, and covertly disparaging of the father."⁹ This analysis and description would seem to be an apt description for Sarah and James Roosevelt.

Roosevelt's thirties were marked by a series of prolonged illnesses. In 1912, while still a state senator, he contracted typhoid fever. The attack was severe but unaccompanied by complications. FDR was severely ill over a period of four to five weeks and required a long period of convalescence.[10] In July 1916, while assistant secretary of the navy, he had an appendectomy. There is no detailed description of the attack except to say that the surgery was of an emergent nature.[11] In 1915 FDR was troubled by a nonspecific type of backache labeled lumbago. This plus a succession of headaches, colds, sinus attacks, and a number of throat infections during 1916 and 1917 kept him in bed three or four weeks at a time. In August 1917 he had to be hospitalized with a tonsillar abscess. Roosevelt, while on an inspection tour in Europe during the last few weeks of the war, contracted influenza which was complicated by influenzal pneumonia. In December 1919, after a series of nose and throat problems, he had a tonsillectomy.[12]

Clearly, however, the most significant illness of Roosevelt's life was the polio contracted in the summer of 1921. Roosevelt was very tired when he and the family arrived at Campobello for a vacation. He had been put under a great deal of stress by a threatened Senate investigation of a scandal which had occurred while he was assistant secretary of the navy. He had gone to Washington to try to defend himself against these accusations. In late July (before the Campobello vacation), Roosevelt visited the New York Boy Scout Camp at Lake Kanowahks. There is conjecture that he may have picked up the virus while visiting the Boy Scout camp. There is also a presumption that overprotection and seclusion as a child may have prevented his acquiring immunity during childhood. It may be added that his exposure and exhausting activities during the time of invasion by the virus may have greatly aggravated his case. His activity during the incubation period and even after that would not be calculated to help protect against a severe attack of the polio virus.

On July 21 Roosevelt woke up not feeling well but went with his family picnicking, sailing, and fishing. At the end of the day the family fought a forest fire for several hours; and in order to remove the soot, dirt, and perspiration, they went swimming in the very cold waters of the bay. At suppertime he developed a backache and went to bed, thinking he had had a recurrence of lumbago. Soon after retiring he had a severe chill. The symptoms were treated but not relieved by extra blankets, hot drinks, and the hot water bottle. The progression of his disease was very rapid, and the next morning he had weakness of his left knee. The family doctor diagnosed his problem as a cold. During that day his muscular weakness became rapidly more extensive, and by evening he had weakness in both lower extremities. On the third day he was aching all over and had a fever of 102 degrees.

The family then called Dr. W. W. Keen, a famous Philadelphia neurosurgeon who had helped operate many years earlier on President Cleveland for throat cancer. Dr. Keen had also seen President Wilson in consultation while Wilson was president. This physician came much nearer to the truth than did the family physician, but he still failed to make the correct diagnosis. Dr. Keen felt that a blood clot had formed in Roosevelt's lower spinal cord, rendering him paralyzed in his lower extremities. By the end of the third day Roosevelt had paralysis from the waist down, and there was transient partial paralysis of the upper extremities, bladder, and lower bowel. It was necessary to empty his bladder by catheter. The function of bladder and bowel returned after two weeks; and then shortly thereafter there was a return of full function in the upper extremities. However, there was residual and permanent paralysis from the hips down.

It was not until August 25 that Dr. Robert Lovett made the correct diagnosis of poliomyelitis. In September Lovett referred the patient to Dr. George Draper of New York who entered him in the Presbyterian Hospital. After FDR was placed in the hospital a release was made to the press. The *New York Times* reported: "FDR ill with polio. Brought on a special car from Campobello.... Doctors say the patient stricken by infantile paralysis one month ago and use of his legs affected." Although the newspaper reported there had been some temporary paralysis of Roosevelt's legs below the knees, the paper assured their readers, "He definitely will not be crippled."[13] This was the beginning, but far from the end, of the splendid deception.

Dr. Draper did not share Lovett's view that there might be full recovery. In fact, he feared that the lower back muscles, which are needed to sustain one while sitting, might never recover. However, there was finally enough recovery that he could be moved to his home at Hyde Park.

After this FDR went through a long period of rehabilitation. In December he started physical therapy. He had developed contractions of the flexor muscles and tendons, and the process of overcoming the contracture was slow and exceedingly painful. In January 1922 he developed swelling of his lower extremities and the contractions were more severe and painful. There was great pain each time Ms. Lake, the physiotherapist, tried to stretch the contracted tendons. In March he was fitted with hip to ankle braces. With the use of braces and crutches he was finally able to stand and walk, even with absence of strength in his legs: "Unable to move without wheelchair or crutches, dependent on nurses and therapists, his body functions exposed to the view of women, Franklin was helpless as a baby."[14]

Roosevelt did not give up, though. In early 1922 he began exercises to strengthen the muscles of his upper extremities. This was needed to give enough strength in his arms and shoulders to support himself on crutches. That summer he began swimming in an outdoor pool. In September 1924 Roosevelt went for the first time to Warm Springs, Georgia, and spent several weeks there. For seven years Roosevelt's single goal was to rebuild the muscles of his legs so that he could walk upright. But most of the musculature left in his feet was hopelessly atrophied, and most of the thigh muscles that stretch the knees never regained their use.

Eventually, Roosevelt was left with his upper body intact. He was paralyzed from the waist down, and could assume the upright position only with the aid of metal braces locked at the knee and the support of crutches. He learned this way to keep his body upright and to carry and swing it forward with his arms, using the crutches as a support and fulcrum.[15] His walking was only a simulation, even though after much training he was able to move with a special cane in one hand and someone supporting his other elbow.

Despite Roosevelt's determination, there was an endpoint to the nature of the disease beyond which he could not go. He did, however, achieve the best possible results with the physical resources that had been left to him. Of course, there was the need to continue the program of rehabilitation designed to maintain even what had been accomplished in obtaining the best muscle tone and muscle mass possible. When Roosevelt returned to public life his appearances were so staged as to conceal, as much as possible, the extent of his disability.

On June 26, 1924, FDR made his first political speech since he had become a victim of polio. This speech, given at Madison Square Garden, was the nominating speech for presidential candidate Alfred Smith. Roosevelt sat with the New York delegates on the crowded floor, determined not to be wheeled in. He had his 16-year-old son, Jimmy, get him in early on crutches before the floor got clogged. Jimmy, as he held his father's arm, matching his stride with his father's ponderous gait, thought of San Francisco and "Pa jumping up and grabbing the state standard." The event occurred in 1920 at the Democratic National Convention at San Francisco, when Roosevelt wrested the New York state banner from a Tammany leader and led a parade around the convention hall. Now just getting into his seat was an ordeal. Jimmy supported him and took his crutches as he lowered himself into place, his legs stiffly extended until the knee joints of the braces were unlocked. Only then could he bend his legs and adjust his sitting position. When he wanted to stand he had to lock the braces again.[16]

When the time came for his speech, he leaned on his son's arm and made his way to the speaker's platform. When the moment came that he had to walk alone, he took the second crutch and moved across the stage. This, or a similar scene, would be repeated time after time in the subsequent years of his public life.

In 1931, while he was still governor of New York, rumors concerning his health were released in an effort to stop his candidacy for the presidency. He countered by releasing to the public the details of a medical examination. Apart from the paralyzed legs the details did not attract much public attention. It was noted that his systolic blood pressure was 140, and the diastolic was 100. The systolic blood pressure of 140 is marginal, but the diastolic pressure of 100 is very undesirable and may be an omen of severe blood pressure problems later. At that time when no great concern was expressed about such levels of blood pressure, the public was not much interested.[17] During the 1932 elections it was rumored that his crippling was due to syphilis. This rumor apparently had no foundation in fact.

He found the means of appearing in public as merely lame rather than crippled. In addition, he and his ever-watchful aide, Louis Howe, had persuaded press photographers and newsreel cameramen not to film him in a wheelchair while locking his braces or while emerging from an automobile.[18] "No movies of me getting out of the machine, boys," he would say. Roosevelt created such an effective illusion that most Americans did not realize that he was a paraplegic.[19]

There is not much to be added concerning FDR's health until the time of his becoming president. One event which was particularly significant at that time was the selection of Admiral Ross McIntyre as his personal physician. The appointment was made on the recommendation of Admiral Cary T. Grayson, who was Woodrow Wilson's doctor. The appointment was made partially because FDR's main medical problem at the time of his inauguration concerned head colds and sinus trouble; and the admiral was an eye, ear, nose, and throat specialist.

The interval of time from between FDR's first inauguration and his final years and days was considerable, and we are left almost in the dark about his health during that time. It was universally known that he had polio with some degree of crippling, but the full degree of his crippling was known to only a few. Dr. Ross McIntyre, the EENT specialist, did continue to treat him for colds and sinusitis.

In 1934 Roosevelt had an attack of respiratory infection, called flu, which lasted longer than an ordinary attack should. In 1937 his records showed that he had a slight blood pressure elevation, an abscessed molar, and a severe attack of gastroenteritis. These illnesses are a matter of record.

Other illnesses, however, apparently were unrecorded. It has been conjectured, for example, that in the late summer of 1938 Roosevelt had the first of a series of "little strokes." One of these, it is presumed, occurred while he was visiting his son at the Mayo Clinic.[20] Small strokes are really transient ischemic attacks which follow a brief loss of adequate blood supply to focal areas in the brain. These, after one or many episodes, may progress to a completed stroke. They may be referred to as a temporary blood deficiency of an area in the brain which does not proceed to completion of a stroke. They are due to arteriosclerotic changes in cerebral vessels. In FDR's case this is very credible if one cares to look at his subsequent history, although Dr. Howard Breunn, his closest and most reliable observer, denied that any strokes had ever occurred.

Following Roosevelt's trip to Tehran in November 1943, a rapid and very obvious decline began. This illness was labeled by Admiral McIntyre as "flu." The "flu" seemed to get no better; in fact, it seemed to be getting worse. Apparently, the only checking Admiral McIntyre had done on the president throughout the years consisted of dosing him on a daily basis with nose drops and sinus sprays, irrigating his sinuses with saline douches, and experimenting with one of the most extreme treatments of the day: cauterization of the sinus tissue with a red-hot loop stuck up the nose. Ironically, the years of dosing with drops which contained vasoconstrictors brought only marginal relief of his sinus difficulties, while at the same time it served to increase his already elevated blood pressure.[21]

While McIntyre was anxious to keep the president well, he was at the same time very jealous of his prerogatives. And although he held the highest rank in the naval medical hierarchy, his medical abilities above treating a cold and sinusitis were dubious. He saw that the president was very ill, but was very uncertain of the illness's cause. Eleanor Roosevelt and her daughter, Anna Boettiger, were concerned enough to ask McIntyre to examine the president more thoroughly. One historian reported that McIntyre then told the family that the president suffered from the flu and bronchitis and was overworked. For the first time, Mrs. Roosevelt rejected the naval doctor's diagnosis and insisted on a second opinion.[22]

McIntyre acquiesced to this idea, but he used the device that would assure his losing no control of the situation. By the end of March 1944 McIntyre had enough concern that he arranged to have FDR admitted to Bethesda Naval Hospital for a complete checkup. The doctor chosen for this task was Howard G. Bruenn, a young naval reserve officer, who specialized in internal medicine and cardiology.

Bruenn was ordered to do a complete heart and lung examination and to report the findings to no one but McIntyre — not even the patient, not even the family. The admiral had also called the commanding officer at Bethesda Naval Hospital to make sure that the examination and findings would be kept private.[23]

The president's chart at the time of admission revealed that he had had a gradual rise in blood pressure from 1935 to 1941. His pressure had gone from 136/78 to 188/105. There were no entries after that date.[24] Also in the chart at the time of admission there was a history of the development of a severe iron deficiency anemia in May 1941. At that time FDR had a hemoglobin of 4.5 gm/100 ml, presumably due to bleeding hemorrhoids. This was a very severe anemia.[25]

Bruenn's initial examination revealed a drawn, gray, and exhausted individual, who became short of breath on the very slightest exertion. The examination of his eyes revealed some changes due to arteriosclerosis and hypertension. There were rales (indicating fluid in both lungs). His heart was enlarged, and there was a heart murmur of valvular insufficiency (mitral valve). The aortic valve closing sound was loud—a finding which is frequently found in hypertension. His blood pressure was 186/108. His liver palpated as normal in size. The electrocardiogram showed nonspecific T-wave abnormalities. His chest X ray showed pulmonary congestion and cardiac enlargement. Bruenn's diagnosis and recommendations were published in the *Annals of Internal Medicine* 25 years after the fact by Dr. Bruenn:

> In view of the low-grade pulmonary infection, cough, and dyspnea on effort, it appeared that these symptoms might well be due to left ventricular failure. Accordingly, diagnoses of hypertension, hypertensive heart disease, cardiac failure, and acute bronchitis were made. These findings and their interpretation were presented to Surgeon-General Ross McIntyre. These findings had been completely unsuspected by McIntyre up to this time. A memorandum of recommendations was presented to McIntyre. It was suggested that: 1) The patient should be put to bed for one to two weeks, with nursing care. 2) Digitalization should be carried out with 0.4 gm. of digitalis every day for five days, followed by 0.1 gm. every day by mouth. 3) A light, easily digested diet. Portions were to be small and salt intake was to be restricted. Potassium chloride, in salt shaker, could be used as desired for seasoning. 4) Codeine 0.5 gm. should be given as needed for control of cough. 5) Sedation should be taken to insure rest and a refreshing night's sleep. 6) A program of gradual weight reduction.[26]

This was in no sense a drastic regimen; considering the president's condition, it was a very mild approach to a very serious problem.[27]

Bruenn, from his examination and report, viewed the president as a desperately ill man, who, even with proper treatment, had not long to live. However, when he presented his diagnosis and treatment proposals to McIntyre, the admiral responded by saying that the information might alarm and antagonize the patient. He also stated that the president, due to his heavy workload, would not agree to it. McIntyre, indeed, was reluctant to accept the diagnosis. He recommended alteration of the treatment regimen until it amounted to no more than treating a cold. The admiral was apparently protecting his own turf. He knew that the family, the patient, and all concerned would wonder why the diagnosis was not made before. In his report 25 years later Bruenn stated in his reference to his findings: "They had been completely unsuspected up to this time."[28] However, at that time McIntyre asked Dr. Bruenn to serve under him as the president's physician in attendance. There was a clear understanding that all medical reports should be issued through the admiral himself.

After rejecting the rational treatment suggested by Bruenn, McIntyre agreed to give the president some cough syrup containing codeine and ammonium carbonate. He balked at the bedrest, digitalis, and salt restrictions. Four days after Bruenn's initial examination FDR showed no improvement. In fact, Bruenn added in his clinical notes that even without an X ray he could tell that Roosevelt's heart was grossly enlarged to the left with a heaving systolic impulse at the apex. Once more he urged McIntyre to give the president digitalis.[29]

Not capitulating to Bruenn's proposed regimen but alarmed, the admiral decided to call in an a team of consultants—Dr. James A. Paulin, an internist from Emory University, and the prominent Boston surgeon, Dr. Frank Lahey. Both of the consultants agreed with Bruenn, but Paulin questioned the wisdom of using digitalis. Bruenn was very forceful in his insistence that the cardiac drug should be given, and finally Paulin and Lahey acquiesced. McIntyre was more difficult to convince, but he too finally conceded.

All of this happened just a few weeks before the Democratic National Convention which was to name FDR for the fourth time as its candidate for the presidency and a little more than ten months before Yalta, when this man, FDR, was to be the primary representative of the free world to help decide the fate of Eastern Europe.

The digitalis was begun on the same day, and within a week the president was symptomatically much improved. The electrocardiogram and chest X rays were improved. His blood pressure, however, showed no improvement; indeed, the blood pressure now was higher than ever. His pulmonary congestion improved, but his blood pressure continued to rise—from a systolic blood pressure of 180 on the first examination by Dr.

Bruenn to 210 in the next two weeks. By April 3 the reading was even
higher — 220/118.[30]

The only treatment at that time for hypertension was a combination
of salt restriction and sedation, which was not too effective. The president's blood pressure remained alarmingly high at a level of 210/120. At
that time blood pressure this severe was called malignant hypertension
and carried a grim prognosis. In April 1944 FDR with his retinue left
Washington for a trek to the enormous estate of Bernard Baruch in South
Carolina. McIntyre and Bruenn were part of the followers. At this time
McIntyre was making his notes which minimized the extreme seriousness
of the president's illness: "A moderate degree of arteriosclerosis, although
no more than normal for a man of his age."

After two weeks at Baruch's home, the Hobcow Barony, although the
president seemed rested, his blood pressure readings were quite disturb-
ing. In the early morning his readings were 230/120 and by bedtime it had
dropped to 190/90. Bruenn then restarted the phenobarbitol and increased
the amounts of digitalis given. The week afterward FDR had what seemed
clinically to be acute cholecystitis; however, abdominal symptoms disappeared after a few days. After the president's return to Washington X rays
were made of his gallbladder which showed some gallstones.[31]

The blood pressure problem continued to be very serious; and by early
May Bruenn's readings showed elevations of 240/130. For the first recorded time Roosevelt began to complain of a dull pain in the back of his
neck and of a throbbing sensation throughout his body. These symptoms
were apparently due to his severe hypertension.[32]

It is very difficult to imagine why some writers have wandered so far
afield in discussing the possible reasons for FDR's sickness and death.
After Breunn's article on the illness and death of FDR, it is impossible to
understand how anyone could have ascribed his death to any other cause
than arteriosclerosis and hypertensive cardiovascular disease.

Dr. Harry Goldsmith did a remarkable bit of medical sleuthing in an
attempt to prove that FDR may have died of a malignancy. Goldsmith
reported that he had attended a lecture at Sloan-Kettering Institute in
1963, in which time the lecturer is presumed to have said that Dr. Lahey
had told him he had seen FDR in consultation in 1944, and had told the
president that he should not run for the presidency in 1944 because he had
a metastatic tumor and would not survive his fourth term. He, Goldsmith,
based part of his speculation on picture evidence. He stated,

> A hypothetical case can be constructed that a pigmented lesion over the
> left eye could have been a melanoma. I have studied many pictures of

> FDR during his early life at Groton and his early days in politics and have never observed a pigmented area over his left eye. However, by about 1932, a definite pigmented lesion had developed in the supraorbital region of the left eye. The supraorbital lesion continued to enlarge over the years in association with his apparently robust health. After the Tehran meeting in 1943, I have never seen a picture which showed the pigmented area over his left eye.

He was implying that in the interval after the pictures no longer showed the pigmented lesion over the left eye some surgery had been done in that area.[33] The theory was that FDR had a malignant lesion, a melanoma, which developed after 1932 and was removed surgically in or before 1943. This was a very clever bit of medical detective work. His hypothesis is, however, blunted by the problem of vanishing records. FDR's records were put in a safe at Bethesda Naval Hospital from whence they disappeared. It is probable that his heirs, both blood and political, felt that his image would be better served if the truth were not known about the state of his health and the attempts to cover up the situation. Bruenn himself had a premonition that something might happen to the records, so he kept a file for himself. There is also the added fact that no autopsy was done. Although Goldsmith did not actually say that the pigmented lesion over his eye was the cause of death, he did raise some interesting speculation and made a plea that the full truth about FDR's health be allowed to surface.

It is now known that Roosevelt was absent from the White House for a total of nine weeks in the first five months of 1944. Throughout March he had been so ill that he rarely left his bedroom. Between January and the end of May the president, unknown to the public, had been away from the Oval Office roughly half the time.[34] From March 1944 until the end of the year, moreover, FDR had a large number of admissions to Bethesda Naval Hospital under assumed names. The reason for admission and what occurred after admission are still unknown.

During his last campaign there were many rumors about the state of Roosevelt's health. When he made his acceptance speech, just before the departure for the Pacific tour in July 1944, a photograph was made in which he appeared haggard, glassy-eyed, and querulous. The photograph had been given very wide publicity in the press and in the pamphlets with which the Republicans were flooding the country.[35]

Roosevelt and his advisers, of course, were doing all they could to defuse the rumors. Admiral McIntyre, less than a month before the election, made a statement about Roosevelt's health: "The President's health is perfectly OK. There are absolutely no organic difficulties at all."[36] This was not the first time nor the last that the admiral lied to the press, to the Roosevelt family, and to all concerned.

In this effort Roosevelt was helped by the press. The managing editor of *Life,* Luce, for example, was shown some 200 pictures of FDR for up-coming issues: "In half of them he was a dead man," recalled Luce. "We decided to print the ones that were least bad and thereby—by trying to lean over backwards to be fair or something, or kind—we infringed our contract with the readers to tell the truth." Actually, the truth was in the pictures. The big irresponsibility of the U.S. press, confirmed Luce, "came when we did not indicate ... that Roosevelt was a dying man."

On Roosevelt's return from his Pacific trip he made a speech at Brem-ington Navy yard in Seattle. During the speech he sounded hesitant and uncertain. And no wonder. During the early part of the speech, as his heart specialist Dr. Bruenn revealed years later, Roosevelt began to suffer, for the first and only time in his life, from an anginal attack—an excruciat-ing pain in his chest extending up into both shoulders and, after 15 minutes, very slowly subsiding.[37]

Lord Moran, Churchill's private physician, made several observations in his diaries regarding the visible decline in the president's health. At an airfield in Malta just before taking off for the Crimea he noted: "The Presi-dent looked old, and thin, and drawn; he had a cape or shawl over his shoulders and appeared shrunken; he sat looking straight ahead with his mouth open as if he were not taking things in. Everyone was shocked by his appearance and gabbed about it." This was February 3, 1945, just before departing for Yalta.[38]

On February 7, 1945, at Sebastopol, Moran again recorded: "To a doctor's eyes, the President appeared a very sick man; he has all the symp-toms of hardening of the arteries of the brain in an advanced stage, so that I can only give him a few months to live."[39]

It has been alleged by some that the hardened arteries supplying the blood to FDR's central nervous system were responsible for his allowing Stalin to take over large areas of Eastern Europe. Whatever may be said, we are left to believe that we were represented at Yalta by a man who was terminally ill.

On March 29, 1945, the president and his retainers left Washington for Warm Springs. While there, according to Bruenn, his physical findings were unchanged except for his blood pressure; which varied greatly from time to time, ranging between 170/88 to 240/130. If one reads the de-scription of events on the morning of his demise, he need look no further than Roosevelt's blood pressure readings to find a cause for the terminal event.

At 1:15 P.M. he was seated in a chair, being sketched by an artist, when he suddenly complained of a terrible occipital headache. "When I saw him 15 minutes later," said Bruenn, "he was pale, cold, and sweating profusely—he was totally unconscious.... His pupils at first were equal, but in a few moments the right pupil was widely dilated and ... his heart rate was 96, blood pressure systolic was well over 300, diastolic pressure was 190.... He voided involuntarily. It was obvious that the President had suffered a massive cerebral hemorrhage. At 3:35 I pronounced him dead." No autopsy, at the request of Mrs. Roosevelt, was obtained.[40]

The belated revelation by Bruenn of the president's clinical course leaves not much mystery regarding his terminal illness. Of course, an autopsy would have eliminated any trace of doubt.

Roosevelt, Kennedy, and Wilson—their illnesses and the successful coverups bear a great deal of resemblance to each other.

References

1. Ted Morgan, *Franklin Delano Roosevelt*, p. 21.
2. Kenneth S. Davis, *FDR: The Beckoning of Destiny*, p. 61.
3. Rudolph Marx, *The Health of the Presidents*, p. 353.
4. Davis, p. 118.
5. Goeffrey C. Ward, *Before the Trumpet*, p. 337.
6. Morgan, *Franklin Delano Roosevelt*, p. 105.
7. Ibid.
8. John A. Sours, "Somnambulism," *Archives of General Psychiatry* 9 (October 1963): 400.
9. Ibid., p. 409.
10. Marx, *The Health of the Presidents*, p. 356.
11. Ibid., pp. 356–57.
12. Nathan Miller, *An Intimate History*, p. 126.
13. Hugh Gregory Gallagher, *FDR's Splendid Deception*, p. 19.
14. Morgan, *Franklin Delano Roosevelt*, p. 250.
15. Marx, *The Health of the Presidents*, p. 361.
16. Morgan, *Franklin Delano Roosevelt*, p. 271.
17. Hugh L'Etang, *The Pathology of Leadership*, p. 89.
18. Frank Freidel, *Franklin Delano Roosevelt: A Rendezvous with Destiny*, p. 47.
19. *New York Post*, November 7, 1928.
20. Marx, *The Health of the Presidents*, p. 366.
21. Gallagher, *FDR's Splendid Deception*, p. 179.
22. Kenneth R. Crispell and Carlos F. Gomez, *Hidden Illness in the White House*, p. 77.
23. Kim Bishop, *FDR's Last Years*, p. 3.
24. Crispell and Gomez, *Hidden Illness in the White House*, p. 78.

25. Howard G. Bruenn, "Clinical Notes on the Illness and Death of FDR," *Annals of Internal Medicine* 72 (March 1970): 579–91, passim.

26. Ibid., p. 584.

27. Ibid., p. 579.

28. Ibid., p. 581.

29. Crispell and Gomez, *Hidden Illness in the White House*, pp. 79–80.

30. Ibid., p. 80.

31. Bruenn, "Clinical Notes on the Illness and Death of FDR," p. 584.

32. Crispell and Gomez, *Hidden Illness in the White House*, p. 82.

33. Harry S. Goldsmith, "Unanswered Mysteries in the Death of FDR," *Surgery, Gynecology, and Obstetrics* 140 (December 1979): 904.

34. Crispell and Gomez, *Hidden Illness in the White House*, p. 83.

35. Robert E. Sherwood, *An Intimate History — Roosevelt and Hopkins*, p. 820.

36. Homer F. Cunningham, *The Presidents' Last Years*, p. 246.

37. Freidel, *Franklin Delano Roosevelt*, p. 545.

38. Lord Moran, *Churchill: The Diaries of Lord Moran*, p. 234.

39. Ibid., p. 242.

40. Bruenn, "Clinical Notes on the Illness and Death of FDR," p. 591.

32

Harry S Truman

Harry S Truman was born May 8, 1884, in Lamar, Missouri, the first president to take office during a war.

Truman had very few health problems in his lifetime — mostly minor. He apparently was blessed with good genes, for his grandparents lived into their nineties and most of his ancestors lived to an advanced age.

As a boy Truman did, however, develop diphtheria, in 1894 at age ten, which left him paralyzed for several months, during which he had to be wheeled around in a baby carriage.[1] Truman was drinking a glass of milk when his throat closed in a diphtheritic paralysis. The paralysis finally extended to his entire body, both arms and legs; and the recovery was slow.

There was no diphtheria antitoxin in those days. He was treated with ipecac and whiskey, and at that age he developed a severe distaste for both.[2]

This attack of diphtheria apparently had nothing to do with Harry's visual defect, hyperopia, which had been discovered five years earlier. He was fitted for glasses at age eight. Because of his glasses he engaged very little in rough play and spent a great deal of time reading and taking piano lessons.[3]

Margaret Truman, his daughter, gave one account about Truman's eye troubles. She wrote about his terrible vision: "His mother noted that when he was five years old she found he was able to see the large print in the family Bible, but when she pointed out objects at a distance, he couldn't see them."[4] His mother took him to an eye doctor in Kansas City where it was discovered that Harry had a rare eye problem — described as flat eye balls. The doctor prescribed thick, very expensive glasses, and warned him against any roughhouse activity, such as football.

Stories about his eyesight are not in agreement regarding the cause and age of onset of his problems, but it seems reasonable that Margaret would be the one best informed about her father. However, it is strange that Margaret did not mention her father's attack of diphtheria. It was her husband, Jonathan Daniels, who stated that the diphtheria attack had left him with the eye problem, and had left him totally paralyzed for a time.[5]

Perhaps due to Harry's impetuous nature he was subject to accidents. At one time, while engaged in the act of combing his hair, he fell out of his chair and broke his collar bone. He had barely recovered from the diphtheritic paralysis when he lopped off the end of his big toe. He accomplished this by slamming the cellar door on it. The family physician put the two separate parts back together with a coating of iodoform, with good results. On another occasion he got a peach pit hung in his throat, and his mother saved his life by quick thinking and quick action when she forced the pit down his throat.[6] Truman said, "I was eating a peach and swallowed the seed. I almost choked to death, but Mama pushed the seed down my throat with her finger and I lived to tell about it."[7]

Truman's poor eyesight kept him out of West Point. His vision was too poor to allow him to serve in any branch of the military, but he chose to volunteer almost immediately after Wilson's call in 1917 for a declaration of war. He served in the National Guard with a final rank of captain.[8]

Despite his eye problems, Truman did manage to exercise regularly. In the early 1920s, when Truman and Edward Jacobson were engaged in the haberdashery business, Truman joined the Kansas City Athletic Club where he learned to swim. "With relentless determination he taught himself to swim using a strange, choppy, self-styled side stroke, his head above water so he could keep his glasses dry."[9] Eventually, in his active years he walked two miles every morning at a fast pace. He also enjoyed playing poker and was a talented pianist. Truman did not smoke, and he drank moderately — mostly bourbon and white wine.[10]

During his adult life Truman's health was generally very good, although not perfect. In 1938, for example, while a member of Congress, he had a car accident. His daughter Margaret related that he always drove too fast. "It was a Sunday morning and a stop sign at a key intersection was obscured by a parked car. A man in another car plowed into us as we went through the intersection. Our car was completely wrecked. It was a miracle that we escaped alive. Dad had a cut over his forehead and Mother had a wrenched back."[11]

There are also many reports regarding President Truman's headaches. When he was judge in Jackson County, Missouri (1924–34), he complained of headaches which were accompanied by dizziness and sleeplessness. The headaches were apparently precipitated by stress and were made worse by added stress. When he was relaxed, there were no headaches. During Harry's first term as senator, he became involved in the fight over Roosevelt's attempt to stack the Supreme Court. In the July heat and the stress of the court struggle, his headaches returned. Mrs. Truman, who was herself suffering from the terrible heat, worried about Harry's ability to sustain his health.[12] Margaret wrote that her father's health was good, but it was not perfect. "He had a tendency to ignore his illness until it either went away, or floored him." In July 1946 he wrote to his mother: "Early last week, after our trip to Shangri-la, I cultivated a sore throat and infected ear, but both are all right now. It's the first time I ever had a bad ear. But couldn't let up."[13]

Truman, in 1948 at age 64, ran for a full term as president. His weight was then 175 pounds, his blood pressure 120–128/80, which is a very good level. He still continued his daily walks, which he did at a fast pace.[14] He seemed to be in excellent health. However, in 1950 the constant attacks by Joseph McCarthy put such a stress on even a healthy man that Bess insisted on a retreat to Florida to recuperate.[15] In addition, he had intestinal flu in 1952 and was hospitalized at Walter Reed for a short time. He had a slow pulse nearly all of his life, which his doctors attributed to his absence of tension.[16]

Since assassinations and attempted assassinations have played such an important part in the history of our presidents, it is felt necessary to mention the attempt on Truman's life. On November 1, 1950, the Trumans were residing in the Blair House, while the White House was being renovated. Two Puerto Rican nationalists tried to break in and assassinate Truman while he was taking a nap. In 3 minutes 32 shots were fired, and one White House policeman was killed. When Truman was later asked about the attempt, he said, "Well, I'll tell you, getting shot at was nothing I worried about when I was President. It wouldn't have done the slightest bit of good if I had. My opinion has always been that if you are in an office like that, and someone wants to shoot you, they'll probably do it, and nothing much can help you out."[17]

When Truman left the White House in the spring of 1953 he was still in good health. In fact, at 68, he was leaving office in better health than when he first took office.[18] His retirement was one of the longest during the twentieth-century history of the presidency. He lacked three weeks of having a full 20 years of retirement. Only Hoover had a longer retirement as an ex-president—31.5 years. There were three presidents who ended their terms at an older age than Truman: Andrew Jackson, William Henry Harrison, and James Buchanan. All of these were a few months older than was Truman when he ended his second term.[19] Until Truman was past 80 he remained active both physically and mentally. He still used walking as his main exercise, which he did at a good pace. If he ever golfed it is not recorded.[20]

In 1954 Truman had a gallbladder attack, which came on while he was attending a performance of *Call Me Madam*. He was rushed to the hospital and operated on soon thereafter. The surgery was a great success, but postoperatively he had a very severe reaction to the antibiotic given him. Truman had what he called "hives inside and out" and was unable to retain his food for a time. However, in a few days he had a sudden recovery, and within two months he was back at work, six days a week.[21]

About a year after his gallbladder surgery Truman fell on some ice while he was taking his morning walk but sustained no severe injury. At that time he was told that he should do no more walking on ice and snow.

Early in 1963 Truman developed some discomfort in his abdomen and was diagnosed as having an intestinal hernia. Surgery was recommended for the condition, which was done without complication, and his recovery was uneventful.[22]

After having passed his eighty-third birthday, Truman had another fall. This time the fall was not on the ice but in the bathroom. In this accident he sustained two broken ribs, a lacerated forehead, and broken glasses. His return to normal was longer after this accident.

By the latter part of 1970 Truman's health obviously had become less good. His morning walks were less brisk and less frequent. He moved more slowly, read less, and in general was at a lower level of activity. However, he still enjoyed talking to his friends. Although he still seemed to enjoy life, other health problems began to arise. He had less energy, recurrent vertigo, and a continued problem with arthritis.

During his eighty-eighth year he developed some pulmonary congestion, obviously due to heart failure. He was hospitalized on December 5, 1972. Early on he showed some improvement, but this was not sustained. The ex-president went into a coma during the night after Christmas and died about 8:50 A.M. on December 26, 1972. The cause of death was heart failure.[23]

References

1. Jonathan Daniels, *The Man of Independence*, p. 21.
2. Ibid., p. 53.
3. David C. Whitney, *The American Presidents*, p. 280.
4. Margaret Truman, *Harry S Truman*, p. 47.
5. Daniels, *The Man of Independence*, p. 21.
6. Alfred Steinberg, *The Man from Missouri: The Life and Times of Harry S Truman*, p. 24.

7. Harry S Truman, *The Autobiography of Harry S Truman*, p. 6.
8. David McCulloch, *Truman*, p. 104.
9. Ibid., p. 148.
10. William A. Degregorio, *The Complete Book of U.S. Presidents*, p. 510.
11. Margaret Truman, *Harry S Truman*, p. 98.
12. McCulloch, *Truman*, p. 227.
13. Margaret Truman, *Harry S Truman*, pp. 335–36.
14. McCulloch, *Truman*, p. 585.
15. Ibid., p. 768.
16. Steinberg, *The Man of Missouri*, pp. 423–24.
17. Merle Miller, *Plain Speaking*, p. 368.
18. McCulloch, *Truman*, p. 918.
19. Roy Jenkins, *Truman*, p. 208.
20. Ibid., p. 212.
21. Margaret Truman, *Harry S Truman*, pp. 563–64.
22. Homer F. Cunningham, *The Presidents' Last Years*, p. 263.
23. Ibid., p. 264.

33

Dwight David Eisenhower

Dwight David Eisenhower, the thirty-fourth president of the United States, was born October 14, 1890, in Denison, Texas. He and Ulysses S. Grant were the only West Point graduates ever to complete two terms in the White House; and Eisenhower, Reagan, and Grant were the only Republican presidents to serve two full terms.[1]

Eisenhower was the third child born in a household of seven children, all boys. He grew up in Abilene, Kansas, where the family had moved when Eisenhower was two years of age. The Eisenhowers were very poor and had to struggle to survive.

Eisenhower demonstrated bravery and a stubborn will more than once during his early years. Perhaps most often related is the story of his infected left knee at age 16 and his refusal to have his leg amputated. In the beginning the injury appeared to be very minor — a scratch incurred while he was running home from school. For two days there was no apparent problem, but on the third morning when he awoke his left leg was very painful. By evening, his foot was discolored and swollen. The family physician, Dr. Conklin, was called. The good doctor examined the extremity and declared the condition to be serious — blood poisoning. Conklin discussed the case with Ike's parents and stated that it might be possible to avoid amputation. He deferred the decision until the next day. That night was spent by Ike in great pain, and the next morning the problem was worse. The blackness and swelling had advanced to the knee. The doctor wanted to remove the leg immediately, but Ike would have none of it. He adamantly refused to have any surgery. The doctor told Ike that it was the only possible way to save his life. "No," said Dwight, in a strangled voice, "I'd rather die."

After the doctor left, Dwight grabbed his brother's hand and sobbed, "You've got to promise you won't let them do it. You've got to promise. I won't be a cripple. I'd rather die." His brother Edgar stood guard for two days and nights while his brother suffered terrible pain. Through the feverish night while the blackness and swelling advanced to his groin, Ike persisted in his refusal to allow the amputation. Finally, after he had sunk into unconsciousness, the fever, swelling, and blackness began to subside. Three weeks later, though still pale and weak, he walked out of his room.[2]

Another occurrence which is related in almost all biographical sketches of Ike happened when he was in high school. Related Ike's brother Arthur, "Every new school year each side, the North and South, selected its champion; and the two had to fight it out with bare knuckles for supremacy. Ike's brother Edgar had fought the year before and won. Now it was Ike's turn. Ike's opponent was bigger, stronger and heavier. Shortly after the battle began, Dwight's face was swollen and bleeding. His eyes and lips suffered the most injury. The fight lasted over two hours and ended in a draw. His foe finally blurted out, 'Ike, I can't lick you.' Ike stammered back, 'And I cannot lick you.'"[3] This fight became part of the Abilene and Eisenhower lore. Ike was unable to attend school until three days after the fight.

Apparently, among Ike's characteristics was a very violent temper when aroused. When he was 12 he had a sudden spate of anger over a small matter against his brother Arthur. A brick was handy, and before he could regain self-control, he picked it up and heaved it toward Arthur's head. Arthur ducked just in time; his brother had fully intended in that moment to do damage with that brick. Apparently, his further training helped him to learn to hold that violent temper in check.[4]

In 1912, when Eisenhower was a cadet at West Point, he twisted his knee while playing football against Tufts University. There was some pain and swelling and he spent some time in the hospital. He had some hope of being able to recover enough to return to the lineup for the navy game. However, during the Monday drill that week and during the riding hall (the exercise of leaping off and on the back of a galloping horse), his knee gave way when he hit the ground. The cartilage and tendons in his knee were torn. The extremity was put in a cast and he was, of course, unable to play in the navy game. Ike was further depressed when the doctor removed the cast and told him that he would never play football again.[5]

When Eisenhower graduated from West Point in 1915, he was told that his injured knee might keep him from being commissioned. The doctor did say that he could have a commission in the Coast Artillery, which would require less exertion and less strain on his knee. When Ike refused the Coast Artillery, the doctor finally compromised by telling him that if he applied for the infantry he could have his commission.

In 1934 Ike was assigned as an assistant to MacArthur in the Philippines where he had some health problems. He lost weight, had bursitis, and a painful intestinal ailment for which a bland diet offered some relief.[6]

In mid–November 1940, when there was much uncertainty about what Ike's role in the army would be, he developed a severe case of shingles. At that time Eisenhower was pulled in several different directions. General Leonard T. Gerow, chief of the War Department Planning Division, wanted him; General George Patton wanted him and his unit; and General C. F. Thompson, commanding the Third Division at Fort Lewis, also wanted him. After Ike went to Fort Lewis, the shingles disappeared.[7]

In June 1942 Ike was named commanding general of the U.S. forces in Europe. The week before he left for Europe he was bedridden as a result of taking all of his immunization shots in one day. This problem was very short-lived. In the summer of 1943 while preparations were being made for the invasion of Europe, Ike came under more stress. "I feel as if my stomach were a clinched fist," he told an aide. Outwardly, he was cheerful, buoyant, and brimful of confidence. Only his habit of consuming 60 or 70 cigarettes per day revealed his tension.[8]

Eisenhower and Lyndon Baines Johnson, both heavy smokers, died of cardiovascular disease. Grant, another heavy smoker of cigars, died of throat cancer. Cleveland, also a heavy cigar smoker, developed throat cancer, but was operated on successfully.

In the fall of 1943 Eisenhower came near to having a fatal plane accident and sustained a severe knee injury. He had been at Chartres for a conference with Patton and General Omar Bradley; on the return trip to Granville he took a small, two-seater plane. His pilot, Captain Dick Underwood—due to bad weather and low gas supply—had to make an emergency landing on the beach near Granville. The plane was landed successfully, but neither Ike nor his pilot could recall whether the German mines had been removed from the beach, so they had to tread carefully as they walked across. Ike slipped, fell, and painfully injured his knee. The army physician prescribed a rubber brace and bedrest.[9] In spite of his knee injury Ike held conferences, attended luncheons, and had visitors.[10] The convalescence period lasted for several days. He was still not fully recovered in late October, which was seven weeks after the accident.

In August 1943 the directive came to General Eisenhower to have a physical examination prior to his promotion to full colonel in the regular army. The army doctors found he had a tendency to be hypertensive and ordered the Allied commander in chief to bed for a rest—a week if possible, at least two to three days.[11]

Here is an early omen of more severe health problems that occurred later. His driver, Kay Summersby, made reference to his health problems while he was commanding general in Europe and undergoing a great deal of stress: "True, he was inclined to suffer from high blood pressure, and neuritis was likely to visit his shoulder." The all-powerful general was so afraid of an army medic's possible orders that he slipped down to a London Clinic for injection treatments. The likely problem was bursitis since he did have injections for it.[12]

Summersby also made some comments on Ike's habits: "With General Ike liquor was only a social custom, necessary, but pleasantly enjoyable after one becomes hardened to it; he treated it lightly but with respect. There is no likelihood that anyone will ever see General Eisenhower drunk. He handles liquor as respectfully and carefully as an old soldier handles a gun—a loaded gun." His smoking habits were different, according to Summersby: "He had the habit to an intensity which approached the old chain fashion stage. Two packs a day were quite normal."[13]

Eisenhower's excessive addiction to cigarettes was still present after the war when he was chief of staff. As John Gunter observed, "For years he smoked like a furnace—60 cigarettes a day or more. I remember lunching with him in Washington when he was chief of staff, and between 10:45 A.M. and 3:00 P.M. he certainly smoked at least 15 cigarettes."[14]

Eisenhower continued his pattern of smoking until after he became president of Columbia University. In 1948 he developed a cardiac arrhythmia, and his doctors recommended that he cease smoking. Ike apparently complied, at least for a while, with the doctors' advice. At the time of his illness he stayed in Augusta, Georgia, for more than a month. His friends were struck by the fact that Ike had quit cold turkey.[15]

It would be very important in discussing the health of any individual to know to what he turned for relaxation, enjoyment, and exercise. Ike was an avid bridge player, a reader of westerns, and an avid golfer. His interest in golf, and the time he spent playing the game, caused a great number of Americans to feel that he should have spent more time as president and less as a golfer. Ike also did some oil painting. Churchill may have introduced him to this form of relaxation.

In March 1949, while Ike was still at Columbia University as president, he had one of the attacks that had troubled him for decades. These episodes were characterized by fever, malaise, and cramping pains in his abdomen. From time to time the pain, located in the right lower abdomen, resembled an attack of acute appendicitis. In 1949 Ike was sick enough to accept bedrest at the Statler Hotel in Washington, D.C., and remained there for several days. He was attended by General Howard Snider, whose impression was that Ike suffered from enteritis. Ike actually suffered from chronic ileitis or Crohn's Disease. The true diagnosis was not made until several years later, when he was operated on for this. He was kept in bed for several days on a diet of liquids, and then was sent to Key West for rest and recuperation. By April 7 he was back at the Augusta National, playing golf and bridge.[16]

Early in Ike's first term as president of the United States he had a recurrence of ileitis. In early April 1953 Ike and his family flew down to Augusta, Georgia, where Ike and Mamie stayed at Bobby Jones's cottage, and played a round of golf with Ben Hogan. Ike was not feeling well. He had abdominal discomfort so severe that he was compelled to use a golf cart. After Eisenhower returned to Washington, he was scheduled to speak at the Statler Hotel to the American Society of Newspaper Editors. He called his lecture "The Chance of Peace." During the speech he began to perspire and had a feeling of faintness. Then he began chilling. He had to hold on to the podium to steady himself. Ike had had the onset of the attack the previous evening, and on the morning of the speech General Snider had given him a sedative. But the attack was now much more severe. Ike finally concluded his speech and afterward went to the ballpark to throw out the first ball of the Senators' opening game. He later flew to Augusta to recuperate from the gastrointestinal problem.[17] It is noted that General Snider had not yet made the proper diagnosis.

For the first recorded time in the history of the presidency, the full truth about a president's illness was made known to the public when Eisenhower had his first heart attack on September 27, 1955. For three decades before he had become president, Eisenhower had had some problems with his health. From 1925 on Eisenhower had recurring attacks of fever and abdominal cramps. His hypertension dated from World War II. Most of his severe problems, however, occurred after he became president.

In a period of a little over two years, he had three major illnesses. The first occurred on September 27, 1955 — a coronary thrombosis. In late August the Eisenhowers flew to Denver for their summer vacation. He had reservations at that time about whether he should run for a second term. He was not sure that he could survive the stress that an added term might bring.

On the morning of August 27 he played golf at Cherry Hills, his favorite golf course. Two times during the morning his playing was interrupted by calls from Secretary of State John Foster Dulles. There was difficulty on the line, so the calls could not go through. That day at lunch he had hamburgers with slices of Bermuda onions, and then returned to the course. He was again called to the clubhouse to take a telephone call from Dulles, only to be told that it was a mistake. He was having a bad game of golf, he was having stomach spasms, and his temper flared.[18]

At 2:30 the next morning Ike was restless and complained to Mamie of indigestion pains. Mamie called Dr. Snider who ordered him to Fitzsimmons General Hospital in Denver for a diagnostic workup. He was placed in an oxygen tent, and then his specialist arrived and made the diagnosis—Ike had sustained a heart attack. He recalled the time of Woodrow Wilson and the impenetrable wall of secrecy which surrounded the illness. Ike ordered Haggarty, his press secretary, to keep the public informed about his health problems. He was later embarrassed when he learned that the public was being supplied with information in detail about his bodily functions, including bowel movements. The press secretary gave out the doctor's daily report. Vice President Nixon functioned just as he had done when Ike was out of town; he presided over meetings of the cabinet and the National Security Council.[19]

There was some lack of agreement among the doctors at Fitzsimmons General Hospital about how early he should be started on ambulation. The school of early ambulation won out, and Ike soon thereafter got up in a chair. The idea of getting a patient with a heart attack up in a chair and moving about was just beginning to be put into practice at that time. The doctors in attendance were Colonel Tom Mattingly, U.S. Army Medical Corps; Colonel Byron Pollack, Director of the Heart Clinic at Fitzsimmons General Hospital; and Dr. Paul Dudley White, the famous heart specialist from Boston. Ike noted that the most annoying part of his hospitalization was being stuck with the needle every few hours to get blood samples. This had to be done since Ike was on the anticoagulant heparin, which required frequent blood samples.

According to Eisenhower's personal account, shortly after the mobilization regimen was begun, he had some progression of his problem— extension of his infarct. "I was sitting in my chair when a doctor came in, and finding me looking a bit white about the nose and mouth, ordered me back to bed without delay—instantly. He said that the exercise routine was abandoned momentarily because my cardiogram showed that the heart wound which initially was very small indicated some enlargement, and I needed more complete rest."[20]

After this initial setback the president's convalescence was smooth. He was able to walk out of Fitzsimmons General Hospital on November 11. He flew to Washington, but left there after four days and retreated to Gettysburg, where his aides were setting up a temporary White House. Three weeks after November 28, Dr. Paul Dudley White announced that the president's recovery was "excellent and encouraging." His increased activity had left no symptom of heart strain.[21]

As far back as 1947 Ike had had recurrent attacks of fever and severe abdominal cramps. In 1947 a diagnosis of partial small bowel obstruction was made. In May 1956 X rays of his bowel confirmed a diagnosis of regional ileitis. He had another severe attack of abdominal pain in June 1956. Diet and sedation were not adequate to relieve his symptoms. Surgery was done at Walter Reed Hospital to create a bypass of the affected area of his small bowel.

On the fifth day postoperative the stomach tube was removed and he was fed by mouth. Eisenhower made a rapid recovery and was able to attend a meeting of the American presidents on July 21; however, for several days after the surgery he was in great pain and looked more ill than he had looked after his heart attack.[22]

One of the prime reasons for the failure to make the correct diagnosis until so late is that typically the disease ileitis has its onset in young adults with a history of fatigue, weight loss, right lower quadrant pain, and diarrhea.[23] Eisenhower had the onset of his problem at the age of 57, so it is easy to see why there may have been some confusion in arriving at the correct diagnosis.

The heart attack and the surgery for ileitis slowed him down for a few weeks. Neither of these in any way reduced his mental capacity; but in November 1957 Eisenhower had a stroke. This was the third major illness in a little over two years. The stroke came as he sat working at his desk on November 25, 1957. The cerebral accident was mild. At the onset he suffered from giddiness, transient weakness of his right hand and arm, and some considerable speech difficulty. He couldn't command the proper words to express his thoughts. His doctors labeled it a transient ischemic attack, affecting the speech center in the left hemisphere of his brain. The apparent rapid recovery made it very difficult to dissuade him from going to a state banquet that evening. Eisenhower never fully recovered from his speech defect and thereafter had some problem in word selection, reversal of syllables, and enunciation. The diagnosis given by the doctor was undoubtedly euphemistic in nature. The symptoms, signs, and progression of his disease pointed to more than a transient ischemic attack. Ike almost certainly had a stroke with a residual speech defect.

In November 1965, a little more than ten years after his first one, Ike had a second heart attack. At the time of his second attack he and Mamie were in Augusta, Georgia. He was moved immediately to a nearby army hospital where two days later he suffered his third heart attack. Two weeks after he had his third heart attack he was moved to Walter Reed Hospital. His recovery was slow, but he did well for a 75-year-old man who had suffered three heart attacks. Soon the doctors were allowing him to play golf again, although they restricted him to a cart and a three-par course.[24]

In the four years prior to Eisenhower's second heart attack he had had 11 admissions to Walter Reed Hospital. There was no statement of a major problem on any of these admissions; the admissions were called "check-ups." However, after January 1966, just a few weeks after Ike's second heart attack, his decline showed an acceleration. He began to reduce his physical activities, though he continued to travel and golf. In 1966 and 1967 Ike was beset with numerous severe health problems. In December 1966 he was hospitalized for gallbladder surgery in Walter Reed Hospital. After the gallbladder surgery he did quite well for a man who had had all the previous problems plus three heart attacks. During the two years before going into Walter Reed Hospital the last time, arthritis added to his problem of trying to remain active.

In April 1968 while in Palm Desert, Eisenhower suffered his fourth heart attack. He was immediately admitted to the base hospital at March Air Force Base. For apparently two weeks Ike lay in March Air Force Base Hospital, where most of his time was spent in an intensive coronary care unit. He had specialists imported from Washington, D.C., to supervise his treatment regimen. His condition finally stabilized enough that he could be transferred by air to Walter Reed Hospital.[25]

On May 15, 1968, the former president entered Walter Reed Hospital where he remained for the last 11 months of his life.[26] There he had three more attacks and several episodes of difficulty with cardiac arrhythmias. There was an unsuccessful attempt at pacemaker implantation.

Ike addressed the Republican National Convention on TV from his hospital bedroom in August 1968. Two months after the convention he suffered yet another heart attack.

In February 1969 the former president had emergency surgery to correct a blockage of the small bowel. Pneumonia followed the surgery; and to the amazement of all, he recovered. For a while he seemed better, but bouts of cardiac irregularity and congestive heart failure took their final toll. He expired March 28, 1969, at 2:15 in the afternoon.[27]

Some of Ike's biographers credit him with having seven heart attacks. Technically, this number is highly unlikely. The lay person who has had heart trouble is likely to label any acute episode, whether an arrhythmia or chest pain, as a heart attack. Some of these seven episodes were likely prolonged episodes of chest pain when the myocardium did not have a progression to a completed infarct. Eisenhower undoubtedly did have a tremendous amount of cardiovascular and cerebrovascular disease, but there is no point in ascribing to him more problems than he actually had.

References

1. David C. Whitney, *The American Presidents,* p. 291.
2. Kenneth S. Davis, *A Soldier of Democracy,* pp. 28, 29, 30, passim.
3. Bela Karnitzer, *The Story of the Five Eisenhower Brothers,* p. 45.
4. Davis, *A Soldier of Democracy,* p. 18.
5. Stephen E. Ambrose, *Eisenhower,* 1:49–50.
6. Steve Neal, *The Eisenhowers' Reluctant Dynasty,* pp. 103–04.
7. Ibid., pp. 126–27.
8. Peter Lyon, *Eisenhower, Portrait of the Hero,* p. 219.
9. David Eisenhower, *Eisenhower at War* (1943–1945), pp. 439–40.
10. Ibid., p. 462.
11. Lyon, *Eisenhower, Portrait of the Hero,* p. 227.
12. Kay Summersby, *Eisenhower Was My Boss,* p. 30.
13. Ibid., p. 29.
14. John Gunter, *Eisenhower, the Man and the Symbol,* p. 29.
15. Lyon, *Eisenhower, Portrait of the Hero,* p. 195.
16. Ibid., pp. 394–95.
17. Ambrose, *Eisenhower,* 2:95–96.
18. Ibid., p. 270.
19. Elmo R. Richardson, *The Presidency of Dwight D. Eisenhower,* pp. 87–88.
20. Dwight D. Eisenhower, *Mandate for Change,* p. 539.
21. Herbert S. Parmet, *Eisenhower and the American Crusade,* pp. 422–23.
22. Hugh L'Etang, *The Pathology of Leadership,* p. 181.
23. Robert M. Glickman, "Inflammatory Bowel Disease: Ulcerative Colitis and Crohn's Disease," in *Harrison's Principles of Internal Medicine,* p. 1742.
24. Ambrose, *Eisenhower,* 2:669.
25. Lyon, *Eisenhower, Portrait of the Hero,* p. 848.
26. Homer F. Cunningham, *The Presidents' Last Years,* p. 274.
27. Ibid., p. 275.

34

John Fitzgerald Kennedy

It is with a great deal of dread and reluctance that I approach this chapter. Several talented investigative writers have been frustrated by the obscuring mask which surrounds and bars any direct approach to the true Kennedy. Besides FDR's illnesses, which were so carefully guarded from public view, nothing in the history of our presidencies has approached the obfuscation which guarded every approach to the true state of JFK's health. Many of the biographers who wrote about JFK were too close to him to be able to give us the true man. Joan and Clay Blair, in their search for JFK, were as objective as possible, but they confessed to having a great number of doors which promised access to much more about Kennedy shut in their faces.

John Fitzgerald Kennedy, the thirty-fifth president, was born on May 29, 1917, in Brookline, Massachusetts. It is recorded that Jack was raised almost solely by his mother, a nurse, and a live-in maid. His father, Joseph (Joe) Kennedy, was practically an absentee parent.

The picture from all sources available to us is that Jack was a sickly child, one who seemed to suffer not only the diseases common to children but some extraordinary ones as well.[1] At age 2, in fact, he almost died from scarlet fever. His mother Rose Kennedy wrote in her memoirs, "Jack was a very, very sick little boy."[2] Generally, he suffered as a youth from jaundice, frequent upper respiratory infections, plus many injuries and bruises sustained trying to achieve in sports where his physique was inadequate — like the bicycle collision with his older brother Joe. Joe came away unscathed; Jack's wounds required 28 stitches.[3] As a young boy his mother remembered him as "bedridden and elfin-like."[4]

The Blairs, during their visit to the Brookline home, copied down the information from Rose Kennedy's card-file index, which she kept on each of her children. She had carefully entered the dates, the illnesses, and the age of children when each became ill. The last notes completed on JFK were as follows:

February 20, 1920, age 2¾ years, scarlet fever, whooping cough, measles, and chicken pox.

Updated: City Hospital, Dr. Hill, Dr. Reardon, took care of ear.

1928: German measles, Schick test, bronchitis occasionally.

June 15, 1930: Examined by Lahey Clinic, tonsils and adenoids OK.

October to December, 1930: While at Canterbury, his weight fell from 99¾ to 99½ lbs.

December 31, 1930: Examined by Dr. Schloss. Good condition. Loss of weight attributed to lack of milk in diet.

May 2, 1931: Appendicitis operation, surgery done by Dr. Verdie of New Haven. Performed at Danbury Hospital.

March 21, 1931: Glasses prescribed for reading by Dr. John Wheeler.

August 31, 1933: Tonsils and adenoids out—Dr. Kahill, St. Margaret's Hospital.[5]

JFK had many health problems that we now know about. However, there is still much that we do not know, largely because his family has refused to release his records. There has been a great deal of controversy, for example, about the true beginning of Jack's back problem. According to Dr. Elmer Bartell, who treated him at the Lahey Clinic in Boston, JFK was born with an unstable spine. Unstable spine is defined as a congenital malformation of the spinal column with an attendant lifetime disability.[6] Bartell explained to the Blairs that unstable backs can be normal for a long period of time and then suddenly begin to cause excruciating pain. Bartell was asked expressly: "You say that Jack was born with an unstable back?" "Yes," was his answer. This item was concealed completely by the Kennedys.[7] The statement Bartell made about Jack's back was also substantiated by Dr. Gilbert Haggard also of Boston's Lahey Clinic, who found that Jack was born with a weak back.[8]

Jack's sickliness continued through his adolescence, and his prep school years were filled with a series of illnesses. During Easter of his first year at Canterbury School in New Milford, Connecticut, age 13, he had an attack of appendicitis and was not able to finish the spring semester. His poor health continued after his transfer to Choate Academy in Wallingford, Connecticut. During his junior year there in 1933 he developed what has been described by different observers as hepatitis, jaundice, and a "blood disease." This illness kept him in bed most of that fall term. The recovery period was prolonged and left him weak, debilitated, and lethargic.[9] The headmaster at Choate in later years explained Jack's mediocre performance in the fall of his fifth form as due to a severe illness suffered then.[10]

From the beginning he was a regular visitor to the infirmary, and he made frequent overnight stops there. Colds were frequent and bothered him a great deal in his first year. At times he also did some of his studying in the infirmary. The following winter, 1934, still at Choate, Jack had a health problem which caused him a great deal of pain. He was sent from the Choate infirmary to New Haven to be seen by Dr. Winthrop Phelps, who attributed the problem to muscle weakness and growing problems. "Rose informed the Choate officials that Jack has always been troubled with his arches, a condition which ran in the family. Shoes with supporters apparently relieved the problem."[11]

Other miscellaneous problems plagued him as well. Jack suffered from a number of allergies, such as those to dogs, horses, and some dust. He had periods of skin rash, coughing, and sneezing. While at Choate he had mumps and a severe case of hives. He was asthmatic at times.[12] And he also had trouble with his arches.

The summer after Choate Jack went to the London School of Economics. Although there only a month or less, he developed a case of jaundice which was so disabling that it delayed his entrance to Princeton University.[13] Jack insisted on enrolling, however, even though late; but shortly after Thanksgiving he became ill again.[14] By early December he was unable to attend classes. Under Dr. Murphy's care, he was hospitalized for two months in Boston. After that, in 1936, he went out West to recuperate. It was thought that the sunny, dry climate of Arizona would be good for his health, especially for his asthma.

He returned to the East in July and in the fall of 1936 entered Harvard as a freshman. Early on he had a repetition of the so-called "blood condition," which was presumably the same illness he had had in London and at Princeton. The recurrences of this undiagnosed illness were frequent and cause for alarm. He was described as looking thin and sickly. At the time he enrolled at Harvard he was 6 feet tall and weighed only 147 pounds.[15]

Disregarding his phenomenal and recurring list of health problems, chronic back trouble, and marked underweight, Jack went out for football as a freshman. Not surprisingly, during a practice session he further injured his unstable back. This 145-pound sickly male was carried from the practice field in great pain. Although later accounts by some biographers indicate that this football injury was the beginning of his back problem, doctors who had treated him years earlier at the Lahey Clinic attributed his problem to a congenitally unstable back, which was aggravated by football practice.[16]

After the football injury, he went out for the swimming team. This venture, too, was frustrated by illness. He developed what was called "flu" which kept him in the infirmary for a month.[17]

In addition to such sports as football and swimming, even many of Jack's pleasurable activities were hampered by illness. In the summer of 1935, for example, he and his roommate, Lem Billings, took a tour of Europe in an automobile, but after one month, Billings recounted, Jack became fatigued and nauseated. When they returned to London, he was much worse: "Jack got desperately sick in London. His face was all puffed up and he got a rash all over." Billings suggested that he may have been allergic to a stray cat.[18]

There is some strong indication that while he was at Harvard he was treated for what Rose, his mother, called a delicate stomach.[19] This was documented in the Blairs book, for they discovered a prescription at the Kennedy Library from Jack's doctor at the Lahey Clinic, at that time Dr. Sarah Jordan: "Continue care in diet, take Trasentine tablets before each meal and in the early morning upon first awakening. Apply heat to stomach in the first awakening for 15 minutes before rising. Take no A.M. Amphiozel [probably Amphogel] except for distress. Continue taking Ceritraine acid tablets and Vitamin B faithfully."[20]

After graduating from Harvard and in the process of getting his book *Why England Slept* published, Jack went to the Mayo Clinic for a checkup and was advised to take a year's leave to recover from his illness. Nothing is known concerning the physicians' reasons at that time for such advice. But, whatever the reasons, Jack did not take the advice and instead registered at Stanford University's School of Business. Soon after enrolling he fell ill and had to withdraw. He returned to Boston to the Lahey Clinic and in January 1941 was admitted to the New England Baptist Hospital in Boston, again with a serious illness. However, there has been no revelation of the nature of that illness except in general terms[21] — terms which were totally unrevealing. The Kennedy family's stock answer was that he had had a recurrence of his malaria.

While Jack was still at Stanford, he registered for the draft on October 16, 1940. As a college student he could defer until July 1941. However, his health continued to be a matter of serious concern. He went back to the Lahey Clinic for treatment by Dr. Sarah Jordan. He spent part of January in the New England Baptist Hospital. In the summer of 1941 Jack volunteered for the Army Officers Candidate School. He failed the physical, presumably because of his bad back. He then tried the navy, which at that time failed to pass him. He reapplied and got a commission in the navy in the early winter of 1941. It has been reported that Jack used powerful influence — namely his father — to accomplish this.[22]

Jack's war record was as much obscured as was his medical history. He did work in naval intelligence until the attack on Pearl Harbor and then was suddenly transferred. According to Jack, he had requested the transfer on account of the boredom attached to his desk job. There were others who insisted that the reason lay elsewhere. For some time he had been dating Inga Arvad, a Swedish journalist with strong ties to the Nazis, and had been under FBI surveillance. There was a concern that Jack had broken security and that his superiors had had him transferred to a public relations job away from classified material. The transfer was to Charleston, South Carolina. He spent most of the winter in this job before he requested a transfer to Officers Candidate School. His request was finally honored and he attended the OCS at Northwestern University beginning in July 1942.[23]

In the late summer of 1942 he was recruited by John D. Bulkeley of Philippine PT boat fame to serve on the PTs in the Pacific. He was selected because he was an intercollegiate sailing champion, had graduated from Harvard cum laude, and had made a favorable impression through his appearance and personality. He did not have to take a physical for this assignment. John Harley, later a retired admiral, related that he did not know until later that Jack had a bad back.[24]

He finished his training at Northwestern University September 27, 1942. Four days later he reported to the PT training school in Melville, Rhode Island. He was made an instructor there and remained for a few weeks until he was transferred to Squadron 14 in Jacksonville, Florida. On the way to Florida one of the PT boats went aground. Kennedy, commanding PT 101, went to his assistance and tossed a tow line which became entangled in PT 101's props. Jack, according to the story, dove into the icy water and cleared the line. When PT 101 reached Florida, he had a high fever and was hospitalized for several days. By another account, that of Whipple, one of his naval biographers, Jack did not make the trip south. According to Whipple, PT 101 got underway from Melville January 8, 1943, but the CO, Kennedy, did not go with his craft. "Jack," Whipple said, "had wrenched his troublesome back in a rough sea, and was hospitalized." Jack caught up with his boat in Jacksonville on January 2, 1943.

According to the log, that afternoon PT 99 went aground in the waterway. When Jack attempted to give her a tow line, PT 101 went aground, too. One of the machinist's mates first class, A. D. Tucker, "suffered a sprained ankle in the release of the tow line." At 6:30 P.M. PT 101 anchored in the waterway. There was no mention of Jack going overboard to free the tow line. The next day, January 12, the boat reached Morehead City. The log noted that on the same day Jack was entered in the base hospital for two days.[25]

Jack's squadron was apparently assigned for permanent duty in Panama until he pulled strings again. This time he received orders for the war zone. Through his actions and with the help of others he found himself in a real shooting war.

While he was on patrol in the Solomons, Kennedy and his boat, PT 109, became involved in an action in Blachett Strait, between two islands in the Solomons. Here, through neglect on Kennedy's and the crew's part, PT 109 was cut in half by a Japanese destroyer, the only such mishap in the entire history of World War II.[26]

On that night PT 109 had two separate contacts with the Japanese boats about two and one-quarter hours apart. In the first one, with the Japanese Express southbound, the PT 109 failed to follow the leader to attack and "bugged out" toward Gizo Island. In the second, when the Japanese Express was headed north, the PT 109 was rammed and sunk.[27]

It is very difficult to determine from studying several accounts whether Jack did indeed reinjure his back. Some of his shipmates who were involved in the encounter with the Japanese destroyer were unable to recall that during or after the collision he had complained of any back injury. Apparently, several members of the crew were either thrown into the water or ordered to abandon due to fear of an explosion. Several of the crew members were involved in a rescue, Kennedy among them. He has been reported to have gone into the water to rescue two of his crew, one of whom was badly burned, although it is difficult to believe that anyone with a badly injured back could have performed such heroics.

PT 109's encounter with the Japanese destroyer was the end of JFK's active naval career. The crew, with Jack, were taken to an evacuation hospital and given treatment for infections, lacerations, malnutrition, and exposure. One of the doctors who examined Kennedy would recall that X ray machines picked up a problem with Jack's back. He had an injured intervertebral disc in the lumbar region, not a fracture but what is called a chronic disc disease of the lumbar area.

JFK remained for several months in the Pacific, and the ship log of PT 59, Kennedy's new assignment, November 18, 1943, read, "Lt. Jack Kennedy left the boat as directed by the doctor at LAMBU." It is possible that JFK also had malaria. It is quite reasonable to suppose that he did, since malaria was such a common illness in the Pacific at that time.

Very much in need of further medical treatment, JFK left the South Pacific before Christmas on military leave. A friend in Los Angeles described him as looking "ghastly, thin, and drawn."[28] His request for transfer to the mainland was formally approved in January 1944.[29]

Two days before JFK's twenty-seventh birthday, May 27, 1944, he was transferred from Miami to Chelsea Naval Hospital in Boston. Back surgery was apparently performed in mid–June at the New England Deaconess Hospital. Something apparently went wrong with the operation, however, and there were many long weeks of postoperative convalescence.[30] The operation, even after a long recovery period, was not a success. Very thin and sickly, he was discharged from the navy for disability, in spite of his history of disability prior to his naval service.

He then went to Arizona to further recuperate and was described at that time as being very yellow and very thin. He was also reported as having a lot of indigestion. After two months in Arizona he felt much better, and worked for a while as a news correspondent. After his newspaper experience he found himself, at the behest of Joe Kennedy, Sr., in politics, running for Congress in the eleventh district in Massachusetts. At that time during the campaign his sister, Eunice, noticed that Jack was thin, sickly, and yellow.[31]

Kennedy was thought to be the sickest newcomer to the Congress in March 1947. One colleague thought he looked decrepit. His illness and back pain caused him to be absent from his seat several times for prolonged periods. For most of the time he was restricted to bland food, nor did he drink much except for an occasional daiquiri.[32]

At the adjournment of Congress in July 1947 Jack went on what was expected to be an extended tour of Europe. The first stop was in Ireland, where his sister, Kathleen, was visiting at Lizemore Castle, which belonged to her father-in-law, the Duke of Devonshire. During Jack's visit to Lizemore Castle, he had not been feeling well and when in England a few weeks later, about to begin his European trip, he was seriously ill. At the suggestion of Pamela Churchill, Jack went to a London doctor for medical advice, and there the problem which he had had for years was finally diagnosed as Addison's Disease.[33]

This diagnosis, in all probability, was to become the most lied-about illness of any suffered by any public figure. All of his symptoms and signs, excepting backache, could be attributed to this one illness: weight loss, fatigue, gastrointestinal disturbances, pigmentation, and lack of resistance to infection. By the time he reached London, he had reached the most severe stage of the disease. He was rushed to a clinic and was given what was then the only treatment available, a shot of DOCA (desoxycorticosterone acetate). The doctors' prognosis at that time gave Jack less than one year to live.

On October 11, 1947, Jack sailed for the United States on the *Queen Elizabeth* where, in the ship's hospital, he was actually given last rites. By the time he reached New York, the DOCA had brought some improvement, but he was still very ill. He was flown to a hospital in Boston. All of the Boston papers were told that Jack had suffered from a relapse of his malaria.[34]

Jack began taking cortisone in 1947 in addition to DOCA shots. Cortisone had just been found to be effective in Addison's Disease. After surviving the initial dangerous period of his disease, he was advised by Dr. Bartell, who had treated him since the age of 11, to slow down.

Kennedy did fairly well until late 1951, when he took an around the world trip with his brother Bobby. Bobby Kennedy later reported that when they reached Okinawa Jack came down with a sudden, high-grade infection and that his temperature was 106 degrees. The doctors at the hospital did not expect him to live.[35]

His doctor from the Lahey Clinic prescribed over the phone extra doses of cortisone and antibiotics. The hospital records were not made available to the Blair investigative writers who did perhaps the most thorough investigation in trying to find out the truth about Jack's illness. According to the Blairs, no two stories were alike. Some records, as in the case of FDR, were missing, and people close to him who could have made this information available refused to do so. The supposition that he had malaria and the PT boat story were used to excess.

The 1944 back operation had given some relief, but he continued to deteriorate. By early 1954 Kennedy was in such great pain that he could barely walk. Painkillers in ordinary treatment doses still left him in much pain. He consulted with the orthopedic surgeons at Lahey Clinic about surgery, but they were reluctant to operate in the presence of Addison's Disease.[36]

Jack apparently was in a state of desperation, so a second opinion was sought. He was admitted to the New York Hospital for special surgery on October 10, 1954; and on October 21, 1954, he was operated on by Dr. Philip D. Wilson with Dr. Ephraim Shorr of the New York Hospital advising. After what was essentially uneventful surgery, he did well until the third day postoperatively. He then developed a severe infection which did not respond to antibiotics. Jack lapsed into an unconscious state and was considered critical. The family rushed to the hospital where Jack was again given last rites of the Catholic Church. His problem had been compounded by his insisting that the surgery be done in one stage instead of two as recommended by the surgeons.[37]

Gradually, however, he recovered. The surgery had been a big gamble, and his convalescence was prolonged. After the crisis, he remained in the hospital for another two months. By mid–December he was released from the hospital and continued his recovery at the Kennedy Palm Beach home. He spent his Christmas there in great pain. After several weeks passed, it seemed that the surgery had failed and that Jack might not be able to walk again.[38]

The true severity of this and JFK's other illnesses has been so shrouded in secrecy that one has to grope here and there for fragments. His family and his colleagues conspired to keep the truth from being known. The Kennedy family, the doctors, and all close to JFK denied that he had Addison's Disease. However, there have been some crevices in this wall of secrecy which have allowed some of the truth to seep through. At the time that JFK was operated on at New York Hospital, facts were unknown concerning the reason for admission and what happened after he was admitted.

On July 28, 1955, the *Archives of Surgery* accepted for publication an article by James A. Nichols and others of New York. The subject of the article was an anonymous patient whose time of admission coincided with that of Kennedy. The description in the journal was of a 37-year-old male who had had Addison's Disease for seven years, had been under treatment with DOCA implants 150 mg. for three months, and cortisone 25 mg. by mouth daily. Orthopedic consultation suggested that he might be helped by a lumbosacral and sacroiliac fusion. Dr. Ephraim Shorr of the New York Hospital provided advice in the management of the case. The operation was done on October 21, 1954, the same day as Kennedy's surgery. There was a detailed description of the surgical procedure and the management of his Addison's Disease.[39]

On February 26, 1955, the *New York Times* reported that Senator Kennedy had undergone a spinal operation in October 1954, for an injury received to his spine in World War II, and had entered the hospital February 10, 1955, for removal of a metal plate. This plate had apparently made his condition worse. He had developed a staphylococcal infection around the plate requiring its removal.[40]

In a follow-up article in the *Journal of the American Medical Association*, July 10, 1967, Dr. James Nichols wrote, "It is most unlikely that two persons of the same age and clinical history of the late President would have undergone similar surgery in the same hospital at the same day and returned exactly four months later for the removal of the plate."[41]

In 1960, when JFK was running for president, the question of whether or not he had Addison's Disease arose. Kennedy forces, including his doctors, denied that he had Addison's Disease. His brother, Robert, Jack, and Dr. Jannette Travell, all denied that he had the illness.

A statement from JFK's doctors and coworkers was issued by Robert Kennedy as follows:

John F. Kennedy has not, nor has he ever, had an ailment described classically as Addison's disease, which is a tuberculous destruction of the adrenal gland. Any statement to the contrary is malicious and false.... In the post-war period he had some mild adrenal insufficiency and this is not in any way a dangerous condition. And it is possible that even this might be corrected over the years since ACTH stimulation tests for adrenal function was considered normal in 1958. Doctors have stated that this condition might have arisen out of his wartime experiences of shock and malaria.[42]

This was undoubtedly one of the most cleverly laid smoke screens ever put down around a politician. Undoubtedly, Jack had every symptom and sign which could be ascribed to Addison's Disease. This disease as described in Williams's textbook on endocrinology enumerates: "Fever, weight loss, lethargy, nausea, vomiting, diarrhea, and pigmentation.... Although tuberculosis and fungus disease accounted in earlier days of 90% of the cases, such is not at present the case. It is in most cases due to atrophy perhaps due to autoimmune disease."[43]

In addition, Harrison's stated: "Addison's disease results from progressive adrenocortical destruction which must involve more than 90% of the gland before clinical signs of insufficiency occurs."[44] Thus, saying that someone has a mild case of adrenal insufficiency, not Addison's, is similar to saying that someone is a little bit pregnant.

A bulletin issued when he left the hospital in 1954 announced that Kennedy planned to resume his seat in the Senate in March. The convalescence in the Palm Beach family home required another two months. His recovery was delayed there further by a bad back. For several weeks he was in such pain that he couldn't sleep well.[45]

The two episodes of major back surgery did not end his pain. On a trip to Rome with Jackie he was photographed on crutches at the time of his audience with the Pope. There had been times in the spring of 1955 when it was rumored that he might have to give up his seat in the Senate.

On Tuesday, May 4, 1955, Kennedy returned to the Senate. On that day he walked slowly and with difficulty but without crutches. However, when he arrived at the office of Dr. Jannette Travell on May 25, he was again on crutches. Travell recommended that he be hospitalized; on June 1 he was back in the Senate, but for months afterward he spent the weekends in New York Hospital for treatment. He was admitted to New England Baptist Hospital on July 3 of the same year, where he spent a week for checkups. Thus, when he was not in the Senate he was somewhere else having medical treatment.[46]

There is no doubt that Jack, after his surgery and treatment of his

Addison's, was better, but he still suffered a great deal from back pain. Dr. Travell was responsible for the major part of his treatment for a considerable period of time. Travell decided that his back pain was largely due to spasms of weak muscles in his back. She employed novacaine injections at frequent intervals to relieve the spasms. However, this type of relief was only temporary. Travell then discovered that his left leg was three-quarters of an inch shorter than the right. This she considered to be an aggravation to the spasm of his back muscles. He was prescribed shoes which corrected the difference between the length of his lower extremities. He also wore a small brace to support his back.[47]

In May 1961 Kennedy made a trip to Canada. After he had been greeted by Prime Minister Diefenbaker, Kennedy walked out on the lawn of Ottawa's government house to plant a red oak tree. This tree was to go along with those planted by other U.S. presidents. As Kennedy bent down to shovel some dirt, there was a sharp pain in his back, deep down in the lower lumbar region. The severe pain omened more problems with the back he had thought was cured. That night at a grand reception his previously experienced pain set in again.[48] The pain did not leave him for more than six months, and for weeks it was often severe and exhausting.[49]

Actually, during the summer of 1961, after his visit to Canada, his condition was the worst it had been in years. He had been relatively free from pain for some time; now he was in agony. This presented special problems since it came at the same time as the Berlin Crisis.[50]

In June 1961 JFK developed a severe infection. The illness involved a sore throat, cough, chills, and a fever that reached 105 degrees. He was treated with large doses of penicillin, IV injections, and cold sponges. After a few days he recovered from this episode; however, his medical history is replete with recurrent infections.

Initially, Kennedy's treatment was in the hands of Dr. Jannette Travell, who continued to relieve his back pain with novacaine injections. Travell's continued use of novacaine began to raise some medical eyebrows among other specialists involved in JFK's care. There was some concern that as he grew more tolerant of the novacaine he might require more narcotics for relief. Dr. Eugene Cohen, who was involved in the follow-up of his Addison's Disease, recommended a consultation with Dr. Hans Kraus be sought. There is some evidence, too, that JFK himself was beginning to express some dissatisfaction with the progress of his back pain. Travell, for some time, resisted the suggestion to call Dr. Kraus, but Dr. George Burkeley, a naval admiral and also on the White House medical staff, threatened to call Dr. Kraus if she did not.[51]

This in-fighting somewhat resembles the protective shield with which

Admiral Ross McIntyre surrounded himself on his job as White House physician to FDR.

Soon Dr. Kraus made very frequent commuting trips to the White House. He was concerned that the president was getting an increasing number of injections—as many as two or three each day. Kraus suggested beginning physiotherapy treatments three times per week. When Kraus began his treatment, he found that JFK's abdominal muscles were flabby and his back was stiff. Daily swimming was added to the regimen. By December Kennedy had made great progress, and had greatly improved his muscular development. Travell remained on the White House staff, but Dr. Burkeley was put in complete charge of JFK's medical care.[52]

In later days it was related by some reporters of the *New York Times* that Jack Kennedy had been treated early in his administration by Dr. Max Jacobson with injections of amphetamines to combat his fatigue. Dr. Jacobson was one of the unofficial White House visitors. Only later was there concern about the adverse effects of amphetamines, which included addiction and psychiatric problems.[53] The knowledge that JFK was using amphetamines arouses a lot of speculation. Dr. Raymond D. Adams and Maurice Victor have described the effects of these drugs:

> Undoubtedly the initial effect of a moderate dose of amphetamine is to relieve fatigue, reduce some of the need for sleep, and elevate mood; but these effects are not entirely predictable and the user must pay for the period of wakefulness with even greater fatigue and often some depression. The IV use of a high dose of amphetamine produces an immediate ecstasy.... The chronic administration of large doses of amphetamine may give rise to hallucinations, delusion, and changes in the effect and thought process, a state that may be indistinguishable from paranoid schizophrenia.[54]

It gives one cause for concern to think of a president sitting in the White House who is taking mood-altering, addictive drugs that may, in excess, produce psychotic symptoms. Some of the symptoms ascribed to this drug are both euphoria and an after effect of depression. It is frightening to think that such a leader would have the power to initiate an atomic war. It was only later that the severe side effects were known. In the late 1930s or early 1940s students who desired to stay up all night and study would sometimes use amphetamines to keep themselves awake. As a junior medical student, I used oral amphetamines a few times in ordinary doses or small doses. It kept me awake, but it also made me drymouthed and very jittery. I was in no condition, after taking even a small dose, to face any great crisis.

Although this matter touched only indirectly on JFK's health, many writers have touched at least tangentially on JFK's sexual prowess. Jack had Old Joe, his father, for a role model, and Jack followed his role model in matters of sex. "Montaigne said that some aristocrats not only claim a license for themselves but arrange a similar freedom for their sons. It is the fashion in our country to put sons in the best homes as pages where they may be trained in noble manners, and it is called a discourtesy to refuse any gentleman his wishes."[55]

And again, perhaps to overwork Montaigne, another quote from him: "The ill or aging sometimes must rely on the tickle of lust to reanimate them." This might be applicable to the ailing JFK.[56]

After Kraus assumed the job of rehabilitating Kennedy through exercise and physiotherapy, the president's physical condition improved. He had never looked as fit or felt better before. Dr. Kraus was making frequent visits to the White House. In early 1963 Kennedy was in much better shape to do his work. His improved condition was maintained up to the time of his assassination on November 22, 1963.

The mysteries behind Kennedy's assassination were probed in volume after volume in the Warren Report. We have no reason to believe that we can add anything else to the solution of that mystery. We only know that on that day he was shot and on that same day he died. However, the exploiters are not content to allow JFK's remains to rest in peace. There have been many since he was assassinated in 1963 who were not content with the findings of the Warren Commission and insist that there were those who conspired to end the life of JFK. *High Treason,* written by Robert J. Groden and Harrison Edward Livingstone and first published in 1980, purports to be an authority on what happened in Dallas's Parkland Hospital in the emergency room and in the autopsy room at Bethesda Naval Hospital after JFK was shot. There is also the recent book written by Charles Crenshaw, *JFK, Conspiracy of Silence.* Crenshaw was presumably among several others who were in the emergency room at Dallas and observed the futile attempts to save Kennedy's life. He alleged that the bullets fired in the assassination struck Kennedy from the front instead of the rear, as reported by the Warren Commission. Such statements brought into question the possibility of more than one assassin and more than three bullets fired. There is also the sensational Oliver Stone film *JFK* which makes the overall statement that there was a grand conspiracy not only to murder JFK but to cover up the facts afterward.[57]

Dr. Mark Micozzi makes the point that the difference between the feeling about Lincoln's assassination and that of JFK is that all available facts about who shot Lincoln and how he was shot became fully known almost immediately. Micozzi states: "Part of the problem had been access to correct information. We have relied on the media to communicate the critical information to the public at large. As conspiracy theories have spread, the public has not been satisfied with the information. Open access to the medical information (in JFK's case) had until recently been denied, leaving only speculation."[58]

The recent confirming evidence provided by the doctors present in the Parkland Hospital emergency room in Dallas who tried to resuscitate JFK and the autopsy report from Bethesda Naval Hospital reminds one of the article in the March 1970 *Annals of Internal Medicine,* written by Dr. Howard G. Bruenn. This was written 25 years after the death of FDR. The report by Bruenn did much to help lay to rest the suspicion and rumors which had surrounded the illness and death of FDR. Bruenn was in constant attendance during the president's last 11 months of life. He was not only the most competent observer during those last months—he was the most reliable.[59]

Now, after 29 years, we have the facts about the findings in Parkland Hospital where an attempt was made to resuscitate JFK. Four doctors were the principals at Parkland: Dr. Malcolm Perry, who did the tracheotomy; Dr. Jim Carrico, a surgical resident, the first to treat JFK and who observed that an exit wound on the front of his neck was present before the tracheotomy; Dr. M. T. "Pepper" Jenkins, chief of anesthesiology, who attempted to ventilate the patient; and Dr. Charles Baxter, a surgeon who assisted in the resuscitation attempt. These four were the principal actors in the operating scene at Parkland. All of these four physicians have emphasized that Crenshaw was wrong about the direction from which the bullets came.

Dr. Perry says, "In 1963 Charles Crenshaw was a junior resident and he absolutely did not participate in a meaningful way in the attempt to resuscitate the President. . . . I do not even remember seeing him in the room." These four doctors who cared for JFK in their emergency room in Dallas are confirming in every way the autopsy findings at Bethesda Naval Hospital.[60]

Dr. Dennis L. Breo contends that there are two, and only two, physicians who know exactly what happened—and didn't happen—in the autopsy room at Bethesda Naval Hospital on November 22, 1963. These are the former U.S. Navy pathologist James Joseph Humes, and J. "Thornton" Boswell. Their story was obtained in a two-day interview with a *JAMA* editor, George D. Lunberg, a former military pathologist.

The evidence produced in the four-hour autopsy at Bethesda Naval Hospital "provides irrefutable proof that the President was struck by only two bullets that came from above and behind from a high velocity weapon which caused the fatal wounds."[61]

The autopsy proof, combined with the bullet and rifle evidence found at the scene of the crime and the subsequent detailed documentation in a six months' investigation involving the enormous resources of the local, state, and federal law enforcement agencies, proves the Warren Commission's conclusion that Kennedy was killed by a lone assassin, Lee Harvey Oswald.[62]

References

1. Herbert S. Parmet, *Jack: The Struggles of John F. Kennedy*, p. 15.
2. Ibid., p. 16.
3. Judy Mills, *John F. Kennedy*, p. 19.
4. John H. Davis, *The Kennedys, Dynasty and Disaster*, p. 114.
5. Joan Blair and Clay Blair, Jr., *The Search for JFK*, p. 23.
6. Davis, *The Kennedys, Dynasty and Disaster*, p. 114.
7. Blair and Blair, *The Search for JFK*, p. 25.
8. Parmet, *Jack: The Struggles of JFK*, p. 16.
9. Kenneth R. Crispell and Carlos F. Gomez, *Hidden Illness in the White House*, p. 168.
10. Ibid.
11. Parmet, *Jack: The Struggles of JFK*, p. 39.
12. Davis, *The Kennedys, Dynasty and Disaster*, p. 114.
13. Arthur M. Schlesinger, Jr., *A Thousand Days: John F. Kennedy in the White House*, pp. 81–82.
14. Mills, *John F. Kennedy*, pp. 29–30.
15. Ibid., p. 30.
16. Davis, *The Kennedys, Dynasty and Disaster*, p. 117.
17. Mills, *John F. Kennedy*, p. 30.
18. Blair and Blair, *The Search for JFK*, p. 106.
19. Crispell and Gomez, *Hidden Illness in the White House*, p. 170.
20. Blair and Blair, *The Search for JFK*, p. 58.
21. Davis, *The Kennedys, Dynasty and Disaster*, pp. 120–21.
22. Parmet, *Jack: The Struggles of JFK*, p. 86.
23. Crispell and Gomez, *Hidden Illness in the White House*, p. 174.
24. Blair and Blair, *The Search for JFK*, pp. 157–58.
25. Ibid., p. 168.
26. Davis, *The Kennedys, Dynasty and Disaster*, p. 96.
27. Blair and Blair, *The Search for JFK*, pp. 232–34.
28. Parmet, *Jack: The Struggles of JFK*, p. 115.
29. Crispell and Gomez, *Hidden Illness in the White House*, p. 177.
30. Blair and Blair, *The Search for JFK*, p. 337.
31. Mills, *John F. Kennedy*, p. 78.
32. Parmet, *Jack: The Struggles of JFK*, p. 165.

33. Mills, *John F. Kennedy*, p. 87.
34. Ibid., p. 89.
35. Crispell and Gomez, *Hidden Illness in the White House*, p. 189.
36. Ibid., p. 191.
37. Parmet, *Jack: The Struggles of JFK*, pp. 309–10.
38. Mills, *John F. Kennedy*, pp. 118–19.
39. James A. Nichols, et al. "The Management of Adrenal Cortical Insufficiency During Surgery," *Archives of Surgery* (1955), pp. 737, 742.
40. *New York Times*, February 26, 1958, p. 28.
41. James A. Nichols, "President Kennedy's Adrenals," *Journal of the American Medical Association* 201, no. 2 (July 10, 1967): 26.
42. Blair and Blair, *The Search for JFK*, pp. 573–76.
43. Robert H. Williams, *The Textbook on Endocrinology*, pp. 1042–43.
44. Gordon H. Williams and Robert A. Dluhy, "Diseases of the Adrenal Cortex," in *Harrison's Principles of Internal Medicine*, p. 651.
45. Mills, *John F. Kennedy*, p. 120.
46. Parmet, *Jack: The Struggles of JFK*, p. 317.
47. Schlesinger, *A Thousand Days*, p. 97.
48. Hugh Sidey, *John F. Kennedy, President*, pp. 165–66.
49. Schlesinger, *A Thousand Days*, pp. 343–44.
50. Herbert S. Parmet, *JFK: The Presidency of John F. Kennedy*, p. 119.
51. Ibid., pp. 120–22.
52. Ibid., pp. 122–23.
53. *New York Times*, December 4, 1972.
54. Raymond D. Adams, and Maurice Victor, "Sedatives, Stimulants, and Psychotropic Drugs" in *Harrison's Principles of Internal Medicine*, pp. 1300–01.
55. Gary Wills, *The Kennedy Imprisonment*, pp. 19–20.
56. Ibid., p. 32.
57. Dennis L. Breo, "JFK's Death, Part 2: The Plain Truth from the MDs Who Did the Autopsy," *Journal of the American Medical Association* 267, no. 20 (May 27, 1992): 2794.
58. Mark S. Micozzi, "Lincoln, Kennedy, and the Autopsy," *Journal of the American Medical Association* 267, no. 20 (May 7, 1992): 2791.
59. Howard G. Bruenn, "Clinical Notes on the Illness and Death of FDR," *Annals of Internal Medicine* 72 (March 1970): 579–91, passim.
60. Breo, "JFK's Death, 2," p. 2804.
61. Ibid., p. 2794.
62. Ibid.

35

Lyndon Baines Johnson

Lyndon Baines Johnson, the thirty-sixth president of the United States, was born on the August 27, 1908, near Stonewall, Texas. Johnson was the eighth vice president of the United States to succeed to the presidency. At birth he was described as having all of the characteristics of his father: "Dark eyes, black curls, and white skin." He was also noted as having the characteristics of his mother's family, the Buntons, large ears and heavy eyebrows.[1]

Rebekah, his mother, at times would display an excess of affection and then would completely reject him. Lyndon never experienced her love as a reliable force, but as a conditional reward, alternately given or taken away according to how he complied with her wishes. Lyndon unconsciously followed this pattern of overwhelming regard for an individual and then a complete withdrawal of his love. In return for all the favors he gave, he expected absolute gratitude and loyalty.[2]

It is well known that Johnson had in his early days the usual childhood diseases, including whooping cough. Some of these illnesses were helpful in satisfying his desire to stay at home from school.

When Lyndon finished high school, at the age of 15, he was tired of studying. He and some of his friends thumbed their way to California, where he lived for a while the life of a migrant worker — washing dishes, picking oranges, and experiencing in general the difficulties of surviving during a depression. After a year in California he returned home and worked at hard labor on a road gang. At the age of 18 he entered Southwest Texas State Teachers College, in San Marcos. Lyndon worked his way through college and graduated in 1930 at the age of 21. At San Marcos he became "big man on campus" and demonstrated early what great political potential he had.

After Lyndon graduated from college in 1930, he taught public speaking and debate in Sam Houston High School in Houston. He showed a great aptitude for teaching and was apparently able to bring out the best in his students. While he was teaching, he manifested the same drive that he would show throughout his life. The opportunity which pointed most clearly to the career he had in mind finally came: U.S. Representative Richard Kleberg invited Johnson to come to Washington as his secretary. Lyndon held this secretarial job until 1935. In the meantime, in 1934, he married Claudia Alta Taylor, "Lady Bird." In 1935 an opportunity came for him to broaden his political base in Texas. President Roosevelt established the National Youth Administration. Johnson applied for and got a job in this New Deal apparatus. He made the most of the chance, making literally thousands of contacts which were calculated to boost his political ambitions. Lyndon held the NYA job until he ran for U.S. representative in 1937.

Lyndon developed early the traits that he was to carry throughout his life. As a congressional assistant he drove himself and those around him without mercy. This tendency to push himself and others persisted throughout his political life. He was never satisfied with what he or his colleagues were accomplishing.

His smoking began while he was at San Marcos in college. His introduction to smoking at that time was by way of the pipe. This habit in the beginning was just an attraction-getter—he was a big man on campus, and big men on campus smoked pipes. Progressively, LBJ smoked more until he was, at least at times, a chain smoker.

His table manners when he was a child were so atrocious that at times his mother was in tears. At San Marcos fellow students noted that he grabbed his food and gulped it down. He had long arms and he would reach, if necessary, to the other end of the table. While he was a congressional assistant to Richard Kleberg, he ate in a cheap cafeteria (Child's). He would rush ahead of everyone else, grab a tray, rush to select his food, rush to his table, and gulp down his food. His unusual eating habits persisted throughout his career. When he was Senate majority leader he ate poorly and irregularly, but he was still overweight and flabby.

There is no record that LBJ ever took regular exercise of any kind. From the time that he worked as Kleberg's congressional assistant until he was Senate majority leader, 1955–60, he worked very late in the evening and allotted no time at all for exercise or recreation. On top of the other problems mentioned, he had a very poor family history for heart disease. According to family history passed on to Lyndon from early times, all of the men in the Johnson family had died early of heart disease. His own father developed coronary heart disease at an early age and died of it. Johnson was obsessed with the idea that he had inherited his fatal tendency and was wont to relate to Lady Bird, Sam Rayburn, and others, that he too would die early of heart disease.

A present-day physician would label him as a Type-A personality. He drove himself and everyone else mercilessly. In 1935, while he was still a congressional assistant, he received some attractive job offers, one of which was that of a lobbyist. He turned the offer down because it was not consistent with his overwhelming political ambitions. This apparently was a time of great mental stress and crisis for LBJ. The time of the crisis coincided with or was associated with his first major illness, pneumonia. This attack of pneumonia sent him to the hospital. The coincidence of illness with periods of stress could be later noted in several instances.[3]

During Johnson's congressional campaign of 1937 he ran true to form — he drove himself mercilessly. He was described by his colleagues as being gray and hollow-cheeked with fatigue and sleeplessness. His fingers were stained yellow with nicotine, and he seemed always to be holding a cigarette in his hand.

Lady Bird blamed his loss of weight on improper eating habits. He had grown thinner and thinner throughout the campaign. "He ate very irregularly and had very unbalanced meals, which made me very angry because I'm a great believer in nutrition. He would just stop at some country store and buy a can of sardines and some crackers, or some cheese. But when he was fed a proper meal he would gag on it. He didn't get much down, and what he did he couldn't keep down. He seemed to be vomiting more frequently. He kept complaining about stomach cramps, and was at times doubled over with pain. However, he was not lessening his activity, he was working more, not less."[4] This campaign in many respects resembles that of Nixon when he ran for the presidency for the first time in 1962. Nixon also campaigned ceaselessly night and day, with a great compulsion to cover every single state even after he had spent two weeks in the hospital due to an infection in his left knee.

On April 8, 1937, LBJ woke up, two days before the election, with nausea and abdominal pain. That evening at 8:00 P.M. Johnson was scheduled to give a speech at the Travis County Courthouse. Still in much pain, Lyndon began his speech, holding onto the rail while speaking. Soon he doubled over very pale and sat down, but he got up after a short while, apologized, and finished his speech. He ended by shaking hands with the audience. Sherman Birdwell, Lyndon's congressional assistant who came up to congratulate him, noted that "he was covered with perspiration." He finally had to sit down again. This time he couldn't stand up. He was put in a car, driven home, and from there taken to Seaton Hospital, where he was operated on for acute appendicitis. The doctors there said that his appendix was on the point of rupturing.[5]

The United States entered World War II in late 1941 and Johnson, while serving as a congressman, requested active duty in the navy. He served for a while as special deputy secretary of the navy under James Forrestal as part of a fact-finding mission for Roosevelt. Johnson's South Sea tour was interrupted by a bout of febrile illness, which had its onset in Hawaii, and ended with pneumonia in a Fiji Island hospital.[6] After Johnson's mission was finished, he returned to his seat in the House.

During his last years in the House, Johnson experienced periods of severe depression. He seemed to feel that the House was a dead end. His ambition did not end there. LBJ was still driving himself and his staff unmercifully. From time to time in those years he suffered a severe rash on his hands. The rash recurred and made his hands very dry, scaly, red, and uncomfortable. His doctors prescribed various ointments, and he often had his hands in gauze dressings. He used Lubriderm, a purple-colored ointment, which gave him temporary relief. Johnson kept a container of Lubriderm on his desk and would often dip his hands in it. Then at times there would be some bleeding of his hands when he would handle correspondence. The edge of the paper made small cuts in the already greatly irritated skin. The rash seemed to be related to periods of greater stress. At this time Johnson was smoking more and more—at least three packs per day. His fingers were stained yellow with nicotine.[7]

In his later years in the House, periods of great stress were accompanied by periods of sickness. In 1946 he was hospitalized for what was variously labeled by Johnson and associates as flu, pneumonia, and exhaustion. Many excuses were given for his absence from his seat in the House. No one had a definite answer. The illness extended from New Year's Day 1946 until mid–February.

In March 1946 he was hospitalized for an attack of renal colic, and again in October 1946 for the same thing. He was first hospitalized at Seaton Infirmary, then at the Mayo Clinic.[8]

When Johnson's disenchantment with his seat in the House finally led him to run for the Senate in 1948 against Coke Stevenson, he had, while making up his mind to run, a period of deep depression. He had a deep fear that if he ran for the Senate he might lose and if he lost he would be neither senator nor congressman. He finally decided to run. The campaign was conducted in the same manner as his previous ones.[9] As before he went night and day, weekdays, and weekends. He would spend 16 hours a day in a car, becoming so exhausted that he would fall asleep in it. In order to cover more territory, he even went by helicopter, landing any place where there was a flat surface.

However, the candidate of 1948 was different in some respects from the one of 1937. When he took off his jacket, it was apparent that the only part of LBJ that was still thin was his shoulders, conspiciously narrow in proportion to the middle of his body which had become quite wide. His belt sagged around the beginning of a paunch, and his rear was now quite large. The gaunt face of 1937 now was a broad, heavy face. There was a full-fledged double chin, and his big jaw jutted out of heavy jowls.[10]

Three weeks before the election he developed a severe left flank pain, which turned out to be due to kidney stones. He was not willing to be operated on for the stones, insisting that no one should know he was in the hospital. He had had previous attacks of renal colic and had always passed the stones, so he assumed that he would do the same this particular time. He was admitted a few days later to the Mayo Clinic.[11]

His stay at the Mayo Clinic was one that all who were engaged in his care would never forget. Almost immediately on admission to the clinic he became its star (and most irritating) patient. He stayed one week until the stone had passed, but one doctor at the clinic said that if a poll had been taken of the staff, it would have undoubtedly been shown that it seemed more like a year. He had the doctors issue an almost hourly statement that he was not going to die.[12]

In January 1955, early in his tenure as Senate majority leader, Lyndon had a recurrence of his kidney colic and returned to the Mayo Clinic for surgery. During several weeks after surgery Lyndon returned many times to the Mayo Clinic for treatment. He also spent considerable time in convalescence but finally returned to the Senate on March 9, 1955. In the meantime, his first major effort as majority leader, a tax reduction bill, had been defeated.[13]

As Senate majority leader LBJ was an obsessive-compulsive worker. He rarely got home at night before 10:00 or 11:00 P.M. He drank too much and he smoked too much—at least three packages per day. He was described as holding a cigarette in his hand at all times, inhaling deeply, and holding the smoke in his lungs for a prolonged period of time.

The heart attack, which was probably inevitable, soon came. Toward the end of June 1955 LBJ began to feel tired all the time. On the night of July 1 he had dinner with Sam Rayburn and Stuart Symington. Rayburn noted that LBJ's drinks were larger, stronger, and more frequent than usual. Rayburn also noted that the circles under his eyes were unusually dark.[14]

On July 2 Lyndon had a very hectic morning. At noon he had two frankfurters on buns, baked beans, and one half of a cantaloupe. After lunch he had a news conference, during which he had a cigarette in his fingers and had a very rancorous exchange with newsmen.

He was so tired that he took a vacation over the weekend at the home of George Herman Brown, a friend and supporter, near Middleburg, Virginia. On the way to Middleburg he felt faint, short of breath, and later became nauseated. LBJ was certain that it was indigestion. He blamed it on the cantaloupe he had eaten for lunch. Senator Clinton Anderson, who happened to be at the Brown estate, had himself suffered a heart attack, and he warned Johnson that his symptoms indicated that he also had suffered a heart attack.[15]

A doctor was called, and LBJ was rushed to Bethesda Naval Hospital. Somewhat later that evening LBJ went into shock and nearly died. He was, for several days, in critical condition. The diagnosis was myocardial infarction. He was at Bethesda Naval Hospital for six weeks, followed by three months of convalescence at home.[16]

In the 1960 campaign between LBJ and JFK, Jack Kennedy made a political issue of health. Kennedy was the one whose health was in more jeopardy even than Johnson's but just before the convention he made a statement that the presidency required the "strength, health, and vigor of a young man." This was interpreted as an oblique reference to Johnson's heart attack in 1955. Kennedy made the statement, in spite of the fact that he was being treated for Addison's Disease.

The Citizens Committee for the Election of LBJ would not sit still and take this not-so-subtle reference to his health. John Connally, not so subtly, also announced that Kennedy had Addison's Disease. The reply to this allegation by Connally was followed by a statement from Robert Kennedy which was one of the most skillful bits of obfuscation ever uttered by a politician.[17] Thus in 1960 we had two badly flawed candidates for the highest office in the land.

In 1964, while Johnson was presumably trying to make up his mind whether he would run again for the presidency, he stated that among other things the constant uncertainty of whether he could stand up to the rigors of a full four years' term was on his mind. "The strain of my work in the Senate had helped to bring on my heart attack when I was only forty-six. Now I was nine years older. I felt a strong inclination to go back to Texas while there was still time to enjoy life with my wife and daughters."[18]

On Labor Day weekend, 1965, LBJ suffered a gallbladder attack. After the X rays and other examinations, the doctor recommended surgery. At this time Lyndon was greatly concerned with secrecy. He had not allowed anything about his illness to leak to the press. Eisenhower, however, recommended openness and candor and pointed out the advantage of openness. Johnson informed the vice president, Hubert H. Humphrey, of what he should do in case of his incapacity. He even told him what he should do under certain circumstances. He announced at a cabinet meeting that he would enter Bethesda Naval Hospital for his surgery.

The surgery was done on October 8, 1965. There were 10 doctors and 3 Secret Service men in the operating room, besides the nurses who scrubbed in. The surgery required 2 hours and 15 minutes, and involved removal of the gallbladder and gallstone, and also the removal of a stone in his ureter. While still in the hospital he received visitors to whom he exhibited a long surgical scar on his abdomen.[19]

Of course, Johnson's stresses were not ordinary ones. He was confronted with the seemingly unending war in Vietnam, and the great and growing unrest on the domestic scene. Understandably, the effects were mental as well as physical.

In 1967 LBJ underwent a highly secret operation for cancer. Not until 1977, after LBJ's physician, Admiral Burkley, had denied the published reports, did a navy spokesman confirm that Johnson had undergone surgery for skin cancer on the left ankle.[20]

On December 17, 1968, LBJ developed pneumonia and was admitted to Bethesda Naval Hospital by Dr. Burkley. This attack of pneumonia was essentially uneventful. During his hospitalization he did sit in his room and watch the launching of an Apollo mission.[21]

One factor helping Johnson to decide not to run again in 1968 was his health. He had a secret actuarial study run to determine how long he was likely to live. The prediction was made that he would probably not see his sixty-fifth birthday.[22]

LBJ had troubling dreams to which he attached much significance. His dreams and his concern with their meaning would remind one of Lincoln, who had recurring dreams of such dark and gloomy content. During the convalescence from his heart attack he had recurring nightmares in which he dreamed of being paralyzed. While he was vice president he dreamed again and again of physical incapacities—incapacities which he interpreted as a repetition of the powerlessness he had felt during the day.

During one dream at this time he started to get up from a chair, but found himself unable to move. He looked down at his legs and saw that he was shackled to his chair. During the Vietnam days LBJ was again dreaming dreams about paralysis. In these dreams he was lying in bed in the Red Room of the White House; his head was still his, but his body from the neck down was the thin, paralyzed body that had been the affliction of Woodrow Wilson and his own grandmother in her final years.[23] All of his dreams seemed related to a feeling of being pent up, caged, and frustrated.

After Johnson retired to his ranch, he was depressed at times. His heart condition had deteriorated, and he was having anginal attacks which were both severe and frequent. He was observed to take a lot of nitroglycerin pills. In spite of his doctors' advice, he was driving his car. Soon after his first heart attack he had ceased to smoke; but now he had resumed the habit, and was smoking excessively. At the time he retired he was not in any worse condition than he had been a year or two earlier, but observers now noted that he was perceptively aged and worn.

After LBJ retired his physical problems became worse, and he had to depend more and more on Lady Bird. In the four years after his retirement he showed more and more the signs of aging. His activities around the ranch became more and more restricted. He continued to smoke excessively, took naps, and used oxygen as needed. The January 21, 1973, *Washington Post* carried the story of Nixon's inauguration. The next day the media carried the story of the passing of LBJ.[24]

January 22, 1973, dawned as any other winter day might in the hill country of Texas. The ex-president had a fairly good night, although there were always the chest pains and shortness of breath. His doctor at Brooke Medical Center spoke briefly with him on the phone that morning. Neither the patient nor the doctor saw any unusual reason for concern, but Lady Bird noted that he was unusually quiet. She needed to do some shopping and take care of some business matters in nearby Austin, so she left her husband who had planned to putter around the ranch. In the afternoon he went to his room for his usual nap. At 3:50 P.M. he called the switchboard and asked for Mike Howard, one of the Secret Service agents at the ranch. Howard was not in his office at the moment, so two other agents responded immediately, and when they arrived found Johnson on the floor of his bedroom, apparently dead. However, the ex-president was rushed by air to the Brooke Medical Center where he was pronounced DOA. The autopsy performed the next morning at Brooke General found that death was caused by a large coronary occlusion.[25]

It was not at all fitting that this man who greatly desired to be surrounded by people at all times, and who manifested a fear of being alone, should die with no one near.

References

1. Robert A. Caro, *The Path to Power: The Years of LBJ*, p. 66.
2. Doris Kearns, *Lyndon Johnson and the American Dream*, p. 25.

3. Caro, *The Path to Power,* p. 334.

4. Ibid., p. 434.

5. Ibid., pp. 435–36.

6. Merle Miller, editor, *Lyndon: An Oral Biography,* pp. 99–100.

7. Robert A. Caro, *Means of Ascent: The Years of LBJ,* p. 139.

8. Ibid., pp. 139–40.

9. Kearns, *Lyndon Johnson and the American Dream,* pp. 100–01.

10. Caro, *The Path to Power,* p. 694.

11. Kearns, *Lyndon Johnson and the American Dream,* p. 101.

12. Miller, *Lyndon: An Oral Biography,* p. 153.

13. Ibid., p. 236.

14. Ibid., p. 232.

15. Kearns, *Lyndon Johnson and the American Dream,* p. 125.

16. Ibid.

17. Hugh L'Etang, *The Pathology of Leadership,* p. 184.

18. Lyndon Baines Johnson, *The Vantage Point: Perspectives of the President, 1963–1969,* p. 93.

19. Miller, *Lyndon: An Oral Biography,* pp. 567–68.

20. *Greensboro News and Record,* New York Times News Service, January 10, 1982.

21. George Christian, *The President Steps Down,* pp. 215–16.

22. Homer F. Cunningham, *The Presidents' Last Years,* p. 301.

23. Kearns, *Lyndon Johnson and the American Dream,* pp. 40, 125, 167, 341, 342, passim.

24. Cunningham, *The Presidents' Last Years,* p. 304.

25. Ibid.

36

Richard Milhous Nixon

Richard Milhous Nixon, the thirty-seventh president of the United States, was born January 9, 1913, in Yorba Linda, California, and is the first president to resign and avoid impeachment.

At birth, Richard M. Nixon was described as an 11-pound boy, "roly-poly" with brown eyes, and a thick crop of black hair. The new son would be known to the family as a screamer.[1]

In general, as a child Nixon was a healthy person. He was small for his age but developed a strong set of shoulders and a tough physique. His hair was dark and long. He had a full share of baby fat in his cheeks. Nixon had dark, deep-set eyes, dark eyelashes, and a hard-set, determined mouth. His movements were generally awkward, except at the piano.[2]

Nixon did have some childhood medical problems, however, and his first memory is of a childhood accident. His mother had taken the children out in a buggy to pick grapes. On the return trip, Nixon refused to sit on the buggy seat and stood up on the dashboard. When the buggy turned a sharp corner, he fell out, and the buggy wheel lacerated his scalp on the left side. He was taken to a doctor and required many stitches to close the cut. The scar was a permanent mark. The following year he went through a siege of pneumonia, his only serious childhood ailment.[3]

During his teenage years Nixon developed undulant fever and had a temperature running as high as 104 degrees. His mother nursed him through weeks of recovery.[4] As a teen he also developed a serious sinus infection and was sent to Prescott, Arizona, for the climate.[5]

But the most serious medical problem of these years concerned Nixon's brother, Harold, who developed pulmonary tuberculosis. Harold was treated in Prescott, where his mother nursed him. She and Harold, along with four other tuberculosis patients coughing up blood, stayed in a small "lunger cabin" built by Fred Nixon, Richard's father.[6]

Harold died while Nixon, age 19, was at Whittier College. This was a brother to whom Nixon was greatly attached. After Harold's death, Nixon became deeply depressed. The loss of Harold had a lasting effect on him.[7]

At Whittier College Nixon remained very active physically. He especially loved football, which he depended on for his recreation. He played on the freshman team but never made the varsity. He dressed for the home games, but did not go on trips. Although he seldom got in a game, he was so emotionally involved that he could not eat before one. He was 5 feet 11 inches tall and weighed 155 pounds. One of his teammates, also on the third team, recalled: "Nixon and I were cannon fodder."[8]

In the social arena while Nixon was at Whittier, and later at Duke Law School, some of his traits began to emerge, which a psychiatrist made a great deal of later. One of his early girl friends in college said, "He was smart and sat apart." She added, "I think he felt unsure of himself deep down."[9] Someone else described Nixon this way: "He never smiled. What an extraordinary thing for a young man who actually had a very nice smile and a great deal to smile about."[10]

While at Duke, Nixon lived a very spartan existence. With meager funds, he barely subsisted, eating what he could. In fact, he found an abandoned building in the Duke forest which was not equipped with heat or plumbing. While he lived there, Nixon studied in the library and took his showers in the gym. One of the Duke grounds caretakers discovered that Nixon was using the building without authorization, but did not make him vacate. Through most of the three years at Duke Law School, he boarded without a chest of drawers or even a closet, living out of an old trunk which he had hauled from California.[11]

Apparently, however, Nixon suffered no ill effects from such a harsh regimen and remained in good health during these years. But back in California, studying for the California bar, he caught influenza. He had not lost a single day from sickness during his three years at Duke Law School.[12]

During Nixon's first term in Congress, 1947–48, Nixon served on the House Committee for Un-American Activities. During February 1948 Nixon had to be absent during a critical period of the hearings. Nixon was at Bethesda Naval Hospital with a fractured elbow. He had received the injury from a fall on some icy steps while carrying his little daughter, Tricia.[13]

Generally obsessive-compulsive working habits, disregard for proper hours, lack of exercise, and poor eating habits characterized Nixon's congressional career. While a senator, he often worked very late at his office, at times spending the night there. He would, at times, sleep for a few hours on the couch in his office. He ate irregularly and apparently had very little regard for what he ate. He often subsisted on just a tuna fish sandwich and a glass of milk. He had no hobbies and at that time played no games. He tried golf for a while but did not pursue it regularly. Nixon was not a regular drinker but at times he could be a heavy drinker.[14]

After moving into a new home and after only a few months in the Senate in 1950 Nixon developed what his daughter described as "severe back and neck pains." After seeing several physicians and being told that the problem was due to severe tension, he consulted Dr. Arnold Hutschnecker, "an internist specializing in psychosomatic medicine." Dr. Hutschnecker would deal with the emotional conditions, the tensions, the unhappiness. For four years Nixon made frequent visits to Hutschnecker's office in New York. These visits ended following the threat of public exposure by columnist Drew Pearson.[15] The Hutschnecker-Nixon patient-doctor relationship was aired before the election in 1968 by Pearson, who called Hutschnecker on a tip that the internist, psychosomatic medicine specialist, and later psychiatrist, had treated the then vice president Nixon. Pearson implied that Nixon had turned to Hutschnecker for treatment of a mental problem. Hutschnecker denied that he had given any psychiatric treatment to Nixon and pointed out that at the time he treated Nixon he was only licensed to practice as an internist, not as a psychiatrist. Hutschnecker's records showed that he had mainly given Nixon routine physical examinations, and treated him for severe headaches. "During the entire time that I treated Mr. Nixon," Hutschnecker wrote in *Look* magazine, "I detected no signs of mental illness."[16] Hutschnecker later told Klein that he believed the source of Pearson's rumor regarding the treatment of Nixon was a former patient whom he described as a "paranoid schizophrenic who hated Nixon with the same passion with which he hated his own father."[17]

Nixon also encountered many medical problems connected with his numerous election campaigns. In 1956, for example, when Nixon was running for the second time as vice president, he was hit in Cheyenne with an upper respiratory infection which gave him great difficulty in speaking. Ashen faced, he was barely able to finish his address in Cheyenne.[18]

In the campaign of 1960, when he was running for the office of president against Kennedy, one of Nixon's campaign trips took him to Greensboro, North Carolina, where he bumped his left knee while getting into a car. The knee was later treated with hot compresses while he wrote his speeches. The pain, tenderness, and swelling became so intense that one week after the accident he entered Walter Reed Hospital for a diagnostic tap of his left knee joint space. On August 29, 1960, a physician, Dr. Walter Tkach, called Nixon from Walter Reed and advised him to come to the hospital right away. Nixon rejoined that he could not afford to take time away from his campaign. Tkach answered, "You had better come to the hospital right away or you might be campaigning on one leg." The infection in his left knee was due to hemolytic streptococci. He was urged to enter the hospital for two weeks for rest and antibiotic treatment with massive doses of penicillin. Nixon later noted that the pain in his knee was bad enough, but the mental anguish was infinitely worse. Kennedy was out on the trail campaigning while Nixon was in bed.[19]

After Nixon left the hospital his compulsive nature took over. He tried to make up for the lost time which he had spent in the hospital with his infected knee. He had made a commitment to himself to campaign in all the states. He was determined to do just that, even though the rigors of such a schedule kept him on the road campaigning night and day up until the time of his first debate with Kennedy, on September 26, 1960.

Nixon's arduous campaigning took its toll. When he arrived at the studio for the first debate, he was physically exhausted. He was ten pounds underweight, and his shirt collar was very loose around his neck. As he got out of his car to go into the television studio, he struck his left knee again on the automobile door, just as he had with the first injury to his knee in Greensboro, North Carolina. An observer noted that his face went all white, but he quickly recovered himself and regained his composure.[20]

During the debate itself, Nixon was described as tense, almost frightened, at times glowering, and occasionally haggard-looking to the point of sickness. "Probably no picture in American politics tells a better story of crisis and episode than that famous shot of the camera on Vice-President Nixon as he slouched, his 'lazy-shaved' powder faintly streaked with sweat, his eyes exaggerated hollows of blackness, his jaw, jowls, and face drooping with strain."[21] The camera showed the cumulative effect of recent severe sickness, the great fatigue from his compulsive campaigning, and poor makeup.

Nixon's physical problems, however, have not interested biographers nearly as much as has that elusive Nixon which psychiatrists have tried to analyze from afar. Different ones have had a field day trying to describe Nixon's mental state. David Abrahamsen, for example, has examined his childhood and found false the image Nixon presented of the saintly mother. Instead, says Abrahamsen, Nixon's mother, Hannah, was a "domineering, castrating woman.... The boy was cheated out of love.... Rejection by her was a direct threat to his good image of himself." He also "feared his father and began at an early time to compete with him." Nixon was a tense, frustrated, isolated, and angry child who felt abandoned by his mother and father.[22]

Bruce Mazlish was impressed with Nixon's body rigidity and his mechanical gestures which suggested a desperate need for control of himself, which in turn meant compulsive control of his situation.[23] (In recently viewed flashbacks of old films of Ed Sullivan shows, I was amazed at the resemblance between the robot-like movements, the stance, the rigidity to that of Nixon.) Mazlish felt that Nixon was partly aware of his need for control, and he quoted Nixon, "I have a fetish about controlling myself."[24]

Feeling neither loved nor likable, Nixon was unable to form a healthy relationship with anyone. He desired relationships with others without knowing how to go about forming them or how to respond emotionally and spontaneously to a woman. A deep gulf between surface and depths, between surface love and depth hate, remained within Nixon.[25]

Nixon was described as having had three father figures: his own father; his football coach at Whittier College, Wallace Newman; and Dwight D. Eisenhower.[26] Wallace Newman, his football coach, gave Nixon license to be dirty, sweaty, and bloody, the license to get angry, to smash at bodies, and be smashed by other bodies, which had been denied him by his domineering mother and his own resentment against his yelling father.[27]

Eisenhower has been identified as a father figure by some who have tried to analyze the relationship from a distance. According to Mazlish, "Eisenhower presented Nixon with a crisis of feeling, involving emotions about Ike as a beloved and admired father figure to whom death wishes as both father and as President became attached." But Mazlish went further: "These, we would need hardly add, would be on the unconscious level."[28]

Nixon was, however, the apparent victim of depression from time to time. Critics of Nixon ascribed his dark moods to his being a "black Irishman." Whatever the cause of the adult Nixon's dark moods and introspection, it was not Irish blood.[29] One episode of severe depression occurred after Harold, his older brother, died. At the end of 1967, while he was going through an agony of indecision as to whether he would run again for president, on Christmas Day he decided to tell his family that he was not running. His daughter, Julie, recorded in her diary that "Daddy called Tricia and me in separately and told us that he had decided almost definitely not to run. He was very depressed. I had never known him to be so depressed before, not even after 1962." The year 1962 was when he failed to be elected as governor of California.[30] There was another rather prolonged period of depression in May 1972 during the Vietnam War. He was depressed because of the North Vietnam Tet offensive, and the great difficulty in ending the war.

Nixon, according to many of those who wrote about him, employed anger quite often. The news writers were a frequent target. Staff gave him daily some selected items to read. Nixon did some jotting on the margin of his news summary items. In these scribblings he revealed his true feelings. According to Stephen Ambrose, the first thing that stands out in his commentary is his word choice; his verbs were almost always violent. "Get someone to hit him," Nixon would write about one reporter, or "Fire him," or "Cut him," or "Freeze him," or "Knock this one down," or "Fight him," or "Dump him," or "Don't back off."[31]

There are those who have insisted that any diagnosis of Nixon's mental state would require a whole new glossary of psychiatric terms and an entire new set of rules for analyzing what was happening in his mind. Such assessments were made by persons who were not psychoanalysts—and most frequently by writers and reporters, the most blatant of whom was Norman Mailer. These writers, if not antipathetic, were at best not sympathetic. We must remember that the subject, Nixon, was not only under the usual stresses of the presidency but the added ones imposed by the revelations of the Watergate scandal. The fact that he was always viewed under a glaring spotlight by an antagonistic press would tend to make the ordinary mental aberrations seem too much beyond the ordinary.

Billy Graham, after he learned something about the true content of the tapes and something about Nixon's true involvement in Watergate, said "I think it was sleeping pills—sleeping pills and demons. I think there was definitely demon power involved. He took all those pills that would give him a low in the morning and a high in the afternoon. You know all through history drugs and demons have gone together."[32]

The biographers and psychobiographers have written much more about the mental problems, supposed and real, of Nixon's life than about his physical ills. Those psychobiographers who have attempted to reveal the mental problems of Nixon seem to be wandering in a maze. Among the many labels put on Richard was survivor guilt complex, presumably brought on by the death of two brothers. The second effect of his brothers' deaths was presumed to bring on Richard the threat and fear of his own death. Mazlish theorized that Richard Nixon, who so resembled his mother in many traits, eventually turned these traits to use in terms of identification with the father—almost mimicry at times. Both had a keen distaste for writers and newspapermen. Also, in his identification with his father, Nixon sought to redeem his father, a failure, by being successful himself. Mazlish went further to state that Nixon must always have been haunted by fear of his own failures.[33]

We have trouble with so many Nixon watchers who have attempted from afar to evaluate the psyche of this man. Perhaps Eli Chesen's analysis agrees in most respects with those of others, but Chesen's approach is both more logical and more lucid. Beginning with Nixon's childhood, Chesen emphasized that Nixon was "evolving as an immature child, who, with some reluctance, found himself submissive to a fear of an uninspiring father and a domineering mother." Chesen felt that all of Nixon's psychiatric profile fell into an area suggestive of the classification "obsessive-compulsive personality." This was defined by the American Psychiatric Association as follows: "This behavior pattern is characterized by excessive concern with conformity and adherence to standards of conscience. Consequently individuals in this group may be rigid, over-inhibited, over-conscientious, over-dutiful, and unable to relax easily."[34]

Of course, all of the abnormal characteristics of Nixon's mental makeup were accentuated and came under a closer scrutiny during and after Watergate. It would be inconceivable that any human subject to the terrific stress of those days in the White House would not reveal some abnormal and revealing signs of the underlying personality. In this setting Nixon underwent unremitting and relentless scrutiny by the press and by the political opposition.

Nixon went out of office suspected of suffering from severe mental illness. Some of the Nixon watchers wrote of the president's relationship with the press in the last months before he resigned from the presidency. There was a feeling in some circles that he might go "bats" in front of the newsmen at any time.[35] An aura of paranoia, the "bunker mentality," hung around the White House. Nixon's own doctors said he had a "death wish."[36]

The mental stress of Watergate was worsened by physical ailments as well. In mid-1973 Nixon was in Bethesda Naval Hospital in Maryland with viral pneumonia. J. Fred Buzhardt, Leonard Garment, and University of Texas professor Charles Allen White visited him. They wanted Nixon's permission to review the tapes. Nixon refused permission. Two days later he was back at the White House, apparently well enough to return to work.[37] Nixon stated that some of his critics agreed that he had made the wrong decision. "If I had been up to par physically, there is certainly a chance that I could have stepped up to the issue and ordered the tapes destroyed." No one can be actually sure what might have happened in these cases had illness not intervened.[38]

Under various circumstances and at different times, we are told something about Nixon's alcoholic consumption. One instance was shortly after his loss to Pat Brown for the governorship of California. He was in the Beverly Hilton Hotel in Los Angeles, watching the returns after the polls were closed. Nixon refused to concede until the early morning. The reporters were waiting for Nixon to come down and make a statement. Herb

Klein, Nixon's press secretary, was urged to bring Nixon down to a press conference. Klein tried several times to get Nixon to go down, but Nixon, who had been consuming alcohol and taking tranquilizers, refused to come down and did not do so until later.[39]

At 10:10 A.M. Klein stepped onto the platform. "I have the text of two messages I'll read to you," he said. "The boss won't be down.... He plans to go home and be with his family." What Klein did not say was that Nixon was upstairs and was in such a distraught state from fatigue, disappointment, and, according to reports, the perversely stimulating effects of tranquilizing pills on top of some drinks, that his aides had been struggling to prevent him from coming down.[40]

In 1966, while Nixon was in the Northwest, John Erlichman met with him to discuss Nixon's political future and offered his support. John Erlichman: "I said that all being equal he had my support, but that I was very much troubled by his drinking. I was in no position to ask him to stop, nor would I ever intrude that way into anyone's personal life, but I continued, I did not want to invest time in a difficult presidential campaign that might well be lost because the candidate was not fully in control of himself."[41]

On December 21, 1973, Nixon asked a small group to the White House for dinner. Barry Goldwater was present. In his after-dinner conversation, Nixon displayed a great deal of paranoia. The president felt that he was beset from all sides; he was a victim of circumstances of uncontrollable forces; the democrats and the press were now working together to get him; and he had inherited a much-abused office, flagrantly misused by Kennedy and Johnson, but the liberals and press hated him. Pat Buchanan, who was present, thought "the old man is tired and can't hold his liquor well, especially when he is exhausted." The next day Goldwater called Bryce Harlow and asked, "Is the President off his rocker?" Harlow replied, "No, he was drunk." Alexander Haig felt the president was drinking more than usual.[42]

In May 1974, after Julie Nixon Eisenhower gave an interview to the press just four months before Nixon's resignation, her interviewer had been most supportive. The White House switchboard was flooded with calls, praising her performance. Later that evening Helen Smith encountered the president on the White House elevator and she thought, "He does not look well, he does not look strong or vigorous, [his] face [looks] damp from sweat.... This man does not look in control of the situation."[43]

In August 1974, when it became almost definite that the president was resigning, Thomas Eagleberger and Henry Kissinger were conversing.

The phone rang during the conversation. It was the president. Eagleberger picked up the phone to listen. He was shocked. The president was slurring his words, he was drunk, and he was out of control. At that time Nixon told Kissinger about his decision to leave.[44]

On August 6, 1974, Edward Cox, Nixon's son-in-law, was worried about Nixon's mental status. Cox sounded distraught. The president was not sleeping, and he had been drinking and behaving irrationally. "The President," Cox began, his voice rose momentarily, "was walking up and down the hall last night talking to pictures of former Presidents — giving speeches and talking to pictures on the wall."[45]

William Safire stated, "Nobody who worked with Nixon can read the taped transcriptions without a sinking, disgusted feeling. Sometimes they show Nixon in his own words, 'a dumb turkey.' At other times they show a vacillating abandoned man, and then mean spirited and vengeful."[46]

Harvard's late professor Richard Hofstadter, author of *The Paranoid Style in American Politics*, wrote: "Paranoid is a strong word to use in connection with the President of the United States and Nixon's critics used it frequently to describe him." Hofstadter used the word to describe a style, not a man. "No other word," he wrote, "adequately evokes the qualities of heated exaggeration, suspiciousness, and conspiratorial fantasy that I have in mind." The central fact about the paranoid style as applied to Nixon is this: here is the first time in presidential politics that the paranoid style has been used by the leader of the majority.[47]

Whether or not Nixon was suicidal was a recurring theme in the last several months of his presidency. Nixon had made some indirect references to ending one's own life. The first week in August 1974 he made less than subtle approaches to the subject. Once when Haig and Nixon were alone, the president stated, "You fellows in your business," he began — meaning the army — "you have a way of handling problems like this. Somebody leaves a pistol in the drawer." Haig waited. "I don't have a pistol," the president said sadly.[48]

When Nixon made his trip to the Middle East in June 1974, he was already suffering from phlebitis in his leg. He made the trip to take the heat off his domestic problems at home. His personal physician, Dr. Tkach, accompanied Nixon on the trip. At Salzburg Nixon called for his physician. His leg was inflamed and swollen. Examination revealed that a blood clot had formed in one of the left leg veins. Tkach warned Nixon that the clot could break loose and go to his lungs and that the result could be fatal. Tkach warned him of the possible consequences of continuing the trip and urged him to be hospitalized long enough to ensure the clot had stabilized. Nixon was advised that he should then return to

Washington for further treatment. He refused to take his doctor's advice: "The purpose of this visit is more important than my life. I know the risks." Tkach put on a support hose, but it was too uncomfortable and Nixon couldn't wear it. After this exchange, the doctor went to Haig's room and related to him the diagnosis. Tkach inquired of Haig how much standing and walking would be required during the trip. The schedule called for him to be on his feet a great deal of the next day. Actually, the next day was in Cairo and appeared to be particularly rough. Henkel Williams, the White House chief of advance, advised Tkach that there was no way that they could alter the schedule. Tkach said that "Nixon belonged in the hospital, he should never have made the trip. The President has a death wish." The advice of Nixon's other physician, Rear Admiral William Lukash, was sought. After Lukash's examination, he came to the same conclusion. He tried to persuade Nixon to end the trip, but Nixon was still of the same opinion and just as determined to continue. On June 12, 1974, Nixon and his entourage made their way to Cairo by plane and from there to Alexandria by train. On the way to Alexandria Nixon persisted in standing in the window of an open-sided observation car with Sadat, waving to the crowd. Lukash could see that Nixon was in great pain. The doctor gave him a painkiller and urged him to get off his feet. The president's exposure to the huge crowds seemed a reckless risk to the Secret Service people. Dr. Tkach sought out Dick Keiser, head of the special units guarding Nixon, and expressed his alarm at Nixon's reckless behavior. "You can't protect a President who wants to kill himself," Keiser responded.[49]

Nixon visited the pyramids, then crossed the Red Sea on a plane to Saudi Arabia. He then flew east to Damascus, Syria, Israel, and Jordan, and then on June 17 he headed home. He had heeded neither the advice of his doctors nor that of the security contingent. He had walked when he should have ridden and stood when he should have sat.

The third week in June Nixon went to Camp David to rest and further plan his trip to Russia. His leg, in spite of his not taking medical advice, was somewhat improved. His doctors begged him to cancel the Russian trip but again he refused. He flew to his first stop in Brussels with his leg elevated to reduce swelling. After Brussels he proceeded to Russia, where he remained for several days, largely in communion with Brezhnev. Just before Nixon left for Brussels the story of his phlebitis appeared in the U.S. newspapers. The reporters watched Nixon for signs of pain or limp. Nixon said in his diary, "In fact, my leg was still swollen and painful. . . . I feel at the present time, however, we have it relatively under control."

Nixon gave his ideas on the relationship between mental and physical health in his book *In the Arena*.

I've always believed that there is a direct relationship between mental
and physical health.... Twenty years have passed since I had suffered
from phlebitis.... Just before my trip to the Mid-East in June 1974, my
left leg began to swell. I have a rather high pain threshhold and did not
report it to the doctor for several days. When I did, he did not advise
me, as was later reported in the press, to cancel the trip to the Mid-East.
Hot and cold compresses reduced the swelling, but it increased alarmingly when I had to stand too long at the various ceremonies. It became
even more aggravated when I went to the Soviet Union in July and
visited a memorial in Minsk. I had to walk for almost a mile and a half
over cobblestone paths. The pain was excruciating.[50]

In August 1974 Nixon resigned as president, and during the first
several weeks of his retirement there was a return of his old chronic problem — the phlebitis flared up.

When I returned to Washington the pain subsided, but a few days after
the pardon the swelling returned. I consulted my family doctor. He urged
me to go into the hospital for treatment with heparin and coumadin
(coumadin and heparin are drugs used to prevent clotting in blood vessels), saying that if a clot should break loose and go to the lungs it would
be fatal. That got my attention. I went to the hospital. I was there for
almost two weeks, sleeping very little because the nurses came in every
hour to refill the intravenous heparin medication. When I went home
I told Pat that I would never go to a hospital again. Within three weeks
I was back. [Dr. John] Lungren had warned me that sharp pain in the
abdomen would be a dangerous sign. After x-rays the doctors decided
an operation should be performed immediately. I remember the pin
prick of the needle administered by the anesthetist, and being wheeled
to the OR, but for six days I was in and out of consciousness.... When
I woke up again Lungren was taking my pulse.... I told him I was anxious to go home. He said, "Listen, Dick, we almost lost you last night.
You are not to go home for quite a while." He told me that I had gone
into shock after the operation and that my blood pressure had dropped
to 60 over 0. Only after four transfusions over a period of three hours
were the doctors able to push it back to normal.

After Nixon left the hospital he returned to San Clemente.[51]

After Nixon returned to San Clemente, Judge John Sirica wanted
him in the courtroom to testify against John Mitchell. He sent three doctors to examine Nixon to see if he was really unable to appear. They reported back to Sirica that Nixon was not under any circumstances to travel
to Washington.

One further notable health problem has occurred. In 1983 Nixon
contracted shingles. He said, "My high pain threshhold did not help this

time. My doctor, Harvey Klein, said that it was one of the worst cases he had ever seen. The condition was aggravated by the fact that coumadin, a blood thinner given to avoid another attack of phlebitis, caused the sores to bleed so heavily that my sheets and pajamas had to be changed several times a day."

Later, Nixon wrote, "Sometimes I am asked what a 78-year-old former president does for exercise. Again, I do not set a very good example. I have never gone hunting or fishing, just isn't my bag. . . . I do not ski or play tennis. . . . I quit golf ten years ago. . . . In 1969 I asked President Eisenhower what he did for exercise. He told me that he believed that walking was the best thing a leader could do for mental, physical, and emotional health. I now follow his advice and walk four miles per day."[52]

So far as can be determined, Nixon presides in New Jersey as an elder statesman and sought-after adviser in foreign affairs. There are no available reports that he has had any recurrence of his health problems.

References

1. Roger Morris, *Richard Milhous Nixon: The Rise of an American Politician*, pp. 41–42.
2. Stephen E. Ambrose, *Richard M. Nixon*, 1:30.
3. Morris, *Richard Milhous Nixon*, pp. 42–43.
4. Ibid., p. 110.
5. Fawn Brodie, *Richard Nixon: The Shaping of His Character*, p. 98.
6. Ambrose, *Richard M. Nixon*, 1:42.
7. Ibid., p. 41.
8. Ibid., p. 65.
9. Brodie, *Richard Nixon*, p. 80.
10. Ambrose, *Richard M. Nixon*, 1:76.
11. Morris, *Richard Milhous Nixon*, p. 163.
12. Herbert S. Parmet, *Richard Nixon and His America*, pp. 83–84.
13. Ibid., pp. 153–54.
14. Ambrose, *Richard M. Nixon*, 1:245–46.
15. Morris, *Richard Milhous Nixon*, p. 654.
16. Arnold Hutschnecker, "The Health of Our Leaders," *Look*, July 15, 1969, pp. 51–54.
17. Herbert Klein, *Making It Perfectly Clear*, pp. 409–17.
18. Ambrose, *Richard M. Nixon*, 1:412.
19. Richard M. Nixon, *Six Crises*, p. 326.
20. Theodore H. White, *The Making of a President*, p. 343.
21. Ibid., pp. 346–47.
22. David Abrahamsen, *Nixon vs. Nixon: An Emotional Tragedy*, p. 25.
23. Bruce Mazlish, *In Search of Nixon: A Psychohistorical Inquiry*, p. 124.
24. Earl Mazo, *Richard Nixon — A Political and Personal Portrait*, p. 5.

25. Abrahamsen, *Nixon vs. Nixon,* p. 140.
26. Brodie, *Richard Nixon,* pp. 111–12.
27. Ibid., p. 111.
28. Mazlish, *In Search of Nixon,* p. 99.
29. Ambrose, *Richard M. Nixon,* 1:112.
30. Ambrose, *Richard M. Nixon,* 2:131.
31. Ambrose, *Richard M. Nixon,* 1:409–10.
32. Marshall Frady, *Billy Graham: Profile of American Righteousness,* p. 275.
33. Mazlish, *In Search of Nixon,* pp. 27, 28, 29, passim.
34. Eli S. Chesen, *President Nixon's Psychiatric Profile,* pp. 79, 80, 201, passim.
35. John Osborne, *The Last Nixon Watch,* p. 5.
36. Brodie, *Richard Nixon,* pp. 17–18.
37. Bob Woodward and Carl Bernstein, *The Final Days,* pp. 46–49, passim.
38. Richard M. Nixon, *In the Arena,* p. 168.
39. Gladwin Hill, *Dancing Bear: Inside Look at California Politics,* p. 164.
40. Ibid., p. 164.
41. John Erlichman, *Witness to Power,* pp. 37–38.
42. Woodward and Bernstein, *The Final Days,* pp. 100–01.
43. Ibid., p. 175.
44. Ibid., p. 472.
45. Ibid., p. 438.
46. William Safire, *Before the Fall,* p. 274.
47. Ibid., p. 275.
48. Woodward and Bernstein, *The Final Days,* p. 449.
49. Ibid., pp. 229–30, passim.
50. Nixon, *In the Arena,* p. 22.
51. Ibid., pp. 22–23.
52. Ibid., pp. 163–65, passim.

37

Gerald Rudolph Ford

Gerald Rudolph Ford, the thirty-eighth president of the United States, was born July 14, 1913, in Omaha, Nebraska. Ford was the first president ever to reach that office from the vice presidency to which the aspirant had been appointed by a retiring or resigning president—Richard Nixon. There were a great many accusations and recriminations after Gerald Ford granted Nixon "a full, free, and absolute pardon for all offenses committed during his administration." After the news media had shown its displeasure, it recalled a comment attributed to LBJ: "Jerry Ford is a nice guy but he played too much football with his helmet off."[1]

Ford grew up in Grand Rapids and East Grand Rapids, Michigan, in a household that was not wealthy. He was described as a spirited, industrious, and athletic youngster. His biological father and his mother were separated when he was close to three years of age. Ford saw his biological father only twice.

Generally speaking, Ford had a very healthy childhood. When he was five years old he developed a severe abdominal pain and was rushed to the Butterworth Hospital where his illness was diagnosed as appendicitis. A decision was made to operate on an emergency basis. The appendix turned out to be healthy and his parents were furious.[2]

In his autobiography Ford related that as a child he had a bad temper which his mother helped him to control. He also related that his stepfather as well as his mother were strict disciplinarians. His stepfather was not such a strict disciplinarian, however, that he didn't have a good time. When Gerald was a toddler, his father would toss baseballs and footballs with him during the summertime. His father owned a cabin on the Little South Broad and Pere Marquette River where Gerald and his father fished and engaged in a number of outdoor activities.

As a young child Ford developed a stuttering problem which went away when he was almost ten years of age. He stated that the stuttering problem could perhaps be ascribed to his ambidexterity: "For as long as I can remember, I have been left handed sitting down and right handed standing up, and as strange as it may sound I throw a football with my right hand and write with my left."[3]

The stuttering may also have had something to do with the emotional trauma incurred at the time his biological father and mother separated. The fact that the stutter left him at the age of ten would lead one to believe that the happy household established by his stepfather and his mother in all likelihood caused his speech defect to go away.

Ford's education in general was marked by good performance both athletically and scholastically. At the end of his junior year in high school he made the National Honor Society and ranked in the top 25 percent of his class. Ford was a star center on the South High football team and was named to the All-City squad. He graduated from high school in 1931 and entered the University of Michigan that fall on a partial scholarship. He earned part of his expenses by working in the university hospital dining room. Ford made the freshman football team at Michigan and was named outstanding freshman on that team. He played second-string center on the football team as backup to All-American center Chuck Bernard. As a senior Gerald was first-string center and was named most valuable player. Ford graduated in the top 25 percent of his class at the University of Michigan.[4]

After Ford's graduation he played center on the 1935 college All-Star team which played a game against the Chicago Bears. He was offered a professional contract to play by both the Detroit Lions and the Green Bay Packers, but he passed up professional football to study law. Ford maintained a B average while studying law at Yale University and finished in the upper one-third of his class.[5]

Ford was described as being 6 feet tall and weighing about 195 pounds. He had blond hair, which he combed straight back, and small blue eyes. He has largely retained the trim, muscular figure of earlier years, and except for weak knees, the result of football injuries, his health generally has been sound.[6]

Ford began his military service on April 20, 1942. He was given a commission as an ensign and placed in a program designed to recruit athletes as physical training instructors. He was, after six weeks, sent to Chapel Hill, North Carolina, where he spent a year giving physical instruction to navy aviation cadets. In the meantime, Ford was seeking to be assigned to duty. He was finally assigned to sea duty on a light aircraft carrier, *The Monterey*. He survived his naval service without wounds, but had a narrow escape when he was almost blown overboard in a typhoon in December 1944.[7]

After Ford's release from the navy, he practiced law in Grand Rapids,

Michigan (1946–48). In 1948 he married Elizabeth (Betty) Bloomer Warren. From 1949–73 he was a U.S. representative from Michigan, and was minority leader in the House, 1965–73. On December 6, 1973, Ford was sworn in as the fortieth vice president of the United States under Richard Nixon. He was, when he replaced Spiro Agnew, the first person ever appointed to that office under the Twenty-fifth Amendment. He became the thirty-eighth president of the U.S. on August 9, 1974, when Nixon resigned following the Watergate scandal.

There is no record that Gerald Ford suffered any illness during his long term as a member of the House of Representatives, his vice presidency, or his partial term as president which ended in March 1977.

Gerald Ford, from his early years until the present, has been involved in many sports and outdoor activities which keep him physically fit. He enjoys swimming, golf, tennis, and skiing. His skiing was and is usually done in Vail, Colorado. While president he rode an exercise bike and lifted weights in the president's study before breakfast. Ford smokes a pipe — about eight bowls of Sir Walter Raleigh or other blends in a day's time.[8]

Richard Reeves went into more detail in describing Ford's daily routine in the White House. He said, "Ford is an early riser and newspaper reader and becoming President did not change his routine. He gets up each day between 5:30 and 6:00 A.M., after six to seven hours of sleep, and begins reading the *Washington Post*. After exercise his breakfast is served."[9]

His exercise consists of a mile on a stationary bike, leg lifts, 40 pounds strapped on his left leg, then 25 strapped on his right leg, 20 situps, and 25 pushups.[10]

Every movement of a president is scrutinized closely by the media who are assigned to cover the chief executive. Should he happen to stumble the reporters can, if they are short of something to write about, build up the incident greatly by speculating on all possible causes. When President Ford flew to Salzburg from Spain on May 3, 1975, for a meeting with Sadat, Ford related: "The weather in Spain had been fair; rain clouds hung low over the Salzburg airport, however, and when the airplane taxied to a stop, I tumbled down the ramp, literally. What happened is this, Betty and I were descending the steps. I had my right arm around her waist to help her, and I was carrying an umbrella in my left hand. Two or three steps from the bottom of the ramp the heel of my shoe caught on something. I had no free hand to grab the rail, so I took a tumble to the tarmac."[11]

Ford was unhurt. He got to his feet immediately. Presidential secretary Ron Nessen told the president later that he—Nessen—had been quizzed by the reporters who were assigned to the trip about Ford's misstep. They wished to know if Dr. Lukash had examined him. Ford was not concerned about the questions of the reporters who were obviously probing to find out if there was some physical reason for his stumble. Ford said, "There was no doubt in my mind that I am the most athletic President to occupy the White House in years."[12]

All presidents are undoubtedly on the hate list of someone. Many of our presidents have been shot at. Several of the assassination attempts have been successful. Ford narrowly escaped being shot on September 5, 1975. He had flown to the West Coast to deliver speeches and gave one of his most important speeches before the joint session of the California legislature in Sacramento. On the morning before the speech, Ford walked across the Capitol grounds toward the office of Governor Jerry Brown. The morning was clear and pleasant. A great number of people had turned out to greet and applaud the president. There were many people behind a rope which restrained the crowd to his left. Ford said,

> I was in a good mood until I started shaking hands. That's when I spotted a woman wearing a bright red dress. She was in the second or third row moving right along with me as if she wanted to shake hands. When I looked down I noticed immediately that she thrust her hand under the arm of another spectator. I reached down to shake it and looked into the barrel of a .45 caliber pistol pointed directly at me. I ducked. "This country is in a mess. This man is not your President," she was reported to have yelled, but I didn't hear her. I did remember seeing Secret Service agent Larry Buendorf reach for the woman's hand and wrestle her to the ground.[13]

Described elsewhere, the attempt at assassination was as follows: "As Ford shook hands with the crowd a red-haired woman named Lynette Alice Fromme, nicknamed 'Squeaky,' a follower of Charles Manson, pulled a loaded .45 caliber pistol from beneath her skirt, raised it between two spectators in front of her, and pointed it directly at the president from two feet away. Secret Service agent Larry Buendorf grabbed the gun and twisted it out of the woman's hands. With the help of another agent and a local policeman, Buendorf subdued the woman, handcuffed her, and sent her off to jail."[14]

A second attempt on Ford's life came just over two weeks later. Following the assassination attempt at Sacramento, Ford went back to California for a series of speeches. The talks ended September 22, 1975, in San Francisco. There were premonitions by several that it was not safe for Ford to remain in the Bay area. An NBC cameraman, David Kennerly, warned, "Get him out of town as fast as you can. These are not good people." Ford was ending his last San Francisco event, a 30-minute taped interview with a local TV station. Kennerly went down to size up the crowd waiting for the president. The cameraman did not like what he saw. He suggested that the Secret Service should not allow Ford to shake hands in the crowd. After the TV interview Ford descended by the elevator to a small side-street lobby of the St. Francis Hotel.

Outside, the president started toward the front of his limousine as if he were going to cross the street and shake hands with the crowd on the other side; but he followed the Secret Service's advice and walked to the rear of the car. The door was not open. While the agent reached to open it the president waved to the crowd. There was a loud pop. "I tried to persuade myself that it was a firecracker, but I knew it was a gun," said the agent. For one instant there was absolute silence and nothing moved.

The news photos froze the moment. It showed Ford starting to crouch, his eyes glassy with shock and fear. Ford was bundled into the White House limousine. The motorcade took off immediately at high speed. The agent continued: "As we raced away from the scene I caught a glimpse of a gray-haired woman being carried out of the crowd in a horizontal position by police. She was Sara Jane Moore, a middle-aged woman, whose .44 caliber pistol and 113 bullets had been confiscated the day before by the police as a threat to Ford. She had obtained another gun, a .38 caliber revolver to fire at the president."[15]

Gerald Ford was not only the first president who was the target of a female would-be assassin; he was the intended victim of two pistol-wielding women inside of two weeks.

It is not a complete record if we do not relate something concerning Betty Ford, the wife of Gerald Ford. She became an alcoholic, but she faced her problem squarely and sought help. She has been very active in helping others who faced the same problem. She also sought aid for the handicapped and mentally retarded.

Soon after Gerald became president, Betty had a radical mastectomy for breast cancer. After her breast surgery she became an open advocate for public education in early detection of breast cancer.[16]

During Ford's retirement he has, to date, remained in good health. He may be the fittest, healthiest president ever to occupy the White House.

According to the media, he is still an avid golfer and maintains his physical fitness through exercise.

References

1. David C. Whitney, *The American Presidents*, pp. 364–65.
2. Gerald R. Ford, *A Time to Heal*, p. 43.
3. Ibid., p. 45.
4. William A. Degregorio, *The Complete Book of U.S. Presidents*, pp. 605–06.
5. Ibid.
6. Ibid., p. 603.
7. Bud Vestal, *Jerry Ford, Up Close*, p. 68.
8. Degregorio, *The Complete Book of U.S. Presidents*, p. 606.
9. Richard Reeves, *A Ford Not a Lincoln*, p. 121.
10. Ibid.
11. Ford, *A Time to Heal*, p. 289.
12. Ibid.
13. Ibid., pp. 309–10.
14. Ron Nessen, *It Sure Looks Different from the Inside*, p. 180.
15. Ibid., pp. 185–86.
16. Degregorio, *The Complete Book of U.S. Presidents*, p. 606.

38

James Earl Carter

James Earl Carter, the thirty-ninth president of the United States, was born on October 1, 1924, in Plains, Georgia. His birth was totally uncomplicated. However, Lillian Carter, his mother, did experience a great deal of pain, but she knew from her experience in aiding other women to give birth that this was a normal event. She noted that Jimmy was colicky and cried often. She often related that he had pneumonia at a very early age and at 20 months almost died of bleeding colitis.[1] During the colitis he screamed and screamed for a goat. A goat was found and kept in a box by his bed. Paul H. Elovitz used this incident with the goat to illustrate the oral rage characteristic of a narcissistic personality in Jimmy, and the goat may have served as a transitional object, a security blanket, to compensate for the impending further loss of his mother's attention. His mother was at the time expecting the first of three sibling arrivals.[2]

It is recorded that as a young child Carter was very small for his age. "I was a little guy," said Carter. "They called me baby dumpling." He was told by his father not to let himself be pushed around and consequently got in a lot of fights. "I kindly enjoyed the physical combat, but I was real little for my age."[3] His small size continued into young adulthood, and at his high school graduation in 1941 he was 5 feet 3 inches and 141 pounds.[4]

Carter feared that his size would keep him out of Annapolis, so he gave up a job to rest more and also ate a lot of bananas. He worried about other physical "defects" keeping him out of Annapolis as well. He was much concerned, for example, that his teeth did not coapt properly or meet exactly in front. This malocclusion interfered with his proper enjoyment of food. He was also concerned over the navy's abstruse wording for the act of bed-wetting—"retention of urine." He wondered if the last clinging drop on his penis after urination might leak and cause his disqualification. Another of his fears concerned flat feet and fallen arches. His fear caused him to use his own remedy—rolling the soles of his feet on a Coca-Cola bottle for hours each day in an attempt to raise his arches.[5]

Carter's anxiety over the last clinging drop of urine and his attempt to alter his flat feet are perhaps symptomatic of what has been described as his fantastic drive for control. The authors in *Jimmy Carter and American Fantasy,* an attempted psychohistorical study, describe Carter in terminology similar to that used about Richard Nixon. Carter is said to have a great desire to control his own oral and anal rage and is further described as having a narcissistic personality whose "emotional life was shallow."[6]

In 1966 Carter ran against Lester Maddox for governor and lost. The election went to the state's legislature because Howard H. (Bo) Calloway, the leader, did not have a majority. Carter lost considerable weight during the race and after the defeat retired for a while to the operation of his family plantation. He became involved in some of the actual labor and, while working on a cotton gin, seriously injured a finger. The end result was a flexion contracture, a "mallet" finger, with permanent flexion contracture.[7] During his successful campaign for governor in 1971 Carter used his injured finger to political advantage. When addressing a group of farmers, he would display the injured finger to indicate that he was "one of them."

At the time of Carter's inauguration as president in 1977 he was described as weighing just above 160 pounds and being 5 feet 7 inches tall. He was small but not delicate. His arms and legs were sinewy, lean, and hard. He had the thick chest of a welterweight and a firm, flat abdomen — betraying only a slight evidence of middle age.

Carter dieted to maintain his weight and exercised regularly for fitness and weight maintenance. A temperate man, he smoked only a rare after-dinner cigar and was a very light drinker of alcoholic beverages — a couple of beers after a tennis match and a light scotch in the evening. He had occasional problems with hemorrhoids, however, and was allergic to swiss cheese.[8]

In December 1978, in Plains, Georgia, Carter was reported to be suffering from an attack of hemorrhoids. His problem was severe enough to cause him to cancel his appointments for December 21, 1978. On December 22 he was reported to be better.[9]

The most frightening medical event of his presidency occurred on September 15, 1979, when Carter, pale with exhaustion, dropped out of a 6.2 mile race near Camp David. Carter, an avid jogger, was kept from collapsing by Secret Service agents who held him erect as he staggered to the top of a long hill. This occurred on the fourth mile of the race. The president was assisted to a golf cart, where White House physician, Dr. William Lukash, examined him and urged the president not to run any farther. Carter moved to the White House car and was taken to Camp

David to recover. Dr. Lukash gave Carter a comprehensive medical checkup on September 16, 1979, and declared him fit.[10]

There was not the stir in the media after Carter collapsed, however, like that which occurred 12 years later when George Bush collapsed while engaged in the same sport in May 1991. The difference lay in that Carter's collapse was not caused by any underlying medical problem, and apparently the incident was caused purely by Carter running out of steam. It is recalled that Bush's collapse was precipitated by a cardiac irregularity—atrial fibrillation.

Like every other president, Carter aged significantly in office. Hamilton Jordan, a Carter aide, described Carter's appearance at the time of his leaving the White House: "I thought about the President's physical appearance. The boyish look of his early forties had disappeared. The formerly sandy hair was gray, and wrinkles were creeping across his face."[11]

Carter has enjoyed good health since leaving office, however, although on December 20, 1980, he fell and broke his left collar bone while crosscountry skiing near the presidential retreat at Camp David, Maryland.[12]

References

1. Betty Gladd, *In Search of the Great White House*, p. 32.
2. Lloyd DeMause and Henry Ebel, editors, *Jimmy Carter and American Fantasy: Psychohistorical Explorations*, p. 54.
3. Victor Lasky, *Jimmy Carter, the Man and the Myth*, p. 30.
4. Bruce Mazlish and Edwin Diamond, *Jimmy Carter: A Character Portrait*, p. 92.
5. Ibid., pp. 92–93.
6. DeMause and Ebel, *Jimmy Carter and American Fantasy*, p. 54.
7. Ibid., pp. 149–50.
8. James Wooten, *Dasher*, p. 22.
9. Journal of Facts on File, December 21, 1978, p. 1000.
10. Ibid., September 15, 1979, p. 700 D3, and September 16, 1979, p. 701 A1.
11. Hamilton Jordan, *Crisis: The Last Year of the Carter Presidency*, p. 417.
12. *Journal of Facts on File*, December 27, 1980, p. 989.

39

Ronald Reagan

Ronald Reagan, the fortieth president of the United States, was born on February 6, 1911, in Tampico, Illinois. Reagan's birth was described as being long and difficult. His mother was attended by a midwife until the family doctor arrived. His birth weight was 10 pounds, and Reagan's father bragged about his fat little "Dutchman." He called his son this because of his robust appearance.[1] At the time Reagan was born, the homicide rate was one-third the present level, but infant mortality was 30 times higher than at present. Childhood diseases were often fatal.[2]

Reagan's brother, Neil ("Moon"), had recollections of his boyhood with Ronald; he remembered the family itinerancy, poverty, and uncertainty inflicted by their father's alcoholism. He remembered sleeping with Ronald in a cramped bed which they both wet. "Our big meal on Sunday was fried liver. We ate soupbone all the rest of the week."[3]

During the winter of 1918 "The Dutch," along with thousands of other Americans, developed pneumonia. His mother in that winter recovered from a severe case of flu which nearly killed her.[4]

Apparently, in spite of the rather stark poverty of his family, Reagan's childhood was almost free of illness. "We were damn poor," Reagan has said. He wore the hand-me-downs of his brother Boone, who was two years older. At the dinner table one of Dutch's favorites was "oatmeat," which was hamburger stretched out with meal.[5]

Reagan attended Eureka College, Illinois, where he played football and acted in the school's plays. In college he was so nearsighted, he said, that his vision on the football field was limited to the square yard of turf occupied by the other team's guard. This visual defect was corrected by corneal lenses.

During Reagan's days at Eureka College he was very active in athletics. His achievements on the football field were not great, but he did very well on the swimming team. In his freshman year during the big meet he came in first in every event except the breaststroke.[6]

Reagan was disqualified from serving in combat units during World

War II because of his nearsightedness. He did wear a uniform, and was assigned to the first motion picture unit of the Army Air Corps.[7]

There are numerous references to Reagan's loss of hearing, apparently caused by the loud gunfire endured during the filming of numerous Hollywood westerns. Donald Regan, the White House chief of staff, wrote of the powerful hearing aid which Reagan wore in both ears. And again, Regan referred to a Reagan and Mikhail Gorbachev conference at which the chief of staff was present. The chief of staff brought a message to the president, but Reagan could not hear since Regan was talking into Ronald's deaf ear.[8]

President Reagan was reported to drink very little. Donald Regan cited an instance in which President Reagan invited leaders of Congress to the White House for a drink at the end of the day to discuss the budget. "The President, who drinks very little alcohol, sipped his favorite cocktail, a weak orange blossom."[9]

Reagan undoubtedly maintained a program of physical fitness. He related something about his White House routine: "About 5:00 or so each afternoon, or whenever the work was done, I went upstairs, peeled down, and put on my trunks; I then crossed the central hallway to a great bedroom which we had converted into a gym with exercise equipment. I worked out an hour or more and then took a bath."

On March 30, 1981, two months after his inauguration, there was an attempted assassination. Reagan was shot after delivering a speech at the Washington Hilton. John W. Hinckley, Jr., a disturbed young man carrying a "Saturday night special," fired the weapon a number of times in an attempt to assassinate the president. Only one bullet struck Reagan. Several others were wounded, including press secretary James Brady, who received a severe wound in his head. The bullet which entered the president's chest was a long-nosed .22 caliber, meant to be used in a .22 rifle—lethal when fired from a pistol. It was determined that the bullet which had struck the president ricocheted from the car which he was starting to enter. After the shooting, Reagan was rushed to George Washington Hospital. The early information about the president was erroneous and incomplete.

Initially, it was reported that the president was not seriously injured, but the nation soon found that Reagan's injury was quite serious, even life threatening. Urgent surgery was needed. The ricochet bullet had penetrated to within an inch of his heart. It was not an ordinary bullet but one which was supposed to explode after penetration. Fortunately, in this case the bullet failed to explode. The greatest threats came from the severe loss of blood, shock, and a collapsed lung.[10]

When the bullet struck the car, it was flattened to the size and shape of a small coin. The pellet then entered Reagan's body under his left arm, and in entering made a slit-like wound. The Secret Service agent who pushed Reagan into the car had attempted to find the bullet wound but found none, but he did see that there was bright red blood coming from Reagan's mouth. The president walked into the emergency room at George Washington University Hospital, assisted by the agent. After he was in the emergency room, he fell on one knee, collapsing, and said, "I cannot breathe. Please tell me you are Republicans." Soon after he entered the emergency room, an endotracheal tube was inserted to help him breathe.[11]

The assailant accused of shooting the president was born in 1955 and was reared in the Highland Park section of north Dallas, in a community known as "The Bubble." The Bubble was built in the early 1900s as a haven for the wealthy. Hinckley attended college in Lubbock at Texas Tech University, without getting a degree. He was described as an aimless drifter with no fixed address. On October 19, 1980, John Hinckley had been arrested at the Nashville airport trying to get through the metal detectors with three handguns concealed in his luggage. He was released on bond — no charges pressed. At that time, during the presidential campaign, President Carter was in the Nashville airport two hours before Hinckley's arrest. Reagan was scheduled to be in Memphis that day, but the appearance was canceled. When arrested, Hinckley was trying to board a plane for New York, where Carter was scheduled to appear on October 13 and Reagan on October 16. The arresting police confiscated his guns but did not make a report to the Secret Service as required by federal guidelines.[12]

On the seventieth day of his presidency, Reagan underwent three hours of surgery at George Washington University Hospital to remove the bullet that entered in his left armpit, struck the seventh rib, and burrowed three inches into his left lung. At 7:25 P.M., 3 hours later, the president was out of surgery and in stable condition.[13] Reagan survived the surgery and made a good recovery. We can speculate how history might have been changed had Garfield and McKinley had access to modern medicine. Reagan's wound, from what can be learned, was at the onset much more life-threatening than that of Garfield and McKinley, who would both have almost certainly survived had proper attention been given to prevent infection.

According to Reagan's surgeon at George Washington University Hospital, if Reagan had been taken to the White House instead of George Washington Hospital he could have been killed by the bullet which lodged only an inch from his heart. The implication was that emergency surgery was required to save Reagan's life. Dr. Benjamin Aaron stated that it was only because Reagan received immediate and highly skilled modern shock trauma therapy that he was in no danger of dying. The surgery to recover the bullet was more difficult than anticipated, and the effort to find the bullet was almost given up three times.[14] The president was on the edge of a precipitous drop in blood pressure and dangerous shock. When Reagan came into the hospital, he was bleeding internally very vigorously and at an alarming rate. He had lost 30 percent of his blood volume according to Dr. Aaron.[15] Reagan did recover fully from his wound.

In 1985 Reagan required surgery again. On July 13 Larry Speakes, the White House spokesman, reported: "Doctors at Bethesda Naval Hospital found a large precancerous growth in Reagan's lower intestine yesterday and scheduled surgery for mid-day today. This type of growth, or polyp, can develop into cancer in about ten to twenty percent of cases; and the risk grows as the polyp becomes larger," Speakes said. "Doctors called Reagan's polyp large."[16]

On July 12, 1985, Nancy Reagan called Donald Regan from Bethesda Naval Hospital to tell him that Ronald would require colon surgery to remove a large polyp; she also added that the surgery would be delayed for a day and a half. Regan feared that the first lady was choosing the date for surgery after consultation with an astrologer. Soon thereafter Dr. Barton Smith, White House physician, called Regan to tell him that the tumor was not malignant but could become so. The mass was described by Smith as being as large as a golf ball.[17] However, the mass did turn out to be malignant. After the surgery Reagan spent much of July recovering from the operation. He was reported to have said following the surgery that he had not had cancer as such. "I didn't have cancer," he told Lou Gannon, "I had something inside of me, with cancer in it, and it was removed."[18]

On July 12, 1985, Reagan had a CAT scan and some other tests. The scan was delayed twice by power surges due to storms. At 11:00 P.M. Reagan was told that the scan showed no evidence of liver involvement by the tumor—which was good news indeed. Mrs. Reagan had already instructed Larry Speakes, the White House spokesman, not to use the word "cancer" or "masses."

The surgery was a success. The surgeon removed a polyp 0.5 cm. across and two smaller polyps, plus a section of his colon. The president slept from 11:28 A.M. until about 7:00 P.M.; and during that time interval Bush was president, empowered by a letter written before surgery by Reagan and covering the provisions of the Twenty-fifth Amendment.[19]

The president's letter read as follows:

I am about to undergo surgery during which time I will be briefly and temporarily incapable of discharging the Constitutional powers and duties of the office of the President of the United States. After consultation with my counsel and the Attorney General, I am mindful of the provisions of Section III of the 25th Amendment to the Constitution and of the uncertainties of its applications to such brief and temporary periods of incapacity. I do not believe that the drafters of this amendment intended its application to situations such as the instant one. Nevertheless, consistent with my long-standing arrangement with Vice-President Bush, and not intending to see a precedent binding to anyone privileged to hold the office in the future, I have determined, and it is my intention and direction, that Vice-President George Bush shall discharge these powers and duties in my stead commencing with the administration of anesthesia to me in this instance.

I shall advise you and the Vice-President when I determine that I am able to resume the discharge of the constitutional powers and duties of this office.

May God bless this nation and us all.

Sincerely, Ronald Reagan.[20]

This was the first time that such delegation of power had been made. Before, when Eisenhower had tried to make arrangements to give temporary presidential powers to Nixon during his illnesses, there were no such clear-cut provisions as were made by Reagan. In fact, the wording of the agreement between Eisenhower and Nixon left much more reason for confusion than for clarification.[21]

As Reagan emerged from the operating room, the doctors remarked on his remarkable physique. He was 74 at the time and already the oldest man ever to serve in his office. The surgeons exclaimed, "This man has the insides of a forty year old."[22]

Reagan's recovery from his surgery was uneventful and no radiation therapy was required. He did spend most of July 1985 recovering from the surgery. The cancer had penetrated the wall of the intestine but apparently had not spread further. This was a degree worse than a malignant polyp with no spread beyond the polyp itself. His abdominal lymph nodes were free of metastases, and the scan showed no liver involvement. There was only a good but not an excellent chance that it would not recur. The very nature of the lesion and the extent of tissue involvement would require a close periodic checkup by scoping, X rays, and scans of his intestines and liver.[23] Since the bowel surgery, Reagan has reported periodically to Bethesda Naval Hospital for checkups. To date, there has been no evidence of recurrence.

Reagan did, however, have trouble later with other polyps and with skin cancer. On July 28, 1987, two small, apparently benign polyps were removed from the president's gastrointestinal tract. The procedure was performed at the White House during a routine medical examination and colonoscopy. Reagan was given CAT scans every six months since his cancer surgery in 1985. His physician, Colonel John E. Hutton, said the polyps were small and apparently benign.[24] On June 31, 1987, President Reagan had a small skin cancer removed from his nose. Biopsy showed the lesion to be a small basal cell carcinoma. The president then had a large area of tissue excised surrounding the lesion. The surgery was done under local anesthesia at Bethesda Naval Hospital.[25]

In November 1987 surgeons found that the president had an enlarged prostate. He was told that the condition could be relieved by a transurethral resection, a technique which is less difficult and less apt to cause complications. Mrs. Reagan wished to have it seem that the problem and the surgical procedure were not of any great significance and that he should be viewed by all as being able to resume a normal routine after he was discharged from the hospital. Donald Regan assumed that she had consulted her astrologer; and she wished on the one hand to have the public believe that Reagan could resume full duties immediately, but on the other hand she advised the chief of staff that her husband would not be allowed to fulfill very important engagements already scheduled. Reagan's surgery went well as do most such cases.[26]

Susanne Jeffers, the author of *Hard Bodies*, depicts the Reagan administration as one whose success pivoted on the ability of Ronald Reagan and his administration to depict themselves as distinctly masculine, "not merely as men but as decisive, tough, aggressive, strong, and domineering men. Ronald Reagan became the premier masculine archetype for the 1980's."[27]

It is the presumption of the writer, Jeffers, that Reagan had an image of himself as a macho, "hard bodied" individual. He had played such roles in his years as a movie actor and had carried that image of himself into his presidency. "In the broadest terms, whereas the Reagan years offered the image of a 'hard body' to contrast to the soft bodies of the Carter years."[28]

"Whereas the hard body was, like Reagan's own, male and white, in Reagan's self promoted image—chopping wood at his ranch, riding horses, standing tall at the presidential podium—his was one of those hard bodies not subject to disease, fatigue, or aging."[29]

On January 15, 1988, Reagan was pronounced fit and in excellent condition by White House physician, Dr. John Hutton. The president's annual physical had revealed no evidence of any recurrence of his colon cancer and there were no intestinal polyps. Chest X rays, brain scans, and stress tests were all negative. There had been some concern after Reagan experienced an overnight bout of gastroenteritis.[30]

President Reagan has had periodic six-month checkups since his colon surgery, and no evidence of recurrence has been found. He is, according to all reports, at present in excellent physical condition.[31]

References

1. Anne Edwards, *Early Reagan: The Rise to Power,* pp. 34–35.
2. Lou Gannon, *Ronald Reagan,* p. 12.
3. Ibid., p. 23.
4. Edwards, *Early Reagan,* p. 40.
5. Ronnie Dugger, *On Reagan: The Man and His Presidency,* p. 2.
6. Edwards, *Early Reagan,* p. 99.
7. Bob Schieffer and Gary Paul Gates, *The Acting President,* pp. 178–79.
8. Donald T. Regan, *For the Record,* p. 318.
9. Ibid., p. 278.
10. Ibid., pp. 163–70, passim.
11. Gannon, *Ronald Reagan,* p. 406.
12. Ron Scheiffer, *Washington Post,* March 31, 1981, p. 1.
13. David S. Broder, *Washington Post,* March 31, 1981.
14. Victor Cohn, *Washington Post,* April 16, 1981.
15. Ibid.
16. Roger Rensberger, *Washington Post,* July 13, 1985.
17. Regan, *For the Record,* pp. 4–5.
18. Schieffer and Gates, *The Acting President,* pp. 230–31.
19. Regan, *For the Record,* pp. 7–9.
20. Kenneth R. Crispell and Carlos F. Gomez, *Hidden Illness in the White House,* p. 217.
21. Ibid., p. 207.
22. Regan, *For the Record,* p. 9.
23. Ibid., p. 15.
24. *Journal of Facts on File,* June 26, 1987, p. 482, E1.
25. *Journal of Facts on File,* July 31, 1987, p. 551.
26. Regan, *For the Record,* pp. 67–73.
27. Susan Jeffords, *Hard Bodies: Hollywood Masculinity in the Reagan Era,* p. 11.
28. Ibid., p. 13.
29. Ibid., p. 25.
30. *Journal of Facts on File,* January 15, 1988, p. 19A.
31. *Journal of Facts on File,* February 9, 1988, p. 934, D1.

40

George Herbert Walker Bush

George Walker Bush, the forty-first president of the United States, was born June 12, 1924, in Milton, Massachusetts. The son of an affluent family, Bush attended the Greenwich, Connecticut, Country Day School, Phillips Exeter at Andover, and Yale University.[1]

At his private prep school, Bush was quite active in sports, playing baseball, football, soccer, and tennis. At the age of 13 he entered Phillips Academy at Andover, Massachusetts, where he was captain of the baseball team and the soccer team. In addition, he managed the basketball team. He was voted third-best athlete, third-most popular, and third-most handsome.[2]

Bush's only reverse while at Phillips Exeter came in his senior year when he developed a staphylococcal infection in his right arm, which "turned out to be a brush with death." Apparently, no sulfa drugs were given, although sulfanilamide was available, as well as sulfapyramide, in 1938. It seems unusual that none was tried on George during his stay at Massachusetts General Hospital, where he spent weeks recovering.[3]

After graduation from Phillips Academy Bush went almost directly into the Naval Air Force as an ensign. He had what can be called a very distinguished service record, having his plane shot out from under him on two occasions. The first time Bush was flying his VT 51 off the deck of the *Jacinto,* which was engaged in an attack on the Marianas preparatory to the invasion of Saipan. Under attack by Japanese aircraft, Bush and the other flyers of the squadron were ordered to get their planes off the flight deck. The planes were armed with TNT-filled depth charges and as such presented a great hazard to the *Jacinto* if an armed plane were hit on the deck by enemy fire. Bush did get his plane airborne, but it was soon crippled by either enemy or friendly fire. Bush did land his plane safely in the rough sea; he and his two crew members were rescued in about 30 minutes.

His second downing, and most frightening adventure as a pilot, came on September 2, 1944. The VT 51's assignment on that day was to destroy a radio station on Chichi-shima, one of the Bonin Islands. The radio installations there were sending out signals of approaching U.S. ships which were en route to their targets. When Ensign Bush reached Chichi-shima with his load of TNT bombs, he noted heavy antiaircraft fire. Bush was about to undergo his most severe test of that war in the Pacific. About halfway through its 60-degree dive, the plane was struck, and smoke filled the cockpit. The engine began to cough, and his controls weakened. His plane was not yet close enough to his objective to bomb effectively, and he felt at that time his plane was damaged beyond recovery. Bush fought to continue his dive and released his bombs only at the last minute. He made an effort to keep the plane flying in order to get as far away from the enemy as possible, in order to escape capture, and also to put himself and his crew in a position to be recovered by U.S. forces. When his plane reached an altitude of 1,000 feet, Bush opened the canopy and was ejected from his plane. In being ejected his forehead struck the tail of the plane, and he sustained a deep gash. The two crew members with Bush were lost. Bush floated in a rubber raft which was ejected from the plane at the same time he was. He landed only 10 miles from Bonin Island, and he feared the Japanese would reach him before his own rescuers. He made a great effort to paddle his raft away from the island. His wound, the smoke in his cockpit, and swallowed seawater made him very nauseated. Several hours later he was rescued by a U.S. submarine.[4]

The escapades of the very youthful George Bush under such circumstances served to indicate that he was brave and that he kept his head under very difficult circumstances. After his exploits at sea he received the Distinguished Flying Cross.

After the war Bush, already married to Barbara Pierce, entered Yale, finishing in two and a one-half years. As a first baseman at Yale he was known as an outstanding fielder but only a fair hitter. He played in 51 games during his 2 years on the varsity, which won the Eastern regional both years but lost to California and USC for two years. George hit for a .256 average, with 2 home runs and 23 RBIs, while making 442 putouts and 24 assists and committing only 9 errors. He made Phi Beta Kappa before he graduated from Yale.[5]

Bush is an avid sportsman and apparently stays physically fit. Throughout the years he has kept in shape with a number of physical activities. He has been a tennis player since the age of five. He developed his skills as a tennis player in group lessons under Czech pro Karel Kozeluh. His golf game is hampered by poor putting. He also plays racquetball and pitches horseshoes.[6]

It was while CIA director, at age 51, that Bush began regular jogging as a means of keeping fit. He said, "Some lunch hours I would be joined by one or two other fitness-types from the agency on a three mile run along nearby side roads. On bad weather days we would use an indoor track set up in the basement corridor."[7]

Bush's great liking for sports and his wish to keep physically fit seem to have been passed on to him by his father and mother. In his autobiography he related that his dad, his mother, and his paternal grandmother were first-rate athletes. About his mother's athletic prowess, he said, "She wasn't big, but she was a match for anyone in tennis, golf, basketball, or baseball—for that matter I don't recall a foot race Mother was ever in that she did not come in first."[8]

After graduating from Yale George chose to move with his wife to Texas and work as a trainee with Dresser Industries in Odessa, Texas. After less than one year in Texas, he transferred to California where he worked at several jobs with the same company before his return to Texas in 1958. The Bushes had two children by the time they had returned to Texas. A daughter, Robin, born in 1949, died at three and a half years of age of leukemia. Bush described the child's death as one of the most difficult experiences of his life.[9]

In 1951 Bush and a friend, John Overby, formed their own company, Bush-Overby Oil Development. He remained in the oil business until 1964.

Bush has been characterized as being highly competitive, whatever the arena: he pushed himself. Such competitiveness, of course, has consequences for one's health. In the early 1960s for example, he pushed himself so hard that he responded adversely during his time with Zapata, the oil-drilling company with which his own company was merged. Some of his coworkers related that on trips to Europe George would take a dose of Pepto-Bismol before retiring in order to treat his heartburn.

There were two intervals during which he suffered from bleeding ulcers. The first episode was during his later days with the oil-drilling company in Texas. The last ulcer episode was in 1960 during a congressional race. His intestinal problems have improved since then. At present he has had no relapse of his illness. "Indeed, his fondness for pork rinds, hot tamales, and chili dishes seemed to have settled his stomach."[10]

In 1962 Bush became interested in politics. He challenged Senator Yarborough in 1964 for a seat in the U.S. Senate but was defeated. In 1966 he ran successfully for U.S. House of Representatives. In 1971–72 he served as ambassador to the United Nations. In 1973–74 he was chairman of the Republican National Committee. In the years 1974–75 he served as chief of the U.S. liaison office in Beijing, China. Bush was director of the CIA

1976–77, and was vice president of the United States under Ronald Reagan, 1981–89. During the interval 1962–88 Bush suffered no serious illness and maintained a good state of physical fitness.

Very early in life Bush became an advocate of physical fitness. In 1990 he gave his views on physical fitness to a group of health and fitness writers: "Some people think that I kind of put it on in terms of sports and physical activity, but I have done this my whole life. An example of an athletic presidency can set a tone for this concept of ideas."

As president he usually ran three days a week. He also played horseshoes. He installed a stationary bicycle outside his Oval Office, and he also liked to work the Stairmaster exercise machine. He believes in physical fitness for all Americans and decries the notion held by some that exercise is a high access, elitist occupation. "I think anybody can participate in certain kinds of fitness," he said. "Some can afford snappy apparatus like cycles and plenty of others can't, but the concept of an individual doing some form of calisthenics to stay fit transcends economic lines. They may not get as much fun out of it. They may not get the exhilaration that comes from competitive sports, but the point I want to try to emphasize is that even someone who is not doing so well economically can stay physically fit." Bush runs about 2 miles in 20 minutes. "I used to do four miles in about eight minutes and fifty seconds per mile," he said, "but age has been catching up with me. That's what gets me. When I run on the hard stuff I don't feel it when I'm running, but that night I have to put a pillow between my legs."[11]

Bush is the first president since Jefferson to make a clear-cut statement of his views on physical fitness and health. Jefferson wrote a letter answering Dr. Vine Utley, who was conducting what we now call a clinical survey of some of the great men of his time to determine their mode of living. The letter dated March 2, 1819, was quoted in Chapter 3 on Jefferson.[12]

But even avid exercisers can have medical problems: "Bush Hospitalized with an Irregular Heartbeat." This headline from the *Washington Post* for Sunday, May 5, 1991, sent a sort of shockwave throughout the country. The significance of the president's irregular heartbeat was variably interpreted. In fact, some of the local radio stations reported that the president had suffered a heart attack while jogging at Camp David. Immediately after the news break there was widespread speculation about the status of the president's health. Part of the alarm occurred among those who felt that vice president Dan Quayle might become president and were worried about his ability to take over in case of Bush's disablement. There was a thought that if Bush became no longer able to serve as president, it would be necessary to invoke the Twenty-fifth Amendment. The scenario reminded one of Garfield's wounding by an assassin in 1882 when Garfield lay ill for 11 weeks before he died. At that time the country in general, and the president's party in particular, were as much concerned by the possibility of Chester A. Arthur's succeeding to the presidency as they were about Garfield's health.

Bush was jogging, as was his custom, at about 4:20 P.M. on May 4 with his Secret Service agents when he complained of fatigue and shortness of breath. Bush then walked to the Camp David infirmary where Dr. Michael Nash, one of his team of physicians, determined that Bush had atrial fibrillation.[13]

Here began a real round of speculation. The label "atrial fibrillation" needs much explaining. The initial thought in the mind of a nonmedical person was that the president had serious heart disease underlying the atrial fibrillation.

Atrial fibrillation is really a rapid, irregular heartbeat which arises in the atrium itself and is conducted to the ventricle in a more or less chaotic fashion. The list of causes is very long and includes arteriosclerotic heart disease, rheumatic heart disease, several forms of congenital heart disease, electrolyte imbalance, pulmonary embolism, congenital heart disease, and certain types of thyroid disease.

The speculation on the cause of the president's atrial fibrillation was ended after a number of tests were run at Bethesda Naval Hospital and it was determined that the president was suffering from a not unusual cause of atrial fibrillation — thyrotoxicosis.

When the president arrived at Bethesda Naval Hospital, his ventricular rate was 150 and grossly irregular. The White House physician diagnosed the irregular rhythm as atrial fibrillation. Bush was given an electrocardiogram, an echocardiogram, and several blood tests, which indicated no underlying heart disease. The next step taken was to give the president medication to slow his heart rate. The first drug given for that purpose was Digoxin, a form of digitalis. The second drug given was Pronestyl (procainamide), which may help to convert the heart to normal rhythm, but it is not always successful. By Sunday night the treatment had returned his heart to normal rhythm. The use of electric shock, or cardioversion, was ruled out. Bush went back into atrial fibrillation soon after he left the hospital, but was back in normal sinus rhythm by 9:45 A.M. on May 7.[14]

Bush's physicians, after further tests, announced that the cause of his atrial fibrillation was hyperthyroidism (Grave's Disease). This is a disease in which the signs and symptoms are produced by an excess of the thyroid hormone. The cause of Grave's Disease is unknown. One of its manifestations is cardiac arrhythmias, including atrial fibrillation. The diagnosis seems a bit unusual since the president's wife, Barbara, had been treated for Grave's Disease in 1989.[15]

The president had another short run of his atrial fibrillation after returning to the White House on Tuesday, May 7, but the rhythm returned to normal in minutes. Bush was started on coumadin, an anticoagulant, to prevent clots in the atrium and subsequent possible emboli to the brain. Emboli from clots formed in the atrium during atrial fibrillation are a dreaded complication of this arrhythmia.

Bush returned to Bethesda Naval Hospital on Wednesday, May 8, where he swallowed a dose of radioactive iodine. This atomic cocktail takes about 24 hours to concentrate selectively in the thyroid where it can be scanned by X ray. His thyroid function was determined to be 10–20 percent above normal, and on May 8 and 9 he drank doses of radioactive iodine which selectively destroyed thyroid function.[16] Bush told reporters that the doctors had advised him to slow his athletic activities, but that he would not have to alter his work schedule.[17]

Bush's condition did, however, produce a delicate political dilemma. After the president's atrial fibrillation persisted through Sunday night and on into Monday, May 6, there was speculation among the doctors about ending the atrial fibrillation by electrical defibrillation in case his rhythm did not return to normal on drugs. There were, of course, two things which could cause some hesitation to perform this procedure. First, there is a small, but real risk, to this form of treatment. Second, the president, if only briefly, must be put to sleep, which would involve the Twenty-fifth Amendment. Presidential authority would have to be briefly transferred to the vice president, Dan Quayle. Fortunately, the reversion to a normal sinus rhythm obviated the need for the use of such procedure.

Bush's health again became the focus of national political attention in January 1992 while the president was on a trade mission to Japan. Bush must have known very well the risks of combining jet lag, overwork, alien food, and alien viruses; but he chose to hazard them all in an attempt to achieve a better trade atmosphere between the United States and Japan. If Bush did not succeed in the latter, he established an absolute first in American foreign relations. No president from Washington up to the time of George Walker Bush had ever vomited on a Japanese prime minister. In fact, no American president had ever vomited on any foreign representative, at any level.

The headlines read: "Bush Collapses in Japan" and sent another shock of anxiety through the land similar to the incidents of early May 1991. The collapse occurred at a state dinner in the residence of the

Japanese premier, Kiichi Miyazawa. The president had told his physician, Dr. Burton Lee, earlier in the evening that he did not feel well. The doctor diagnosed Bush as having a "brush with the flu" and recommended that he not go to the dinner.

Bush arrived at the premier's residence at about 7:50 P.M. and at approximately 8:20 P.M. he became pale and slumped in his chair. He then vomited and collapsed into the arms of the premier of Japan, who was seated by Bush and who cradled Bush's head in his lap briefly. Bush was then lowered to the floor by the Secret Service men who had rushed to his aid. Within three minutes Bush became conscious, rose to his feet and declared that he felt fine. "I just wanted to get some attention," he quipped, according to the press secretary, Marlin Fitzwater. Secret Service agents smoothed his hair, helped him put on his coat, and drove him back to his hotel.[18]

On the morning after Bush collapsed at the abode of the Japanese premier he canceled some appearances. With the campaign for reelection just around the corner, there arose the same sort of speculation as had occurred in May 1991 when Bush had his temporary problem with atrial fibrillation. The concern level was elevated somewhat by the on-the-scene video coverage as Bush collapsed at the banquet table, vomited, and with his mouth agape slumped into the lap of the prime minister.

Marlin Fitzwater, the White House spokesman, announced on Thursday morning that Bush was still weak, but feeling better, and that he would go back to the prescribed schedule late in the day.[19] Barbara Bush, the president's wife, maintained her composure throughout the entire episode. The Japanese prime minister later sent Barbara a note praising her action throughout the evening. She was able to preserve some calm among those around her by her evident aplomb and spontaneous wit. She jokingly blamed his distress on losing a tennis match earlier in the day to Emperor Akihito and Crown Prince Naruhito. She said, "We Bushes aren't used to that, so he felt much worse than I thought."[20]

The Associated Press reported that a caller who claimed to be the president's physician reported to CNN on Wednesday that the president had died. The CNN Headline News was on the verge of reporting it when the editors realized that the call was a hoax.[21]

At a press conference January 9 Marlin Fitzwater repeated that Bush's illness was no more than a 24-hour gastrointestinal flu. Bush, a 67-year-old man, had pursued a grinding schedule on the 10-day trip. He had worked a 16-hour day and had flown 19,000 miles. After his return from Japan Bush was proclaimed to be over his spate of illness and returned to his normal schedule.

In a related medical incident, the White House announced on February 5 that the president would no longer take the sleeping pill Halcion. The drug had been banned in Great Britain in 1991 after critics alleged that it caused a variety of behaviorial side effects in some persons, such as depression, paranoia, and hallucinations. Newspaper writers had questioned whether Bush's well-known tangled syntax or his sudden illness in Japan on January 8 had been due to the pill.[22]

On March 26 Bush underwent a comprehensive medical checkup, after which his physician pronounced him to be in perfect health. However, he said that the president was under a great deal of stress and needed a more relaxing schedule. Doctors removed four small noncancerous skin growths, called keratoses, from Bush's face.[23]

Since leaving office, Bush has continued in good health. He jogs and plays tennis to keep in shape. He has a periodic checkup for his heart problem.

References

1. David C. Whitney, *The American Presidents*, p. 433.
2. William A. Degregorio, *The Complete Book of U.S. Presidents*, p. 22.
3. Fitzhugh Green, *George Bush: An Intimate Portrait*, p. 22.
4. Ibid., pp. 38–39.
5. Degregorio, *The Complete Book of U.S. Presidents*, pp. 667–68.
6. Ibid., pp. 668–69.
7. George Bush and Victor Gold, *Looking Forward: An Autobiography*, p. 169.
8. Ibid., p. 26.
9. Whitney, *The American Presidents*, p. 436.
10. Green, *George Bush*, p. 82.
11. Abigail Trafford, "Health," *Washington Post*, May 7, 1991, p. 12.
12. William Cope and Adrian William Bedees, editors, *The Life and Selected Writings of Thomas Jefferson*, pp. 690–91.
13. *Washington Post*, Sunday, May 5, 1991, p. A-1.
14. Larry Thompson and Carol Krukcoff, "Health," *Washington Post*, May 7, 1991, p. 10.
15. *Journal of Facts on File*, "Hosp. for Thyrotoxicosis and Irregular Heartbeat," May 1991, p. 336, D2.
16. William Booth, "Bush Begins Tests to Find Cause of Thyroid Disease," *Raleigh News and Observer*, May 9, 1991, p. 9A.
17. *Journal of Facts on File*, "Bush checked for thyroid function and irregular heartbeat," May 9, 1991, p. 336, D2.
18. *Journal of Facts on File*, "Bush Collapses in Japan," January 8, 1992, p. 18E.
19. *Greensboro News and Record*, January 9, 1992, p. 7A.
20. Ibid.

    21. Ibid.
    22. *Journal of Facts on File,* "Question Whether Drug Halcion Caused Collapse in Japan," February 5, 1992, p. 188, B1.
    23. Ibid., "Doctors Urge More Relaxation for Pres. Bush," March 28, 1992, p. 226, A2.

41

William Jefferson
Blythe Clinton

President William Jefferson Blythe Clinton, the forty-second president of the United States, was born on August 19, 1946, in Hope, Arkansas. Hope is in the Bible belt of the South and in earlier days was very depressed economically.[1]

In Bill Clinton's family history, it is related that his mother, Virginia Kelly, recently deceased, was operated on earlier for breast cancer. His paternal grandmother died at the age of 62 of a stroke; his maternal grandfather died at the age of 57 of emphysema; and his natural father drowned in a freak accident before Clinton's birth.[2]

After his natural father, William Blythe, died, Clinton was left with his maternal grandparents while his mother studied in New Orleans to become a nurse anesthetist. Apparently, Clinton's life with his grandparents, other relatives, and friends was pleasant, and he suffered from no feeling of loss or desertion. No recorded evidence exists of any significant childhood health problem except his having had a tonsillectomy at the age of six.

Clinton's mother married Roger Clinton, an alcoholic who was sometimes abusive to Clinton's mother. There was a deposition for divorce proceedings because Bill's mother feared for her own and her son's safety: "He has continually tried to do bodily harm to myself and my son Billy." Eventually, Clinton got to be too big to allow himself to be beaten and threatened his stepfather, "telling him never to lay a hand on his mother again."[3]

Bill Clinton entered Georgetown University in 1964 at the age of 18, receiving his bachelor's degree in 1968. It is not recorded that he engaged in any sports while an undergraduate at Georgetown. He was a Rhodes Scholar at Oxford University, England, from 1968 to 1970. From 1971 to 1973 Clinton attended law school at Yale University. He is said to have begun jogging while he was at Yale Law School.

Clinton returned to Fayetteville, Arkansas, and taught law at the

University of Arkansas Law School, 1973–77. He was elected attorney general of Arkansas in 1976 and governor of Arkansas in 1978 where he served from 1979 to 1992 except for a two-year interval, 1981–82. During these years Clinton's health was generally good. He is married to Hillary Rodham Clinton and has a daughter, Chelsea.

President Clinton does have a few medical problems, none major, which are chronic and persistent—not life threatening. One of these was quite evident during his arduous speaking schedule in the 1992 presidential campaign: his hoarseness. He has also been troubled by gastrointestinal symptoms which have been attributed to reflux esophagitis. The latter condition is caused by the failure of the sphincter between the stomach and the esophagus to prevent the acid contents of the stomach from entering the lower esophageal area. The lower esophagus is not anatomically suited to the high acid content occurring in the stomach. The tendency for the acid reflux to occur is aided by a low pressure in the lower esophagus, increased intraabdominal pressure, a recumbent position, bending, tight binders or girdles, obesity, or most importantly, loss of tone of the sphincter (valve) between the stomach and esophagus.

The president saw several physicians for his health problems during his presidential campaign: Susan M. Santa Cruz, an internist; Andrew G. Kumpuris, a cardiologist; Kelsy J. Caplinger, an allergist; and James Y. Suen, an otolaryngologist, all of Little Rock, Arkansas. Dr. Suen is professor and chairman of Head and Neck Oncology at the University of Arkansas Medical Center.

On October 15, 1992, the Associated Press reported, "Clinton's Health Generally Strong." It was stated that Clinton was in excellent health and was winning his battle against high cholesterol. His physicians were reported to have said that his worst health problems were bouts of heartburn and hoarseness due to overuse of his voice.[4] The medical report issued by Susan Santa Cruz on October 13, 1992, indicated that Clinton was at that time without specific medical complaints. Dr. Santa Cruz did state that Clinton had been seen by Dr. Kelsy Caplinger for evaluation and treatment of his environmental allergies. Clinton was taking a prescription antihistamine, Hismanal, for treatment of these. Symptoms from his allergic reactions were reported to be sinus congestion, nasal drainage, and occasional swelling of the temporal area, the latter resolving after a couple of hours. The report indicated no serious allergic reactions such as anaphylaxis.[5]

Past medical history given by Dr. Santa Cruz included surgery to create sinus windows in 1979, a tonsillectomy in 1952, left knee ligament strain in 1984, and a colonoscopy for rectal bleeding in 1984, which showed no evidence for significant pathology including polyps or tumorous growths.[6] Physical findings recorded by Dr. Santa Cruz after her physical examination of Clinton revealed a well-developed, well-nourished white male. His blood pressure was 118/70. Pulse rate 78 beats per minute and regular. His weight was 226 pounds. He was noted to have a ruddy complexion. His pupils were equal and reactive to light and accommodation. His fundoscopic examination was normal. There was no excessive redness of the nasal musosa. No sinus tenderness was noted. His neck examination showed no venous distension, bruits, thyroid enlargement, or enlarged lymph nodes. His pulmonary examination was normal. His cardiovascular examination showed a regular rhythm without any evidence of murmurs, gallops, or rubs. His heart size was normal by palpation. Abdominal and back examinations were normal. Genital and rectal examinations were normal—including a normal prostatic examination. Stool was negative for occult blood.[7] This report showed only negative findings with the exception of his being overweight.

There was also a medical report issued by Kelsy J. Caplinger, also of Little Rock, who saw Bill Clinton in the fall of 1991 for an allergy evaluation: "He has a history of nasal congestion, swelling of his eyes, and difficulty breathing through his nose. His nasal congestion was so severe in the spring of 1991 that he had difficulty running. There is no history of wheezing, asthma, or severe allergic reaction. His signs and symptoms are worse in the fall. He is noted to be a nonsmoker."

Allergy skin tests showed moderate reaction to house dust, mold spores, cat dander, weed pollen, grass pollens, beef, and milk. He was begun on allergy injections with an extract containing the inhalants to which he was reactive. He tolerated the injections well. Included in the medical report was the notation that he was on the usual maintenance dose and was taking his injections every two weeks, depending on symptoms. The diagnosis was allergic rhinitis without complications. His food allergies were handled by elimination of certain foods in his diet. He was last seen by Dr. Caplinger on September 30, 1992, and was showing satisfactory improvement. He was scheduled for a complete checkup in the fall of 1992.[8]

A third medical report, written by James Suen, of Little Rock, dated October 13, 1992, stated that Dr. Suen had been following Bill Clinton for the preceding 12 months for voice problems. There was a history of hoarseness when he talked excessively—especially during campaigns. The hoarseness was due to a combination of nasal allergies and esophageal reflux. His allergy symptoms were fairly well controlled with allergy shots, antihistamines, and avoiding certain foods.

For his esophageal reflux, he was on a diet to eliminate certain foods. He left out caffeine and took medications to reduce gastric acid production. He also took antacids and slept on a wedge.[9] The wedge is employed to elevate the upper part of the body while he is reclining. This device through the effect of gravity reduces the tendency of acid gastric juices to reflux into the lower third of his esophagus.

A fourth and perhaps the most significant medical report was issued by Andrew Kumpuris of Little Rock, in which he gave additional information regarding President Clinton's health. Under "Medical Habits" he related the president gave no history of cigarette smoking and that he drank socially. He also reported that he jogged regularly. Dr. Kumpuris also related that he did a physical examination on Clinton on August 27, 1991. His physical examination at that time was totally unremarkable. Clinton's blood pressure was 130/70. His pulse rate was 75 beats per minute. His weight and height were acceptable for his age. A battery of blood chemistry tests were done in which it was found that his sodium was 140, his potassium was 4.2, his chloride was 99, his CO_2 content was 30, his urea nitrogen was 15, his creatinine was 1.0, his fasting glucose was 104, his calcium was 9.9, his fasting cholesterol was 184, his fasting triglycerides were 59, and his uric acid was 6.3. Hematological tests showed a white blood count to be 5.5, hemoglobin 15.8 grams percent, hematocrit 45, platelets 223,000, platelet estimate normal, and a recent electrocardiogram performed August 27, 1992, was unremarkable (all of the above tests were perfectly normal).[10]

One of the most significant bits of medical information regarding the president's physical state was that obtained from Dr. Kumpuris in which he reported the results of Clinton's stress tests. A recently done stress test by Kumpuris using a standard Bruce protocol showed that Clinton achieved 91 percent of his maximum heart rate and was able to go for 14 minutes on the treadmill. There were no electrocardiographic changes either during or after the test. The results were completely normal and demonstrated an excellent exercise tolerance.[11] In fact, the treadmill test was very good. In the Bruce protocol 14 minutes carried the president 2 minutes into the fifth stage which is quite good for a man of 46. It is good that Bill Clinton became aware of his moderate cholesterol elevation and now has it under control. Regarding his weight problem, it is reported that he lost 10 pounds during the year prior to his election. The gastric reflux and the allergies are apparently under control. Clinton began his term as president in much better physical condition than most of those who have occupied the Oval Office.

During the 1992 presidential campaign the electorate were very concerned about the fitness of the candidates. The candidates, including Clinton, seemed quite anxious to project an image of fitness and leanness. Both candidate Clinton and President Bush were careful to be seen as often as possible running and sweating.

Since becoming president, Clinton, when the opportunity arises, still continues to jog. He is still somewhat overweight, but his allergies are better.

References

1. Garry Wills, "Beginning of the Road," *Time,* July 20, 1992, p. 34.

2. Susan M. Santa Cruz, Medical report, September 9, 1991; issued October 13, 1992.

3. Wills, "Beginning of the Road," p. 55.

4. *Greensboro News and Record,* "General News," October 15, 1992, p. 4.

5. Santa Cruz, Medical report, September 9, 1991.

6. Ibid.

7. Ibid.

8. Kelsy J. Caplinger, "Allergist Reports on William Clinton," Medical report, August 27, 1991; issued October 12, 1992.

9. James Y. Suen, "Allergist Report on Wm. Clinton," Medical report, issued October 13, 1992.

10. Andrew G. Kumpuris, "Report on Cardiovascular System," Medical report, issued October 12, 1992.

11. Ibid.

Bibliography

Books

Abrahamsen, David. *Nixon vs. Nixon: An Emotional Tragedy.* New York: Farrar, Straus, and Giroux, 1977.

Adams, Charles Francis. *Familiar Letters of John Adams and His Wife Abigail Adams, During the Revolution,* Vol. 1. Boston: Houghton Mifflin and Co., 1875.

Adams, John. *Correspondence of John Adams and Thomas Jefferson.* Indianapolis: Bobbs-Merrill, 1925.

Adams, John Quincy. *Diary of John Quincy Adams, 1794-1845.* Ed. Allan Nevins. New York: Scribner, 1951.

Adams, Samuel Hopkins. *The Incredible Era: The Life and Times of Warren Gamaliel Harding.* Boston: Houghton Mifflin, 1939.

Agnew, D. Hayes. *The Principles and Practices of Surgery.* Philadelphia: J. B. Lippincott, 1878.

Alden, John R. *George Washington: A Biography.* New York: Dell, 1987.

Alexander, Holmes M. *The American Talleyrand.* New York: Harper, 1935.

Ambrose, Stephen E. *Eisenhower: The President,* Vol. 2. New York: Simon & Schuster, 1984.

_____. *Eisenhower: Soldier, General of the Army, President-Elect,* Vol. 1. New York: Simon & Schuster, 1983.

_____. *Nixon: The Education of a Politician, 1913-1962,* Vol. 1. New York: Simon & Schuster, 1987.

_____. *Nixon: The Triumph of a Politician, 1962-1972,* Vol. 2. New York: Simon & Schuster, 1989.

Ammon, Harry. *James Monroe: The Quest for National Identity.* New York: McGraw-Hill, 1971.

Anderson, Judith Icke. *William Howard Taft, an Intimate History.* New York: Norton, 1981.

Anderson, Nancy Scott. *The Generals Ulysses S. Grant and Robert E. Lee.* New York: Knopf, 1988.

Arnett, Ethel Stephens. *Mrs. James Madison: The Incomparable Dolly.* Greensboro, NC: Piedmont Press, 1972.

Baker, Ray Stannard. *Woodrow Wilson: Life and Letters,* Vols. 1 and 2. Garden City, NY: Doubleday, Page, 1927.

Barnard, Harry. *Rutherford B. Hayes and His America.* Indianapolis: Bobbs-Merrill, 1954.

Bassett, John Spencer. *The Life of Andrew Jackson.* New York: Macmillan, 1928.

Bates, Richard O. *The Gentleman from Ohio: An Introduction to Garfield.* Durham, NC: Moore, 1973.

Bauer, K. Jack. *Zachary Taylor.* Baton Rouge: Louisiana State University Press, 1985.

Beale, Howard K. *The Critical Year: A Study of Andrew Johnson and Reconstruction.* New York: F. Ungar, 1958.

Bergeron, Paul H. *The Presidency of James K. Polk.* Lawrence, KS: University Press of Kansas, 1987.

Bishop, Jim. *FDR's Last Year, April 1944–April 1945.* New York: W. Morrow, 1974.

Bishop, Joseph Bucklin. *Theodore Roosevelt and His Time Shown in His Own Letters,* New York: C. Scribner's Sons, 1920.

Blair, Joan, and Clay Blair. *The Search for JFK.* New York: Berkley, 1976.

Boller, Paul F. *Presidential Wives.* New York: Oxford University Press, 1988.

Boorstin, Daniel. "The Mythologizing of George Washington." *George Washington: A Profile.* Ed. James M. Smith. New York: Hill and Wang, 1969.

Boritt, Gabor S., editor, and Norman O. Farness, associate editor. *The Historian's Lincoln.* Urbana: University of Illinois Press, 1988.

Bowen, Catherine Drinker. *John Adams and the American Revolution.* Boston: Little, Brown, 1950.

Bragdon, Henry Wilkinson. *Woodrow Wilson: The Academic Years.* Cambridge, MA: The Belknap Press of Harvard University Press, 1967.

Brant, Irving. *The Fourth President: A Life of James Madison.* Indianapolis: Bobbs-Merrill, 1970.

————. *James Madison: Vol. 6, Commander in Chief, 1812–1836,* Indianapolis: Bobbs-Merrill, 1961.

Brodie, Fawn M. *Richard Nixon: The Shaping of His Character.* Cambridge, MA: Harvard University Press, 1983.

————. *Thomas Jefferson, an Intimate History.* New York: Bantam, 1975.

Bruce, Robert V. *Alexander Graham Bell and the Conquest of Solitude.* Boston: Little, Brown, 1973.

Burner, David. *Herbert Hoover, a Public Life.* New York: Knopf, 1979.

Busch, Noel F. *T. R.; The Story of Theodore Roosevelt and His Influence on Our Times.* New York: Reynal, 1963.

Bush, George, with Victor Gold. *Looking Forward.* Garden City, NY: Doubleday, 1987.

Butt, Archibald W. *Taft and Roosevelt, the Intimate Letters of Archie Butt,* Vol. 1. Garden City, NY: Doubleday, Doran, 1930.

Butterfield, L. H., editor-in-chief. *Adams Family Correspondence,* Volumes 1 and 2. Cambridge, MA: Belknap Press of Harvard University, 1963.

Cannon, Lou. *Reagan.* New York: Putnam, 1982.

Caro, Robert A. *The Years of LBJ: Means of Ascent,* Vol. 2. New York: Knopf, 1990.

————. *The Years of LBJ: The Path to Power,* Vol. 1. New York: Vintage, 1983.

Castel, Albert E. *The Presidency of Andrew Johnson.* Lawrence, KS: Regents Press of Kansas, 1979.

Chesen, Eli S. *President Nixon's Psychiatric Profile.* New York: P. H. Wyden, 1973.

Christian, George. *The President Steps Down.* New York: Macmillan, 1970.

Clark, Leon Pierce. *Lincoln: Psycho-biography.* New York: C Scribner's Sons, 1933.

Cleaves, Freeman. *Old Tippecanoe.* New York: C. Scribner's Sons, 1939.

Coletta, Paolo E. *The Presidency of William Howard Taft.* Lawrence, KS: University Press of Kansas, 1973.

Coolidge, Calvin. *The Autobiography of Calvin Coolidge.* New York: Cosmopolitan, 1929.

Cresson, W. P. *James Monroe.* Chapel Hill: The University of North Carolina Press, 1946.

Crispell, Kenneth R., and Carlos E. Gomez. *Hidden Illness in the White House.* Durham, NC: Duke University Press, 1988.

BIBLIOGRAPHY

305

Cunliffe, Marcus. *George Washington, Man and Monument*. Boston: Little, Brown, 1958.
Cunningham, Homer F. *The Presidents' Last Years*. Jefferson, NC: McFarland, 1989.
Curtis, George Ticknor. *The Life of James Buchanan*, Vol. 2. New York: Harper & Brothers, 1883.
Dana, Charles A. *The Life of Ulysses S. Grant, General of the Armies of the U.S.* Springfield, MA: Gurden, Bill, 1868.
Daniels, Jonathan. *The Man of Independence*. Philadelphia: Lippincott, 1950.
Davis, Burke. *George Washington and the American Revolution*. New York: Random House, 1975.
Davis, John H. *The Kennedys: Dynasty and Disaster, 1848–1983*. New York: McGraw-Hill, 1984.
Davis, Kenneth S. *FDR: The Beckoning of Destiny, 1882–1928*. New York: Putnam, 1972.
_____. *General Eisenhower, Soldier of Democracy*. Garden City, NY: Doubleday, 1949.
DeGregorio, William A. *The Complete Book of U.S. Presidents*. 3rd ed. New York: Barricade, 1991.
de Mause, Lloyd and Henry Ebel, eds. *Jimmy Carter and American Fantasy: Psychohistorical Explorations*. New York: Two Continents, 1977.
Dichter, Marc A. "Epilepsy and Convulsive Disorders." *Harrison's Principles of Internal Medicine*. 10th ed. Ed. Robert G. Petersdorf. New York: McGraw-Hill, 1983. 2018–27.
Dix, Dorothea Lynde. *The Lady and the President: The Letters of Dorothea Dix and Millard Fillmore*. Ed. Charles M. Snyder. Lexington: University Press of Kentucky, 1975.
Doenecke, Justus D. *The Presidencies of James A. Garfield and Chester A. Arthur*. Lawrence: Regents Press of Kansas, 1981.
Downes, Randolph C. *The Rise of Warren Gamaliel Harding, 1865–1920*. Columbus: Ohio State University Press, 1970.
Duffy, Herbert S. *William Howard Taft*. New York: Minton, Balch, 1930.
Dugger, Ronnie. *On Reagan: The Man and His Presidency*. New York: McGraw-Hill, 1983.
Dyer, Brainerd. *Zachary Taylor*. Baton Rouge: Louisiana State University Press, 1946.
East, Robert A. *John Quincy Adams: The Critical Years*. New York: Bookman Associates, 1962.
Eckenrode, H. J. *Rutherford B. Hayes*, Statesman of Reunion. New York: Dodd, Mead, 1930.
Edwards, Anne. *Early Reagan*. New York: Morrow, 1987.
Ehrlichman, John. *Witness to Power: The Nixon Years*. New York: Simon and Schuster, 1982.
Eisenhower, David. *Eisenhower at War, 1943–1945*. New York: Random House, 1986.
Eisenhower, Dwight D. *Mandate for Change, 1953–1956: The White House Years*. Garden City, NY: Doubleday, 1963.
Falkner, Leonard. *The President Who Wouldn't Retire*. New York: Coward-McCann, 1967.
Fleming, Thomas J. *The Man from Monticello: An Intimate Life of Thomas Jefferson*. New York: Morrow, 1969.
Flexner, John Thomas. *Washington, The Indispensible Man*. New York: New American Library, 1984.
Foote, Shelby. *The Civil War*, Vol. 2. New York: Random House, 1958.

Ford, Gerald R. *A Time to Heal.* New York: Harper & Row, 1979.

Frady, Marshall. *Billy Graham: A Parable of American Righteousness.* Boston: Little, Brown, 1979.

Freidel, Frank B. *Franklin D. Roosevelt: Launching the New Deal.* Boston: Little, Brown, 1973.

_____. *Franklin D. Roosevelt: A Rendezvous with Destiny.* Boston: Little, Brown, 1990.

Freud, Sigmund and William C. Bullit. *Thomas Woodrow Wilson, Twenty-eighth President of the United States: A Psychological Study.* Boston: Houghton Mifflin, 1967.

Fuess, Claude. *Calvin Coolidge, the Man from Vermont.* Boston: Little, Brown, 1940.

Gallagher, Hugh Gregory. *FDR's Splendid Deception.* New York: Dodd, Mead, 1985.

Gilman, Daniel C. *James Monroe.* Boston: Houghton Mifflin, 1883.

Glad, Betty. *Jimmy Carter, in Search of the Great White House.* New York: W. W. Norton, 1980.

Glickman, Robert M. "Inflammatory Bowel Disease: Ulcerative Colitis and Crohn's Disease." *Harrison's Principles of Internal Medicine.* 10th ed. Ed. Robert G. Petersdorf. New York: McGraw-Hill, 1983. 1738–51.

Goebel, Dorothy Burne. *William Henry Harrison: A Political Biography.* Indianapolis: Historical Bureau of the Indiana University and Historical Department, 1926.

Goodwin, Doris Kearns. *Lyndon Johnson and the American Dream.* New York: Harper & Row, 1976.

Grant, Ulysses S. *The Papers of Ulysses S. Grant.* Vol. 16. Ed. John Y. Simon. Carbondale: Southern Illinois University Press, 1967–1991.

_____. *Ulysses S. Grant: Warrior and Statesman.* New York: Morrow, 1969.

Grayson, Cary T. *Woodrow Wilson: An Intimate Memoir.* New York: Holt, Rinehart, and Winston, 1960.

Green, Fitzhugh. *George Bush: An Intimate Portrait.* New York: Hippodcrene Books, 1989.

Green, James A. *William Henry Harrison, His Life and Times.* Richmond, VA: Garrett and Massie, 1941.

Gunther, John. *Eisenhower, the Man and the Symbol.* New York: Harper, 1952.

Hamilton, Holman. *Zachary Taylor, Soldier in the White House.* Indianapolis: Bobbs-Merrill, 1951.

Hammond, John Hays. *The Autobiography of John Hays Hammond,* Vol. 2. New York: Farrar & Rinehart, 1935.

Harrison, Benjamin. *The Correspondence Between Benjamin Harrison and James G. Blaine, 1882–1893.* Ed. Albert T. Volwiler. Philadelphia: The American Philosophical Society, 1940.

Hecht, Marie B. *John Quincy Adams: A Personal History of an Independent Man.* New York: Macmillan, 1972.

Hesseltine, William B. *Ulysses S. Grant, Politician.* New York: Dodd, Mead, 1935.

Hill, Gladwin. *Dancing Bear: An Inside Look at California Politics.* Cleveland: World, 1968.

Howe, George Frederick. *Chester A. Arthur.* New York: Dodd, Mead, 1934.

Hume, Edgar Erskine. *Victories of Army Medicine.* Philadelphia: J. B. Lippincott, 1943.

Irwin, Washington. *George Washington: A Biography.* Ed. Charles Nelder. Garden City, NY: Doubleday, 1976.

Irwin, Will. *Herbert Hoover, a Reminiscent Biography.* New York: Grosset & Dunlap, 1928.

Jackson, Andrew. *The Papers of Andrew Jackson*, Vol. 2.. Ed. Sam B. Smith and Harriet C. Owsley. Knoxville: University of Tennessee Press, 1980.

James, Marquis. *Andrew Jackson, the Border Captain*. Vol. 1. Indianapolis: Bobbs-Merrill, 1933.

Jefferson, Thomas. *The Life and Selected Writings of Thomas Jefferson*. Ed. Adrienne Koch and William Peden. New York: Modern Library, 1944.

Jeffords, Susan. *Hard Bodies: Hollywood Masculinity in the Reagan Era*. New Brunswick, NJ: Rutgers University Press, 1993.

Jenkins, Roy. *Truman*. New York: Harper & Row, 1986.

Johnson, Andrew. *The Papers of Andrew Johnson*, Vol. 2. Ed. Leroy P. Graf and Ralph W. Haskins. Knoxville: University of Tennessee Press, 1967.

Johnson, Gerald W. *Andrew Jackson, an Epic in Homespun*. New York: Minton, Balch, 1927.

Johnson, Lyndon B. *The Vantage Point: Perspectives of the President, 1963–1969*. New York: Holt, Rinehart and Winston, 1971.

Jordan, Hamilton. *Crisis: The Last of the Carter Presidency*. New York: Putnam, 1982.

Kaplan, Justin. *Mr. Clemens and Mark Twain*. New York: Simon and Schuster, 1966.

Ketcham, Ralph Louis. *James Madison: A Biography*. New York: Macmillan, 1971.

Kimball, Marie Goebel. *Jefferson, War and Peace, 1776 to 1784*. New York: Coward-McCann, 1947.

Klein, Herbert. *Making It Perfectly Clear*. Garden City, NY: Doubleday, 1980.

Klein, Philip S. *President James Buchanan, a Biography*. University Park: Pennsylvania State University Press, 1962.

Kornitzer, Bela. *The Great American Heritage: The Story of the Five Eisenhower Brothers*. New York: Farrar, Straus and Cadahy, 1955.

Lasky, Victor. *Jimmy Carter, the Man & the Myth*. New York: R. Marek, 1979.

Leech, Margaret. *In the Days of McKinley*. New York: Harper, 1959.

L'Etang, Hugh. *The Pathology of Leadership*. New York: Hawthorn Books, 1970.

Link, Arthur S. *Woodrow Wilson, a Brief Biography*. Cleveland: World Publishing Co., 1963.

Lorant, Stefan. *The Life and Times of Theodore Roosevelt*. Garden City, NY: Doubleday, 1959.

Ludwig, Emil. *Lincoln*. Boston: Little, Brown, and Co., 1930.

Lunn, Arnold Henry Moore. *Matterhorn Centenary*. Chicago: Rand McNally, 1965.

Lynch, Denis Tilden. *An Epoch and a Man, Martin Van Buren and His Times*. New York: H. Liveright, 1929.

_____. *Grover Cleveland, a Man Four-Square*. New York: H. Liveright, 1932.

Lyon, Peter. *Eisenhower: Portrait of the Hero*. Boston: Little, Brown, 1974.

Lyons, Eugene. *Herbert Hoover, a Biography*. Garden City, NY: Doubleday, 1964.

McCoy, Donald R. *Calvin Coolidge: The Quiet President*. New York: Macmillan, 1967.

McCullough, David. *Truman*. New York: Simon & Schuster, 1992.

McElroy, Robert. *Grover Cleveland, the Man and the Statesman*, Vol. 2. New York: Harper & Brothers, 1923.

McFeely, William S. *Grant: A Biography*. New York: Norton, 1981.

McGee, Dorothy Horton. *Herbert Hoover: Engineer, Humanitarian, Statesman*. New York: Dodd, Mead, 1959.

MacKenzie, Catherine Dunlop. *Alexander Graham Bell: The Man Who Contracted Space*. Boston: Houghton Mifflin, 1928.

Malone, Dumas. *Jefferson and His Time: The Sage of Monticello*, Vol. 6. Boston: Little, Brown, 1981.

Mapp, Alf J. *Thomas Jefferson: A Strange Case of Mistaken Identity.* New York: Madison Books, 1987.

Marx, Rudolph. *The Health of the Presidents.* New York: Putnam, 1960.

Masters, Edgar Lee. *Lincoln, the Man.* New York: Dodd, Mead, 1931.

Mazlish, Bruce. *In Search of Nixon: A Psychohistorical Inquiry.* New York: Basic Books, 1972.

_____ and Edwin Diamond. *Jimmy Carter: A Character Portrait.* New York: Simon and Schuster, 1979.

Mazo, Earl and Stephen Hess. *Nixon: A Political Portrait.* New York: Harper & Row, 1968.

Means, Gaston B. *The Strange Death of President Harding.* New York: Guild, 1930.

Miller, Merle. *Lyndon, An Oral Biography.* New York: Putnam, 1980.

_____. *Plain Speaking: An Oral Biography of Harry S Truman.* New York: Berkley, 1974.

Miller, Nathan. *FDR, An Intimate History.* Garden City, NY: Doubleday, 1983.

Mills, Judie. *John F. Kennedy.* New York: F. Watts, 1988.

Milton, George Fort. *The Age of Hate: Andrew Johnson and the Radicals.* New York: Coward-McCann, 1930.

Mohr, Jay P., Carlos S. Kase, and Raymond D. Adams. "Cerebrovascular Diseases." *Harrison's Principles of Internal Medicine.* 10th ed. Ed. Robert G. Petersdorf. New York: McGraw-Hill, 1983. 2028–60.

Moore, Virginia. *The Madisons: A Biography.* New York: McGraw-Hill, 1979.

Moran, Charles McMoran Wilson. *Churchill: The Struggle for Survival, 1940–1965, Taken from the Diaries of Lord Moran,* Boston: Houghton Mifflin, 1966.

Morgan, H. Wayne. *William McKinley and His America.* Syracuse, NY: Syracuse University Press, 1963.

Morgan, James. *Our Presidents: Brief Biographies of Our Chief Magistrates.* New York: Macmillan, 1924.

Morgan, Kay Summersby. *Eisenhower Was My Boss.* New York: Prentice-Hall, 1948.

Morgan, Ted. *FDR: A Biography.* New York: Simon and Schuster, 1985.

Morrell, Martha McBride. *"Young Hickory," The Life and Times of President James K. Polk.* New York: G. P. Dutton, 1949.

Morris, Edmund. *The Rise of Theodore Roosevelt.* New York: Coward, McCann & Geoghegan, 1979.

Morris, Roger. *Richard Milhous Nixon: The Rise of an American Politician.* New York: Holt, 1990.

Morse, John. *John Adams.* Boston: Houghton, Mifflin, 1884.

Moses, John B. and Wilbur Cross. *Presidential Courage.* New York: Norton, 1980.

Murray, John F. "Diffuse Infiltrative Diseases of the Lung." *Harrison's Principles of Internal Medicine.* 10th ed. Ed. Robert G. Petersdorf. New York: McGraw-Hill, 1983. 1553–58.

Murray, Robert K. *The Harding Era: Warren G. Harding and His Administration.* Minneapolis: University of Minnesota Press, 1969.

Neal, Steve. *The Eisenhowers: Reluctant Dynasty.* Garden City, NY: Doubleday, 1978.

Nessen, Ron. *It Sure Looks Different from the Inside.* Chicago: Playboy, 1978.

Nevins, Allan. *Grover Cleveland: A Study in Courage.* New York: Dodd, Mead, 1932.

Nichols, Roy Franklin. *Franklin Pierce, Young Hickory of the Granite Hills.* Philadelphia: University of Pennsylvania Press, 1931.

Niven, John. *Martin Van Buren: The Romantic Age of American Politics.* New York: Oxford University Press, 1983.

Nixon, Richard M. *In the Arena: A Memoir of Victory, Defeat, and Renewal.* New York: Simon and Schuster, 1990.

_____. *Six Crises.* Garden City, NY: Doubleday, 1962.

Oates, Stephen B. *Abraham Lincoln, The Man Behind the Myths.* New York: Harper & Row, 1984.

_____. *With Malice Toward None: The Life of Abraham Lincoln.* New York: New American Library, 1978.

Olcott, Charles S. *The Life of William McKinley.* Boston: Houghton Mifflin, 1916.

Osborne, John. *The Last Nixon Watch.* Washington: New Republic, 1975.

Osler, William. *The Principles and Practices of Medicine.* New York: D. Appleton, 1892.

Parks, Lillian. *My Thirty Years Backstairs at the White House.* New York: Fleet, 1961.

Parmet, Herbert S. *Eisenhower and the American Crusades.* New York: Macmillan, 1972.

_____. *Jack: The Struggles of JFK.* New York: Dial, 1980.

_____. *JFK, the Presidency of John F. Kennedy.* New York: Dial, 1983.

_____. *Richard Nixon and His America.* Boston: Little, Brown, 1990.

Parton, James. *Life of Andrew Jackson,* Volumes 1, 2, and 3. New York: Mason Brothers, 1860.

Pepper, William. *A Text-book of the Theory and Practice of Medicine,* Vols. 1 and 2. Philadelphia: W. B. Saunders, 1893–1894.

Peskin, Allen. *Garfield: A Biography.* Kent, OH: Kent State University Press, 1978.

Petersdorf, Robert G., ed. *Harrison's Principles of Internal Medicine.* 10th ed. New York: McGraw-Hill, 1983.

Peterson, Norma Lois. *The Presidencies of William Henry Harrison and John Tyler.* Lawrence, KS: University Press of Kansas, 1989.

Polk, James K. *The Diary of James K. Polk During His Presidency, 1845 to 1849.* Ed. Milo M. Quaife. Chicago: Chicago Historical Society, 1910.

Pringle, Henry F. *The Life and Times of William Howard Taft,* Vol. 1. New York: Farrar & Rinehart, 1939.

_____. *Theodore Roosevelt, A Biography.* New York: Harcourt, Brace, 1931.

Putnam, Carleton. *Theodore Roosevelt, A Biography.* New York: Scribner, 1958.

Reeves, Richard. *A Ford, Not a Lincoln.* New York: Harcourt Brace Jovanovich, 1975.

Reeves, Thomas C. *Gentleman Boss: The Life of Chester Alan Arthur.* New York: Knopf, 1975.

Regan, Donald T. *For the Record: From Wall Street to Washington.* San Diego: Harcourt Brace Jovanovich, 1988.

Reid, Edith Gettings. *Woodrow Wilson: The Caricature, the Myth, and the Man.* London: Oxford University Press, 1934.

Remini, Robert V. *The Life of Andrew Jackson.* New York: Harper & Row, 1988.

Richardson, Elmo. *The Presidency of Dwight D. Eisenhower.* Lawrence, KS: Regents Press of Kansas, 1979.

Roosevelt, Theodore. *Autobiography.* New York: Scribner, 1958.

_____. *The Letters of Theodore Roosevelt.* Ed. Elting E. Morrison. Cambridge, MA: Harvard University Press, 1951–1954.

Ross, Ishbel. *Grace Coolidge and Her Era.* New York: Dodd, Mead, 1962.

Russell, Francis. *The Shadow of Blooming Grove: Warren G. Harding in His Times.* New York: McGraw-Hill, 1968.

Rutland, Robert Allen. *James Madison: The Founding Father.* New York: Macmillan, 1987.

Safire, William. *Before the Fall.* Garden City, NY: Doubleday, 1973.

Schachner, Nathan. *Thomas Jefferson, a Biography,* Vol. 1. New York: Appleton-Century-Crofts, 1951.

Schieffer, Bob and Gary Paul Gates. *The Acting President.* New York: Dutton, 1989.

Schlesinger, Arthur M. *A Thousand Days: John F. Kennedy in the White House.* Boston: Houghton Mifflin, 1965.

Seager, II, Robert. *And Tyler Too: A Biography of John and Julia Gardiner Tyler.* New York: McGraw-Hill, 1963.

Seale, William. *The President's House: A History,* Vols. 1 & 2. Washington, D.C.: White House Historical Association with the cooperation of the National Geographic Society, 1986.

Sellers, Charles. *James K. Polk,* Vols. 1 and 2. Princeton, NJ: Princeton University Press, 1957–1966.

Shachtman, Tom. *Edith & Woodrow: A Presidential Romance.* New York: Putnam, 1981.

Shepherd, Jack. *The Adams Chronicles: Four Generations of Greatness.* Boston: Little, Brown, 1975.

Sherwood, Robert E. *Roosevelt and Hopkins: An Intimate History.* New York: Harper, 1948.

Sidey, Hugh. *John F. Kennedy, President.* New York: Atheneum, 1963.

Sievers, Harry J. *Benjamin Harrison, Hoosier Statesman.* New York: University Publishers, 1959.

———. *Benjamin Harrison, Hoosier Warrior,* Vol. 1. New York: University Publishers, 1960.

Smith, Elbert B. *The Presidencies of Zachary Taylor and Millard Fillmore.* Lawrence: University Press of Kansas, 1988.

———. *The Presidency of James Buchanan.* Lawrence, KS: University Press of Kansas, 1975.

Smith, Gene. *Lee and Grant, a Dual Biography.* New York: McGraw-Hill, 1984.

———. *When the Cheering Stopped: The Last Years of Woodrow Wilson.* New York: Morrow, 1964.

Smith, Page. *Jefferson: A Revealing Biography.* New York: American Heritage, 1976.

———. *John Adams,* Vols. 1 and 2. Garden City, NY: Doubleday, 1962.

———. *The Nation Comes of Age.* New York: McGraw-Hill, 1981.

Smith, Richard Norton. *An Uncommon Man: The Triumph of Herbert Hoover.* New York: Simon & Schuster, 1984.

Smith, Theodore Clarke. *The Life and Letters of James Abram Garfield.* New Haven: Yale University Press, 1925.

Socolofsky, Homer E. and Allan B. Spetter. *The Presidency of Benjamin Harrison.* Lawrence: University Press of Kansas, 1987.

Starling, Edmund W. *Starling of the White House.* New York: Simon & Schuster, 1946.

Steinberg, Alfred. *The Man from Missouri: The Life and Times of Harry S Truman.* New York: Putnam, 1962.

Tarbell, Ida. *The Life of Lincoln.* Vols. 1 and 3. New York: Lincoln Historical Society, 1896.

Taylor, John M. *Garfield of Ohio, the Available Man.* New York: Norton, 1970.

Thayer, William Roscoe. *Theodore Roosevelt, an Intimate Biography.* Boston: Houghton Mifflin, 1919.

Thomas, Benjamin B. *Abraham Lincoln, a Biography.* New York: Modern Library, 1968.

Thomas, Lately. *The First President Johnson.* New York: Morrow, 1968.

Trefousse, Hans L. *Andrew Johnson: A Biography.* New York: Norton, 1989.

Truman, Harry S. *The Autobiography of Harry S Truman.* Ed. Robert H. Ferrell. Boulder: Colorado Associated University Press, 1980.

Truman, Margaret. *Harry S Truman.* New York: Morrow, 1973.

Vestal, Bud. *Jerry Ford, Up Close.* New York: Coward, McCann & Geoghegan, 1974.

Victor, Maurice and Raymond D. Adams. "Sedatives, Stimulants, and Psychotropic Drugs." *Harrison's Principles of Internal Medicine.* 10th ed. Ed. Robert G. Petersdorf. New York: McGraw-Hill, 1983. 1295–1301.

Vidal, Gore. *Lincoln: A Novel.* New York: Random House, 1984.

Ward, Geoffrey C. *Before the Trumpet: Young Franklin Roosevelt, 1882–1905.* New York: Harper & Row, 1985.

Welch, Richard E. *The Presidencies of Grover Cleveland.* Lawrence: University Press of Kansas, 1988.

White, Theodore H. *The Making of the President, 1972.* New York: Atheneum, 1973.

White, William Allen. *A Puritan in Babylon, the Story of Calvin Coolidge.* New York: Macmillan, 1938.

Whitney, David C. *The American Presidents.* Garden City, NY: Doubleday, 1985.

_____. *The American Presidents.* Revised and updated by Robin Vaughn Whitney. New York: Prentice Hall, 1990.

Williams, Charles Richard. *The Life of Rutherford Birchard Hayes,* Vol. 1. Columbus: Ohio State Archaeological and Historical Society, 1928.

Williams, Gordon H. and Robert G. Dluhy. "Diseases of the Adrenal Cortex." *Harrison's Principles of Internal Medicine.* 10th ed. Ed. Robert G. Petersdorf. New York: McGraw-Hill, 1983. 634–56.

Williams, Robert H. *The Textbook of Endocrinology.* 6th ed. Philadelphia: Saunders, 1981.

Williams, T. Harry. *Hayes of the Twenty-third.* New York: Knopf, 1965.

Wills, Garry. *The Kennedy Imprisonment.* Boston: Little, Brown, 1982.

Winston, Robert W. *Andrew Johnson, Plebian and Patriot.* New York: H. Holt, 1928.

Wolfe, Harold. *Herbert Hoover: Public Servant and Leader of the Loyal Opposition.* New York: Exposition, 1956.

Woodard, William E. *Meet General Grant.* New York: A Liveright, 1928.

Woodward, Bob and Carl Bernstein. *The Final Days.* New York: Avon, 1977.

Wooten, James T. *Dasher: The Roots and the Rising of Jimmy Carter.* New York: Summit, 1978.

Magazines/Journals

Adler, Selig. "Operation on President McKinley." *Scientific American* Mar 1963: 118–30.

Breo, Dennis L. "JFK's Death—The Plain Truth from the MDs Who Did the Autopsy." *JAMA: The Journal of the American Medical Association* 267 (1992): 2794–803.

Bruenn, Howard G. "Clinical Notes on the Illness and Death of FDR." *Annals of Internal Medicine* 72 (1970): 579–91.

Burwell, C. S., et al. "Extreme Obesity Associated with Alvedar Hypoventilation-Pickwickian Syndrome." *American Journal of Medicine* 21 (1956): 811–18.

Clark, L. Pierce. "Unconscious Motives Underlying the Personalities of Great Statesmen and Their Relation to Epoch Making." *Psychoanalytic Review* 8 (1921): 1–21.

Gardner, Francis Tomlinson. "The Gentleman from Tennessee." *Surgery, Gynecology and Obstetrics* 88 (1949): 405–11.

Goldsmith, Harry S. "Unanswered Mysteries in the Death of Franklin Delano Roosevelt," *Surgery, Gynecology, and Obstetrics* 149 (1979): 899–908.

Hutschnecker, Arnold. "Mental Health of Our Leaders." *Look* 15 July 1969: 51–54.

Ikard, Robert W. "Surgical Operation on James K. Polk." *Tennessee Historical Quarterly* 43 (1984): 121–31.

Marmor, MD, Michael F. "Wilson, Strokes and Zebras," *New England Journal of Medicine* 307 (1982): 528–35.

Micozzi, Mark S. "Lincoln, Kennedy, and the Autopsy." *JAMA: The Journal of the American Medical Association* 267 (1992): 2791.

Nichols, MD, James A., et al. "The Management of Adrenocortical Insufficiency During Surgery." *Archives of Surgery*. 1955.

————. "President Kennedy's Adrenals," *JAMA: The Journal of the American Medical Association* 201 (1967): 129–30.

Sours, John A. "Somnambulism." *Archives of General Psychiatry* 9 (1963): 400–13.

Weinstein, Edwin A. "Woodrow Wilson's Neurological Illness." *Journal of American History* 57 (1970): 324–51.

Wills, Garry. "Beginning of the Road." *Time* 20 July 1992: 32 + .

Newspapers

"Attack of Hemorrhoids." *Facts on File* 31 Dec 1978: 1003.

Booth, William. "Bush Begins Tests to Find Cause of Thyroid Problem." *Raleigh News and Observer* 9 May 1991: 9A.

Broder, David S. "Reagan Wounded by Assailant's Bullet." *Washington Post* 31 Mar 1981: A1 + .

"Bush Hospitalized for Irregular Heart Rhythm." *Facts on File* 9 May 1991: 336–37.

"Carter Breaks Collar Bone." *Facts on File* 31 Dec 1980: 989.

"Carter Drops Out of Foot Race." *Facts on File* 21 Sept 1979: 700–01.

"Clinton's Health Generally Strong." *Greensboro News & Record* 15 Oct 1992: A4.

Cohn, Victor. "Bullet Lodged an Inch from Reagan's Heart." *Washington Post* 16 Apr 1981: A1 + .

"Creates Illusion of Not Being Paralyzed." *The New York Post.* 7 Nov 1928.

Devroy, Ann and Dan Balz. "Bush Hospitalized with Irregular Heartbeat." *Washington Post* 5 May 1991: A1 + .

"Experts Say Delay Would Help Study of Lincoln's Genes." *Greensboro News & Record* 16 Apr 1992: A10.

"Halcion Quitting Reported." *Facts on File* 19 Mar 1992:188.

"Kennedy Undergoes Spinal Surgery." *The New York Times* 26 Feb 1958.

King, John. "Health Questions Revised." *Greensboro News & Record* 9 Jan 1992: A1.

"L. B. J. Surgery Cancer Left Ankle." *Greensboro News and Record.* 10 Jan 1982.

"MD Urges More Relaxation." *Facts on File* 2 April 1992: 226.

"Points About Folger and Arthur." *The New York Tribune* 10 Oct 1882, Vol. XLI, No. 13.

"President Collapses at State Dinner." *Facts on File* 16 Jan 1992:17.

"President Has Nose Cancer Removed." *Facts on File* 31 July 1987: 551.

"President Shot at Buffalo Fair." *New York Times* 7 Sept 1901: A1 + .

"The President's Health." *The New York Herald* 21 Oct 1882: 3.

"Reagan Has Two More Polyps Removed." *Facts on File* 3 July 1987: 482.

"Reagan Passes Checkup." *Facts on File* 16 Dec 1988: 934.

"Reagan Pronounced Fit." *Facts on File* 15 Jan 1988: 19.

Rensberger, Boyce. "Amphetamines Used by a Physician to Lift Moods of Famous Patients." *New York Times* 4 Dec 1972: A1 + .

_____. "Reagan to Undergo Intestinal Surgery Today." *Washington Post* 13 July 1985: A1 + .

Shaffer, Ron and Neil Henry. "Suspected Gunman: An Aimless Drifter." *Washington Post* 31 Mar 1981: A1 + .

Thompson, Larry and Carol Krucoff. "Exercise and the Heart." *Washington Post* 7 May 1991: WH10.

Trafford, Abigail. "Me, Bush and Graves Disease." *Washington Post* 26 May 1991: D1.

Miscellaneous

Caplinger, MD, Kelsy J. Medical report—August 27, 1991; issued October 12, 1992. Little Rock, Arkansas. Re: Health of William Clinton by allergist.

Kumpuris, MD. Andrew G. Medical report—issued October 12, 1992. Little Rock, Arkansas. Re: A cardiologist reports on Gov. Clinton.

A Letter: Taft to J. C. C. Black. December 25, 1922. Re: Relates stone removed from bladder (urinary).

A Letter: Taft to Robert A. Taft. February 15, 1925. Re: Bladder stone removed with cystoscope.

Santa Cruz, MD, Susan M. Medical report—September 9, 1991; issued October 13, 1992. Little Rock, Arkansas. Re: Health of Bill Clinton.

Suen, MD, James Y. Medical report—issued October 13, 1992. Little Rock, Arkansas. Re: Health of Pres. Clinton.

Index

315